HIGHER EDUCATION
IN THE FIFTY STATES

HIGHER EDUCATION
IN THE FIFTY STATES

M. M. CHAMBERS

Department of Educational Administration
Illinois State University

with a Foreword by
HERMAN B WELLS

University Chancellor
Indiana University

THE INTERSTATE
Printers & Publishers, Inc.
Danville, Illinois

Copyright © 1970 by
M. M. CHAMBERS

Library of Congress
Catalog Card Number 70-107847

Printed in U.S.A.

12/2/75 - $10.00

The writer who relies on perceptive understanding cannot avoid being inside his material. He neither could, nor wishes to, be disengaged. In discerning the truth about universities there is no doubt perceptive understanding wins every time.

— Sir Eric Ashby

As a people, we still have a choice. If we want a society on the beehive model, all we need do is relax and we'll drift into it. If we want a society built around the creative possibilities of the self-directing individual, then we have tasks to perform.

— John W. Gardner

FOREWORD

During the last two decades, rapid developments in higher education and the policy questions arising from them have stimulated the growth of institutional research and a literature of higher education. Together, these have become a valuable resource for academic administrators, trustees, and legislators seeking data to guide them in their decisions on educational and institutional policies.

Through his pioneering research and writing, Dr. M. M. Chambers early established himself as a leading authority in such areas of higher education as its administration, its public financial support, and the court decisions that have helped delineate its role.

His professional career, which has spanned the teaching field from high schools to university professorships and included sixteen years on the staff of the American Council on Education, has given him a broad perspective for his work. Frequently called upon as a consultant, he has participated in surveys of higher educational systems of seven states and of New York City; he served as Executive Director of the Michigan Council of State College Presidents for a year; and he has had consulting assignments with the U. S. Office of Education, the Michigan State Board of Education, the Arizona Board of Regents of State Universities, and Southern Illinois University.

From 1963 to 1969, Indiana University had the benefit of Dr. Chambers' expert counsel and distinguished service as a Visiting Professor of Higher Education. In the crucible of student opinion, represented by the "1969 Student Evaluation of Faculty and Courses," he received a superior rating in every category.

The author of more than twenty-five books and pamphlets and some 300 articles, Dr. Chambers is best known for his series *The Colleges and the Courts,* its sixth and latest volume having appeared in 1967, and for his annual publications, "Appropriations of State Tax Funds for Operating Expenses of Higher Education in the Fifty States," widely circulated by the National Association of State Universities and Land-Grant Colleges. These yearly compilations of his unique monthly "Grapevine" issues, reporting the actions of state legislatures in support of higher education, provide comparative data nowhere else available.

The present volume is a unique and invaluable record of the partnership of public higher education and the state. Here in a concise form Dr. Chambers has traced the basic developments in each state underlying the management and degree of the tax support it provides for its state colleges and universities. The accompanying tables facilitate analyses and comparisons of the progress being made in the fifty states. In view of the evident need for the services public higher education can furnish as American society becomes urbanized and technologically oriented, this clear presentation of public support of these services is both timely and essential for the decisions that lie ahead.

Herman B Wells
University Chancellor
Indiana University

PREFACE

My first impulse, upon completing the discourse which is compressed within this one volume of moderate size, is to express humility in the face of a mighty task. The subject could very well supply material for a fifty-volume encyclopedia. Hence the treatment it receives here is sketchy.

Such flashes of history as appear are dealt with more in the manner of the journalist than of the meticulous historiographer. The statistics of appropriations of state tax funds for annual operating expenses of higher education over 1960-1970 are in general accurate, especially where large sums are involved; but they are rounded to the last one thousand and never purport to partake of bank-clerk exactitude. This is all the more true of successive appropriations of somewhat marginal smaller sums such as for special projects, student aids, fringe benefits, and contributions to interstate compacts and interinstitutional consortiums. Such items as these are sometimes appropriated and reported separately for a few years. and thereafter lumped into some larger rubric. Therefore it must not be supposed that the brief tabulations herein will afford a consecutive and systematically detailed history of all these matters. They provide, within reasonable tolerances, the ten-year appropriation history of the state universities and colleges, and of the state-wide totals. Comparisons and contrasts among states and among institutions, if made, must be with comprehension that many unquantifiable variables are unmentioned. Several other types of limitations on the validity and usefulness of interstate and interinstitutional comparisons are indicated in Appendix One, "What the Figures Are Intended to Mean."

All the foregoing applies also to the numerous brief statements in the stories of individual states about total population, growth of population over recent periods, per capita tax investment in annual operating expenses of higher education, ratio of this sum to personal income, the total of state and local tax collections per $1,000 of personal income, the total magnitude of appropriations for annual operating expenses of higher education, and their relative rates of increase over the ten-year period covered. Here an additional explanation may also be due: to avoid presenting a ponderous statistical abstract composed of many lengthy tabulations of data available from other published sources, I have dealt briefly with the types of information just named in the separate stories of the states, where they may assist the reader in getting something of the feel of the local situation without painfully digging the figures out of several massive tabulations. Some, but not necessarily all, the data of these types are included in the stories of individual states, but generally only when they are deemed to have especial point.

There are also sketchy paragraphs about the evolution of state revenue systems in many of the states. Here again, only a few high points of major importance could be aimed at. No comprehensive and detailed tracing of state tax legislation appears herein, because that alone would require a volume larger than the present one. What is new about this discourse, if any novelty can be asserted, is that it suggests, by no means exhaustively, a few ways in which wider ranges of data can be brought into juxtaposition to contribute toward realistic decisions regarding the financial support of higher education in the states, and regarding the conditions which conduce toward rising educational productivity in higher education at all levels, broadly including both quality and quantity.

This discourse contains occasional notes and comments on the place of institutions of higher education in the constitutions of several states, and on the varying relationships between higher education and the legislature as well as numerous statehouse administrative and fiscal offices. To my mind, the preponderance of the evidence is overwhelmingly to the effect that overcentralization of detailed fiscal and administrative controls, though often intended to promote efficiency, is in fact generally self-defeating and detrimental to the progress and productivity of universities and colleges. A distinctly different way of restricting the autonomy of the institutions is that of setting up a state-wide board of higher education (by whatever name) either to supplant and supersede institutional governing boards or to absorb varying portions of their historic powers while leaving the boards intact. My judgments of these practices appear in many places. These matters are controversial. For my opinions no infallibility is claimed. They must stand or fall on their merits. They are based on what seems to me to be convincing evidence, some of which appears at many points in this volume; but no pretense is made that the total discourse is either fully comprehensive or exhaustive. Such studies have been beyond the resources of time and money available to me.

Having tried to make clear some of the limitations of this effort, and voiced my personal humility, I now suggest my hope that this first edition may be useful enough to justify future supplementary volumes which may help to illuminate the advancement of higher education in the interest of all the people of the states and the nation.

Acknowledgments

In some part an outgrowth of the eleven years of continuous circulation of the small monthly mimeographed reports known as *Grapevine*, this present book owes a good deal to at least two hundred key persons distributed among all fifty states, who supplied data on request and volunteered correspondence and documents over greater or lesser numbers of years.

Much is owed, too, to the approximately four hundred advanced graduate students (most of whom earned or are earning doctoral degrees) who voluntarily enrolled in one or more of my courses in administrative, financial, and legal aspects of higher education, successively at the University of Michigan (1958-63) and Indiana University (1963-69). Add to these the twenty-five postdoctoral fellows with whom I had the benefit of being associated at the University of Michigan.

There is also a certain debt to numerous persons in the dozen states and cities which have engaged my services as consultant or as member or chairman of survey staffs at various times since 1939. Let me also not omit mention of the encouragement received from several national associations, including the National Association of State Universities and Land-Grant Colleges, the American College Public Relations Association, and the American Association of State Colleges and Universities.

The intensive work of several months' duration which was required for the drafting of this volume could hardly have been accomplished without the aid of a small grant from the Indiana University Research Committee (Chancellor Herman B Wells, Chairman), which enabled me to obtain the services of Betty (Mrs. Frederick P.) Lucas, of Bloomington, Indiana, as a very competent and conscientious secretary and general assistant for this purpose.

We were able to achieve promptly a necessary preliminary step by assembling and publishing a large amount of fiscal data from the fifty states in *A Record of Progress: Ten Years of State Tax Support of Higher Education, 1959-60 through 1968-69*. This is a large-format (14 by 17 inches), 45-page offset document released in February 1969 by The Interstate Printers & Publishers, Inc., of Danville, Illinois 61832, and now available from that source. It contains vastly more detailed data than would be feasible to include in this present volume.

Lastly, drafts of parts of this volume were privately circulated to key persons in every state, many of whom were generous enough to scan them critically and purge them of occasional errors of fact; and who consented to the appearance of their names herein in acknowledgment of that service. None is to be thought to bear any responsibility for any remaining mistakes of fact, or as necessarily endorsing any of the expressions of judgment or opinion.

Harry S. Allen, Director of Institutional Research, University of Nebraska

Robert S. Babcock, Provost, Vermont State Colleges

James A. Blissit, Vice President and Treasurer, Medical College of Georgia; former Treasurer of the Board of Regents of the University System of Georgia

Edward J. Boling, Vice President for Development and Administration, University of Tennessee

Herman R. Branson, President, Central State University (Ohio)

R. B. Corbett, President, New Mexico State University

Edwin M. Crawford, Director, Office of Institutional Research, National Association of State Universities and Land-Grant Colleges

Wilson H. Elkins, President, University of Maryland

Elmer Ellis, President Emeritus and Professor of History, University of Missouri

John R. Emens, President Emeritus, Ball State University (Indiana)

James L. Fisher, President, Towson State College (Maryland)

Ted C. Gilbert, Executive Director, Kentucky Council on Public Higher Education

Ernest W. Hartung, President, University of Idaho

Richard A. Harvill, President, University of Arizona; President, National Association of State Universities and Land-Grant Colleges

Robert Heussler, President, Trenton State College (New Jersey)

Carl M. Hill, President, Kentucky State College

A. D. Holt, President, University of Tennessee

G. D. Humphrey, President Emeritus, University of Wyoming

Neil D. Humphrey, Chancellor, University of Nevada System

Martin D. Jenkins, President, Morgan State College

William A. Johnstone, Acting President, Montana State University

Frank L. Kidner, Vice President for Educational Relations, University of California

Gerald S. Leischuck, Director of Institutional Research, Auburn University (Alabama)

L. R. Lunden, Vice President and Consultant to the President, University of Minnesota

Robert R. Martin, President, Eastern Kentucky University

William E. Morgan, President, Colorado State University

David W. Mullins, President, University of Arkansas

Allan W. Ostar, Executive Director, American Association of State Colleges and Universities

William H. Patterson, Provost, University of South Carolina

Edward Rutkowski, Associate Professor of History and Philosophy of Education, University of Northern Iowa

Ernest E. Rydell, Coordinator of Public Relations, Trenton State College

George W. Starcher, President, University of North Dakota

Wayne Stumph, Dean of Business Services, Belleville Area College (Illinois)

Robert Taylor, Vice President, University of Wisconsin

Stuart A. Taylor, Assistant Professor, Southern Illinois University; White House Fellow assigned to the U. S. Department of Housing and Urban Development, Washington, D. C.

Edsel E. Thrash, Executive Secretary and Director, Mississippi Board of Trustees of Institutions of Higher Learning
Catherine M. Warrick, Assistant to the Dean, General College, University of Minnesota
William R. Wood, President, University of Alaska
Roy A. Young, Acting President, Oregon State University

Let it be reiterated that none of these persons is responsible for any shortcomings of this work. None is to be understood as necessarily endorsing it in whole or in part. Entire responsibility is mine.

Normal, Illinois   *M. M. Chambers*
June 1970

CONTENTS

I. INTRODUCTION

II. STORIES OF THE FIFTY STATES

I

INTRODUCTION

THE MID-POINT OF TWENTY YEARS, 1960 - 1980

The year 1970 was preceded by a decade of unprecedented expansion and change in public higher education. So far as the volume of the enterprise is concerned, as measured by the numbers of persons and of dollars directly involved, 1970 will be followed by another 10 years in which current trends will continue without much deflection.

The number of persons aged 18-24 in the United States, estimated at 24 million in 1970, will increase to more than 29 million in 1980.[1] Additional millions of adults beyond that age will be taking opportunity for some type of formal education beyond the high school.

The annual crop of high school graduates will continue to increase at least until 1979, after which it may show a slight recession on account of the tapering of the annual numbers of births which occurred in 1957-1962 but was not of any substantial significance until after 1962.

The ratio that the total number of first-year enrollments in formal education beyond the high school will bear to the annual crop of high school graduates may be expected to increase each year of the decade 1970-1980. This ratio, nationwide, was already above 50 per cent in the late 'Sixties (in California, above 80 per cent). Nationally, it may well reach the order of 75 per cent or more by 1980. Total enrollments at all levels beyond high school in 1980 have been conservatively estimated to be 12 million students—more than twice what they were in 1965 (5,920,000). In 1970, the total was guessed as 7.3 million, of whom 72 per cent were in public institutions and 28 per cent in private.[2] In 1980, the estimate has it that these proportions will have changed to 77 per cent public, 23 per cent private.

---

[1] P. 9068 of *A Fact Book on Higher Education*, Second issue, 1969. Washington: American Council on Education, June 1969. Pp. 9057-9112

[2] The basic figure of 7.3 million was a projection made by the U.S. Office of Education, appearing on page 1 of *Education in the Seventies*. Washington: Government Printing Office, May 1968. 44 pp.

The author records his personal opinion that all the estimates mentioned here will turn out to be below the mark, partly because they are generally based on "degree-credit" students in colleges and universities, and because there is an increasing margin of students not in that classification, especially in vocational-technical schools and occupational programs in junior colleges.

This means that during the decade, public enrollments will have gone up from 5,256,000 to 9,240,000, a gain of 76 per cent. Private enrollments will have gone from 2,044,000 to 2,760,000, a gain of 35 per cent. The total 10-year added increment will be substantially larger than it was for the 10 years preceding 1970, meaning that more students will be added during 1970-1980 than were added during 1960-1970.

Although the total number of students graduating from high school annually may temporarily level off at about the year 1979, as previously noted, the total enrollments in all levels above the high school (combined) will continue to increase to a peak at about the year 1982. This will later turn out to be a plateau rather than a peak, because the anticipated continued increase in population will push the general trend upward to the end of the century.

As to the total annual current operating expenditures excluding capital outlays, by institutions of higher education in the United States,' the figure was reported as $4 billion in 1955-56; $5.3 billion in 1958-59; $15.1 billion in 1968-69; and projected to $22.5 billion in 1975-76. Thus over the 20-year period the figure will have become more than five-fold what it was in 1955-56.[3]   The figures as reported are "of 1965-66 dollars," and hence reduce somewhat the actual rate of growth in current dollars for each year thereafter, on account of gradual general inflation.

Without attempting to project any precise figure to represent total annual operating expenditures of all higher education in 1980, it is possible to suppose that they may aggregate $35 billion upwards.[4] Certainly the portion coming from tax funds will increase year by year. Probably the federal share will grow most rapidly of all. The state tax support will also increase greatly. Support from local taxing sub-divisions (cities, counties, junior college districts) does not appear likely to keep pace, but will continue to be of some importance.

The appropriations of state tax funds for annual operating expenses of higher education in the 50 states, by fiscal years, *in billions of dollars*, have been:

---

[3]Pp. 68-70, 72 of *Projections of Educational Statistics to 1975*. Washington: Government Printing Office, 1966. 113 pp.

[4]Howard R. Bowen (president, University of Iowa, 1964-1969), whose scholarship and judgment merit the highest confidence, has estimated total current income for higher education in 1979-80 at $33 billion: page 77 in his article "The Financing of Higher Education: Issues and Prospects," which appeared on pages 69-83 of *The Academic Community: Continuity and Change*, a 170-page paperbound volume published by the American Council on Education in 1968 as "background papers" for its annual meeting of that year.

On this important, complex, and controverted subject, the most meritorious recent document is Howard R. Bowen's *The Finance of Higher Education*. Berkeley: Carnegie Commission on Higher Education, 1968. 36 pp.

1960	1961	1962	1963	1964	1965	1966	1967	1968	1969	1970
1.4	1.5	1.7	1.9	2.2	2.4	3.0	3.5	4.4	5.0	6.1⁵

Within 10 years, the figure for fiscal year 1959-60 was quadrupled. Probably the rate of increase from 1970 to 1980 will not be quite so rapid; but it will be very substantial, for annual institutional operating expenses necessarily increase faster than enrollments, for reasons which need not be detailed here.[6] This says, of course, that the institutional expenditure *per student per year* must continue on a rising scale.

This has been documented by the U.S. Office of Education in a report showing that these average annual expenditures (for "educational and general" purposes only, excluding auxiliary enterprises) *per student* by all institutions were $1,240 for fiscal year 1955-56, and $1,737 for fiscal year 1965-66. The same document projected them to $2,034 for fiscal year 1975-76.[7] If they go to $2,500 for 1980, and 12 million students are enrolled, then total "educational and general" expenses alone will be $30 billion. Adding auxiliary enterprises will bring the total up to $35 to $40 billion. This would be about 2½ per cent of a Gross National Product of perhaps $1,500 billion, which is not unreasonable to anticipate. (Some estimates of Gross National Product in 1980 run as high as $2,000 billion.)

What proportion will come from the 50 states alone? The biggest and most uncertain variable is in a related question: What proportion will come from the federal government? There is little doubt that the federal contribution will increase rapidly, though perhaps after a brief slowdown at the beginning of the decade. But in any event this should not cause any flight from responsibility on the part of the states. During 1960-1970 the appropriations of state tax funds for annual operating expenses of higher education reached in the vicinity of 30 per cent of the grand total of income for that purpose. If they were to continue at that ratio to 1980, apparently they would arrive at $10 to $12 billion—twice that in fiscal year 1968-69. By 1980 the federal contribution through all channels should go above 45 per cent of the total, so that the aggregate would be, say, $15 billion. Then the additional $8

---

[5] All figures except for 1970 are from *A Record of Progress: Ten Years of State Tax Support of Higher Education, 1959-60 through 1968-69.* Danville, Illinois: The Interstate Printers & Publishers, Inc., 1969. 45 pp. outsize format, offset.

[6] The reasons are set forth in some detail at pages 196-197 in *Higher Education: Who Pays? Who Gains?* Danville, Illinois: The Interstate Printers & Publishers, Inc., 1969. 302 pp.

[7] Derived from data on pages 9 and 82-85 of *Projections of Educational Statistics to 1975-76.* Washington: Government Printing Office, 1966. OE-10030-66, 113 pp.

billion to $12 billion required would come from local taxing sub-divisions, gifts from private sources, endowment earnings, student fees, and miscellaneous institutional receipts.[8] These figures do not include capital outlays. With financing of capital expenditures added, total annual income for all higher education in 1980 may well exceed $50 billion.

If the state and federal contributions were to continue at about equality in volume, they would be about $12½ billion each in 1980, and the state total would thus be two and one-half times what it was in fiscal year 1968-69. This is neither unreasonable nor improbable. The states can easily provide support of this magnitude by updating their revenue systems and giving higher education the priority it merits during this period of swift progress, and they are likely to do so. [9]

The preceding paragraphs ought not to be concluded without a remark that the projection of most sorts of data 10 years ahead is hazardous business. Unforeseen catastrophe could conceivably change the picture enormously. Uninterrupted increases in produc-tivity at rates faster than anticipated could cause the tentative figures to be far surpassed before 1980 is reached, so far below the mark as to become a laughingstock. (This latter has indeed been the fate of many predictions made during the late 'Fifties and early 'Sixties.)

But as the foregoing estimates show, progression on more than an ordinary arithmetical ratio will continue at least until 1980. The point is that in 1970 no pinnacle had been reached;—only the mid-point of a 20-year period of tremendous advancement. The backward look was down a steep gradient. The forward gaze was upward along a rise only a little less steep.

The test of the 'Sixties had been met; but the distant goal had been only half won. The 'Seventies presented an equal challenge.

---

[8] These projections assume that by 1980 more than 75 per cent of the total support will be from tax sources—federal, state, and local. The other sources named will continue to have important roles, but there appears to be no other possible source of great magnitude except a vast system of student loans (urgently advocated in some quarters) which would open the way for unlimited increases in student fees and conduce toward charging the total cost of his education to the student. Any such scheme is so flatly contrary to the national and state commitments to make education available on reasonably equal terms to all capable of using it to the benefit of themselves and of society, and is of so reactionary a tendency, that the author does not believe it can ever be put into operation in this country. It is discussed in somewhat more detail in pages 117-125 of *Higher Education: Who Pays? Who Gains?* Danville, Illinois: The In-terstate Printers & Publishers, Inc., 1969. 302 pp.

[9] A pertinent reference document: Kenneth E. Quindry, *State and Local Revenue Potential.* SREB Research Monograph No. 15. Atlanta: Southern Regional Education Board, 1969. 108 pp.

THE POINT OF THE DISCOURSE

The aim here is to discover something of the nature of higher education as a function of society, and inklings of an optimum *modus vivendi* for the partnership of public higher education and the state. Elsewhere the author has written that a key to productivity in higher education is good morale among those immediately engaged: students, faculty members, administrative officers, and members of governing boards. This indispensable *esprit de corps* is derived in part from the judicious trust and confidence of parents, donors, taxpayers, legislators, and governors. "Morale cannot be forced; it can only be fostered."[1]

This sentiment is not original. It is and has been understood and held by many. Observe, for example, the words of Arthur G. Coons, late revered educational statesman of California:

"In the midst of controversies over finances, or structures, or functions, or programs . . . , it is important to remember that what takes place in fact rests on the attitudes and intentions of the persons who are involved. Dependence primarily on power, whether by directives or by demonstrations, will fail."[2]

On the matter of public confidence, consider what was written in 1967 by Terry Sanford, a recent governor of North Carolina, known for his breadth of wisdom concerning educational issues:

"In at least one activity, it is undisputed that over the years the money from the states has achieved excellence. That is public higher education. The nation has become strong through the support the states have given public higher education. . . . Much of our preeminence as a social and governmental system has come from our unrivaled state-based university and college system. . . . The university capacity of America couldn't have been put together in a crash program. It has grown over many years by state nurture."[3]

In many states this clear view has been clouded somewhat by distrust, some real and some feigned, by some legislators and state

---

[1] P. 210 in *Higher Education: Who Pays? Who Gains?* Danville, Illinois: The Interstate Printers & Publishers, Inc., 1969. 302 pp.

[2] In Arthur G. Coons, *Crises in California Higher Education.* Los Angeles: Ward Ritchie Press, 1968. 246 pp.

[3] Pp. 63-64 in Terry Sanford, *Storm Over the States.* New York: McGraw-Hill Book Company, 1967. 218 pp.

7

administrative officers who grumblingly question the efficiency of the management of state universities and colleges and the efficiency of state-wide development of public higher education. Only rarely are such innuendoes reducible to a specific complaint. Rarely is any factual evidence adduced in their support.

It is well to be candid and recognize that some of this alleged lack of confidence is sincere, even if mistaken; and that some of it stems solely from a power struggle by overambitious office-holders and would-be office-holders for control of the expenditure of large sums of state tax money.

Early in the present century the effort to remove some of the confusions and abuses of nineteenth-century state governments took hold. One of the thrusts was to reduce the large numbers of miscellaneous state agencies, departments, bureaus, and commissions, and compress them into a much smaller number of major departments whose heads would be appointed by the governor and directly responsible to him.

Another thrust was to introduce detailed administrative and fiscal controls emanating from a state department of finance, a state personnel board or civil service commission, a state department of public works, and often central agencies such as a state printer, a state architect, a state engineer, and others.

Granting that the motive was good (but not without noting that a state administrative reorganization almost invariably meant opportunity for an incoming governor to "throw the rascals out" on a large scale, and install his own followers), and conceding that state governments are now generally better than they were half a century ago, it is nonetheless important to notice that the push toward centralization has led to vast increases in unnecessary paperwork, delayed decisions, and harmful rigidity in administration.

These are especially damaging in public higher education, where half of the total of annual operating expenditures is on contracts for salaries of persons at high levels of professional training and general education. Inflexibility and undue delays in the management of recruiting and of changes in salary and rank can cause failures in obtaining or retaining prized talents—to say nothing of depressed morale—, with resultant imponderable losses in productivity and quality.

These matters are managed generally with skill and dispatch, and in admirable style, by the leading private universities, and by the great constitutionally independent state universities, all of which are free of any vast overlay of smothering officiousness from the statehouse. A study team for the Southern Association of Colleges and Schools, reporting in 1968, was eloquent on this point:

"Effective higher education absolutely requires a maximum of freedom for the exploration of ideas and concepts. This makes wholesome relationships between higher education and state government even more necessary than may be true with other functional areas of state service and makes direct political involvement in the control of institutional personnel and operations intolerable. The uniqueness of higher education should be recognized in organizational patterns and relationships with other agencies of the state."

More specifically, the report concludes: "An educational institution can neither conduct a sound educational program if its operational procedures are set by legislative act, nor can it be properly administered if an agency outside the institution exercises undue and restrictive financial control. Once funds have been appropriated for an institution (either for building construction or operations), budget-making, establishing priorities, and control of expenditures should be entirely within the institution under the jurisdiction of the governing board subject to general policy provisions enacted by the legislature and to the commitments represented through budgetary requests by the institution.

"State financial and administrative officials adversely affect the educational and academic process when they exercise specific and detailed control over matters which can and should be handled within the institution. Recognition by educational representatives of the responsibility of state officials for the post-audit function and the general enforcement of reasonable budgetary law is imperative; however, the educational function of an institution must not be controlled through the use of budgetary techniques or controls by financial officials outside the institution."

This statement, a studious revision of an earlier one after the completion of the study, was recommended for inclusion among the Association's *Standards for Colleges*.[4]

The other and related thrust toward bundling the governance of all or many of a state's public universities and colleges into the hands of one state-wide governing board, or the alternative of superimposing a power-laden "coordinating board," deserves equally careful examination and monitoring. To the extent that this movement diminishes or destroys the autonomy of the university or college by removing decision-making from the campus to the statehouse or some other remote point, creating a species of "absentee landlordism," it tends to short-change and insult the constituency, and to debase the institutions.

---

[4] The quotations are from *Higher Education and Financial Control by State Governments in Southern Association States*. Atlanta: Southern Association of Colleges and Schools, March 1968. 20 pp. unpaginated. Edward J. Boling and J. Jefferson Bennett were joint chairmen of the committee making this report. Robert Cornett and Joe Johnson were staff members.

To be sure, the interests of all the people of the state are superior to those of any institutional constituency; but state-wide public interest can be well served without the power-play involved in the abolition of governing boards or their reduction to impotency. The solution is in the limiting of the state-wide central agency to the work of facilitating interinstitutional *liaison*, performing data-gathering, research reporting, making planning studies, disseminating of public information, and aiding in the representations of state-wide public higher education to the governor, the legislature, the institutional governing boards, and the general public—all in an advisory capacity and by means of permissive and persuasive methods, free of the exercise of raw power.

A state university is not properly conceived as an inanimate *mechanism* which can be operated by remote control, with Big Brother pushing the buttons on the control panel on the twentieth floor of the state office building. Instead it is a living *organism* with its own complex skeletal and muscular structure, its own circulatory and nervous systems, its own capacities for encouraging initiative and inventiveness and maintaining the atmosphere of expectancy which is most conducive toward discoveries in various fields of learning. Its morale, and its productivity, can be greatly diminished or destroyed by rude "chopping off of fingers and toes" by a power-laden "super-board."

A distinguished state university president wrote in 1966: "The disadvantages of a 'super-board' setup, in extra overhead cost, in added but unproductive work at all levels, in impairment or even loss of flexibility in an era of rapid and often major change, in interference with faculty control of courses and curricula, in lost time of·administrators, in standardization of important things some of which can only become and others of which are likely to become mediocre if standardized, in the frequent and almost inevitable 'substitution of rules for brains,' in the erosion of responsibility right along with authority, to my mind far outweigh any presumed benefits from supposed avoidance of unnecessary duplication of programs within a state system."[5]

Fear of "duplication" of general undergraduate programs is a relic of Depression days and earlier, when public higher education was a very thinly-spread enterprise. Virtually all undergraduate curriculums and courses, whatever their labels, contain large in-

---

[5] Elvis J. Stahr, president of Indiana University 1962-1968, in his *State of the University Address to the Faculty, 1966*. (Mimeographed paper, unpublished.) Quoted at page 30 in M. M. Chambers, *Freedom and Repression in Higher Education*. Bloomington, Indiana: Bloomcraft Press, Inc., 1965. 126 pp. (Now out of print, but available in many libraries.)

fusions of liberal arts or general education, which indeed needs to be "duplicated" (or better, diffused, diversified, and dispersed) until it is accessible to all citizens. Wariness of alleged "duplication" would have some point with respect to costly advanced graduate studies and research, were it not for the fact that the scholars and scientists who lead these enterprises are always aware of what their counterparts in other institutions in the same state, if any, are doing and planning. Within the fraternity of top-level scholars and scientists there is intercommunication often unknown to administrators and others, and on a level which would be uninteresting and unintelligible to lay citizens and even to professional persons not immediately concerned in the special fields involved. This is insurance of a sufficient degree of "coordination" without the intervention of uninformed fiscal clerks. Wise governing boards and administrators know their best service is to encourage it, not impede it or clumsily meddle with it. The story of Iowa, *infra*, provides an illustrative example.

Twin menaces to optimum reasonable autonomy of state universities and colleges for more than half a century have been (1) unduly detailed and oppressive central fiscal and administrative controls from a dozen statehouse offices, and (2) the push toward overcentralized state-wide structures for the governance of higher education. These are persistent forms of "over-reaction" to the shortcomings of state governments in the nineteenth and early twentieth centuries. In many states, though by no means all, they have been applied in varying degrees to state colleges and universities in ignorant or willful disregard of the fact that they tend to cause lengthy needless delays, confusions, and frictions; to depress the all-important morale of governing boards and faculties, administrators and students. This can only result in ultimate wasteful losses—diminished educational productivity per tax dollar invested.

Some states have enacted "autonomy bills" which have relieved their state universities or colleges of some of the worst features complained of; for example, Rhode Island (1939), Massachusetts (1956 and 1962), Ohio (1965 and piecemeal in several earlier years, with respect to custody of student fees and other institutional receipts), and New Jersey (1969). But in most instances the gains were only partial, and sometimes were eroded in subsequent years. The analogy between the bureaucracy and an octopus is vivid: cut off one or two tentacles and you are constricted by half a dozen others.

Through the 'Fifties and most of the 'Sixties the press for the abolition of institutional governing boards was dormant; instead many states set up a state-wide "coordinating council" or similar board by whatever name, whose prescribed duties were largely or wholly confined to making studies and recommendations and acting in advisory capacity. Such state-wide councils or boards which are wholly advisory and without any powers of mandate were established in

California (1960), Michigan (1963),[6] Louisiana (1968), Washington (1969), and Alabama (1969). The statutes creating such boards in some twenty other states between 1950 and 1970 were usually cautious and often ambivalent about conferring coercive powers. Almost always the function with regard to institutional budget askings was no more than the duty to examine and make recommendations.

Often in these statutes there is wordage about "approving or disapproving" the addition or deletion of major departments or schools within a university, but it is usually unclear as to whether this authority is intended to be final. This is in fact a rather unworkable idea, because departments and schools are not ordinarily created by fiat, but only labeled and recognized after the essential nucleus of professors, students, books, and apparatus has been painstakingly assembled over a period of several years. Clumsy attempts at such regulation by remote control can also produce very embarrassing problems when it may result in loss of substantial philanthropic grants or governmental subsidies, and consequent departure of one or more distinguished professors and many advanced students.

If the main point of this discourse were to be stated in a single sentence, it would be that state universities and colleges should be extricated (in reasonable degree and with moderate dispatch) from the unnecessary and burdensome mandatory ministrations of statehouse fiscal and administrative offices, and from the rigidities of overcentralized state-wide structures of governance or coercive "coordination."

The myth of "wasteful duplication"—a ceaseless incantation for half a century—has lost its force among knowledgeable persons with the coming of universal education beyond the high school in an economy of abundance, and with the development of interinstitutional and interstate cooperation in many forms. Coordination by consensus is the productive policy, and this is increasingly recognized and practiced everywhere, even by legally power-laden statutory authorities.

---

[6] The Michigan Constitution of 1963 created a State Board of Education and designated it a "coordinating body" for education at all levels, including higher education; but the same Constitution makes each state institution of higher education explicitly autonomous.

WHAT THE READER IS
GETTING INTO

Between these covers are 50 stories, one for each state. Their length varies in rough correspondence to the population and relative magnitude of the general roles of the states. Thus California and New York get perhaps 8,000 words each, while Alaska and Wyoming get 800 words. States of near-average population are covered in about 2,000 or 3,000 words.

Such stories are necessarily condensed and sketchy. The opportunities for error of fact and mistake of judgment are many. The author hopes you will not be too disgruntled if the sketch of your state does not seem to resemble a promotional brochure for the state or its institutions. It is not so intended. It is meant to be critical, and to indicate possibilities of change that enhance the productivity of public higher education; not to imply ratification or fulsome praise of the *status quo*.

Thus the book is tendentious. To some degree it is "personal journalism." But it is based on large amounts of factual data, collected with the generous aid of key persons in every state, some of whom are not named, though many are. The author's belief is that his intellect and his integrity would be questionable if, after handling these data intimately over a long period, he failed to develop some convictions regarding relevant issues. The judgments expressed and implied are not infallible. They are impressions derived from long observations and study by one who, after observing the facts, lets his conscience be his guide.

Components of the State-by-State Sketches

First of all, the emphasis is on the decade 1960-1970; but often small amounts of data from earlier periods are brought in when thought to have particular pertinence. Detailed projections, state-by-state, of estimated populations, student enrollments, and income and expenditures for public higher education during the ensuing decade 1970-1980 do not appear herein. A simple statement of the oncoming nation-wide expansion forms an earlier part of this introductory discourse. The year 1970 is unquestionably the mid-point of a 20-year

13

period of great and steady growth of public higher education. (See the heading, "The Mid-Point of Twenty Years, 1960-1980," *supra*.)

1. *The tabulations* of appropriations of state tax funds for annual operating expenses of higher education are a focal part of the story of each state. Appendix 1 provides some conception of their purposes and limitations.

2. *Relevant statistics* of some usefulness in comparison with those of the appropriations of state tax funds are not tabulated but are indicated in a few sentences in many of the stories, but not in all. Usually they appear where contrasts seem spectacular. They touch upon:

   a. The rates of gain over 10 years.
   b. The average state tax investment *per citizen.*
   c. The ratio of the state tax investment per citizen to the *per capita* personal income.
   d. The total annual state tax receipts per $1,000 of personal income.
   e. Some elementary facts of the evolution of the state's revenue system.

It is recognized that many variables, such as the percentages of resident students attending institutions not receiving state tax funds, and the relative requirements of state functions and services other than higher education, limit the usefulness that the comparisons and contrasts suggest.

3. *State revenue systems*: highlights in their evolution, 1960-1970. Probably this is the first book in which the progress of state support of higher education is coupled with the improvement of state tax systems. The author's observations of the 50 states during many years convinced him that the two need to be considered together, and that this may not be so politically hazardous as it was once thought to be. This is a bonus from a better-educated populace. A noteworthy example is the forthright comment attributed to President William Travers Jerome, III, of Bowling Green State University: "In a state as industrialized as Ohio, a state income tax is inevitable." The remark is equally applicable in some other populous and wealthy states.

While the state revenue systems support many useful and important public services other than higher education, and the relative roles of these different services vary from time to time, it would not be the part of wisdom to discuss state support of higher education without mentioning some of the essentials of modern state taxation.

It is rudimentary that irreversible economic changes have caused the exercise of the taxing power to move increasingly upward to the larger governmental units; that the local taxing subdivisions should have exclusive use of property tax revenues. At the state level several speedy and productive revenue measures have become available: general sales taxes, selective sales taxes (cigarettes, motor fuels, and others), individual and corporate income taxes, severance taxes, and many others of lesser impact.

At the end of 1969 five states had no general sales taxes. A dozen states had no personal income taxes. Nine had no corporation income taxes. The rates at which these major sources of revenue were levied, the methods of their administration, and other features varied widely from state to state. In one state (Louisiana) the severance tax, principally on the extraction of oil and gas, was the state's largest single producer of revenue, though the state also had a general sales tax and both individual and corporate income taxes at modest rates.

Incredible as it may seem, as recently as 1964 six states were getting more revenue from their taxes on gasoline than from any other type of tax (Montana, Nebraska, New Hampshire, New Jersey, Oklahoma, and Texas). At that time the first-named four of these states had no general sales tax. By 1969 Nebraska and New Jersey had general sales taxes in effect.

This is not to imply that all 50 state tax systems should be uniform. It is only to emphasize that they are very diverse, and that technological and economic changes make it necessary to study and revise them almost constantly to keep them optimally equitable and productive without hardship. No state tax system is perfect; and if it were, it would not be so next year, because inevitable changes in the state's economy would outdate it.

Needless to say, none of the 50 stories of the states herein includes any thorough study of any one state's revenue system. They mention only occasional inklings which may be suggestive stimulants to further viewing of the fascinating panorama of 50 states. The states are not "up against a ceiling." They have not exhausted their revenue potentials.[1] They can and will continue to be a major source of support of higher education.

4. *Degrees of statehouse control* of higher education, as provided in state constitutions and statutes, judicial decisions, customs of the legislatures, and state administrative practices.

   a. *Constitutionally autonomous state universities.*

See Michigan, California, Minnesota, Idaho, Colorado, Nevada, Arizona, Oklahoma, Georgia, and Utah for stories of constitutional independence of somewhat varying types and degrees.

   b. *State institutions having much freedom from statehouse interference by virtue of customs of the legislatures.*

Different instances of this characteristic are observed in the stories of Arkansas, Indiana, Missouri, and several other states.

---

[1] Kenneth E. Quindry, *State and Local Revenue Potential*. SREB Research Monograph No. 15. Atlanta: Southern Regional Education Board, 1969. 108 pp.

c. *Unnecessary and self-defeating infringements of institutional autonomy by state central authorities:*

Minute itemization of appropriation acts.

Examples appear in the stories of Illinois, New Jersey, New York, and Texas.

Riders and conditions attached to appropriations.

Indiana and New Mexico provide instances. Others could be cited elsewhere.

Executive withholding of appropriated funds

Varied illustrations are observable in Florida. Louisiana, Massachusetts, North Carolina, and Pennsylvania. This also occurs in some other states.

Statehouse pre-auditing of disbursements; state auditors often exceeding their statutory authority.

Arizona, Florida, Iowa, North Dakota, Vermont, West Virginia, and others.

Inclusion of some or all employees within the jurisdiction of a state civil service commission or state personnel board.

Different histories with varying outcomes in Arizona, California, Delaware, Louisiana, Massachusetts, New Jersey, New York, Rhode Island, Virginia, among others.

Compulsory purchasing through a statehouse office.

Arizona, Delaware, Kansas, Oklahoma, Pennsylvania, Rhode Island, New York, Vermont, West Virginia.

Subjection of land acquisition and building construction to the ministrations of a state board of public works and state engineers and architects.

California, Delaware, Illinois, New York, Nevada, Oklahoma, Vermont. This is prevalent in many other states.

Requiring a system of accounting and financial reporting so different from that used nationally by colleges and universities as to double the work involved.

Delaware, Nebraska, and Pennsylvania. The practice is disappearing, but slowly.

Requiring that printing and publication be contracted by a

state printer or state editor.

Massachusetts. A conspicuous recent historic instance in Wisconsin is not recounted. See *Democrat Printing Co.* v. *Zimmerman,* 14 N.W. 2d 428 (1944).

Prohibiting colleges or universities from using legal counsel except from the staff of the attorney general.

See Illinois for one historic example, in which the University successfully rejected the services of the attorney general, and won a judicial declaration of its right to employ legal counsel.

Requiring student fees and other institutional receipts to be deposited in the state treasury, resulting, in some instances, in their being permanently lost to the institution.

Arkansas, Florida, Georgia, Hawaii, Ohio, Pennsylvania, South Dakota. This practice also occurs in some other states in various forms.

Items of the history of the foregoing practices will be found in this volume, in the stories of the states indicated. Some of the sketches will exhibit a practice at its worst; others will show that it has been mitigated or abolished, wholly or largely. The examples recounted herein are not to be taken as comprehensive or all-inclusive, but as illustrative.

Practically without exception these practices are detrimental to public higher education, and turn out to be wasteful of tax funds, rather than conducive to economy and efficiency. If anything in the 50 stories comprising the bulk of this volume has any influence toward hastening the current progress away from these practices, a service will have been performed.

5. *State-wide top-echelon structure* for public higher education. Distinguishable from the forms of statehouse control detailed in number 4 is the widespread and persistent notion that all state colleges and universities in a given state should be under one administrative "umbrella," with one state-wide board taking over all the powers and duties of the institutional governing boards, which are thereupon abolished. A more popular alternative since 1930, and especially after 1950, has been the setting up of a state-wide statutory "coordinating" board, leaving the institutional governing boards in operation with their traditional powers largely or wholly unimpaired.

The idea of one state-wide *governing board* was implemented, between 1896 and 1970, in 14 states.[2] In these states the board's

---

[2]New Hampshire and Maine, which reorganized the governance of public higher education in 1965 and 1968 respectively, do not appear in this list because they are defined as "states having only one state university and its branch or branches."

jurisdiction covered all state institutions offering programs of four
years or more; but in a majority of them the state's hand in the administration of local public junior colleges, if any existed, was exercised by the State Board of Education which was responsible for the
public elementary and secondary schools.

South Dakota (1896)	Kansas (1915)	Rhode Island (1939)[3]
Florida (1906)	North Dakota (1916)	Arizona (1945)
Iowa (1909)	Oregon (1929)	Utah (1969)
Montana (1913)	Georgia (1931)	West Virginia (1969)
Idaho (1914)	Mississippi (1932)	

Another group of states continues to have a single board governing
several institutions, but not including the principal state university or
the land-grant university, each of which stands apart with its own
governing board. These centralized "subsystems" are listed here
indiscriminately:

California State Colleges	Colorado State Colleges
Wisconsin State Universities	Massachusetts State Colleges
Illinois State Colleges and Universities[4]	Tennessee State Universities
Minnesota State Colleges	Louisiana State Colleges and Universities
Texas State Colleges	Maryland State Colleges
Oklahoma State Colleges	Alabama State Colleges
Connecticut State Colleges	Vermont State Colleges

In most of the 14 states listed, these "subsystems" were once
governed by the respective state boards of education, or by boards
which were closely adjunct thereto; but a long-standing tendency,
accelerated in the decade 1960-1970, divorced most of them from that
agency; so that in 1969 only Tennessee, Louisiana, and Alabama (with
a minority of its state colleges so governed) continued in that manner.
All the other states listed had given this "subsystem" its own governing board, often called board of trustees of state colleges, or given all
or some of the institutions their own separate governing boards, as had
been done in Michigan (1963), Indiana (1965), Alabama (1967), and
New Jersey (1967).

Apart from the idea of one governing board for several institutions
is the more reasonable and practicable concept of a "coordinating

---

[3]See the story of Rhode Island, *infra*, for a plan enacted in 1969, creating a
Board of Regents to govern all higher education and also to have all powers of
the State Board of Education with respect to the elementary and secondary
school system.

[4]In Illinois the two largest state universities have separate governing
boards. The next two in order of size are governed by a recently created single
board—the Board of Regents, which also has under its jurisdiction the new
Sangamon State College. Two smaller state universities and two state colleges
are governed by the Board of Governors of State Universities and Colleges,
formerly the Normal School Board.

board" to promote cooperative planning, without abolishing any institutional governing boards or diminishing their authority to govern their own institutions, except that the "coordinating board" or "coordinating council" is given an advisory voice as to total budget askings, and often some uncertain authority to define the scope of the institutions. Only rarely are such boards or councils given the exclusive and paramount power to allocate appropriated funds among all the institutions, as is the Oklahoma Board of Regents for Higher Education, created by the state constitution of 1941. (Single *governing* boards for several institutions often possess this power, but not always. In several of the states having such boards, the appropriations—at least in substantial part—are made directly to each institution by the legislature.)

Toward the other end of the spectrum, some of the coordinating boards are only purely advisory, as in the case of California Coordinating Council for Higher Education created in 1960, and the Michigan State Board of Education established in 1963. Some are charged largely or exclusively with the duty of conducting studies, collecting statistics, making reports and recommendations, and disseminating public information about public higher education in the state. In 1969, some 26 states had such a board or council:

Alabama[5]	Louisiana[5]	New Jersey	South Carolina
Arkansas[5]	Maryland	New Mexico	Tennessee
California[5]	Massachusetts	New York	Texas
Colorado	Michigan[5]	North Carolina	Virginia
Connecticut	Minnesota[5]	Ohio	Washington[5]
Illinois	Missouri	Oklahoma[6]	Wisconsin
Kentucky		Pennsylvania[5]	

The vagueness of the wording of the statutes, and the fact that many of them are relatively new and have very little history of interpretation in practice or in litigation, make it difficult to classify these coordinating bodies into discrete groupings with finality. Each is described in its appropriate place in the stories of the 50 states.

Ten states in 1969 had either several institutions with no statutory overall coordinating board of any kind, or only one state university and its branch or branches, all under one governing board:

Alaska	Nebraska
Delaware	Nevada
Hawaii	New Hampshire[7]
Indiana	Vermont
Maine[7]	Wyoming

[5] Advisory only.
[6] Receives all appropriated funds and allocates them to institutions.
[7] The system consists of only one state university and branch campuses. Vocational-Technical Colleges continue under the State Board of Education. In Maine the Maritime Academy has its own governing board.

Despite the long-continued surge of "conventional wisdom" demanding overcentralization and bureaucratization in state-wide public higher education, both expert authority and examples of recent changes to the contrary are available.

Thad L. Hungate, in his work on *Management in Higher Education*, wrote in 1964 that: "Each institution should have its own governing board, with the maximum of autonomy that can be provided to it. . . . Only as the board has authority to act can there develop the community of consensus which for higher education is an essential of governance."[8]

In New York, the *Heald-Folsom-Gardner* report of 1960, the *Wells* report of 1965, and Chancellor Samuel B. Gould of the State University of New York have successively recommended urgently that the virtually impotent local advisory boards for each public institution of higher education in that state should be given the powers and duties of local institutional governing boards, but as yet with little palpable result. A struggle toward similar ends in the New Jersey legislature of 1969 achieved partial results. (See stories of New York and New Jersey, *infra*.)

As for actual major changes toward separate institutional governing boards: the Michigan Constitution of 1963 gave separate boards to four universities formerly governed by the State Board of Education; Indiana provided separate boards for two universities formerly governed by a single teachers college board in 1965; New Jersey snatched six state colleges from the governance of the State Board of Education in 1967 and gave each of the six a nine-member board of trustees. Alabama took somewhat similar action in the same year when it took four state colleges out of the jurisdiction of the State Board of Education, renamed them state universities, and gave each its own governing board.

Occurrences such as the foregoing in recent years lead one to suspect that the stampede toward total centralization in state-wide public higher education may not everywhere run to its logical conclusion; that it may indeed perhaps be halted and reversed. John D. Millett has wisely written: "There is no necessity in the academic community for that degree of precise coordination of effort which may be required in a large industrial organization or in a military force. The objective of higher education is realized in the minds and actions of individual students, as inspired by scholars and as influenced by the academic environment." Earlier he had said in the same work: "The essential ideas about business and public administration, such as they

---

[8]Thad L. Hungate, at p. 226 in *Management in Higher Education*. New York: Teachers College, Columbia University, Bureau of Publications, 1964. 348 pp.

are, may actually promote a widespread and unfortunate misunderstanding of the nature of the college and university in our society." [9]

The simple fact is that the mainspring of the academic community is morale—the individual *esprit* which fires men and women to search and discovery, makes baffling problems a pleasure, and renders sustained intellectual effort easy. No proctor or patrolman can enforce it. It flourishes in a community governed largely by an ongoing *consensus* rather than by hierarchic power. This principle applies at all levels of the state-wide academic collectivity. Again and again it has been demonstrated (but little publicized) that a statehouse "Czar" or "Establishment" oligarchy for public higher education, empowered to issue mandatory edicts, cannot effectively enforce such edicts when they run counter to strong and reasonable preferences of an institution's public constituency and of its students, faculty, administration, and governing board.

One example is that of the somewhat headstrong (and sometimes wrongheaded) State Board of Higher Education in North Carolina. Created in 1955 and empowered to dictate deletions and additions to the programs of the institutions, it was deprived of some of that power by the legislature of 1959 after four years of fruitless and damaging controversy between it and the University of North Carolina. Subsequently at least twice major recommendations of the Board regarding the growing design of the state-wide system have been pointedly ignored by the legislature.

In 1967 the Board's attempt to veto the request of East Carolina State College to be named a regional state university soon resulted in the naming by the legislature of not *one*, but *four* regional state universities. Again in 1969 the legislature added two new campuses to the Consolidated University of North Carolina, making a total of six campuses in that complex. Probably the Board might have been beneficently influential in all these matters if it had been more flexible in its attitudes, more inclined to cooperate than to combat, and willing to achieve some of its ends by permissive and persuasive tactics rather than by wielding restrictive power.

Looking back on the record, the Chairman of the North Carolina State Board of Higher Education in March 1969 made a revealing remark. Speaking at a colloquium on state-wide coordinating boards in higher education, he said: "Ours in North Carolina is fourteen years old and always on the verge of being out of business." [10]

---

[9] John D. Millett, *The Academic Community: An Essay on Organization.* New York: McGraw-Hill Book Company, 1962. 265 pp.

[10] Watts Hill, Jr., quoted in "The Direction of Higher Education Coordination: An Assessment," at page 18 in *Compact* (published bi-monthly at Denver by the Education Commission of the States): Vol. 3, No. 3 (June 1969).

It should not be omitted that during the late 'Sixties the staff of the North Carolina Board of Higher Education industriously produced and circulated a good series of statistical reports and other informative documents, including comprehensive planning reports. It may be that either the staff or the Board itself was remiss or unsuccessful in establishing and maintaining cordial working relations with the institutions within its jurisdiction. It may be that both the Board and its staff were too little influenced by the expansive mood of the institutions and of their state-wide constituency. At any rate, the repeated actions by the legislature restricting the Board's power or in disregard of its recommendations will probably ultimately redound to the benefit of the state and its people.

A state-wide board, without coercive power and committed not to engage in political struggles, committed to the flexible development of the state-wide system and not to its restriction and harassment, can serve useful purposes. A style and technique of liaison and intercommunication—not of hierarchical control—is called for. This is appropriate to the nature of the higher educational enterprise. It is suited to conduce toward maximum educational productivity for each tax dollar invested. It is not too difficult a style for existing boards to adopt and develop.

II

STORIES OF THE FIFTY STATES

ALABAMA

To sense something of the history of public higher education in Alabama it is well to know that as early as 1833 the state supreme court propounded with clarity and vigor the concept of the University of Alabama as a strictly public corporation.[1] This was significant as one of the earliest judicial definitions of a state university as a public corporation, with title to all its property belonging to the state, since its founding in 1820.

Incredibly enough, some other states failed to develop this concept for many decades afterward, and occasionally their courts flatly declared that the state university was a private corporation, as in Indiana (1887) and Maine (1909). As late as 1918 the governing board of the Illinois State Normal University from 1857 to 1917 was declared to be a private corporation. Thus the importance of Alabama's contribution to the evolution of the law of higher education is emphasized.

The Alabama Constitution stipulates that the location of the state university shall not be changed except by a two-thirds vote of both houses of the legislature taken by yeas and nays and entered upon the journal. It also specifies that the board of trustees of the university shall perpetuate itself by coöption, subject to confirmation of its appointments by the state senate; but the senate, if it rejects an appointee, is directed to proceed immediately to elect a suitable person to fill the vacancy.[2] In 1968 the only other state having some members of its state university governing board chosen by coöption was Delaware.

The University of Alabama has always had its own board of trustees except for a period of eight years during the Reconstruction period (1868-1876) when it was under the exclusive control of a State Board of Education which headed the entire state educational system and was expressly given the title and functions of "regents of the university." Thereafter the control of the institution was restored to a new board of trustees having no other responsibilities; and the University was judicially held to have been continuously in corporate

---

[1]*Trustees of University of Alabama* v. *Winston*, 5 Stew. and P. (Ala.) 17 (1833).

[2]Alabama Const. 1901, secs. 264, 267.

existence, with its corporate rights and powers unimpaired, since its original incorporation in 1820.[3]

The three other principal state institutions also have separate boards of trustees: the land-grant university, formerly styled Alabama Polytechnic Institute, now Auburn University; the former Alabama College for Women (later Alabama College, now the University of Montevallo), coeducational; and the University of South Alabama. The State Board of Education governs two other state institutions of higher education,—Alabama State College (predominantly Negro), and Alabama A & M College (Negro land-grant college). Four former teachers colleges now designated regional state universities, at Florence, Jacksonville, Livingston, and Troy, were given separate boards of trustees in 1967.

The 1959 legislature created a corporation to be known as the Alabama Education Authority, empowered to borrow up to $100 million for the construction of school and college buildings on its own credit and creating no debt against the state. The bonds of the Authority are negotiable and tax-free, and residue portions of the revenues from the state sales and use taxes are pledged for their payment. The legislature allocated $23½ million of the total anticipated proceeds to nine state colleges and universities, including slightly less than $7 million each to the University of Alabama and the Alabama Polytechnic Institute (now Auburn University), and lesser sums to the other institutions.

At an election December 5, 1961, the voters of Alabama approved a $3 million state bond issue to finance a Space and Missile Research Center for the University of Alabama, and a $2 million bond issue for hospital construction. A constitutional amendment adopted at the same time authorized state institutions to use dormitory room-rentals from buildings already constructed to pledge for payment of institutional bonds issued to finance new income-producing buildings—a question that had been decided to the contrary by an Alabama court decision of 1957.[4] The new amendment was construed in a 1966 decision involving Troy State College.[5]

An act of 1963 provided for development of a system of state junior colleges and trade schools. By 1969 there were 17 state two-year colleges. Their annual state support rose from $3 million for fiscal year 1965-66 to nearly $9½ million for fiscal year 1969-70.

---

[3] Trustees of University v. Moody, 62 Ala. 389 (1878).

[4] Opinion of the Justices, 266 Ala. 78, 93 So. 2d 923 (1957).

[5] Amendment CLX, interpreted in Pincard v. State Board of Education, (Ala.), 189 So. 2d 153 (1966).

Decisions in other states against pledging income from one project to pay for another were: Wells v. Stuck et al., (Ark.), 215 S.W. 2d 697 (1948); and Boe v. Foss, 76 S.D. 295, 77 N.W. 2d 1 (1956).

The general retail sales tax rate was raised to 4 per cent from the former 3 per cent, effective October 1, 1963, at first only for a period of 18 months after that date; but the new rate was subsequently retained. At that time only four other states had the 4 per cent rate: Illinois, Michigan, Pennsylvania, and Washington. This provision for added revenue was coincident with recovery from the slump in appropriations for annual operating expenses of higher education which occurred in 1961 and 1962, to be noticed later.

Meantime, nationally publicized events in the racial desegregation of the state institutions of higher education had occurred. As early as July 1, 1955, federal District Judge H. H. Grooms had issued an order permanently enjoining the dean of admissions of the University of Alabama from denying qualified Negro applicants the right to enroll solely on account of their race or color.[6] In mid-1963, when Governor George C. Wallace publicly declared he would personally "bar the door" to any Negro, the federal District Court, by Chief Judge Lynne, issued a temporary injunction against Governor Wallace, restraining him from obstructing the implementation of its order of 1955;[7] and two qualified Negro applicants, escorted by federal marshals, were enrolled at the University over the governor's protest.

At that time Alabama State College (predominantly Negro) was a nonaccredited institution, and the graduate school at Auburn University refused admission to graduates of all nonaccredited colleges. Harold A. Franklin, a graduate of Alabama State College, who wished to pursue studies leading to a master's degree at Auburn University, was thus denied admission. When he sued on behalf of himself and others in similar circumstances for an injunction against this denial, federal District Judge Johnson reasoned that the state of Alabama was fully responsible for both the operation of the Auburn University graduate school and the unaccredited condition of the state's two colleges predominantly for Negroes; and in these circumstances the rule of the graduate school was in effect unlawfully discriminatory on the ground of race. He issued an injunctive order to be effective with the term beginning January 2, 1964.[8]

The total of appropriations of state tax funds for operating expenses of higher education in Alabama for biennium 1961-63 appears to have been slightly smaller than that for the immediately preceding biennium—affording the rare spectacle of a state allowing its support of higher education actually to be diminished during a period of un-

---

[6]*Lucy* v. *Adams*, 134 F. Supp. 235 (1955); affirmed in 228 F. 2d 619 (1955); and *certiorari* denied, 351 U.S. 931, 76 S.Ct. 790, 100 L.Ed. 1460 (1956).

[7]*United States* v. *Wallace, Governor*, 218 F. Supp. 290 (1963).

[8]*Franklin* v. *Parker*, 283 F. Supp. 724 (1963); affirmed, with slight modification not material here, 331 F. 2d 841 (1964).

ALABAMA

Appropriations for Annual Operating Expenses of Higher Education in Alabama, Alternate Fiscal Years, 1959-60 through 1969-70 (in thousands of dollars)

Institutions	Year 1959-60[1]	Year 1961-62	Year 1963-64	Year 1965-66	Year 1967-68	Year 1969-70
U of Alabama	5,758	8,010	10,453	12,901	16,357	19,673
Med Ctr (Birmingham Br)	2,895				1,145	2,430
Huntsville				800[2]	1,666[2]	2,191
Grad Sch Soc Wk				40	208	
Subtotals, U of Ala	8,653	8,010	10,453	13,741	19,376	24,294
Auburn University[3]	7,887	7,365	9,755	12,000	15,601	19,161
Four state colleges:[4]						
Florence	48	727	1,020	4,327	6,800	1,971
Jacksonville	48	791	1,114			3,374
Livingston	44	362	493			1,072
Troy	44	655	919			1,964
Four Tchr-Tng Insts[5]	2,428					
Subtotals, state colleges[6]	2,612	2,535	3,546	4,327	6,800	8,381
U of South Alabama[7]			509	2,462	3,133	3,650
Alabama State College	1,080	1,010	1,317	1,576	2,029	2,364
Alabama A & M College	888	905	1,265	1,555	2,008	2,339
Alabama College	731	709	962	1,180	1,567	1,826
Tuskegee Institute[8]			552	670	470	470
New Jr Colls & Voc Schls			300			
Northwest Ala Jr Coll			176			
Marion Inst (private)			40	75	75	75
Walker Co JC (private)			43	44	44	44
State junior colleges[9]				3,087	6,747	9,361

Medical scholarships			116	135	135	135
Dental scholarships			99	83	83	83
Student aid programs[10]				99	25	25
Regional Edn (SREB)					99	220
Totals	21,942	20,534	29,133	41,127	58,192	72,518[11]

[1]Figures in this column are one-half of the appropriations for biennium 1959-61.

[2]Appropriations for both fiscal years were conditional; but the $800,000 for 1965-66 was paid, and $1,200,000 for 1966-67 was paid.

[3]Formerly Alabama Polytechnic Institute.

[4]Specific allocations to the four institutions were at the discretion of the State Board of Education until 1969.

[5]This sum is a "Teacher-training equalization fund" to be allocated among the four state colleges, which otherwise receive only token appropriations.

[6]Renamed state universities in 1967.

[7]A new institution at Mobile.

[8]The famous private institution for Negroes receives state funds as indicated.

[9]This is a lump sum largely for the support of prospective new state junior colleges. In the early years lump-sum appropriations were made for the "development of a system of junior colleges and trade schools." Thus exact comparison with earlier years is impossible. New appropriations of $5,558,000 and $6,558,000 for fiscal years 1965-66 and 1966-67, respectively, for "state vocational schools," are excluded from this tabulation. Presumably the former Snead Junior College (Methodist), which the legislature authorized the state to acquire, is included.

[10]These include elementary teachers scholarships ($25,000 per year) and student aid in graduate and professional fields ($91,395 a year).

[11]Includes $90,000 for Alabama Commission on Higher Education.

ADDITIONAL IMPORTANT NOTES: Additional appropriations aggregating $9 1/3 million for fiscal year 1967-68 and $10 1/4 million for 1968-69 were made, *"conditional* upon the condition of the Alabama Special Educational Trust Fund and with the approval of the Governor, provided, however, in the release of the conditional appropriations herein made, the conditional appropriation to the State Board of Education for the use of the Minimum Program Account, the Minimum Program Account—Trainable Retarded Children and Vocational Education shall be paid in full before any other conditional appropriations are released."

Another conditional appropriation of $2 million each year was made to Auburn University "for the construction and equipping of a branch in Montgomery," and $5 million in bond money was also appropriated for that purpose. The present Montgomery extension center of the University of Alabama will be phased out as the new Auburn University branch is developed.

precedented expansion of need;—but recovery from this slump began in 1963, and the appropriations for fiscal year 1968-69 represented a gain of 174½ per cent over the nine years since 1959-60. Measured by rates of gain over this period, this placed Alabama in thirty-seventh place among the 50 states, with 13 states making slower gains. Surprisingly, however, only one of those 13 is a southern state. Ten of them are in a contiguous block extending from Iowa to Oregon and from Oklahoma to North Dakota—mostly in the northwest quadrant of the continental United States.

A notable detail is the comparatively small annual appropriation of state tax funds to Tuskegee Institute, a private college predominantly for Negroes, although the Alabama Constitution forbids any appropriation of tax moneys to any private institution except by a two-thirds vote of each house of the legislature.

Among the developments of the decade were the evolution of the Huntsville and Birmingham branches of the University of Alabama and the establishment of a new regional state university at Mobile, styled the University of South Alabama, which received its first modest annual appropriations of $500,000 and $700,000 for fiscal years 1963-64 and 1964-65, and more than $3 million each year for fiscal years 1967-68 and 1968-69. In 1968 the legislature decided that the extension center of the University of Alabama in Montgomery will be phased out as a new extension campus of Auburn University is developed at that city. A *conditional* appropriation of $2 million for each fiscal year of the biennium 1967-69 was made to Auburn University "for the construction and equipping of a branch in Montgomery," and the use of $5 million of bond money was authorized for that purpose.

The plan to have Auburn University develop a four-year branch in Montgomery was challenged in a federal court by the Alabama State Teachers Association, joined by some students and alumni of Alabama State College, on the ground that it would perpetuate racial segregation by placing two state institutions in Montgomery, one white and one Negro (the Auburn University branch, white; and Alabama State College, Negro), and that it would not do all that could be done to end segregation. Apparently the desired alternative would be to build up and expand Alabama State College as a racially-integrated institution, as had been done, for example, in the case of West Virginia State College.

District Judge Frank M. Johnson, writing for the three-judge federal court, declined to interfere. "In reviewing such a decision to determine whether it maximizes desegregation," said he, "we would necessarily be involved, consciously or by default, in a wide range of educational policy decisions in which courts should not become involved. . . ." This decision was affirmed by the United States Supreme Court January 20, 1969.

Contemporaneously the same issue, arising out of a similar set of facts, came before another federal district court in Tennessee, where plans were afoot to place a four-year branch of the University of Tennessee at Nashville, the location of the predominantly Negro Tennessee A & I State University. While denying an injunction, the court was nevertheless willing to go further than any federal court had gone before. In August 1968 it ordered the Tennessee State Board of Education and the Board of Trustees of the University of Tennessee to submit by April 1, 1969, a plan for complete desegregation of the state's public colleges and universities.

"The fact remains," said District Judge Frank Gray, Jr., in the opinion of the court, "that nothing is being done to dismantle the dual system so graphically illustrated by the enrollment at A & I," which was 99 per cent Negro.

Of Alabama's total appropriations for operating expenses for biennium 1967-69 ($116,654,000) nearly $20 million were made "*conditional* upon the condition of the Alabama Special Educational Trust Fund and with the approval of the Governor. . . ." It was reported in February 1968 that the likelihood of payment of any substantial part of these conditional appropriations was very small, though there was some hope that a minor portion might be paid sometime during the second year of the biennium.

The 1967 legislature provided for separate governing boards for each of the four predominantly white state colleges (Florence, Jacksonville, Livingston, and Troy) hitherto governed by the State Board of Education. A Chicago firm of management consultants was employed to report in March 1968 as to whether the state needed a second medical college, in addition to the University of Alabama Medical College in Birmingham. Organized citizens of Mobile wanted a second medical college in that city, and the legislature made a *conditional* appropriation of $2 million to the new University of South Alabama for "general support" which was generally thought to be intended to further the purpose of planning and accomplishing other preliminaries to the establishing of a medical college. There can actually be little doubt that Alabama, with a population of three and one-half million, urgently needs such an institution.

Again in 1967 Alabama was in trouble with a federal court regarding new state statutes designed to preserve and promote racial segregation in schools. Early in November of that year a court composed of Court of Appeals Judge Richard T. Rives and District Court Judges Frank M. Johnson and H. H. Grooms issued injunctions against the enforcement of two acts of the 1967 legislature: One would have permitted parents to choose the race of their children's teachers; the other would have allowed state funds to be paid to private nonsectarian private schools—the latter being a well-known device by which white racist parents hope to provide segregated schools for their own children. Both acts, said the court, violate the equal protection clause of the Fourteenth Amendment.

For more than 40 years Alabama statutes have provided for an advisory State Council of Education composed of the governor and two members of the State Board of Education chosen by that board, and the president and one member of the governing board of each of the state institutions of higher education not governed by the State Board of Education. The state has not been immune, however, from the bandwagon movement toward coercive centralization or consolidation of control of public higher education; and certain plans of that type have been discussed, in and out of the legislature. Early in 1968 this was summarized by a local commentator as "much talk and no action." Tight consolidation and centralization would not sit well in Alabama, where the University of Alabama has a tradition of a century and a half of academic autonomy, older and perhaps stronger than those of some of its sister institutions in other states of the Deep South; and where the history of cooperation among the major institutions in the public interest is excellent.

In 1969 a special session of the legislature established the Alabama Commission on Higher Education, composed of nine members appointed by the governor with the advice and consent of the senate, and appropriated $90,000 for its operation during fiscal year 1969-70. It is authorized to act primarily in a fact-finding and advisory capacity. The governing boards of public colleges and universities in Alabama retain all their powers and duties.

ALASKA

With the advent of statehood in 1959, the new Constitution and implementing statutes provided for a highly centralized "strong executive" state government, with eleven "executive departments," one of which is Education; but the Board of Regents of the University of Alaska was continued and recognized as the agency for the control of public higher education.

The University of Alaska, founded in 1922, is the youngest principal state university in any state (though there are in some states regional state universities of more recent date, such as the University of South Alabama); and the youngest land-grant institution (except the Federal City College in the District of Columbia, which became a land-grant college in 1968).

With territory two and one-half times the size of Texas, and a population of nearly 300,000, Alaska has enormous developing resources, and some of the characteristics of a pioneer country. Even with much of the scanty population distributed along the south coast and in the southeastern "tongue" or panhandle, distances between small cities and towns are relatively great, and facilities for land travel are few. Hence the University of Alaska has initiated seven community college branches, some of which are very small by usual standards, and all of which are financed in the University budget and operated by the University. There is no other public institution of higher education in Alaska, but a small private college styled Alaska Methodist University is located in Anchorage, the largest city; and the private Sheldon Jackson Junior College is in Sitka.

The University of Alaska has an agricultural experiment station at its main campus and at Palmer, and an experimental fur farm at Petersburg. It also operates the Naval Arctic Research Laboratory at Point Barrow, the northernmost cape. Something of the scope of other research activities is indicated by the names of the several institutes: Geophysical Institute; Institute of Marine Science; Institute of Arctic Biology; Institute for Social, Economic, and Government Research; Mineral Industry Research Laboratory; Institute of Arctic Environmental Engineering; Alaska Cooperative Wildlife Research Unit; and Institute of Water Resources. Some of these units have received philanthropic support; and most of them are operated in cooperation with agencies of the federal government, and to some extent with private industry.

ALASKA

Appropriations for Annual Operating Expenses of Higher Education in Alaska, Alternate Fiscal Years, 1959-60 through 1969-70 (in thousands of dollars)

Institutions	Year 1959-60	Year 1961-62	Year 1963-64	Year 1965-66	Year 1967-68	Year 1969-70
U of Alaska	2,111	3,023	3,425	4,619[1]	6,624	8,865
Ag Exp Station				253[2]	299	417
Coop Ag Exten Serv				182[3]	251	387
Geophysical Institute				308	334	544
Inst of Marine Science				160	177	264
Inst of Arctic Biology				122	138	206
Inst Bus, Econ, & Govt				60	101	147
Mineral Industry Rsch				50	45	
Petersburg Ex Fur Farm[5]				34		
Electronic Tech Prog				25	92	
Arctic Environ'l Eng Lab				18	27	47
Community Colleges[6]				278[4]	531	998
Rental of heating plant and facilities[7]			305			
Totals	2,111	3,023	3,425	6,108	8,619	11,876

[1]Includes $186,711 for salary increases.
[2]Includes $20,468 for salary increases.
[3]Includes $16,310 for salary increases.
[4]Includes $6,511 for salary increases.
[5]This appropriation of $34,000 was contingent upon the discontinuance of federal support of the fur farm; and the latter was continued.
[6]These are small outposts of the University of Alaska, located at Anchorage, Juneau, Ketchikan, Palmer, and Sitka (Kenai added in 1967-68 and Kodiak added in 1968-69).
[7]This item is newly budgeted as an operating expense. The facility is financed by a nonprofit corporation, its cost to be amortized by annual rentals paid by the state.

In 1960 a team of consultants from Stanford University and Chico State College in California, assisted by selected architects, was employed with the aid of a Ford Foundation grant to study the University of Alaska and recommend a general development plan for future years, including not only physical aspects of the main campus at Fairbanks, but also the administrative, instructional, and service aspects of all units of the University, wherever located. Members of the faculty were involved in the effort, and the result was put in the form of four small lithoprinted reports issued between February and October, 1960, all under the title of *Planning for Action*, and aggregating about 100 pages. Plans for the Fairbanks campus contemplated a projected total enrollment of 2,700 in 1970 and 5,000 in 1975, with a probable 8,000 in 1980. By 1968 the projected curve of growth had been substantially exceeded.

In 1961-62 a team headed by an officer of the Canadian Social Science Research Council and including deans of extension at the University of Minnesota and the University of Nevada, working on a subsidy from the Fund for the Advancement of Education, prepared a comprehensive 147-page report on *Continuing Education in Alaska*, in which the state-wide role of the University was stressed.

The record of appropriations of state tax funds for annual operating expenses of the University shows a gain of 393 per cent from fiscal year 1959-60 through 1968-69, meaning that the annual aggregate was only slightly less than quintupled in nine years. This rate of gain gave Alaska eighth place among the 50 states as thus measured. Alaska's gain of 393 per cent was exceeded only by Hawaii, Kentucky, and five northeastern states (New York, Pennsylvania, and three states of New England, where a surge in the expansion of public higher education has characterized the decade).

By 1968-69, however, the $10,400,000 appropriated for operating expenses of the University represented less than 8½ per cent of the total of $124,100,000 appropriated for all state governmental operations. This is distinctly below the average percentage among the 50 states and seems to indicate that a less than appropriate portion of state revenues is currently being devoted to higher education in Alaska. The spectacular north slope oil development should provide a more adequate revenue base than the state has had previously.

By way of improving the state revenue system, the 1968 legislature raised the rate of the oil and gas severance tax to 3 per cent (from the former 1 per cent).

In 1968 the residents approved a general obligation bond issue for $8,500,000 for the University. This was part of a $53 million bond package proposed by the state legislature for improvements of the state's highways, ferry system, airports, establishment of fish hatcheries, and other state programs. The university bond issue was for: (1) $750,000 to improve and upgrade fire protection and fire-fighting facilities and to expand utilities; (2) $5,250,000 to build a high-rise general classroom and office building; (3) $1,000,000 to construct a dining complex to serve 800 students; and (4) $1,500,000 to build a 200-student dormitory. The 1969 Legislature approved à $4,000,000 revenue bond issue for construction of a Student Activities Center.

ARIZONA

The legislature of 1959 raised the general sales tax rate from 2 cents to 3 cents on the dollar, and appropriated a total of $102 million for all state purposes for fiscal year 1959-60, 20 per cent more than for the preceding fiscal year. About two-thirds of the sales tax revenue was earmarked for increasing state aid to local public schools from $127 to $170 per pupil per year.

The year 1960 was marked by the enactment of a statute, effective July 1, 1961, providing a systematic frame for the development of local public junior colleges. Prior to that time there had been two small junior colleges, one at Thatcher and one at Phoenix; and in both 1959 and 1960 the legislature appropriated $150,000 for aid to these two. The act, which became effective in 1961, augured a new era of encouragement and support for local public junior colleges, so that by 1964 there were four in operation, including a large one in Phoenix (Maricopa County), and the state appropriation for fiscal year 1964-65 as aid for annual operating expenses was $3,858,000. By 1967 the Maricopa County college had three campuses, and the annual appropriation of state aid for operating expenses of the six local public junior colleges was $6,310,000. The development of the state-aided junior colleges was an outstanding feature of the decade.

The act authorized any county with at least 320 potential junior college students and an assessed valuation of at least $60 million to establish a junior college district. The state was to pay half the cost of initial construction (up to a maximum of $500,000), and $115 per student per year for continuing capital outlays. It also was to pay, for operating expenses, $525 per year per student for the first 320 students, and $350 per student above that number. This was an advanced junior college statute for its time, being considerably more generous with state aid than most other states, even including California and New York. The 1961 act was amended in 1966, to provide $525 for the first 1,000 students in the junior college, and $350 for each student above that number.

The act also set up a State Board of Junior College Directors, composed of one member of the Board of Regents of State Universities, the State Superintendent of Public Instruction, the State Director of Vocational Education, and 14 other members appointed by the governor, one from each county.

As early as 1927 Arizona had enacted a permissive statute under which certain public school districts could establish junior colleges, and under which the colleges at Thatcher and Phoenix had been created. It seems that the Phoenix Union High School District did not immediately elect to come formally into the "system" contemplated in the act effective in 1961, and as a consequence received no state funds for fiscal year 1961-62. The act provided "any junior college established and maintained (under earlier statutes) *may* become part of a junior college district, provided such district complies with the provisions of this chapter." It transpired that in 1962 the electors of the high school district approved a plan of integration whereby the junior college became a part of the state-wide "system," and this plan was adopted by the legislature—thus ostensibly settling the question, but with no retroactive provision regarding fiscal year 1961-62. The Phoenix high school district sued for a declaratory judgment, holding it was entitled to its quota of state funds for 1961-62, and won in the trial court; and at long last, in 1967, this judgment was affirmed by the supreme court of Arizona. The decision was that a reading of all the pertinent statutes together produced the conclusion that they did not make joining the new system a prerequisite to receiving state aid. Justice Struckmeyer said: "That the legislature has not, and, of course, cannot be compelled to appropriate the necessary funds is immaterial. The action is not moot." [1]

In 1967-68 the sum appropriated for state aid for annual operating expenses of junior colleges ($6,310,000) was more than 13½ per cent of the total appropriated for operating expenses of all higher education. It was said that the amount per student enrolled was more for the junior colleges than it was for the three state universities—a fact that would not argue for any diminution of junior college support, but would point unmistakably to a need for better support of the universities.

Arizona currently has no "tripartite" system of public higher education. There are only two general types of institutions: the state-aided local public junior colleges and the three state universities. Oldest of the three is the University of Arizona at Tucson, which is also the land-grant university. Of nearly equal size is Arizona State University at Tempe, which has evolved from a single-purpose teachers college within the past 20 years with lightning rapidity, due to the influx of approximately a million people into the Phoenix metropolitan area. Northern Arizona University, at Flagstaff, in the sparsely populated north central mountain area, also has escaped from the chrysalis of a teachers college, but is only about one-third as

---

[1]*Arizona State Board of Directors for Junior Colleges* v. *Phoenix Union High School District of Maricopa County*, 102 Ariz. 69, 424 P. 2d 819 (1967).

large as the other two. While it may be said to be an "emerging" university, it could also be appropriately styled "regional state university" for the northern half of its vast state.

One can point to the evolution of Arizona State University at Tempe as one of the three leading miracles of state university growth after the middle of the twentieth century. First among these is Southern Illinois University at Carbondale and Edwardsville; and third is Florida State University at Tallahassee. Only a generation ago each of these three was a small institution of only a few hundred students, with limited offerings and narrow outlook. Now each is a large state university, with doctoral programs and professional schools, permeated with the lusty exhilaration of growth, attracting distinguished faculty members, building great libraries and laboratories and all the related impedimenta of a "city of intellect."

The University of Arizona, at Tucson, has a longer history, also marked by growth in recent years. The Tucson metropolitan area now has one-third of a million people, and its population was nearly doubled between 1950 and 1960. One of the current major additions to the University is a new medical school. Authorized and planned during the middle 'Sixties, and now well under way, it was much needed in a state of one and two-thirds million people with the growth record and growth prospects of Arizona. The population of the whole state was indeed doubled within the 15 years between 1950 and 1965, placing it among the top four states in the nation as measured by rate of population growth. It is this factor that creates a pinch for higher education in Arizona.

Although the annual appropriations for operating expenses of higher education show a gain of 292½ per cent over the nine years from 1959-60 through 1968-69, this rate of gain is exceeded by Colorado (308½); by Kentucky, Georgia, Missouri, Tennessee, Virginia, and North Carolina in the South and the border states; and by seven states of New England and the Middle Atlantic group. None of these had a rate of population growth anywhere near that of Arizona. Arizona's lag was further shown in 1966 by a tabulation of the amounts of state tax dollars appropriated per student in Arizona's three state universities compared with 49 land-grant universities and colleges in other states. Th. University of Arizona (which is a land-grant university) ranked forty-seventh; and Northern Arizona University and Arizona State University (not land-grant institutions) ranked fifty-first and fifty-second, respectively.

The situation was summarized in some detail in a series of seven articles in the state-wide newspaper *Arizona Republic*, December 11-17, 1966, under the byline of the author, and with the general title of "Looking Ahead with Higher Education in Arizona." Earlier in the same year the Arizona Academy, a state-wide organization of some 200 civic leaders, had devoted its semi-annual October meeting to higher education. A 16-page summary report with recommendations was

ARIZONA

Appropriations for Annual Operating Expenses of Higher Education in Arizona, Alternate Fiscal Years, 1959-60 through 1969-70 (in thousands of dollars)

Institutions	Year 1959-60	Year 1961-62	Year 1963-64	Year 1965-66	Year 1967-68	Year 1969-70
U of Arizona	7,726	9,916	12,365	15,388	20,063	28,429
Arizona State U	5,036	6,537	8,821	10,817	14,853	20,982
Northern Ariz U[1]	979	1,399	2,224	3,067	5,055	7,216
Subtotal, state U's	13,742[2]	17,852	23,410	29,273	39,971	56,627
Junior Colleges:						
Maricopa County[3]				4,563	4,557	5,877
Yuma County[4]				693	711	735
Cochise County[5]				475	426	600
Graham County[6]				372	534	574
State Jr Coll Board				84	82	102
Subtotal, Jr Colls[7]				6,186	6,310	8,649[8]
Total	13,742[2]	17,852	23,410	35,459	46,281	65,611

[1]Formerly Arizona State College at Flagstaff; name changed effective May 1, 1966.
[2]Exclusive of institutional receipts from other sources, which are estimated at a total of $6,217,221 for the three institutions, bringing the total operating expense budget up to about $20 million.
[3]Phoenix College, Glendale College, Mesa College.
[4]Arizona Western Junior College.
[5]Cochise College.
[6]Eastern Arizona Junior College.
[7]During the years 1959-1963 very small appropriations were made to one or two local junior colleges, but are not included in this tabulation.
[8]Included in this total are sums for two new colleges: Yavapai County Jr. Coll., $394,000, and Pinal County Jr. Coll., $367,000.

published under the title *Report of Ninth Arizona Town Hall: Higher Education in Arizona*; and a comprehensive 250-page mimeographed report on *Higher Education in Arizona*, cooperatively prepared by all the universities and other collaborating agencies and edited by Arthur T. Grant of the University of Arizona, had been completed for the Academy in June 1966.

The University of Arizona does not have precisely the same constitutional independence as the universities in Michigan, Minnesota, Idaho, and California, but a series of Arizona supreme court decisions has established and confirmed that the Regents have exclusive power to manage the funds of the institution, both before and after the three institutions were placed under a single Board of Regents in 1945. The audit and allowance of a claim by the Regents is recognized as conclusive, as against the interposition of the state auditor.[2] Twice the state auditor has been ordered by *mandamus* to issue warrants to pay claims approved by the Regents: once for the purpose of paying membership fees and assessments in organizations, and of paying travel expenses;[3] and once for payment of expenses of the ceremonial inauguration of a new president of the University of Arizona.[4]

An Arizona civil service act of 1948 would have covered the nonacademic employees of the Board of Regents, but was held unconstitutional to that extent. The unanimous supreme court, by Justice Windes, said: "To permit legislation to throw the employment and supervision of all personnel under the civil service law, except the teaching staff, would necessarily deprive the Board of Regents of a large portion of its constitutional supervisory power. We have no hesitation in holding that such legislation runs counter to Article 11, Section 2, Arizona Constitution."[5]

A special session of the legislature in December 1967 enacted two revenue measures which, though not of tremendous import, indicate interest in improving the state tax system: the tax on cigarettes was raised to 10 cents a pack from the former 6½ cents; and the tax on distilled spirits went up from $1.44 to $2 per gallon.

A recent statute established the office of State Commissioner of Finance and subjected the Board of Regents to increased central control of budget preparation, accounting, data processing, and

---

[2]*Callaghan* v. *Boyce, State Auditor*, 17 Ariz. 433, 153 Pac. 773 (1915). *Fairfield, State Auditor* v. *W. J. Corbett Hardware Company*, (Ariz.), 215 Pac. 510 (1923).
[3]*Frohmiller* v. *Board of Regents of University and State Colleges*, (Ariz.), 171 P. 2d 356 (1946).
[4]*Board of Regents of University and State Colleges* v. *Frohmiller*, 69 Ariz. 50, 208 P. 2d 833 (1949).
[5]*Hernandez* v. *Frohmiller*, 68 Ariz. 242, 204 P. 2d 854 (1949).

purchasing. In view of the doctrine of the state supreme court as enunciated in the five decisions just cited, the constitutionality of some of these provisions may be questionable.

ARKANSAS

The University of Arkansas in Fayetteville dates from 1871. It is the land-grant university as well as the principal university of the state. (According to the custom in 16 southern states, Arkansas also has a separate land-grant college for Negroes predominantly.) The medical school of the University of Arkansas is in Little Rock. It occupied only a single city block until 1947, when it acquired 30 acres from the 160-acre site of the Arkansas State Hospital, where a new plant was built for the medical school and its teaching hospital.

The acquisition of the new site was by agreement between the State Hospital Board and the University of Arkansas Board of Trustees, without the intervention of the legislature or other state authorities. It was immediately challenged by a taxpayer's suit to enjoin both boards, on the ground that they had exceeded their authority and usurped powers belonging only to the legislature. The supreme court of Arkansas readily sustained the boards. Finding no explicit statutory authority for the joint plan, the court pointed out that none is necessary, for boards of trustees have not only all powers specifically delegated, but also such additional or implied powers as may be necessary to carry out the trust to the best advantage of the public.[1]

It was shown that the state hospital and the state university would gain mutual advantages. Medical students would gain by having an abundance of clinical material available in nervous and mental diseases at the adjacent state hospital. State hospital patients would gain by having a general hospital and medical center immediately at hand. The state would get a large and modern medical plant and equipment with economy of expenditure and a minimum of duplication of facilities. As frequently occurs, there were also some offers of substantial philanthropic contributions to the new project.[2]

The rate of gain in appropriations of state tax funds for annual operating expenses of higher education in Arkansas from fiscal year 1959-60 through 1968-69 was 229 per cent. This was definitely below the 50-state average of 261 per cent, and placed Arkansas in thirty-third

---

[1]*Lindsay* v. *White et al.*, (Ark.), 206 S.W. 2d 762 (1947).
[2]*State of Arkansas* v. *State of Texas*, 346 U.S. 368, 74 S.Ct. 169, 98 L.Ed. 80 (1953).

ARKANSAS

Appropriations for Annual Operating Expenses of Higher Education in Arkansas, Alternate Fiscal Years, 1959-60 through 1969-70 (in thousands of dollars)

Institutions	Year 1959-60[1]	Year 1961-62	Year 1963-64	Year 1965-66	Year 1967-68	Year 1969-70
U of Arkansas						
(Incl Ag Exp Sta, Ag Exten Serv, & Grad Inst Tech)	6,260	7,564	8,865	11,792	15,299	17,850
Med Ctr (Incl Child Guid Ctr)	4,800	3,124	3,845	4,676	5,594	6,333
Indus Rsch & Exten Center		127	130	155	375	
Soils Testing Laboratory	99	99	109	118	129	
Night Law School				132		
Loans to medical students	45					
Subtotal, U of Arkansas	11,204	10,914	12,949	16,873	21,327	27,776[2]
Arkansas State U[3] (incl Beebe Br)	989	1,170	1,589	2,914	4,715	5,656
State Colleges:						
Ark A, M & N College (incl Voc Sch)	850	825	1,147	1,714	2,422	2,690
State Coll of Ark[4]	711	884	1,093	1,576	2,383	2,652
Henderson St Coll	629	753	1,027	1,448	2,229	2,460
Southern St Coll	607	628	776	1,108	1,605	1,848
Ark Polytech Coll	598	742	860	1,256	1,622	1,759
Ark A & M College	643	683	768[5]	959	1,436	1,555
Subtotal, State Colleges	4,038	4,515	5,671	8,061	11,697	12,964

Educational TV		10	116	352	459	234
So Reg Educ Bd[6]		84[7]	95	171	188	
St aid to Jr Colls				350	600	1,000
Total	16,230	16,693	20,419	28,722	38,985	47,630

[1]These figures include income from nontax sources and are therefore not comparable with those in the succeeding tabulations.

[2]Includes $3,593,000 for Little Rock campus, former private University of Little Rock.

[3]Formerly Arkansas State *College.*

[4]Formerly Arkansas State *Teachers* College.

[5]Increased to this amount by a special appropriation of $50,000 for Forestry.

[6]Payments to the Southern Regional Education Board, in accord with the interstate compact among 16 southern states.

[7]This figure for the first fiscal year; 87 for the second fiscal year.

place among the states, as measured by percentage of gain over that period. Arkansas is a state of comparatively undeveloped material resources and of relatively low *per capita* incomes. A factor also underlying the slow rate of growth is the nearly stationary condition of the population curve. Slightly under 2 million people in mid-1967, the figure was only a trifle more than it had been in the census of 1960, 7 years before. During some of those years the figure had actually fallen temporarily below what it had been in 1960.

The 1961 legislature created a "Commission on Coordination of Higher Educational Finance," to consist of 10 members appointed by the governor and confirmed by the senate for terms of 10 years, one term to expire each year. The Commission employs a director and small staff, and maintains a central office in Little Rock. Although the Commission is to "receive, evaluate, and coordinate budget requests for the University and state colleges, and present a single budget request containing recommendations for separate appropriations to each of them," this is only an *advisory* function. The act specifically provides that "nothing herein shall be construed to prohibit any institution of higher education from submitting any matter pertaining to the financial operation and needs of such institutions to the General Assembly or to the Governor at any time."

Another section of the act specifies: "The Boards of Trustees of the University and state colleges (each has a separate board) shall continue to exercise their present functions and powers and nothing in this Act shall be construed to deprive, limit, or in any way alter or change any of the existing statutes and constitutional provisions pertaining to or governing said Boards of Trustees."

In the late 1940's a taxpayer's suit was brought to enjoin the University of Arkansas and the several other state institutions from paying out any funds not appropriated by the legislature, and to require them to deposit all their receipts in the state treasury. Also it was sought specifically to enjoin the institutions from using their receipts from nontax sources to supplement the salaries of certain employees so as to exceed the maximum salaries specified in the current appropriation act. The trial court dismissed the case, and the supreme court of Arkansas affirmed the judgment, except as to the last point. Here it was held that the plaintiff was entitled to an injunction against the payment of salaries in excess of those provided for in the appropriation act, but that the injunction should not apply to the use of funds received from sources not controlled by the legislature, such as federal subventions, endowment income, current gifts, and student fees.

Two sections of the Arkansas Constitution of 1874 stipulated that no money shall go out of the treasury except as appropriated by law; but there was no requirement that the funds at issue in this case should go *into* the state treasury. The legislature could so prescribe, but it had not done so. This was the opinion of Justice McFaddin and the entire court except Chief Justice Griffin Smith, who dissented vigorously but on dubious reasoning. He could not believe that the framers of the Constitution had *intended* to omit the deposit requirement.[3]

In their earlier years some of the state colleges in Arkansas were two-year colleges—*state* junior colleges, not based on local taxing districts, and not university branches. The tendency has been for these to become four-and five-year institutions, as the demand for higher education increased. The legislature of 1965, after a permissive constitutional amendment had been adopted, enacted legislation authorizing the establishment of state-aided local public junior colleges based on local taxing districts. Comparatively small appropriations of state tax funds for that purpose appear in the statutes for fiscal years 1967-68 and 1968-69.

The institution known until recently as Arkansas State College has been renamed Arkansas State University. It operates one outlying two-year branch campus at Beebe. Little Rock University, a private college, is being acquired as a branch campus of the University of Arkansas.

------

[3] *Gipson* v. *Ingram et al.*, (Ark.), 223 S.W. 2d 595 (1949).

CALIFORNIA

In considering the decade of the 'Sixties, the first factor to be noticed is that in 1959 California was already at a relatively high point in state support of higher education. The University at Berkeley was, by many evidences, the greatest state university in the world. It was the "flagship" of the multicampus University of California, with other campuses in San Francisco, Los Angeles, Davis, Santa Barbara, Riverside, and La Jolla. The 14 state colleges had long since broken the narrow mold of the normal school or the teachers college and become multipurpose institutions. Half a dozen of the older and larger among them were already larger and better supported than half the nation's state universities.

Some sixty-five local public junior colleges dotted the state—twice as many as in any other state except Texas. California was the leader in the development of the two-year college. Altogether the California system of public higher education was larger than that of any state in the Union and also noted for its excellence at all levels. These facts are parts of a necessary basis for correct interpretation of an average or less-than-average rate of gain in state support during 1959-1969.

Even so, it is during this decade that the University campus at Davis has been developed far toward the status of a cosmopolitan university. New University campuses at Santa Cruz, Irvine, and San Diego have been established, each destined to become a full-fledged university of a distinctive style. The California College of Medicine at Los Angeles (formerly a private college of osteopathy) has become a unit of the Irvine campus of the University. The 14 state colleges have become 19, with additional ones in prospect. The approximately sixty-five junior colleges have become approximately eighty, and the goal of having every square mile of the state within the boundaries of some junior college district has been nearly achieved.

A declaration of public policy regarding the support of education at all levels appears in the form of an amendment to the Constitution of California (Article XIII, Section 15) adopted in 1933, in the depths of the Great Depression: "Out of the revenues from state taxes for which provision is made in this article, together with all other state revenues, there shall first be set apart the moneys to be applied by the state to the support of the public school system and the State University."

The wording should not be interpreted in any sense as intended to omit or downgrade the state colleges or the public junior colleges, for at that time both these types were thought of as parts of the public school system—the state colleges being governed by the State Board of Education, and the junior colleges under the governance of local district boards, with the state's hand represented by a bureau of junior colleges in the State Department of Education.

Equally prominent with the tradition of generous state support of the University of California is the historic thread of the constitutional autonomy of the Board of Regents. Apparently following the precedent established in the Michigan Constitution of 1850 and the Minnesota Constitution of 1858, the makers of the California Constitution of 1879 provided for the independence of the Board of Regents in the following words: "The University of California shall constitute a public trust, and its organization and government shall be perpetually continued in the form and character prescribed by the organic act creating the same passed March 23, 1868 (and the several acts amendatory thereof), subject only to such legislative control as may be necessary to ensure compliance with the terms of its endowments and the proper investment and security of its funds."

The courts of the state have declared that this Constitution elevates the University "to the place and dignity of a constitutional department of the body politic," and have sustained the independence of the Board of Regents again and again.[1] The University has a broad sphere of discretion within which it is held immune from interference by the legislature, and the courts themselves have also on occasion declined to invade that sphere.

When in 1940 a citizen sued for a writ of prohibition to prevent the Board of Regents from continuing their employment and payment of Lord Bertrand Russell as a temporary professor, on the ground of his alleged moral unfitness, the court of appeal refused to intervene, saying, in the words of Presiding Justice Moore: "The conclusions reached by the regents are final in the absence of fraud or oppression."[2] Justice McComb, concurring, said: "The question of Dr. Russell's qualifications to act as an instructor at the University of California is one lying solely within the discretion of the Board of Regents, and their determination of his qualifications is final."

He continued: "Experience has indicated that the people of the state have wisely vested this discretion in the Board of Regents, as it is a matter of international knowledge that the University of California has under the guidance of the Board of Regents become one of the

---

[1]*People* v. *Kewen*, 69 Cal. 215, 10 P. 393 (1886). *Williams* v. *Wheeler*, 23 Cal. App. 619, 138 P. 937 (1913). *Wallace* v. *Regents of University of California*, 75 Cal. App. 274, 242 P. 892 (1925).

[2]*Wall* v. *Board of Regents of University of California et al.*, (Cal. App.), 102 P. 2d 533 (1940).

great universities of the world and that the University possesses a faculty composed of educators of the highest standing."

That there is undoubtedly a causative connection between the autonomy of the University and its eminence is not widely understood or appreciated among the general public, or even among many educators. Too many are content to dismiss it with the fuzzy thought that since the legislature is a major source of financial support, it must be taken for granted that the legislature manages or dominates the management of the University. This is wildly erroneous.

This issue was cleanly clarified in the opinion of Justice Horace Badt of the Nevada supreme court in a 1948 decision involving the governance of the University of Nevada, which also has a sphere of independence defined in the state constitution. He said:

"Respondent insists that the unquestioned right of the legislature to appropriate the required funds for maintaining the university indicates that the elected board of regents was not vested by the constitution with exclusive and plenary control. However, the two processes are distinct. The power of the legislature to provide the requisite money and to limit and decrease the amount considered by the regents to be necessary is entirely a different function from the administration and control of the university itself." [3]

The Efficiency of Freedom

State university autonomy means many things, legally, administratively, and academically. It *does not mean* that the state university is immune from participation in the making of the annual or biennial state budget, or from making its requests for appropriations of state tax funds, accompanied by suitable statistical and other data in support thereof, and submitting them to the designated state fiscal office and ultimately to the governor and the legislature.

Wherever the state university has a large sphere of independence, whether by virtue of the state constitution as in California, Michigan, Minnesota, and half a dozen other states, or only by virtue of the custom of the legislature and the courts, it means a number of crucial freedoms:

1. The university governing board has custody and control of the university funds, and none must be deposited in the state treasury.

2. The board is not required to accept the state treasurer as its *ex officio* treasurer, or to depend on the attorney general for legal services, or to have its financial affairs audited by the state auditor (for the essential annual *post*-audit it may employ a private accounting firm) or *pre*-audited by any state officer.

3. The legislature does not make "line-item" appropriations to the

---

[3]*King* v. *Board of Regents of University of Nevada*, (Nev.), 200 P. 2d 221 (1948).

board, but instead makes "lump-sum" appropriations and leaves the allocations to specific items of university operating expenditure to the discretion of the board.

4. No employees of the university are subject to the regulations of the state civil service system for classified state employees.

5. The university is not required to make purchases through a state purchasing office.

6. No state editor or state printer or other similar functionary has any voice whatever in determining what the university shall print and publish.

7. The university governing board has sole authority to fix the fees to be charged for tuition and other services, and the salaries and wages and perquisites of all university employees, including president, faculty members, and all others.

The list is not complete, but it is sufficient to illustrate. These elements of autonomy appertain universally to private institutions of higher education, and traditionally they belonged to all state universities as well; but in many states (especially in the Northeast) they have been somewhat eroded by the fad for tidy and symmetrical overcentralization in state governments, including rigid fiscal controls, which flourished for half a century (about 1910 to 1960) in the sacred name of "economy and efficiency."

The benchmark for the return to sanity was the publication in 1959 of the succinct report of Milton Eisenhower's Committee on Government and Higher Education, entitled *The Efficiency of Freedom*,[4] and its supporting volume, *The Campus and the State*.[5] The facts had been presented many times, and many years earlier, in the annual *Proceedings* of the National Association of State Universities and elsewhere—but with apparently little effect on the rampaging craze for centralized state fiscal control.

One classic statement was the speech of Lloyd Morey, then president of the University of Illinois, at the annual meeting of the National Association of State Universities in New York City, May 2, 1955. Under the title of "Governmental Control of Public Higher Education" he made clear that external control is acceptable in two important fiscal functions: (1) incorporation of the institutional requests into the over-all state budget, and (2) annual *post*-audit by an outside agency. Beyond these, Mr. Morey showed cogently that interference by state fiscal officers in university purchasing, *pre*-auditing, property control, physical planning and construction, and especially publication, is generally self-defeating, wasteful, and damaging to the institutions.

---

[4] Baltimore: The Johns Hopkins Press, 1959. 44 pp.
[5] Malcolm Moos and Francis E. Rourke. Baltimore: The Johns Hopkins Press, 1959. 400 pp.

A rudimentary and very important fact in California is that the constitutionally autonomous university is free of these annoyances, but that the state colleges operate under tight and multiform state fiscal controls, even including substantial authority of the State Personnel Board (Civil Service Commission) in faculty personnel management.

State-wide Studies of Higher Education

The legislature of 1931 provided for a general survey of state-supported higher education in California, and invited Henry Suzzallo, then president of the Carnegie Foundation for the Advancement of Teaching, to assemble a commission of nationally-known experts and conduct the study. Reporting in 1932, Suzzallo and his group recommended that the governance of the state teachers colleges be transferred from the State Board of Education to the Board of Regents of the University of California. This recommendation was never implemented.

Suzzallo also recommended creation of an Advisory Commission for Educational Planning, to be composed of the president of the University, the chief state school officer, the state director of finance, two members of the Board of Regents, two members of the State Board of Education, and four educational experts chosen by these members. The legislature of 1933 came out with a "State Council of Educational Planning and Coordination" consisting of the State Superintendent of Public Instruction, the president of the University, and seven others, at least five of whom must not be engaged in any way with the practice, supervision, or control of education—thus insuring its failure.

By 1945 the Regents and the State Board of Education had initiated voluntarily their joint Liaison Committee. In 1951 the legislature appropriated funds for the work of the Liaison Committee, thus making possible the beginning of a permanent Joint Staff, headed jointly by a Special Consultant on Higher Education employed by the Regents and a Specialist in Higher Education employed by the State Board of Education. During its 15 years of existence the Liaison Committee and its Joint Staff accomplished much by way of studies, reports, and recommendations which were approved by both boards, and when needing legislative action, submitted to the legislature, often with affirmative results.

The authors of the *Master Plan for Higher Education in California, 1960-1975* wrote of the Liaison Committee: "No action taken during the past half-century has had a greater impact on the development and direction of higher education than has the establishment of the Liaison Committee of the two boards in 1945."

In March 1961, when the Liaison Committee was in desuetude because it was about to be superseded by the Coordinating Council for Higher Education created by the Donahoe Act of 1960, Thomas C. Holy, who had served long as the chief representative of the University in the

Joint Staff, completed and published a 27-page mimeographed *Summary of the Work of the Liaison Committee of the Regents of the University of California and the State Board of Education, 1945-1960.* Thirty-two reports for the Liaison Committee are listed. The earliest was *A Survey of the Needs of California in Higher Education* (Berkeley: University of California Press, 1948), bearing the names of Monroe E. Deutsch, Aubrey A. Douglass, and George D. Strayer, and generally known as the *Strayer Report.* The next landmark (thirteenth in the series) was the voluminous *Restudy of the Needs of California in Higher Education* (Sacramento: California State Department of Education, 1955), by T. R. McConnell, T. C. Holy, and H. H. Semans.

Latest were the *Master Plan for Higher Education in California* (twenty-sixth in the series) prepared by the specially-constituted Master Plan Survey Team headed by the late Arthur G. Coons, president of Occidental College (who subsequently served as a member of the Coordinating Council for Higher Education and as its president 1965-68); and several subsidiary reports produced by staff committees, all in 1960.

In his summary of the 15-year career of the Liaison Committee, Thomas C. Holy noted that during that period the Committee made 121 major recommendations which received the approval of both the major boards; and that among these there were 56 which contemplated action or nonaction by the legislature. Among these 56, the subsequent behavior of the legislature was in accord with the intent of the recommendations in no fewer than 50 cases.

This record impelled him to recognize the obvious question: Why should such successful coordinating machinery be replaced? His answers, though no doubt true to the prevailing climate of opinion, seem a trifle lame: (1) rapid growth of enrollments, (2) inadequate representation of the junior colleges and the private colleges, and (3) "since the coordinating machinery is voluntary, it has no power to insist that agreements reached by the two boards are actually observed."

He says, and correctly, that this third feature—power—was the most important element underpinning the push to rigidify the vast, varied, and flexible California system of public higher education in the statutes—a main outcome of the Master Plan recommendations as partially implemented in the Donahoe Act of 1960. It is the old urge to "knock heads together"—quite inappropriate in the organization and administration of higher education, which should certainly not be petrified in state statutes.

Fortunately the California Coordinating Council for Higher Education, created by the Donahoe Act, is only an *advisory* body, with no powers of coercion. It has continued the work of making many studies and recommendations. Among available summaries of its performance, all from sources inherently favorable to it, are: (1)

Progress Report on the Coordinating Council for Higher Education to the Governor and the 1962 Legislature, a highly condensed 8-page mimeographed fragment dated March 1, 1962, but bearing no evidence of its authorship or source (though obviously prepared by the Council's staff); (2) "The Coordinating Council for Higher Education in California—A Review of Its First Two Years," by T. C. Holy, in the *Journal of Higher Education* for June 1964, pages 313-321; (3) *California's Coordinating Council for Higher Education,* by James G. Paltridge, a 1966 publication of the Center for Research and Development in Higher Education, headquartered at the Berkeley campus of the University; (4) "College by Plan—California Institutions of Higher Education Operate and Grow Under a Master Design," by Edmund G. Brown, then Governor of California, in *American Education* for March 1965, pages 9-11; and (5) *The Master Plan Five Years Later,* a 53-page document designated Number 1024 of the Council, dated March 1966 (containing as an Appendix a 4-page full text of the Donahoe Higher Education Act of 1960, as amended).

The latter two of the documents just named relate to the implementation of the "Master Plan," and not exclusively to the work of the Council. Another and more recent source is the 246-page volume by Arthur G. Coons, *Crises in California Higher Education* (Los Angeles: Ward Ritchie Press, 1968), prepared and published with the aid of a grant from the Haynes Foundation. This is partly memoir, partly history, and partly aggressive defense of the "Master Plan" by the private college president who was in a central position in its formulation and operation throughout the decade—in position to know as much about it at first hand as any one person who could be named; and whose views, though admittedly carrying some favorable bias, are unquestionably sincere.

The "Master Plan" and the Donahoe Act

All the state-wide studies and reports named herein had in general recommended more centralization of control of public higher education in California, in deference to the cost-conscious "business in government" mystique which was nationally dominant from 1910 to 1960. It is not surprising that the Master Plan Survey Team of 1959-60 continued in this tradition, not, however, by recommending a single all-powerful board of higher education, but by urging that the rigid outlines of a "three-segment" system be ossified in the state statutes, and that ongoing surveys and recommendations be entrusted to a representative Council which would have no duties other than advisory.

Only parts of the recommendations were adopted by the 1960 legislature. The Survey Team proposed that the governance of the state colleges be taken from the State Board of Education and placed in a new Board of Trustees of State Colleges, and that this board be given constitutional autonomy equal to that of the Board of Regents of the University of California. The Board of Trustees was created, but the legislature declined to submit a constitutional amendment that would give it the independence recommended. A Joint Resolution was passed declaring it to be the policy of the legislature that the new Board of Trustees of State Colleges should be given more freedom from state administrative and fiscal agencies than present statutes allowed; but progress in that direction has been made with only glacial speed, if at all.

The Survey Team recommended that the constitution be amended to permit members of the Board of Trustees to have terms of 16 years, as is the case with the Regents. The only result was an amendment to allow terms of eight years instead of the four to which the constitution limits other state officers. It was also recommended that the new Coordinating Council itself be given constitutional status. No step in this direction was taken.

In brief, the Donahoe Act declared the University to be the "primary academic agency for research"; authorized it to "provide instruction in the liberal arts and sciences and in the professions, including the teaching profession"; and gave it "exclusive jurisdiction over instruction in the profession of law, and over graduate instruction in the professions of medicine, dentistry, veterinary medicine, and architecture."

It gave the University "sole authority to award the doctoral degree in all fields of learning, except that it may agree with the state colleges to award joint doctoral degrees in selected fields." By 1968 only two of the highly impracticable "joint doctoral" programs had come into being; no money had been appropriated by the state for research in the state colleges; and a half dozen of the older and larger of these institutions, each located in heavily-populated metropolitan areas and each being larger than most state universities, were increasingly chafing under the "second-class" status imposed by these restrictions which made it difficult for them to obtain good faculty replacements. Independent of these matters, there was a movement on foot demanding the name and style of "university" for these institutions, which was approved and advocated by their Chancellor (chief executive officer of the Board of Trustees of State Colleges).

The state colleges were assigned as their primary function "the provision of instruction for undergraduates and graduates, through the master's degree, in the liberal arts and sciences, in applied fields and in the professions, including the teaching profession." They were to avoid invading the fields of the local public two-year colleges: "Presently established two-year programs in agriculture are authorized but other two-year programs shall be authorized only when mutually agreed upon by the Trustees of California State Colleges and the State Board of Education." (Then and until 1968, the State Board of

Education was the state agency to which the local public junior colleges reported.)

There was a strong doctrinaire obsession that no institution other than a junior college should perform a junior college function, and no junior college, under any circumstances, should ever offer any instructional program of any kind extending more than two years. This may be feasible in large urban localities where institutions of many types necessarily exist and are about equally accessible to all residents of a concentrated area; but it manifestly may hamstring the development of higher education in more sparsely populated areas where at different stages of population growth the sensible and practicable thing to do may be to allow and encourage an existing four-year college or university to offer two-year college programs, or an existing junior college to extend some programs upward to three and four years to accommodate local demand.

The first sentence of the first section of the act declares: "Public higher education consists of (1) all public junior colleges . . . ," but the first section of its fourth chapter (on Junior Colleges), as amended in 1963, says: "The public junior colleges are secondary schools and shall continue to be a part of the public school system of this State." They shall offer instruction "through but not beyond the fourteenth grade level."

The ambivalency as to terminology is not too important in itself, but it is symptomatic of another confrontation which was left unresolved. The junior colleges are indeed based on local taxing districts, and although the "Master Plan" recommended that the fraction of their support from state tax sources be greatly increased, little has been accomplished in that respect. This means that a large part of their support continues to be derived from local property taxes. This is one factor, indeed the principal one, which gives rise to an incipient demand that the entire support of public junior colleges be taken over by the state. Such moves have recently occurred in Minnesota, Washington, and Colorado, and may be the wave of the future.

Meantime the Survey Team recommended (but the legislature did not enact) measures to divert, by 1975, a full 50,000 freshmen per year from the state colleges and the University to the junior colleges. This was apparently motivated by the nostalgic and incurable impression that "a university campus can be too big," which led to the impracticable recommendation (not enacted) that the number of students on any one campus should never exceed 27,500.

On this recommended diversion of freshmen to the junior colleges several comments are possible. First, note that if the state greatly increases its support of the junior colleges, or takes over their entire support, the argument about saving state money evaporates unless it can be shown that it is less costly to the taxpayers to educate students at junior colleges than in the first two years at a state college campus;

and this is not the case, in a junior college that is worthy of the name. Attendance at a local junior college can effect very substantial personal savings for the student and his family; but in the best of junior colleges, though the educational experience may be precisely appropriate for those who want it, yet by and large the opportunities available to the student must be far less diversified and stimulating than those accessible to students in the lower division of a university or college, at no greater, or only negligibly greater, cost to the taxpayers.

Arthur G. Coons noted that as early as June 3, 1959, before the Survey Team had been appointed, the Liaison Committee adopted a study guide listing several inquiries, and that prominent among these was: "How many lower division students who would normally enroll in a State College or University campus can be shifted to the junior colleges, and how can the districts meet additional costs resulting therefrom?"

He commented: "The reader should note that no query as to the desirability of such a policy action was written in this question. It appears that in the light of previous reports and discussions in California desirability was taken for granted. Also, one suspects that uncertainty as to the state's ability to bear all the costs of the two other public segments as they might otherwise develop even though not yet defined, created for many persons an *a priori* favorable judgment on the wisdom of diverting some lower division students, one way or another, to an as yet undetermined number, to the junior colleges." [6]

A most perceptive and convincing discussion of this matter appears in a letter of September 27, 1965, from Frank L. Kidner, a vice-president of the University of California, to Willard B. Spalding, then director of the Coordinating Council for Higher Education:

"The doubts concerning this issue do not stem from any reservations having to do with the essential role played by the most outstanding system of Junior Colleges in the nation. They stem, instead, from what I believe to be a mistaken conception, either in principle or in language, which beset the authors of the relevant section of the Master Plan.

"To be specific: It is possible by a variety of means, some appropriate and some less so, to deny admission to the University (or the State Colleges); but it is not demonstrably possible to assure that those thus denied will in fact go to the Junior Colleges. The combination of circumstances, motivations, and wishes which direct a prospective University (or State College) student to begin his work in the Junior College are not wholly understood. . . .

"In any case, I doubt whether (apart from the adoption and maintenance of Master Plan admission requirements) efforts should

---

[6] Pages 30-31 in Arthur G. Coons, *Crises in California Higner Education.* Los Angeles: Ward Ritchie Press, 1968. 246 pp.

CALIFORNIA

Appropriations for Annual Operating Expenses of Higher Education in California, Alternate Fiscal Years, 1959-60 through 1969-70 (in thousands of dollars)

Institutions	Year 1959-60	Year 1961-62	Year 1963-64	Year 1965-66	Year 1967-68	Year 1969-70
U of California	95,331	133,024	154,742	192,899	243,670	314,427
Berkeley					63,244	75,630
Los Angeles					59,325	76,831
Davis[1]					33,510	44,331
San Francisco[2]					19,144	24,735
Santa Barbara					18,433	24,547
San Diego					15,832	25,241
Riverside					14,521	18,198
Irvine					8,966	16,967
Santa Cruz					6,278	9,169
Calif Coll of Med[3]					2,864	
Agricul Sciences						10,171
U-wide Adminis					1,552	4,008
Salary increases			642	10,871		
Subtotal, U of Calif	95,331	133,024	155,384	203,770	243,670	329,828

State Colleges:

San José		10,584	13,822	16,556	21,396	26,718
Calif Polytech[4]		8,062	10,393	12,929	19,519	26,529
Los Angeles		7,494	10,384	12,058	18,766	26,622
San Diego		7,493	10,451	13,000	18,391	24,987
Long Beach		6,422	8,654	11,867	17,932	22,711
San Francisco		7,851	10,352	12,317	13,737	21,075
San Fernando Valley		4,402	6,794	9,574	11,766	18,626
Fresno		5,551	6,657	8,133	11,078	16,677
Sacramento		4,152	5,350	7,302	11,576	17,196
San Luis Obispo[4] (Cal Poly)						
Chico		3,451	4,275	5,635	9,115	13,803
Hayward (Alameda)		1,217	2,274	4,285	7,908	13,555
Fullerton (Orange Co)		1,378	2,465	4,455	8,433	13,338
Kellog-Voorhis[4] (Cal Poly)					8,463	12,456
Humboldt		2,777	3,512	4,165	6,100	9,309
Sonoma		414	892	1,606	3,011	5,952
San Bernardino		128	210	1,057	2,515	3,848
Dominguez Hills[5]		128	215	458	1,759	3,938
Stanislaus		817	765	1,250	2,151	3,564
Kern Co[6] (Bakersfield)					357	799
Salary increases			51	9,949		13,148
Chancellor's Office		938	1,190	1,623[7]	3,020	3,508
Other expenses				3,489[8]		2,985
Subtotal, St Colls	57,618	73,257	98,706	141,708	196,993	288,194
Hastings Coll of Law		399	459	522	662	981
Calif Maritime Acad		383	474	542	618	788
Calif Coll of Med				1,367		
Coordinating Council HE		227	281	353	496	542
Scholarship & Loan Comm		1,793	2,620	4,141	6,453	14,024
WICHE					15	15
Bd of Govs for Com Colls						790

(Continued)

CALIFORNIA (Continued)

Institutions	Year 1959-60	Year 1961-62	Year 1963-64	Year 1965-66	Year 1967-68	Year 1969-70
State aid to Jr Colls (est)	26,539	33,189	37,460	60,700	85,300	114,000
Add'l sal increases Other purposes	9,116	4,691	5,920[9]			
Total	188,604	247,172	301,304	413,103	534,209	749,162

[1]Originally the agricultural college; now a cosmopolitan university, including the agricultural college.

[2]Chiefly the Medical Center.

[3]Formerly a private college of osteopathy, now state-supported and state-controlled as a part of the Irvine Campus.

[4]California State Polytechnic College now has two campuses—San Luis Obispo and Kellogg-Voorhies, the latter in Pomona, reported separately herein.

[5]Formerly South Bay State College and later changed to Palos Verdes State College.

[6]A projected new institution.

[7]Previously reported as "State College Trustees."

[8]Includes: New and improved programs, Year-round operation, NDEA and nursing loan funds, international program, and work-study programs.

[9]A Special Session appropriated additional sums for salary increases, effective January 1, 1964, and through the second half of the fiscal year 1963-64, amounting to approximately $3.8 million for the University of California and $2.12 million for the state colleges.

be made to 'divert' a measurable number of students to the Junior Colleges.

"I do believe it to be appropriate in the University (and in the State Colleges) that increasing emphasis be placed upon the development of programs at the upper division level. I would expect, moreover, that the University would continue its long-standing practice of calling to the attention of the prospective student the possible advantages to him of beginning his collegiate work in the Junior College. I would expect, too, that the University will continue to seek all reasonable means of enhancing the ease of transfer. But there, I think, the matter should end."[7].

Passing over the details of the structure of the Coordinating Council and some small subsequent changes therein, it should be remarked that it is an attractive thought that a statewide agency of liaison should include in its membership representatives of the private colleges and universities, perhaps roughly in proportion to their quantitative place in the state-wide scene, as the California Coordinating Council does; but after reflection upon experience the wisdom of this scheme becomes doubtful. Due to the wholly admirable tradition of almost unlimited autonomy for reputable private colleges in the American states, this means that their representatives on the state-wide agency will have a voice and a vote in decisions which are extremely unlikely to affect their own interests in any significant way, but may be of the most vital importance to the public institutions.

There are some issues in public higher education and in state-wide responsibility for higher education wherein up to the present, though not necessarily forever, there have regularly appeared to be strong conflicts of interest between the private and public sectors. For example, often private college representatives will advocate measures impairing the autonomy of public colleges, knowing that their own independence is quite unlikely to be affected thereby; and devise or support restrictive and repressive measures aimed at institutions in the public sector, feeling sure that such measures cannot be applicable to private institutions.

Moreover, many private college and university representatives apparently believe a policy of low-fee or tuition-free public higher education is inimical to the interests of private colleges, and will vote for measures intended to force higher fees in the public sector, as the candid Arthur G. Coons wrote that he would. Many private educators have expended much ingenuity in devising schemes of scholarships and loans whose principal tendency is to encourage fee-raising in both

---

7Published on page 46 of *The Master Plan Five Years Later*. Sacramento and San Francisco: California Coordinating Council for Higher Education, March 1966. 53 pp.

sectors. The outcome of this is to restrict the expansion of higher educational opportunity, and to remove it farther from the grasp of children of low-income families and of average academic competency than it is now.

All this adds up to the spectacle of a minority of private college representatives exercising a very influential hand in the shaping of plans and often in the formulation of mandates directed at the public institutions, but from which their own private institutions are entirely immune. Some of these private college men, like the respected Arthur G. Coons, are of unimpeachable probity, but it may be impossible to shed the influence of a lifetime of devoted labor in the private sector and look with level gaze at the fundamental principles of universal higher education with opportunity for all.

It seems logical to say that in the planning of state-wide systems which in fact threaten no inroads upon the autonomy of private institutions, and actually bear exclusively upon the public sector, it would be appropriate for private college men to function as observers only, and not to exercise a decisive voice in matters of policy wherein their special interests strongly predispose them to hold pre-formed adverse opinions regarding the expansion of higher educational opportunities for the whole people.

Foiling the Red Tape Monster

A court of appeals decision of 1966 affords a change of pace, amusing and pathetic, illustrative of the kind of petty hair-splitting likely to follow in the train of a major administrative change such as the transfer of the governance of the state colleges in 1961.

A constitutional amendment of 1934 (Article XXIV, section 4, subdivision a) exempted employees of the "state teachers colleges" from civil service. At that time these colleges were governed by the State Board of Education through its division of state colleges and teacher education. Employees in that division were under civil service. In 1960 the Donahoe Act abolished that division and transferred its functions to the new Board of Trustees of State Colleges. Some of the employees were transferred from the old central office to the new, but gave up their civil service status. As to campus employees of the colleges themselves, they were consistently ruled exempt from civil service in a series of at least five opinions of the attorney general, spread over a quarter of a century from 1938 to 1961.

Now came an effort to impugn the transaction of 1960 by maintaining that it is unlawful to reduce the coverage of the civil service system by abolishing jobs and transferring their functions; and that even the campus employees of the state colleges should be under civil service because in 1934, when the amendment was adopted, they were actually employees of the division (central office) and not of the "state teachers colleges" in the language of the amendment. (They were at that time appointed by the State Director of Education, but only on the recommendation of their respective college presidents.)

The pleading was dismissed in superior court, and this disposition was affirmed in the district court of appeal, in an opinion by Justice Devine in which his two colleagues concurred. To sustain the plea would be in effect to say the amendment of 1934 was meaningless and useless from the moment of its adoption, the court pointed out. Said the forthright Justice Devine: "A person is generally considered employed by the institution for which he works." Showing a keen understanding of higher education, he then quickly refuted the contention that the size and offerings of the state colleges have expanded so greatly that they are no longer the institutions meant by the words "state teachers colleges":

"It cannot be gainsaid that the institutions have grown enormously, as what has not? Their curricula are vastly expanded, and their organization is much more centralized. But they do educate teachers, together with aspirants to other vocations. But more than this, the colleges are part of the prized system of higher education. The exemption from civil service, it would appear, is not made because *teachers* were and are educated in these institutions of advanced learning, but because *people* were and are provided with higher education in these colleges, and because it has been thought that the whole system should be in control of persons responsible for proficiency in education.

"The exemption has to do with the function of education, rather than with any particular profession for which the students may be trained. This appears from the cognate exemption, contained in the preceding sub-division of the article in the Constitution, of all employees of the University of California.

"The exception, constitutionally granted, should not be deemed lost merely because the functions of the teachers colleges have been greatly enlarged and the colleges' title has been changed."

A companion case, decided at the same time, challenged the right of the state colleges to employ architects other than those who are civil service employees. The court of appeal held that architects employed by the state colleges are within the same constitutional exemption as other nonacademic employees. Moreover, said the court explicitly, it is not necessary, prior to such employment, to make any factual finding that the work could not be adequately performed by the state architect.[8]

Events of 1967 and 1968

The Survey Team of 1959-60 raised no question concerning California's century-old policy of tuition-free public higher education;

---

[8] *California State Employees' Association v. Board of Trustees of California State Colleges*, (Cal. App.), 47 Cal. Rptr. 73 (1965); and companion case, 47 Cal. Rptr. 81 (1965).

but this became an issue after the election of Governor Ronald Reagan in 1966 and his proposal in early 1967 that the university and the state colleges should make tuition charges for the first time in history.

As is also done in some other states whose constitutions prohibit charges for tuition, the University of California and the California state colleges charge a modest total of fees to students for purposes other than tuition. In 1967 these fees appeared to aggregate about $200 to $275 per year at the University campuses, and substantially less at the state colleges. The junior colleges appeared to be virtually free of any fees, as the makers of the constitution intended.

Governor Reagan's proposal of tuition fees was greeted coldly by the Regents of the University and the Trustees of State Colleges, and was actively and zealously opposed by many trustees and administrators in the junior colleges. The Board of Regents voted to reject the idea of tuition charges, but agreed to consider the feasibility of some slight escalation of other fees. This brought a blast of disapproval and an intimation of double-dealing from Jesse Unruh, Speaker of the Assembly (and member of the Board of Regents *ex officio*) and chairman of the legislative Joint Committee on Higher Education, which initiated a study of the organization, governance, and financing of the state's universities and colleges.

In a report of some of its preliminary findings, this committee rejected the idea of tuition fees, and opposed any circumvention by any increase in "student fees" which would accomplish essentially the same result under another name. Speaking critically of the meat-cleaver strokes which separated the whole system into three parts under the "master plan" of 1960, the Committee said: "Functional assignments to classes of institutions rather than to individual institutions may be a bar to flexible educational planning." It proposed to study alternative ways of "breaking down the barriers that have been built up."

This Committee, though temporary, was financed and authorized to continue through the first half of 1969. Whether it would recommend new statutes to the legislature of 1969 or address its report to a later legislature could not be ascertained in 1968. Among many other matters to be brought to its attention, undoubtedly there would be the question of a revised composition of the Coordinating Council, and a study of what its appropriate functions should be.

Although as first constituted the Council included only three representatives of the general public (not connected with any institution or "segment" of higher education), the number was raised to six some years later, and there was some pressure to increase it further. The sapient Arthur G. Coons connected this with the push to make the Council a power-laden "superboard" with coercive authority over the whole system, and deplored both: "There is the possibility that if the public members were larger in number and were to have clear control of action, the Coordinating Council might become a 'superboard'. At this juncture any increase of the public members of the Council might tend to eclipse the status of either the Regents of the University of California or the Trustees of the State College system; a development which as of this time I would deplore." [9]

Aside from questions of organization and structure which were boiling beneath the surface, the 1967 legislature enacted measures, mostly to go into effect August 1 of that year, estimated to produce at least $1 billion per year of additional revenue. The general sales tax rate was raised to 5 per cent from the former 4 per cent. The graduated personal income tax rates were raised, mostly in the middle and upper brackets, to accomplish an over-all rise of nearly 60 per cent.

The corporation income tax was raised to 7 per cent from the former 5½ per cent. The tax on cigarettes went from the insignificant 3 cents per pack to 7 cents until October 1, 1967, and thereafter to 10 cents. The tax on liquors was increased by 50 cents per gallon.

California thus stepped into the ranks of the leaders in the use of the general sales tax. At that time the 5 per cent rate was the highest in the nation, and was in effect in three states—California, Pennsylvania, and Rhode Island. In 1968 it was raised to 6 per cent in Pennsylvania.

State tax support of higher education in California, never having reached the national average rate of gains during the years 1959-1968, was braked down somewhat with the advent of the Reagan administration. The percentages of gain in appropriations for annual operating expenses for one year over the immediately preceding year were 18 in 1966, nine in 1967 (the first Reagan year), and 11 in 1968. The low figure for 1968 is partly due to the fact that the governor vetoed some $14 million in the appropriation bills for higher education after they had been passed by the legislature. Speaker Unruh hoped enough strength might be mustered in the legislature to override the veto, and he induced the Board of Regents formally by majority vote to request the legislature to do so; but it turned out that the necessary two-thirds vote in both Houses was not forthcoming, and the veto stood.

An interesting reflection on the relative size and importance of California and its higher educational system arises from the observation that the $14 million vetoed was a sum larger than the total appropriations for higher education in the same year by any one of six of the smaller states: Alaska, Delaware, Nevada, New Hampshire, Vermont, and Wyoming. Yet it reduced the California total by only about 2¼ per cent—from $652,369,607 to $637,788,000. Even such a slowdown is, however, a catastrophe in a state of rapid increase of population and a time of huge increase of need and demand for the facilities of public higher education.

---

[9] Arthur G. Coons, ibid., p. 103.

All things pass. The period of influence of any one governor is comparatively brief. California will probably long retain first place among the 50 states for the largest and best-supported state system of higher education in the nation. As to its organization and operation, currently it suffers from the rigidity of the "master plan" (fragments of which are imbedded in the statutes) and from gross over-centralization of the governance of the nine-campus University of California in the Board of Regents and its hierarchy of University-wide administrators.

The system of state colleges, sad to say, continues to be seriously hampered by too much centralization of two distinct kinds: (1) the incredible anomaly of a single lay Board of Trustees charged with the governance of 19 (soon to be more than 20) thriving institutions, half of which are as large or larger than most state universities; and (2) the equal or greater handicap of constant detailed interference in the administration of these institutions by several state administrative and fiscal agencies, chiefly the State Department of Finance and the State Personnel Board (the latter retains jurisdiction to hear and decide appeals from demotions, dismissals, and other disciplinary actions against faculty personnel of the state colleges).

Although a legislative Joint Resolution of 1960 declared the intent of the legislature that the state colleges should be relieved of these restraints, virtually nothing has been done to implement the policy except by an occasional piecemeal one-shot rider appended to an annual appropriation bill, usually providing only for an extension of marathon "cooperative studies" to determine how the obvious can be accomplished.

Senate Concurrent Resolution No. 29 of 1965 reiterated the principle, but with apparently little effect thus far. Among its numerous "whereases" the Resolution of 1965 included the eloquent statement: "The Legislature firmly believes that fiscal flexibility is an integral part of the responsible operation of institutions of higher learning and is considered the hallmark necessary to enrich the diversity of higher education." But a score of splendid institutions continue their futile struggles within a fishnet of useless and damaging restraints from non-educational fiscal officers at the state capital. This is all the more galling because the University, in sharp contrast to the state colleges, is free of such harassments because of the constitutional autonomy of the Regents.

Making a single governing board responsible for the governance of 19 large institutions has an inescapable tendency to degrade the executive heads of the separate institutions, and an unavoidable propensity for escalating all local problems, including petty ones, to a state-wide level, where the job of state-wide chief executive (chancellor of the state colleges) becomes an impossible one and compels the creation of a growing bureaucracy to support him and to make the decisions that should have been made at the local level. This seems hard to avoid because full legal authority and responsibility resides in the single governing board.

Can these boards (The Regents of the University and The Trustees of the State Colleges) successfully confine their own activities to those of "an inspecting and consenting body" as defined by President Charles F. Thwing of Western Reserve University half a century ago, and delegate all else for decision at the institutional level, freeing the colleges (or the University campuses) to manage their own affairs as befits a flexible and spirited institution of higher education? The "big boards" would still have more than enough to engage their attention in representing the needs of the institutions to the governor, the legislature, and the public, and in mediating the perennial conflicts between the insights of academia and the conventional middle-class wisdom and mores.

One might guess that the foregoing indicates the direction in which the work of the "big boards" will evolve. It would be unrealistic to suppose they can be abolished or reduced in authority for at least a generation, but perhaps they can learn to act with more and more self-restraint, as the best of university governing boards have generally done, and to *decentralize* the administration of the multiple systems they control, recognizing that a university or college is a living organism by nature necessarily flexible and autonomous, and not a chrome-covered mechanism operable by remote control.

After the campus disorders at Berkeley in 1964, *decentralization* of the governance of the University was recommended in the Byrne Report,[10] the Muscatine Report,[11] and others. An almost unlimited degree of decentralization can be accomplished by the governing board of an overcentralized agglomeration of institutions, without the necessity of intervention by the legislature or of any constitution-making body. It is true that the governing board cannot abdicate its own powers, but it can *delegate* to as great an extent as it deems wise. Delegated authority is not lost, but is always subject to recapture.[12]

The principle of extreme self-restraint on the part of the "big boards" in exercising their plenary powers may eventually ameliorate the currently unhappy situation in California and other states where

---

[10] By Jerome C. Byrne, a distinguished young attorney in Los Angeles commissioned by the Regents to study and report on the governance of the University of California.

[11] A faculty committee reporting on the governance of the University of California, headed by Professor Charles Muscatine of Berkeley.

[12] Subject to the limitation that in cases where an innocent third party has made a contract with the board through a subordinate employee whom the board represented to the public as empowered to contract for it, the contract will stand.

the idea of overcentralization is rampant. This principle may need to be brought into play with respect to the junior colleges, for in 1968 a State Board of Governors for Junior Colleges was created, to take this function out of the State Department of Education, as had been done in the case of the state colleges in 1960. Together with the undoubted tendency of the junior colleges to require more and more state support in order to relieve their local taxing districts, and the distinct possibility that they may in time become wholly state-supported, this step may indicate that the junior colleges are now being moved toward the overcentralization kick that has been the bane of California higher education for several decades.

It is well to keep in mind that state-level structure for the organization of higher education is not all-important. What really counts is the wisdom, urbanity, and human understanding of the men and women who man the structure. Fortified with wide-ranging knowledge of the evolving modern society, equipped with capacity for empathy with students, parents, faculty members and administrative officers as well as with the general public, and resolutely committed to act with self-restraint and compassion, there is no reason why such men and women cannot operate the awkwardly overcentralized structure flexibly and smoothly, so that its rigidities do not stand in the way of progress. Gradually, over years or decades, the structure may be reformed to become in harmony with its rightful functions. This seems to be the way of nature.

COLORADO

Several salient features mark the progress of public higher education in Colorado during the 'Sixties: (1) a rate of gain of 308½ per cent in annual appropriations of state tax funds for operating expenses, over the 9-year period 1960-1969, well above the 50-state weighted average of 261 per cent; (2) spectacular development of public junior colleges from meagerly supported small beginnings to a well-distributed network of eight such schools, generously subsidized by the state and soon to become fully state-supported; and (3) striking development of voluntary coordination among the state institutions, which was nevertheless superseded by a statutory State Commission for Higher Education as a coordinating body in 1965.

With a total of approximately two million people in 1967, Colorado is the most populous of the mountain states, and is only slightly exceeded by the West Coast states of Oregon (2 million) and Washington (3 million); but its population is scarcely more than a tenth of that of imperial California's more than 19 million. Metropolitan Denver, with a million people, has long been in many senses the capital of the vast mountain region extending from Canada to Mexico. Most of the people of Colorado are in a comparatively compact northeast-central region, with the principal state institutions of higher education located at the towns of Boulder, Fort Collins, Greeley, and Golden.

Other state colleges are at Alamosa, Gunnison, Pueblo, and Denver. Until 1965 Denver had no state institution of higher education other than the medical and dental schools of the University of Colorado, and some scattered extension offerings of each of the four major institutions. The situation was clouded by the fact that many ye. ago it had been deemed necessary to amend the state constitution in order to authorize the location of the medical and dental schools of the University of Colorado at Denver;[1] and the attorney general stoutly insisted that since the location of the major institutions was fixed in the state constitution, none of them could be authorized to establish a degree-program branch in Denver without an amendment to the constitution.

---

[1] *People ex rel. Jerome* v. *Regents of University of Colorado*, 24 Colo. 175, 49 P. 286 (1897).

This impasse was broken in 1966 by the opening of a new state institution, styled Metropolitan State College, in Denver. At first a two-year college, it is now in process of becoming a four-year institution, in harmony with the modern maxim that no urban community of more than a quarter of a million people can be deprived of at least a four-year public college.

A constitutional amendment of 1922 which permitted the University of Colorado to conduct all its instruction in medicine, dentistry, and pharmacy in Denver, also expressly authorized all the state institutions to carry on extension instruction in any place in the state. Thus if some coalition of graduate extension classes and Metropolitan State College occurs, Denver will indeed be on the way toward having a full-fledged public university, such as is needed in any urban concentration approaching it in size.

The period of the early 'Sixties was a lively one for public higher education in Colorado. The Association of State-Supported Institutions of Higher Education, in existence since 1926, took on a new lease of life by employing a staff director, at first part-time and then full-time. It cooperated with a newly-created Joint Legislative Budget Committee and the State Division of Accounts and Controls in devising new budget request forms suitable for use by universities and colleges, thus freeing the institutions from bondage to the archaic and inappropriate forms previously required to be used by all state departments and agencies. The Association also carried on studies of enrollment trends, instructional programs, and space utilization.

Concurrently a Legislative Committee for Education Beyond High School, composed of nine members of the legislature with a staff director and an assistant director, was at work. It issued reports to the legislatures of 1960 and 1961 carrying much current data and well-formulated projections into future years. These undoubtedly had much to do with the impetus to the development of local public junior colleges at the beginning of the decade, including the doubling of the per-student allotment of state funds in aid of their operation, by the 1960 session. The state appropriation rose from $464,600 for fiscal year 1959-60 to an approximate $1,050,000 for 1960-61.

Having a "separate" (non-Morrill Act) state university, a separate land-grant university, and a school of mines, Colorado has three state-supported schools of engineering. Appropriate divisions of labor among these constituted a principal element in a detailed report prepared and issued by the Association of State-Supported Institutions of Higher Education in December 1962, containing a continuing series of agreements as to the respective roles of the eight state colleges and universities.

The University of Colorado would have sole responsibility for programs in aeronautical engineering, architecture and architectural engineering, and chemical engineering. Colorado State University would have programs in the engineering subfields related to agriculture, forestry, and watershed management; and in the areas of climate, water, land, and forests, with increasing specialization in hydrology, environmental engineering, nuclear engineering, fluid mechanics, heat transfer, and irrigation. The Colorado School of Mines would have programs in its historic fields dealing with minerals and related materials, geological engineering, mining engineering, petroleum, and oil-refining engineering. A feature of the understanding was that the University of Colorado would have a certain freedom to develop in other general fields of engineering not conflicting with the agreed specialties of the other two schools.

Outside the field of engineering, the more general elements of the plan provided that the University of Colorado would have "the broadest range of graduate and undergraduate programs, and the widest range of doctoral and research responsibilities"; but would not offer degree programs in such areas as special education, industrial arts, the vocational fields, and certain other specialties available at the other institutions.

Colorado State University would increase its stress on the humanities, and carry forward in the physical and biological sciences and engineering. The School of Mines would expand its work in earth sciences and materials engineering. Colorado State College at Greeley would concentrate its doctoral programs in professional education, and build up the liberal arts and sciences at the undergraduate level. The four other state colleges (at Alamosa, Durango, Gunnison, and Pueblo) would offer a variety of undergraduate programs, including some technical and subprofessional courses of less than four years. At Alamosa and Gunnison masters' degrees would be offered in subject fields for secondary school teachers. All four of these "general colleges" would be somewhat more flexible as to standards of admission than the four older institutions.

Journalism, law, medicine, pharmacy, and physical therapy would continue to be offered only at the University of Colorado. In general, new doctoral programs at any institution would be inaugurated only after consultation with other concerned schools and with the Association. This report was released to the 1963 legislature and the public at the request of the Legislative Committee on Education Beyond High School.

Two years later (in December 1964), the Association issued a 170-page lithoprinted *Program for the Development and Coordination of Higher Education in Colorado, 1964-1970*, recommending that a statutory coordinating council be created. The legislature of 1965 established the Commission on Higher Education to exercise certain specified liaison functions, but to recognize and respect the powers of the institutional governing boards and to act largely in a leadership and advisory capacity. All functions not specifically delegated to the

COLORADO

Appropriations for Annual Operating Expenses of Higher Education in Colorado, Alternate Fiscal Years, 1959-60 through 1969-70 (in thousands of dollars)

Institutions	Year 1959-60	Year 1961-62	Year 1963-64	Year 1965-66	Year 1967-68	Year 1969-70
U of Colorado						
Colorado Genl Hosp		7,988	10,601	11,585	15,542	19,496
School of Medicine		2,851	6,619[1]	8,311[1]	10,912[1]	12,001[1]
Colo Psychopathic Hosp		1,652				
School of Nursing		1,107				
School of Dentistry		394			71[2]	
Dentistry Scholarships		90				
Subtotal, U of Colorado		14,082	17,220	19,896	26,525	31,497
Colorado State University		4,023	5,128	7,344	10,459	13,740
Ag Experiment Station		880	1,455	1,556	1,921	2,292
Coop Ag Exten Service		685	935	1,033	1,281	1,719
State Forest Service						264
Subtotal, Colorado St U		5,588	7,518	9,933	13,661	18,015
Five State Colleges[3]						18,915
Colorado St College		2,302	2,912	3,465	4,869	
Southern Colorado St Coll[4]			1,099	1,736	3,114	
Metropolitan St Coll[5]				750	2,087	
Western State College		1,107	1,274	1,457	1,831	
Adams State College		906	1,265	1,421	1,817	
Trustees of St Colls						119
Subtotal, 5 St Colls		5,315	6,550	8,829	13,718	19,031

	1	2	3	4	5	6
Colorado School of Mines	1,719		2,016	2,128	2,531	2,978
Fort Lewis A & M Coll	341		629	882	1,199	1,624
State Community Colleges					220	6,387[6]
Planning for new Jr Colls						
Occupational Education						1,525
St Bd for Comm Colls & Occup Edn						146
St aid to Jr Colleges (local)				2,405	4,014	4,794[7]
Colo Commission on HE					90	283
WICHE					15	
Colo Assoc'd U Press						57
Total	17,271	26,099	33,933	44,073	61,856	87,094[8]

[1] This figure includes the medical school, hospitals, nurses' school, and other units of the Medical Center.

[2] Establishment of a dental school was authorized by statute.

[3] For the first time (1968-69) the Board of Trustees now administers a consolidated budget for five state colleges.

[4] Hitherto a locally-controlled junior college at Pueblo. As of July 1, 1963, it became a unit of the state college system, with authorization to become a four-year college.

[5] This two-year college in Denver, established in 1965, was authorized by the 1967 legislature to become a four-year institution.

[6] This sum goes to state two-year colleges at Denver ($2,673,000), Trinidad ($1,195,000), El Paso ($1,102,000), Otero ($833,000), and Lamar ($584,000).

[7] The six community colleges classified as "local district" are Aims, Arapahoe, Colorado Mountain, Mesa, Northeastern, and Rangely. The state aid is $525 per year per academic student, and $1,000 per vocational student.

[8] This total includes: computer program ($400,000), Council of Arts and Humanities ($26,000), and State Historical Society ($366,000).

Commission were to remain in the hands of the boards. Proposed new degree programs were to be subject to approval by the Commission.

In 1967 a statute was enacted offering local public junior college districts the option of coming into a fully state-supported system of *state* junior colleges, and indications were that all junior colleges would eventually, if not soon, join the *state* system, forsaking local tax support. Similar movements had already taken place in the states of Minnesota and Washington.

On account of the great attractions of its climate, scenery, and outdoor life, Colorado has tended to have more than its share of out-of-state (nonresident) students enrolled in the public institutions. This has moved the legislature to take control of the situation with a heavy hand. *Colorado Revised Statutes 1953*, sec. 124-18-1 *et seq.*, as amended by *Session Laws 1961*, Ch. 229, declares:

"It is the intent of the General Assembly that the state institutions of higher education shall apply uniform rules, as herein prescribed and not otherwise, in determining whether students shall be classified as in-state students or out-of-state students for tuition purposes . . .

"An emancipated minor or adult student who has registered for more than five hours per term shall not qualify for a change in his classification for tuition purposes unless he shall have completed twelve continuous months of residence while not attending an institution of higher learning in the state or while serving in the armed forces."

In 1964 the Colorado supreme court declared this statute to be reasonable and not unconstitutional.[2] A suit for $5,500 in compensatory and punitive damages had been brought against the Regents of the University of Colorado by a nonresident student who had completed four years at the university, during which time he had paid some $2,331 in fees in excess of what he would have paid if he had been classified as a resident. In the trial court he was awarded nothing, and the supreme court, affirming the judgment, swept aside all his arguments regarding equal protection and due process under the Fourteenth Amendment to the United States Constiution, the exclusive power of Congress to regulate commerce among the states, the privileges and immunities of citizens of the several states, and the civil rights clauses of the Colorado Consitution. All these are inapplicable, said the court, if the classification prescribed in the statutes is reasonable; and held that it *was* reasonable.

Strangely enough, it seems that neither the statute nor the decision takes account of a student's *intent* as to his future residence. To be sure, many courts in many states have held that a minor who leaves

---

[2] *Landwehr* v. *Regents of the University of Colorado*, (Colo.), 396 P. 2d 451 (1964).

his parental roof and goes to another state for the purpose of attending college there, presumptively intends to leave that state as soon as he has completed his college course; but this presumption is susceptible of being overthrown, and it is weaker in the case of an adult student, or one who is wholly self-supporting, or one who is married and has his family with him; and such students are entitled to an opportunity to declare formally (and to demonstrate with suitable evidence) that they fully *intend* to continue as permanent residents of the state after their college courses are completed. Where they allege that the presumption of nonresidence does not square with the facts, they are entitled to a hearing on that question, and the Idaho supreme court has so held, as has also a federal District Court in a recent Iowa case. These latter decisions are mentioned *infra* in the sketches of those two states.

CONNECTICUT

As is true of most of the other states of New England and the middle Atlantic region, the higher educational scene in Connecticut until recently has been heavily dominated by private institutions. As late as the fall of 1967 a little less than 49 per cent of all students in the state were in public colleges and the state university. In 1963 this percentage had been only 39. Both types of institutions have made swift growth in recent years, with the public ones expanding at a more rapid rate than the private ones.

In the fall of 1963 Connecticut had a net outmigration of 13,000 college students (incomers subtracted from outgoers), and as a percentage of all college students in the state this rate of outmigration was higher than that of any other state except New Jersey. All the northeastern states were heavy "exporters" of students. Within the present decade, however, most of them are making very great strides in the expansion of their own public higher educational facilities, and this may lead to somewhat reduced rates of outmigration.

Connecticut's 9-year rate of gain in appropriations of state tax funds for operating expenses of higher education from 1960 through 1969 was a little more than 401 per cent—a trifle more than quintupling. Only six other states made higher rates of gain: Maine, Kentucky, Massachusetts, Pennsylvania, New York, and Hawaii. Observe that four of these are in the Northeast, including two in New England.

Small in area and having a total population of nearly 3 million, with a population gain of nearly 17 per cent between 1960 and 1968, Connecticut is currently perhaps the liveliest of the New England states. The suburbs of one of the world's largest urban concentrations (New York City) continue to spill over into its southwestern portion, and it has several cities in which light manufacturing industries are abundant, besides the remarkable concentration of national and international insurance company home offices in Hartford.

There is and has been considerable stress on the development of a state system of vocational-technical schools. By 1967 four of these had been designated as technical colleges, and were administered under their own central office at the state capital. There was also an incipient state system of "regional community colleges" for whose annual operating expenses the legislature appropriated approximately $4 million and $5 million for the two successive fiscal years of the biennium 1967-69. The University of Connecticut operated four 2-year branches, at Hartford, Stamford, Torrington, and Waterbury. Its main campus is at the village of Storrs, with its constituent schools of law, social work, and insurance at Hartford, only some 20 miles distant.

For many years there have been four separate institutions in the normal school-teachers college-state college tradition, at New Britain, New Haven, Danbury, and Willimantic. Connecticut was one of the tardiest of the states to authorize and direct these institutions to admit some students not committed to the teaching profession, to develop instruction in the liberal arts and sciences, and to move toward becoming multipurpose state colleges. An act of 1959 initiated this.

Legislation of 1965 removed these four institutions from the control of the State Board of Education and created for them a new single board styled the Board of Trustees of State Colleges. The 1965 legislature also provided for an incipient state-wide system of state-supported regional community colleges, after the pattern of the Massachusetts legislation earlier in the decade; and created a state-level Board of Trustees for Community Colleges. The State Board of Education continued in control of the state technical institutes, and the Board of Trustees of the University of Connecticut continued with its traditional powers and duties. This gave the state four "big boards" in the field of higher education. The act of 1965 explicitly stipulated that "authority and responsibility for the operation of the state's public institutions of higher education shall be vested in" these four governing boards.

In addition, a new state-wide permanent Commission for Higher Education was set up and directed to "encourage the governing boards of the constituent units to initiate necessary plans for development of higher education."

The foregoing developments resulted in part from about four years of preliminaries. In 1961 a new "tax package" had been enacted to produce $122 million a year in new revenues, amounting to something of the order of an immediate increase of 30 per cent in the state's annual income. The general sales tax went to 3½ cents on the dollar from the former 3 cents. Cigarette taxes went to 5 cents per pack from the former 3 cents; telephone taxes to 6 per cent of the charge from the former 4 per cent; domestic insurance company taxes to 2½ per cent from the former 1¾ per cent; corporation taxes to 5 per cent from the former 3¾ per cent.

Liquor taxes were stepped up by 40 per cent, inheritance taxes were raised by a 30 per cent surcharge on current rates, and passenger vehicle registration fees were raised to $10 from the former $8. All this amounted to a substantial step forward; but the U.S. Bureau of the Census report on *Governmental Finances in 1962* showed that Connecticut ranked third among the 50 states in per capita personal income, and forty-eighth in per capita expenditures for state institutions of higher education. In this latter category Connecticut had risen to forty-first place by fiscal year 1968-69, as one would expect from the already noticed high rate of gain in annual appropriations for operating expenses of higher education. These figures seem to say Connecticut is making splendid progress, but started from a very low point and has yet far to go. This condition is characteristic of most of the New England and middle Atlantic states.

In 1969 Connecticut took another step forward in improving the state revenue system. The general sales tax rate was raised to 5 per cent from the former 3½ per cent, and the cigarette tax went up from 8 cents to 16 cents a pack—the highest rate in any state. These and other changes were designed to yield $539 million of new revenue during biennium 1969-71.

The 1963 legislature authorized a temporary study commission on higher education to be set up and to report by December 1964, in time for the 1965 session. This commission contracted with the United States Office of Education to make the survey on which it would presumably base its conclusions and recommendations. Some thirty Office of Education staffers were engaged in this effort. Their *Higher Education in Connecticut: Report of a Survey (Volume II) Summary, Conclusions, and Recommendations* was a 24-page document bearing the date of December 1964. It recommended total consolidation under a single Board of Regents as sole governing board of all higher education in Connecticut. Very different from the California plan of 1960 in that respect, it was in other respects a kind of pale copy of the California arrangement.

Volume I of the same report was long delayed in appearance, and turned out to be a huge compilation of largely irrelevant and undigested data, its principal merit being its poundage; and any resemblance between the data and the recommendations in Volume II appeared to be largely accidental. The Connecticut Study Commission on Higher Education received these reports and recommendations, and proceeded to prepare a report of its own, which was dated February 1965: *Report to the Governor and the General Assembly by the Study Commission on Higher Education*. It rejected the all-powerful Board of Regents idea, and recommended instead that the Trustees of the University of Connecticut continue as formerly; that the State Board of Education have supervision of elementary and secondary education; that each of the four-year state colleges have its own Board of Trustees; and that each state technical institute and each state-supported community college have its own governing board. The first two of these recommendations became law. The latter, as earlier noted, were not enacted.

A coordinating agency to be styled Commission for Higher Education "having full powers of organization" in the state-wide system, but not replacing the institutional governing boards, was recommended. It was to have a full-time chancellor and staff, make studies and surveys, and transmit the budget requests of the several institutions, but in no event interfere with their internal management, within the outlines of the state-wide plan as developed from time to time.

It is noteworthy that William Horowitz, New Haven banker and industrialist, a member of the Study Commission, forthrightly and cogently dissented from its recommendations to the extent indicated by his words: "No such structure as a Commission for Higher Education with a Chancellor is needed." He thought "the development of the state's institutions of higher education, comprising the University and its branches, the four State Colleges and the four Technical Institutes, has been efficient, progressive and in keeping with the allocations voted by the General Assembly." Regarding the proposed regional two-year colleges: "Community colleges supported in their entirety by state funds could properly be placed under the jurisdiction of the State Board of Education, where their growth and geographical distribution could be coordinated with all other institutions of higher learning." Mr. Horowitz is a member of the Yale Corporation and was for a time a member of the permanent Connecticut Commission for Higher Education, though he recommended it not be created.

One admirable feature of the report of the temporary Connecticut Study Commission on Higher Education is a "Statement of Convictions" comprising six items, all of which are quotable, and two of which seem particularly worthy of reproduction here. One of these: "It is not only the top 50 percent of high school graduates who can benefit from higher education. There are many others, whose abilities or motivation emerge later, who should not be denied the chance to develop their full powers." Another: "The future social and economic welfare of the State as well as the greatest fulfillment of each student's potential is dependent upon the development of broader opportunities in higher education." Excellent precepts, both.

Preferring to offer broad principles rather than technical details, let us conclude this brief Connecticut story by noticing an outstandingly wise and thoughtful address delivered by Homer D. Babbidge, Jr., president of the University of Connecticut, at the Sixth Annual Institute on College Self-Study for College and University Administrators, held at the University of California at Berkeley, July 6-10, 1964.[1]

A young man new in the presidency of the University of Con-

---

[1]"Design and Change in American Higher Education," pp. 1-6 in *Long-Range Planning in Higher Education*, edited by Owen A. Knorr. Boulder, Colo.: Western Interstate Commission for Higher Education, 1965. 128 pp.

CONNECTICUT

Appropriations for Annual Operating Expenses of Higher Education in Connecticut, Alternate Fiscal Years, 1959-60 through 1969-70 (in thousands of dollars)

Institutions	Year 1959-60	Year 1961-62	Year 1963-64	Year 1965-66	Year 1967-68	Year 1969-70
U of Connecticut	8,590[1]	9,940	12,549	16,523[2]	26,300	35,242
Medical-Dental School				311	2,063	6,686
Fund-matching & progs				433		
Subtotal, U of Conn	8,590	9,940	12,549	17,267	28,363	41,928
State Colleges:						
Central Connecticut (New Britain)	1,573	1,747	2,257		6,268	8,899
Southern Connecticut (New Haven)	1,411	1,560	2,106		6,112	8,728
Western Conn (Danbury)	634	743	952		2,330	3,513
Eastern Conn (Willimantic)	482	565	721		1,648	2,477
Fund-match g & spec progs					35	
Unallocated				313		
St Bd for State Colleges					153	200
Sal increases—4 Colls[3]		300				
Subtotal, State Colleges	4,100	4,915	6,036	10,053	16,546	23,817
Technical Colleges[4]				1,522	2,187	3,635
Central Office					37	
Reg Community Colleges					4,039	8,506
State Board for Reg Comm Colls					131	252

Coll Student Loans Fdn					
Comm for Higher Edn				1,100	2,039[5]
Comm on Aid to Higher Edn			86	1,117	21
Acceptance & oper of Comm Colls[6]			987	110	
Conn Health & Ed Facil Auth				25	
Total	12,690	14,855	18,585	29,915	53,655
					80,270[7]

[1] Includes $452,000 for equipment; excludes $195,000 allotted to the University for deferred maintenance.

The amounts shown for the state colleges do not include $384,000 for equipment to be allocated among them, nor a fund of $106,000 earmarked for them for deferred maintenance.

[2] Includes, for each fiscal year, half of an appropriation of $199,200 for the biennium, to improve salaries.

[3] Lump sums appropriated to implement the new salary schedule in the four state colleges. Same factor appropriated for the University of Connecticut, but included in its over-all appropriation.

[1] A state-wide system of several technical institutes.

[2] Includes $100,000 for contract services with private colleges.

[3] Scheme contemplates a system of "regional community colleges" to be under a state-wide 12-member board of trustees, which will recommend to the State Commission for Higher Education nominees to be appointed by the Commission as members of a "regional council" for each such community college. This council will have some of the customary powers of a governing board.

[7] This includes $72,000 to the New England Board of Higher Education.

necticut, Babbidge was thrust into the midst of those who would make a state university a branch office of a state bureaucracy and those who would at all costs preserve the autonomy and freedom essential to the spirit and morale of a vital and creative institution of higher education, capable of producing maximum educational returns from the resources invested. His understanding of the issues seems to have been superb, and his ability to put them into convincing words appears to have been unsurpassed.

"There's just too much at stake," said he, "in terms of the future of our system of higher education, to pretend that planning—however or in whatever spirit conducted—is an educational wonder drug, devoid of side effects." Again: "There is something about 'a plan' that is truly ominous, a quality that is somehow compounded when it becomes a 'master plan'. That something that is dangerous about a plan is composed of a number of elements which include at least the following: (a) a tendency to rigidify the course of progress of an institution; (b) a tendency to impart a specious quality of certainty, order and serenity to the life of an institution; and (c) a subtle pressure to conformity, or alternatively, a loss of spontaneity in the life of an institution.

"The plan, in short, can become a conservative, even stultifying influence upon a university. *It can be railroad tracks laid across a meadow meant for meandering.* It can become a device behind which small men hide in an effort to protect themselves against threatening innovation. Every bright new idea can be dismissed as an expensive change order, and leadership can relax the eternal vigilance that is the price of vitality as well as of liberty."

Concerning plans involving several or many institutions in a state or regional system, Babbidge recognized that this can easily become a subject of exaggerated enthusiasm, and aptly quoted the simple words of Robert Frost: "The separateness of the parts is at least as important as the connection of the parts."

He went on: "I think of the *institution* as the basic agency or unit of planning; and that state and regional plans ought to be built out of this stuff, rather than out of a more abstract notion of what constitutes the tidy or the economical in higher education. It is important to say at the same time that our institutions are not sealed private compartments in our society. They do not—cannot— plan in splendid isolation. Some will derive their goals from a sense of involvement in an historic tradition; others will take their cue from contemporary forces. But their planning efforts will in no instance be totally the product of private, internal inspiration. And yet, without responsibility for planning, they are without control of their destinies, and they are no more entitled to be called institutions than is a local postoffice."

Finally: "As we sense a future of turbulent change, it is absolutely incumbent upon us to train our most powerful intellectual searchlights out ahead.

"And yet, I am satisfied that we must be resigned to an imperfect perception of the future. We must acknowledge that in going out to meet an unknown future, the most careful battle plan may be rendered obsolete overnight. And thus I would urge upon all institutions my own conviction that our strongest ally in our foray against the future is not a plan, but *a resolute sense of values*; values that will (among other things) attract and hold leaders of courage and imagination, and inspire and rally academic communities to common cause."

If anyone knows a better statement of the essence of what makes a university great and what makes higher education productive, let him speak.

DELAWARE

Tiny in area and small in population, the home of the world's largest chemical company—E. I. du Pont de Nemours and Company—, Delaware has sometimes been facetiously called "the duchy of du Pont," and the charge has been heard that its state-wide newspapers and its state university are subservient to the whims of members of the numerous and enormously wealthy du Pont family. The University of Delaware is one of the few state universities in the nation having a majority of its governing board members coöpted or "self-perpetuating." (The University of Alabama is another; and this was true of Ohio University for a century, but no more.) As might well be expected, the most distinguished departments of the University of Delaware are reported to be those of Chemical Engineering and of Chemistry. The state is also the home of Hercules, Inc., and of Atlas Chemical Industries, Inc., both of which are large firms split off from du Pont after an antitrust suit in 1912.

In a lively journalistic article in the respected periodical, *Science*, in May 1968, Philip M. Boffey reported that the 32-member Board of Trustees of the University had an executive committee of 14 men, of whom nine were either members of the du Pont family by blood or marriage, or executives of the du Pont company or of a family-owned bank.[1] And he says that when John A. Perkins, president of the University from 1950 to 1967, was asked to name the most influential current trustees, he mentioned eight, of whom six were du Pont executives or family members.

The University of Delaware had an endowment of $65½ million (book value) in 1965-66, as reported by the American Alumni Council and the Council for Financial Aid to Education. This was fourth largest among 183 public institutions surveyed, and in fact equals or exceeds the endowments of all but about 20 of the most prestigious private universities. This is all the more remarkable because among state universities Delaware is only of medium size and average reputation. Boffey says the University's wealth has been built up largely by gifts from members of the du Pont family and not from the du Pont company, which considers itself a nation-wide enterprise with a nation-

---

[1] "Du Pont and Delaware: Academic Life behind the Nylon Curtain." *Science*, Vol. 160, pp. 628-633 (10 May 1968).

wide commitment to support higher education. In 1967-68 the company gave to 145 colleges and universities $2 million, of which only about 10 per cent went to Delaware.

The most exciting event in the recent legislative history of the University of Delaware was in 1964, when an ill-advised attempt was made by the state budget director to impose upon the University the petty fiscal controls from the statehouse that have become customary in most of the northeastern states. Aroused, the multimillionaire Trustees converged upon Dover in what local wags called "Rolls Royce Day" to push through the legislature a statute that is something of a model of its kind in defining the proper fiscal independence of the University.

Amendments enacted in 1964 to the statutes constituting the charter of the University, confirmed and spelled out in detail the long-standing policy of the state:

"(I) Notwithstanding any provisions appearing elsewhere in the laws of this state which might suggest or provide the contrary, the 'entire control and management of the affairs of the University', which is conferred upon the Trustees by the foregoing paragraph, shall be construed, in the area of fiscal and revenue matters, as including but not being limited to, the following powers and duties:

"(a) All authority with respect to salaries and compensatory payments or benefits, as well as other terms of employment, of any and all University personnel, and individual salaries or salary increases or other benefits do not have to be reported or justified to any other official or agency of the state (except to cooperate in the ordinary way with the appropriate officials with respect to income tax or other tax matters).

"(b) The management of all the remaining fiscal affairs of the University, including the establishment of fees and charges, the collection thereof and the adoption of the University's budget, the establishment of all accounting and auditing procedures (subject to the duty to obtain independent certified audits as provided in Section 5109). [The Section 5109 referred to was redrafted to provide '(1) The accounting records of the University may be audited by the Auditor of Accounts of the State of Delaware or such other auditing official as the General Assembly may from time to time appoint. Neither this nor any other law of this State, however, shall hereafter be construed as imposing any duty upon, or creating the occasion for, any state official, with the exception of such state officials as may from time to time also be Trustees of the University, to audit, question, or inquire into the receipt, handling, or expenditure of any funds coming to the University from any source other than a state appropriation, provided, however, that if the University should hereafter commingle funds which came from a state appropriation with other funds, the audit of state-appropriated funds may be made complete even if in the process of

DELAWARE

Appropriations for Annual Operating Expenses of Higher Education in Delaware, Alternate Fiscal Years, 1959-60 through 1969-70 (in thousands of dollars)

Institutions	Year 1959-60	Year 1961-62	Year 1963-64	Year 1965-66	Year 1967-68	Year 1969-70
U of Delaware			5,210	6,533	8,298	10,836
Soc. Sec.[1]					441	536
Pensions[1]					246	270
Insurance[2]					58	
Subtotal, U of Del			5,210	6,533	9,043	11,977[3]
Delaware St Coll			621	782	1,021	1,998
Soc. Sec.[1]					35	
Pensions[1]					12	
Insurance[2]					15	
Subtotal, Del St Coll			621	782	1,083	1,998
Del Tech & Comm Coll					1,062	2,958
Higher Ed Aid Adv Comm for Higher Ed & Voc Loan Program					25	
Out-of-state Scholarships[4]				75	100	
Total	3,731[5]	4,368[5]	5,831	7,390	11,313	16,933

[1]Administered by the State Treasurer.
[2]Appropriated to the State Insurance Commissioner.
[3]Includes $335,000 for various student aids and research services.

[4]This sum is appropriated to the State Board of Education for scholarships to Delaware students attending institutions of higher learning outside the state.
[5]This figure includes the total appropriation for the entire state.

doing so, because of such commingling, non-state funds have to be audited as well. (2) The University shall continue the practice, which has heretofore been followed on a voluntary basis, of obtaining an annual certified audit of all its financial transactions.]

"(c) The authorization, issuance, and repayment of bonds or other obligations of the University; the selection of means and procedures for the investment, deposit, and control of all funds and securities which are now held or which may at any time be received by the University, as well as the allocation, use, and reinvestment of the proceeds and earnings of any such deposits and investments, and the right to commingle funds appropriated by the state with other funds of the University.

"(d) The right to elect whether and to what extent to participate in programs of which all or a part of the costs are provided by the United States of America or by the State of Delaware or any subdivision or municipality thereof; control of all matters having to do with the formulation of the terms of contracts for the construction of buildings or other University facilities, as well as the manner of awarding contracts or purchasing supplies and equipment.

"(e) In respect to the purchase of supplies and equipment, regulations established by the state for bulk or central purchasing are not to apply to the University of Delaware unless the General Assembly expressly so provides, and in that case are to be understood as applying only to transactions involving the expenditure of moneys which have been appropriated from the General Fund of the State; the planning for buildings and improvements and the extension or diminution of the campus or other land holdings, are matters wholly under the control of the Trustees except where inspections or regulations may be provided by law in respects involving the health or safety of the occupants of the buildings.

"(f) Where moneys are appropriated by the General Assembly to the University, unless the General Assembly should expressly provide otherwise, they are intended to be paid to the University in equal monthly installments, and are not in any event to be cumbered by any procedures calling for pre-audit or other administrative control exercised by the Budget Director or other agency or official of the State."

The foregoing is in several respects a classic legislative declaration of state university fiscal autonomy. As such, it is something of a landmark. Compare it with the definition of university independence which forms a part of the story of California, *supra*; and with the "Autonomy acts," described in Massachusetts and New Jersey, *infra*.

FLORIDA

Public higher education in Florida, such as it was shortly after the turn of the century, suffered the blow of having the institutional governing boards abolished by the Buckman Act of 1905. The University of Florida at Gainesville was in an embryonic stage, and was open to men only. The institution at Tallahassee which was eventually to become Florida State University was then a small state college for women. There was a tiny land-grant college for Negroes, and nothing more. Most of the state was in a primitive condition, and its total population was only about 600,000. Envision the contrast between that figure and the estimated 6,160,000 as of July 1, 1968. In 1965 the metropolitan area of Miami alone had more than one million people, nearly 70 per cent more than the whole state had had 60 years earlier.

Florida was apparently the second state to abolish institutional boards of trustees and consolidate the control of several state institutions of higher education (following South Dakota in 1896). The new board, unimaginatively named Board of Control, was placed in an anomolous position (which its recent successor still endures) by being made expressly subordinate to and subject to the supervision of the State Board of Education.

There has never been any certainty as to what types of decisions by the Board of Control will be tacitly approved by the Board of Education, and what types will be reviewed and possibly disapproved. Together with the fact that all of the seven members of the Board of Control were appointed by the governor, and that the State Board of Education was of the most primitive structure, composed only of the governor and a handful of the other principal elective officers of the state, including the Superintendent of Public Instruction, this circumstance would seem to have placed top policy-making for public higher education very largely at the mercy of politicians whose main interests were elsewhere.

The terms of members of the Board of Control were constitutionally limited to four years (along with those of other state officers), and this meant that usually an incoming governor could gain full control of the Board by packing it with his own appointees.

The legislature of 1963 proposed a constitutional amendment which corrected this feature by reconstituting the Board to be composed of nine members appointed by the governor with the approval of the State Board of Education and the consent of the senate, to serve for terms of nine years (if the legislature should so determine); the terms of the first appointees to be from one to nine years so that thereafter one member would be appointed each year. The amendment also renamed the Board, dropping the style of Board of Control and adopting the title of Board of Regents.

The same legislature of 1963 also enacted an implementing act, and provided that it should become effective January 1 of the year following the adoption of the proposed constitutional amendment by popular vote. The amendment was adopted at the election of November 3, 1964, and the implementing act accordingly went into effect January 1, 1965. Although it provided for the nine-year overlapping terms, unfortunately it left the Board of Regents "subject to the supervision and authority" of the State Board of Education as before, and apparently did not go far in any other direction to improve the position of the Board of Regents. Like its predecessor, it is created a corporation, with all the usual powers of an institutional governing board.

In a gesture toward loosening the fiscal strait-jacket imposed by older statutes, the new act provided: "The board of regents and all the institutions and divisions under its control are exempt from any and all supervision or control of the State Budget Commission, except for subsection (1) of section 216.211, Florida Statutes"; but this subsection was subsequently repealed.

Florida statutes provide that if and when the governor believes revenue receipts will be insufficient to finance the full appropriations, then the budget commission or the governor "shall adjust the budget of any department or board," the intent being that there shall be no deficit. This is Florida's salaam to the fetish of the balanced budget. Many other states have somewhat similar provisions. They are destructive of the state university's opportunity to plan for the short fiscal period with confidence. They may severely impair the morale of administrators and professors, thereby causing losses of productivity of greater magnitude than the comparatively negligible sums they withhold, thus becoming excellent examples of self-defeating "false economy."

It is far better from the standpoint of the public interest to pay in full the appropriations for the fiscal year or biennium as planned, even if this creates a small deficit, and then take the deficit into account in planning for the next ensuing fiscal period. Thus if retrenchment becomes necessary, it can be accomplished in orderly manner without abrupt disruption of plans and consequent unavoidable losses.

In the realm of the formulation of annual budget requests, if the wording of the 1965 statute represented the actual practice, it seems that Florida provided for a comparatively short and expeditious trail from the Board of Regents to the legislature: The Board was directed to prepare annual budgets for the state universities, and to transmit these, together with other detailed fiscal data, to the appropriations committees of the two houses of the legislature by December 15. This was in sharp contrast to the lengthening gauntlet of executive budget office, state budget commission, governor's office, joint legislative budget office, and other shoals that have to be negotiated by university budget askings in some other states, particularly California. However, more recent Florida legislation has complicated the process considerably.

Fiscal Relations with State Agencies

The Florida legislature has insisted on keeping in its own hands (and not through any fiscal or administrative intermediary) the control of state funds for capital outlays; but the Act of 1965 wisely embodies very substantial exceptions to this policy on behalf of public higher education.

"No building facilities, except as hereinafter provided shall be constructed or added to by the state university system without prior approval of the legislature." However, any project involving not more than $50,000 of state funds is exempt, as are also all buildings financed from nonstate sources such as federal grants, private gifts, private investment in self-liquidating dormitories or other income-producing auxiliary accommodations; and any buildings of any kind destroyed by fire or other calamity.

Funds for operation coming into the hands of the Board of Regents must be deposited in the state treasury within 40 days after receipt, with certain exceptions, among which are student deposits, student activity funds, scholarship and loan funds, "Federal Point IV Program" (presumably meaning sums received under grants or contracts for assistance to foreign countries), and athletic fees. Probably most important among these exceptions are gifts, grants, bequests, or research contracts from any source other than the state; and "alumni funds of whatever nature or description and however acquired." A wise and experienced university business officer has commented that "A great deal more 'loosening of the strings' is needed." One might add that a simpler and better way of wording the statute would be to except "all funds from whatever sources other than state appropriations."

One of the worst features of the whole fiscal system in Florida is the requirement that disbursements cannot be made until pre-audited by the state comptroller. Generally this practice is now coming to be recognized as unnecessary, likely to be pernicious in its effects on the operation of the institutions, and sure to be annoying. The modern trend is to entrust pre-auditing to the institutional business officers, and it is not regarded as at all necessary to have it duplicated and delayed in any state office. The annual post-audit by an agency outside the institution is a sufficient check on the accuracy and lawfulness of the expenditures.

A feature of *pre-auditing* from the state capital, aside from the delay it entails, is a difficulty that has been demonstrated by years of experience in many states: state fiscal officers have a seemingly unconquerable tendency to exceed their statutory powers (to check for accuracy, lawfulness, and availability of funds), and trespass into the domain of the wisdom and expediency of the expenditures, which is not their province. Several results detrimental to the operation of higher education invariably ensue. Delays and disputes between the institutional president and the statehouse auditing office disrupt the president's plans, cause many of the institution's prior expenditures to be markedly less productive than they would otherwise be, and transfer in greater or less degree the management of the institution from its president to fiscal clerks in the statehouse, with results that might well be expected to be less than admirable.

Some state auditors are prone to seize upon petty matters such as the cost of meals allowable to university professors while traveling in the service of the state, and to encourage reporters to blow these up into headline stories in which the state auditor is posed as the "faithful watch-dog of the treasury" while by implication the university president is portrayed as a congenitally incompetent spendthrift. A well-remembered state auditor of Ohio of a generation ago, who later won election and re-election to several terms as governor, made sensational headlines out of the fact that the price of a baked potato on the menu of a state university employee while traveling had been 40 cents, at a time when Ohio farmers were selling a huge crop of potatoes at 50 cents per bushel.

The Florida act, in order to avoid locking the operation of the institutions at a more or less perpetual standstill awaiting pre-auditing of petty disbursements, allots to each institution a small "revolving fund" out of which payments may be made without delay, and later be audited by the state comptroller who will thereupon reimburse the revolving fund. These institutional "revolving funds" range from $75,000 to $250,000, the largest being for the University of Florida.

Passing the Torch

Although the Act of 1965 improved somewhat the structure of the state-wide governing board, it ran head-on into a serio-comic "snafu" during the early weeks of the year. The term of the outgoing governor, Farris Bryant, extended several days beyond January 1, prior to the inauguration of his successor, Haydon Burns. In literal compliance with the statute, Governor Bryant promptly appointed nine members of the new Board of Regents, for terms of from one to nine years. His appointees included all seven members of the former Board of Control. Governor Burns, who had taken campaign positions opposed to some of the recent decisions of the Board of Control, soon asked the state

FLORIDA

Appropriations for Annual Operating Expenses of Higher Education in Florida, Alternate Fiscal Years, 1959-60 through 1969-70 (in thousands of dollars)

Institutions	Year 1959-60	Year 1961-62	Year 1963-64	Year 1965-66	Year 1967-68	Year 1969-70
U of Florida	22,867	13,847	15,733	15,058	21,240	30,641
Health Center		5,619	5,735	6,141	6,836	11,969
Inst Food & Ag[1]		6,881	8,002	10,088	12,591	16,920
Grad Engrng Sys[2]		395	488	444	595	678
Engrng Exp Sta				500	485	500
Subtotal, U of Fla	22,867	26,742	29,958	32,231	41,747	60,708
Fla St University	8,537	9,678	11,740	12,765	20,816	26,837
U of So Florida[3] (Tampa)	1,315	3,139	5,121	6,658	10,716	16,751
Fla A & M Univ	3,063	3,309	3,579	4,026	4,906	6,693
Fla A & M U Hosp		258	126	161		
Subtotal, Fla A & M U	3,063	3,567	3,705	4,187	4,906	6,693
Florida Atlantic U (Boca Raton)			3,326	3,729	5,677	8,086
U of West Florida (Pensacola)				1,496	3,448	5,418
East Central Fla U / Fla Technolog'l U (Orlando)				361	2,463	4,939
Fla Inst of Continuing University Services[4]			1,637	1,180		
Subtotal, State U's	12,915	16,384	25,529	30,376	48,026	69,374[5]

Board of Regents	1,478[6]					
Gen'l Office		150	240	378	1,940[7]	3,792
Reg'l Educ		454	462		612	730
U of Miami Med Sch		974	990[8]	1,273[9]	1,343[9]	330
Other administered funds		76	53			
147 faculty counselors				1,506		
Faculty salary increases[10]				1,122		
New coll at Pensacola		50	350			
New inst at Boca Raton		50				
Supplem 12-mo apptmts[11]				1,119		
Improvements in U progs				138		
Subtotal, Board of Regents		1,754	2,095	5,536	3,895	4,852
State aid to Jr Colleges			14,333	26,802[12]	53,461	63,202
Total	37,260	44,877	72,043	95,476	147,133	198,438[13]

[1]The Agricultural Experiment Station and the Agricultural Extension Service are now combined in the Institute of Food and Agricultural Sciences.
[2]The Graduate Engineering Education System, often designated GENESYS, serves the middle east coast and Cape Kennedy areas.
[3]This institution received its first students in September 1960.
[4]State-wide general extension service, created in 1963; later decentralized.
[5]Includes $350,000 for Florida International University, and $300,000 for University of North Florida.
[6]Includes administered funds.
[7]Includes the following items which were funded by the special session (biennial sums):

Regents' Scholarships $1,500,000
Planning new inst Dade County 226,000
Planning new inst Duval County 226,000
For transfer to U's for increased enrollments* 200,000
Regional education (TV) 78,000

*To be added to balance of $2 million then undistributed.
[8]State subsidy of $3,500 per student to a private university medical school.
[9]Subsidy of $4,500 per Florida student enrolled in the medical school of the private University of Miami.
[10]These increases are for the Florida State University and the University of Florida only.
[11]At Florida State University and the University of Florida only.
[12]Includes $48,244,786 for existing junior colleges, $1,116,858 for new junior colleges, and $4,243,250 of allocated sales tax receipts.
[13]Includes $301,000 for Dade County Continuing Education Center.

supreme court for a ruling as to whether the outgoing governor could lawfully make the appointments for the terms specified.

The opinion of the court was that the Bryant appointments, having been made before the convening of the legislature, could be only for periods ending with the adjournment of the current session of the senate, or until the appointment and senate confirmation of their successors, whichever came first.[1] Meantime the Bryant appointees had resigned and been succeeded by Burns appointees. Among these latter, it was reported, were a Negro real estate broker of West Palm Beach, a "clubwoman" of Coral Gables, and a physician of Orlando. No Negro had ever been appointed before, and only once had there been a woman member, though the Board of Control had functioned for 60 years as the sole governing board for Florida's universities. These steps toward broader representativeness are probably in a good direction; but the first principle of state university governance was violated, perhaps unwittingly, perhaps craftily, by adopting a constitutional amendment and an implementing statute which made it possible for one governor to appoint an entire new governing board, thus enabling him, if he wished, to dominate the entire Board throughout his whole term, and perhaps beyond. This is an open temptation to any ambitious governor to increase his patronage by accomplishing a reorganization or reconstitution of such boards within his own period of tenure, and is one of the unsolved problems of state government.

Apparently for half a century the old Board of Control was largely inactive so far as the state-wide purview was concerned, and performed in a sort of minimal fashion its unavoidable duties as governing board of each of the separate institutions under its jurisdiction. It had no full-time executive officer of any appreciable stature, and relied chiefly on the institutional presidents, who labored diligently for the development of their own institutions, not by any means without giving some thought to the state-wide scene in higher education. In more recent years the Board built up a strong executive office and staff, and took a much heavier hand.

Sometimes it made the mistake of giving too much of its own time and attention to matters of detailed administration within the several institutions, and sometimes it adopted amazingly arbitrary and unsuitable regulations without sufficient prior consultation with the presidents and faculties. Examples of the latter include a totally rigid ordinance to the effect that any faculty member who became a candidate for public office should be summarily dismissed.[2] Many of the nation's greatest universities have no rule on this subject, and others

---

[1] *In re Advisory Opinion to the Governor*, (Fla.), 171 So. 2d 539 (1965).
[2] *Jones* v. *Board of Control*, (Fla.), 131 So. 2d 713 (1961)

urbanely provide the faculty member with an option of taking a leave of absence for the duration of his political campaign, so that the governing board will not be in the untenable position of forbidding a qualified person from seeking public office merely because he is a teacher. In suitable alternation these two forms of service may often be compatible in high degree, each reinforcing the other; and this is widely recognized throughout the academic world. Subsequently the Florida Board of Control modified somewhat its inflexible rule on the subject.

Another edict issued during the middle 'Sixties without adequate deliberation and consultation was that all Florida's state universities should promptly go on a uniform "trimester" calendar. This was opposed and resented by many persons within and without the universities, became something of an issue in the gubernatorial campaign of 1964, and eventually had to be rescinded. One result of these and other bull-in-the-china-shop actions of the Board of Control was a high rate of turnover among some of the state university presidents in Florida, at least one of whom resigned in disgust. One of the great dangers of overcentralization is its tendency to derogate and pejorate the university presidency to a degree that superior presidents will not abide.

From many standpoints Florida has made magnificent progress in the support and development of public higher education, including a state-wide group of universities and a state-wide network of junior colleges. In addition to the three older state universities, it has created the University of South Florida at Tampa, Florida Atlantic University at Boca Raton, University of West Florida at Pensacola, and Florida Technological University at Orlando. Plans are also under way to open new universities at Jacksonville and Miami. Florida International University at Miami and the University of North Florida at Jacksonville will open in 1972.

The number of state-aided locally-based public junior colleges was 28 in 1969, and almost no really populous county in the state was without such an institution. The estimated total of state aid for operating expenses of the junior colleges for fiscal year 1968-69 was $53½ million, second to that of no other state except California's $96 million.

The total appropriation for operating expenses of all higher education grew from a little more than $40 million in 1959-60 to $156 million for 1968-69—a gain of 288 per cent, which is well above the national average rate of gain among the 50 states for the same 9-year period (261 per cent), but not so far above it as could rightfully be expected in view of Florida's very rapid gain in population.

The legislature of 1963 relieved the Board of Control (now Board of Regents) of the governance of the Florida School for the Deaf and the Blind, leaving the Board's functions concerned exclusively with higher education. This was a belated step away from the error of centralizing in one board not only the governance of all the universities, but also that of various other eleemosynary institutions. Other states of comparatively small population, such as Iowa, Kansas, and North Dakota, made the same error in earlier years, but most of them have rectified it.

1963-65 Was an Eventful Biennium

The legislature of 1963 proposed, and the electorate approved in a subsequent general election, a constitutional amendment authorizing the state to issue $75 million in bonds for construction of university and junior college buildings during the next two years, and authorizing similar issues of up to $50 million every two years thereafter. The bonds were to be issued by the State Board of Education on behalf of the state, and the proceeds of the state-wide gross receipts tax on public utilities were declared a trust fund pledged to their retirement.

The same legislature of 1963 authorized expenditure of about $88 million for capital improvements at universities, junior colleges, and area vocational-technical schools. This was contested in litigation because the total sum exceeded the amount of the bonds ($75 million) authorized to be issued in that biennium; but the court readily decided that the constitution limits only the amount of bonds issued during a specified fiscal period, and not the total of expenditures authorized. [3] Hence, both the statutory authorization of $88 million expenditures and the bond issue of $75 million within the biennium 1963-65 were valid.

The 1963 legislature also enacted a statute intended to effect a state-wide consolidation and centralization of all university extension instruction, to be placed under the control of a newly-created Florida Institute for Continuing University Studies. This quickly proved to be an ill-starred venture, and the legislature of 1965 abolished the Institute and made all off-campus instruction again a function of each of the universities, as of July 1, 1965, subject only to general oversight of the Board of Regents.

The same 1965 legislature also enacted a measure smacking of wise paternal instruction to the Board of Regents, and perhaps amounting to a slight slap on the wrist of the predecessor Board of Control. The measure declared it to be the legislative intent that the Board of Regents *is primarily a general policy-making board*. This in effect advises the Board not to try to manage each of the universities in detail. For the first half-century of its existence the Board apparently did very little; thereafter it developed a history of doing too much in detail, resulting in unhappy and unnecessary collisions with university presidents, faculties, and constituencies.

The eventual outcome over future years, one might hope, would be

---

[3] *State v. State Board of Education*, (Fla.), 165 So. 2d 161 (1964).

the creation of a governing board for each of the universities, and the limiting of the powers of the state-wide Board of Regents to the functions of state-wide *liaison*, public information, fact-gathering, surveys, and recommendations. Lacking this, or until it occurs, it is all the more important that the Board of Regents and its staff should limit themselves to larger matters of state-wide concern, abstain from impulsive and ill-considered edicts that would make of the system an overcentralized authoritarian bureaucracy wholly inimical to the genius of university education, and devote itself to cultivating understanding of the nature and role of higher education among the politicians and the public, and improved morale among faculties, students, and friends of the universities. In pursuing such tasks, the Board has an opportunity for magnificent service to the people of Florida and the nation.

In 1951, incredibly, there was no medical school within the state. The legislature, balking at the idea of financing a medical school at the state university, settled upon the device of enacting a measure authorizing payment of $3,000 per year for each Florida student enrolled, in the first accredited medical school to be opened in the state by a municipality or by a private nonprofit corporation. The act required that the student and his parents must have resided in Florida for seven years, and that the school must not admit more than 10 per cent of its students from outside the state. It appropriated $225,000 to subsidize the school in this manner for the biennium 1951-53.

The private University of Miami then began its medical school, having previously obtained assurances from the American Medical Association that the standards of accreditation could probably be met. But accreditation is never conferred until a school has been in operation at least four years; and thus the Florida supreme court had to stretch a point by construing the appropriation of 1951 to be payable to the University of Miami medical school.[4] The practice of paying state tax funds for this service has continued and grown, so that the state payments to Miami University for this purpose for the biennium 1967-69 were at the rate of $4,500 per year per Florida medical student, for a total of $2,687,000, having increased about twelvefold within 16 years.

Meantime a state-supported medical school has been established as a part of the University of Florida, and is now the nucleus of a Health Center which received $13½ million of state tax appropriations for biennium 1967-69; and initial state support has also been appropriated for the beginning of a new school of medicine and nursing at the University of South Florida. Thus Florida may soon have three centers of medical education. There is no question but that a rapidly

---

[4]*Overman* v. *State Board of Control*, (Fla.), 62 So. 2d 696 (1952) and 71 So. 2d 262 (1954).

growing state of more than six million people needs all these facilities, and more.

An event of great significance to public higher education in Florida was the enactment of a "tax package" by the special session of the legislature in early 1968, to raise an estimated $350 million of new revenue during the final 15 months of the biennium 1967-69. The general sales tax rate was raised to 4 per cent from the former 3 per cent; the cigarette tax to 15 cents a pack from the prior 8 cents; and a new 4 per cent tax on commercial leases was established. Beer and liquor taxes were also raised. These measures became law without the signature of the reluctant governor.

While about its work, the special session also supplemented the appropriations for operating expenses of higher education for the biennium 1967-69 (originally made in early 1967) very substantially. The new state-wide total for the biennium was $38 million larger than the original—the change being from $256 million to $294 million approximately. All the universities, and the community colleges, gained.

The 1969 legislature made permanent the 4 per cent general sales tax rate, which otherwise would have expired July 1, 1969.

GEORGIA

There is a most unusual "sleeper" in the recent history of legislative appropriations in Georgia. A constitutional amendment ratified in 1952 provided that the legislature in each general appropriation act must make aggregate annual appropriations for highway purposes not less than the total of motor fuel taxes and motor vehicle license fees received during the immediately preceding fiscal year.

The effect of that rigidity was practically to inhibit the enactment of general appropriation bills. Only two were enacted between 1952 and 1960. Instead, the Budget Bureau, seemingly by default, was allowed to allocate substantial parts of the increasing gasoline and automobile license revenues to the support of other essential state services. For example, for fiscal year 1958-59 the revenue from these sources amounted to $95 million. Of this, $75 million was allocated to highways, and $20 million to other state services.

The Georgia amendment of 1952 is a classic example of how great a mistake it is to freeze a specific allocation of specified revenues into a state constitution. The 1960 legislature proposed a new amendment to reduce the mandatory state appropriation for highway purposes.

A provision of the Georgia Constitution of 1871 prohibited the appropriation of state funds to any educational institution above the elementary-school level except departments of the University of Georgia. Hence it was essential that all state-supported institutions have that status, at least nominally. Consequently a statute provided that the chairman of each institutional governing board should sit as a member *ex officio* of the University governing board, and that the University governing board should appoint three of its own members to sit as members of each of the several other separate institutional boards. Up to 1931 the number of state-supported schools of all kinds had reached 26, including some junior colleges and some schools not above high school level.

In 1931, in the throes of the Great Depression, the legislature abolished all institutional governing boards, reduced the number of state institutions to 14 by abolishing some and consolidating others, and placed the whole under the governance of a newly-created Board of Regents of the University System of Georgia, with headquarters at the state capital. This Georgia act of 1931 quite closely resembled the similar action taken by the Oregon legislature in 1929, which became fully effective in 1931.

By 1968 the Georgia system embraced 25 institutions: four major ones (The University of Georgia at Athens, the Georgia Institute of Technology at Atlanta, the Medical College of Georgia at Augusta, and the Georgia State College at Atlanta); 12 four-year state colleges; and nine state junior colleges. There is also one state-aided *local* public junior college which has been in operation several years in the populous Atlanta area (De Kalb Junior College at Clarkston).

In 1949 the Board of Regents contracted for a survey of the system by the redoubtable George D. Strayer, professor emeritus of education at Columbia University, who assembled a staff of seven other nationally-known educators and reported in a 343-page printed document dated December 15, 1949, entitled *A Report of a Survey of the University System of Georgia*. As is the custom of such sages, the staff gazed into the murky future to a depth of 15 years and foresaw what they deemed to be the reasonably expectable financial income of the University system for each of those years.[1] Ten years ahead, for the fiscal year 1959-60, this clairvoyance projected appropriations of state tax funds for annual operating expenses as somewhat less than $11 million. The actual figure for that year turned out to be more than $24 million. For the fifteenth year (fiscal 1964-65) the surveyors projected less than $15 million. The actual figure proved to be nearly $42 million. (And it might well be added that this latter figure was more than doubled for fiscal year 1967-68, only three years later.) Not to say that the calculations of 1949 grossly undershot the mark would be less than candid!

In July 1963 a state-wide survey of broad scope, including education at all levels, was launched by the Governor's Commission to Improve Education. Under Governor Carl Sanders as chairman, this Commission was made up wholly of local talent, being composed of half a dozen members of each house of the legislature and some twenty other prominent citizens of Georgia. The staff director was James L. Miller, Jr. (borrowed from his job as associate director for research of the Southern Regional Education Board at Atlanta). There was also a small panel of three nationally-known educators as consultants.

Regarding state tax financing of higher education in future years, this body selected from carefully drawn recommendations of the Task-Force on Finance headed by James A. Blissit, treasurer of the University System, and adapted them to arrive at projections of state tax appropriations for annual operating expenses over the ensuing

---

[1] Table 65, page 339 in *A Report of a Survey...*, submitted to the Regents of the University System of Georgia, December 15, 1949.

decade that achieved a closer approach to realism. For 1964-65, the projection was slightly more than $50 million; for 1968-69 it was $83½ million; and for 1973-74 it was $133½ million.[2] As already noticed, the actual figure for 1964-65 turned out to be less than this prediction, but the actual figure for 1968-69 was far above the projection—being approximately $103 million without including the $9,643,000 for "employer's contribution to retirement" which had in previous years been appropriated to a state agency other than the Regents. What the figure will be for 1973-74 remains to be seen; but it appears very probable that it will greatly exceed the projection made in 1963.

In fact, a supplemental appropriation by the 1964 session made available for fiscal year 1964-65 approximately $3 million additional, almost wholly for academic salary increases and new positions, making possible average faculty salary increases of 12 per cent over the biennium.

The same supplemental appropriations act provided $3½ million for Building Authority rentals, and the Board of Regents in March 1964 authorized bond issues of $60 million (to be retired by rental payments to the State Building Authority for the University System) and of $11 million to be retired by the proceeds of charges for room and board to students, making a total bond program for 1964-65 of $71 million.

As to the financing of student housing facilities, the Regents adopted a policy of financing one-half the cost from state appropriations and one-half from student charges. This made possible substantially lower charges to students than those prevailing in some other states where the practice is to finance these facilities wholly from the proceeds of their operation. A bit of the history of this matter in Georgia is contained in a letter of March 24, 1964, from James A. Blissit, treasurer of the Board of Regents.

"We have never depended solely on dormitory revenues for the financing of student housing. It was not until the late 1930's that we borrowed funds for the construction of dormitories. Then we borrowed only a portion of the cost and the total auxiliary operation was pooled to provide the debt-service requirements. This practice continued until 1950 at which time we started constructing dormitories with bond issues financed entirely with state-appropriated funds. In 1959 we reverted to a partial self-liquidating program for financing dormitories. Again the auxiliary enterprise operation was pooled to provide funds for debt-service. By this I mean that charges were established at reasonable levels for all facilities and the net income from 'paid for' facilities as well as from the new facilities was pooled for debt-service purposes. The financial leeway available has now

[2]Page 66 of *Educating Georgia's People: Investment in the Future.* Atlanta: Governor's Commission to Improve Education, 1963. 72 pp.

GEORGIA

Appropriations for Annual Operating Expenses of Higher Education in Georgia, Alternate Fiscal Years, 1959-60 through 1969-70 (in thousands of dollars)

Institutions	Year 1959-60	Year 1961-62	Year 1963-64	Year 1965-66	Year 1967-68[1]	Year 1969-70[1]
U of Georgia	4,618	5,579	7,370	11,077	25,772	31,510
Ag Exten Service	1,510	1,820	2,281	2,989	3,870	4,721
Ag Exper Station	1,695	2,037	2,270	2,763	3,545	4,429
Continuing Edn Ctr	268	318	436	656	862	1,148
Subtotal, U of Georgia	8,091	9,754	12,357	17,485	34,049	41,808
Ga Inst of Technology	3,247	3,977	4,804	5,893	8,781	11,403
Engrng Exper Station	510	717	986	1,514	1,940	2,523
Engrng Exten Division	277	20	31	81	135	195
Southern Technical Inst		409	506	643	850	990
Subtotal, Ga Inst of Tech	4,034	5,123	6,327	8,131	11,706	15,111
Medical Coll of Georgia	1,090	1,411	1,696	2,194	3,848	6,304
Talmadge Memorial Hosp	3,000	3,500	3,600	4,330	5,282	6,254
Subtotal, Med Coll of Ga	4,090	4,911	5,296	6,524	9,130	12,558
Georgia State U	1,787	1,938	2,252	3,727	6,279	9,675
Ga Southern College	553	670	1,062	1,716	2,879	4,122
West Georgia College	277	375	686	1,322	2,448	3,644
Valdosta State Coll	326	383	495	778	1,637	2,182
Ft Valley St College	650	736	864	1,243	1,698	2,079
Ga Southwestern Coll	174	199	284	517	1,329	1,850
Albany State College	396	494	635	890	1,285	1,649
Ga Coll at Milledgeville	625	712	816	1,016	1,246	1,676
Savannah State College	684	747	847	1,077	1,329	1,653
Augusta College	229	383	440	755	1,206	1,447
Armstrong St Coll	306	323	368	549	993	1,311
North Ga College	438	471	561	689	890	1,036
Columbus College	201	216	279	467	735	1,188

Middle Ga College	185	207	311	567	1,066	1,268
A Baldwin Ag Coll	242	286	406	605	922	1,104
Kennesaw Jr Coll				673	891	1,070
Macon Jr College						932
Albany Jr College					644	752
So Ga College	191	207	262	409	589	785
Dalton Jr College					396	667
Gainesville Jr Coll					474	666
Brunswick Jr Coll				288	506	676
Regents of U System		240	235	400	696	1,175
St Tech Serv Program					300	313
Regents' Scholarships		100	100	200	200	200
Graduate Scholarships					200	140
Scholarships for Negroes		275	225	200		
Regents for Jr Coll Syst					200	200
Regional Education		80	79	75	75	85
Higher Educ Asstnce Corp				168[2]		
St Scholarship Commission				247[2]		
Interest on const debt			8		8	8
Unallocated				274	553	
Soil Conservation		200				
Other activities	745					797[3]
St aid to Jr Colleges				540	810	1,200
Total	24,224	29,046	35,270	50,859	87,369	124,207

[1]Allocations to the several institutions are made by the Board of Regents of the University System of Georgia.

[2]These sums were appropriated directly to the agencies named, not to the Regents of the University System.

[3]Includes $744,000 for Clayton Junior College (a new institution) and $53,000 as a contingency fund for the state junior colleges.

been exhausted and unless room rents are to be materially increased, it will be necessary for us to seek other funds to assist us in financing student housing." Hence the "50-50" policy.

Mr. Blissit continued: "It has always been the thought of the Board that we should not charge rates in an amount adequate to completely finance the cost of student housing. I suppose you could say that this is the first time we have established a firm policy for financing student housing. We believe it is a reasonable approach to the problem and will not place an unreasonable burden on either the State or the student."

The Georgia Education Authority (University), mentioned earlier as the State Building Authority for the University System, is a state agency, a public corporation of a particular type for the special purpose of borrowing money without creating a debt against the state (and thus circumventing any constitutional limitation of state indebtedness), financing the construction of university and college buildings within the public university system, and amortizing the cost of these buildings by receiving agreed payments which are the virtual equivalent of annual rentals from the institutions on whose campuses they are erected. This agency operated up to 1960 under a ceiling of 4½ per cent for the interest payable on bonds issued by it, but a statute of that year removed this limitation. It also removed the dollar limitation ($40 million) on the amount of the bonds to be outstanding at any one time, substituting for it a limitation of the percentages of the total annual income of the Board of Regents of the University System which could be spent on debt service—8 per cent each year for debt service on bonds for "general purpose" buildings, and 7 per cent each year for debt service on bonds for self-liquidating projects.

Still another 1960 statute required the investment in time bank deposits of all state funds not currently needed for operations by state agencies. This was expected to earn $2 million a year for the state. The Regents of the University System had already followed the practice of investing "idle" funds, and in 1958-59 the sum of $520,000 had been earned in that manner.

The constitutional autonomy of the Board of Regents of the State University System is quite clearly spelled out in an amendment to the Constitution of Georgia proposed and adopted in 1943, and saved in the comprehensive constitutional revision of 1945, now standing as Article VIII, Section 4: "The said Board of Regents of the University System of Georgia shall have the powers and duties as provided by law existing at the time of the adoption of this Constitution, together with such further powers and duties as may be hereafter provided by law."

It has been demonstrated that constitutional independence can sometimes be lost merely for want of aggressive defense, as in the case of a decision of the Utah supreme court in 1956 (ambivalent and questionable, and arrived at only after multiple divisions within the court) which interpreted very narrowly the constitutional autonomy of the University of Utah, partly because of long acquiescence in adverse legislative acts and state administrative practices; though two of the judges declared: "The importance and desirability of a high degree of independence of internal function, and of academic freedom, was unquestionably recognized by the founders." [3]

There is also cause for further consideration of the thought that constitutional autonomy need not be bartered away for the favor of legislative appropriations committees, as cogently declared by Justice Horace Badt of the Nevada supreme court in a famous 1948 decision, quoted herein *supra* in the section on California. [4]

From some standpoints it seems that the Georgia Board of Regents may have been subject to less controversial attack, and may have created fewer discords among its constituency, than any consolidated state-wide governing board in any other state. Nevertheless the 1963 Governor's Committee to Improve Education took care to admonish the Regents as follows: (1) The Board of Regents should take steps to de-emphasize its detailed administrative functions, and to emphasize cooperative study, long-range planning, coordination, and public advocacy of the needs of higher education. (2) "The expanded staff (of the Board of Regents) must encourage and protect institutional initiative, authority, and autonomy within the scope of the authorized roles and functions of each institution."

The Commission added pointedly: "There is a strong tendency for central staffs as they are expanded to invade the rightful prerogatives of the institutions. This can lead only to destruction of their effectiveness." [5]

In his message to the legislature January 15, 1964, Governor Carl E. Sanders proposed tax changes which made possible the supplemental appropriations mentioned earlier herein. Taxes on cigarettes and cigars, alcoholic beverages, and malt drinks, as well as on general sales and corporation incomes, were adjusted upward to produce about $9 million of additional revenue for fiscal year 1963-64 and $32 million for 1964-65. These gains were not enormous; but this coup, together with subsequent accomplishments in the support of higher education, has given the governor a place among "education governors" in the South, and has placed Georgia among five southern states (along with Kentucky, Tennessee, Virginia, and North Carolina) which have more than quadrupled their appropriations for annual operating expenses of higher education during the nine years between

---

[3] *University of Utah* v. *State Board of Examiners*, 4 Utah 2d 408, 295 P. 2d 348 (1956).

[4] *King* v. *Board of Regents of University of Nevada*, 65 Nev. 533, 200 P. 2d 221 (1948).

[5] Page 49 of *Educating Georgia's People...*, *supra*, Footnote 2.

1960-61 and 1968-69. The Georgia legislature of 1969 raised the corporate income tax rate to 6 per cent, from the former 5 per cent.

These five states form a contiguous bloc extending from the Virginia shore westward to the Mississippi River above and below Memphis, and from the Ohio, Kanawha, and Potomac rivers southward to Georgia's southern boundary. Their 9-year percentages of gain range from 303 per cent to 450 per cent,—each far above the comparable nation-wide average of 261 per cent for the same period. To embellish the picture, it may be said that the two most populous southern states—Texas and Florida, also show 9-year gains above the national average, but only moderately so—Texas, 265 per cent; Florida, 288 per cent. Tiny Delaware, northernmost of the southern states, made gains of 227 per cent.

Georgia's 9-year gain, 367 per cent, ranks second among the southern states, and tenth among all the 50 states. Georgia has made spectacular gains since 1965. The 2-year gain from 1966 to 1968 was 72 per cent—equaled for that period only by Connecticut with 72 per cent, and surpassed only by Ohio with 77 per cent, Massachusetts with 80 per cent, and Virginia with 83 per cent. Georgia is becoming a leader in development of public higher education in the South. Half a dozen southern states and about the same number of northeastern states have led the nation in percentages of gains over nine years; and in general for the same reasons, both of these regions had public higher education relatively little developed in 1959, and both are now on the way to coming up fast.

HAWAII

Affected by the exhilaration of recent admission to statehood, and fortified by a 23 per cent increase in population between 1960 and 1968, Hawaii made dramatic progress in the support of higher education. From approximately $5 million in fiscal year 1959-60 to nearly $31 million in 1968-69, the percentage of gain over the 9-year period (in appropriations of state tax funds for annual operating expenses) was 525—a multiplication of more than sixfold.

The state government is highly centralized. One feature is that the receipts from student fees and other institutionally-collected income of the University of Hawaii must be deposited in the state treasury and held there until appropriated by the legislature. This gives rise to the custom of making annual appropriations which include estimated institutional receipts, and are thus not *net* appropriations of state tax funds, hence not comparable with appropriations of state tax funds in other states. This confusing practice is also found in some other states in one form or another, among which Massachusetts and South Dakota come immediately to mind as perhaps the most flagrant examples.

Apparently a majority of the states allow their state universities to function as custodians and accountants of their own institutionally-collected receipts, and to apply them to their annual expenses in such manner as the university governing boards direct. But not Hawaii. Thus for fiscal year 1968-69, the total legislative appropriation for operating expenses of the University of Hawaii (a little less than $36½ million) becomes roughly comparable to that of most other states only after the deduction of a little less than $5½ million representing student fees and other non-state-tax receipts.

The theory of the practices just indicated as prevailing in some form in Hawaii, Massachusetts, South Dakota, and some other states apparently is that university governing boards are not to be trusted with the custody and disbursement of their own funds without the intervention of the state treasurer. It is all of a piece with other practices of fiscal overcentralization which usually accompany it—such as the requirement that all university expenditures be pre-audited in the statehouse, and no disbursements made except upon the signature of a state functionary at the capital. These and other related practices go far indeed toward covertly transferring the management of the universities to fiscal clerks in the statehouse. They often cause damaging delays and annoying petty disputes which should not occur.

HAWAII

Appropriations for Annual Operating Expenses of Higher Education in Hawaii, Alternate Fiscal Years, 1959-60 through 1969-70 (in thousands of dollars)

Institutions	Year 1959-60	Year 1961-62	Year 1963-64	Year 1965-66	Year 1967-68	Year 1969-70
U of Hawaii Research Studies	4,958	7,254	10,867	16,928[1]	31,984[2]	43,799
WICHE[3]					25	114
Less estimated student fees and other nonstate tax receipts					-5,772	-5,333
Community College System				78[4]	83	
Total	4,958	7,254	10,867	17,006	26,320	41,782[5]

[1] Does not include the East-West Center, which is supported wholly from federal funds, currently of the order of $5½ million annually.

[2] Includes community colleges and the educational TV network, but excludes the East-West Center, which is wholly supported from federal funds, estimated at $5,800,000 for current year.

[3] Western Interstate Commission for Higher Education.

[4] Operated by the University of Hawaii. Now largely in the planning phase.

[5] Includes $2,702,000 for faculty pay increases, and $500,000 for student loan assistance program.

In some of the states where student fees are kept in special funds in the state treasury for reappropriation intact to the institutions from which they came, the connection between the fees and the purposes for which they were paid is properly maintained; but if and when such fee receipts in whole or in part are commingled with the general fund of the state, then the connection is largely lost and student fees are being treated as taxes for the general support of state government, which is indefensible.

The state of Hawaii supports and controls directly all public schools of elementary and secondary level in the islands; and the University of Hawaii embraces all public higher education, which by 1968 included four two-year "community college" branches of the University, located respectively in Honolulu (2), Maui, and Kauai. The University also operates a branch campus (not a community college) at Hilo, a considerable city on the large island of Hawaii. There are also two small denominational colleges (Roman Catholic and Latter-day Saints) and one private junior college in the islands.

The East-West Center, a university-level public institution in association with the University of Hawaii, is not state-supported, but is wholly financed by federal funds, approximating some $6 million a year in 1969. It is a place where the United States can be host to scholars and teachers from both hemispheres, and promote intercultural studies at the "crossroads of the Pacific."

With a population of 778,000 as of July 1, 1968, Hawaii had nearly three times as many people as Alaska, and was also larger than four of the mountain states, two Great Plains states, two New England states, and Delaware. Population growth in Hawaii may be volatile for several reasons, such as the role of the islands as a strategic outpost of the United States, the probably rapid expansion of their tourism and resort industry, speedier transport and communication with the mainland, and others.

A committee of faculty members and administrators at the University prepared an academic development plan in 1963-64 in which they projected total operating costs as $24 million for fiscal year 1965-66; $42 million for 1970-71; and more than $62 million for 1975-76.[1] Although the definition of "total operating costs" as used by that committee may not be precisely identical with that used in our reports, the differences cannot be great; and our evidence that the University had at least $36 million of state tax funds for annual operating expenses in fiscal year 1968-69 indicates that the committee's projections for future years probably undershoot the mark.

---

[1]Page 89 of *An Academic Development Plan for the University of Hawaii* (January 1964). 132 pp. large format.

IDAHO

During the decade just past, state university fees for out-of-state students have been repeatedly raised by large increments, and there has been some talk in a few state legislatures about charging the nonresidents the *full cost* of the educational activities to which they are admitted. (This would involve very detailed unit-cost accounting by the institution.) The state and federal courts have as yet tended, with some important exceptions, to cling to an old and somewhat outmoded concept of determining the residence of a student for this purpose when it becomes a subject of dispute: namely, that when a minor leaves his parental household to attend college in another state, he is presumed to intend to leave the latter state when he terminates his college attendance there; and hence, even though he may attend the college continuously for several years, he does not acquire a legal residence in that state at all.

The presumption under the old doctrine is susceptible of being overthrown by evidence of actual intent to remain in the state after leaving college; and it is also increasingly undermined by the fact that many university students admitted to the institution for the first time are not minors, but mature persons often having spouses and children of their own; are wholly self-supporting; and have no legal or physical residence elsewhere to which they might presumably intend to return.

Idaho provides two recent court decisions of much interest regarding the foregoing matters. (First notice that Idaho has an antique and unusual structure at the top of the state-wide educational system. A single group of appointed persons constitutes and functions as at least two entirely separate and distinct public corporations: (1) the State Board of Education, and (2) the Board of Regents of the University of Idaho (at Moscow) which also governs Idaho State University at Pocatello, as the Board of Trustees of Idaho State University. This single group of appointees, constituting two separate corporations and acting in two entirely distinct capacities, is officially styled Idaho State Board of Education and Board of Regents of the University of Idaho.)

A young man aged 25 and fully self-supporting, whose former home had been in Vermont prior to his spending four years in the armed services, registered at the Idaho State College (now Idaho State University) for the academic year 1957-58 and paid fees as a nonresident. He continued during succeeding academic years, but after his first year he vainly sought to be classified as a resident for fee-paying purposes, or at least to be heard on the matter. His case reached the Idaho supreme court in 1960, resulting in a decision declaring that the current rule of the Board was arbitrary, capricious, and invalid.[1] The regulation thus invalidated read: "Any person who is properly classified as a nonresident student retains that status throughout continuous term attendance at any institution of higher learning in Idaho." Excluding, as it did, any opportunity for any declaration and showing of intent on the part of the student, it was, indeed, arbitrary.

A very different type of suit came to decision in an Idaho county court in January 1967. A taxpayer sought to restrain and prohibit the Board from establishing any policy regarding the fees of out-of-state students other than one which would require them to pay fees substantially equal to the entire cost to the state of Idaho of providing their education.

The opinion of District Judge Merlin S. Young concluded that: "The nonresident tuition policy (of the Board) is within its discretion and cannot be said to be a spending of public money for the private benefit of nonresidents of Idaho, as a matter of law." Judgment was against the plaintiff.[2] Although perhaps of somewhat less persuasive weight than if coming from a higher court, the opinion is full of pertinent facts and cogent reasoning.

The judge noted that about 20 per cent of the students at the University of Idaho were nonresidents, mostly from 10 western states, and somewhat more than half from the adjacent state of Washington. In the graduate programs the percentages were higher—as high as 50 per cent in some instances; and instructional costs per student per year were markedly higher in the graduate programs than in the undergraduate schools. The minimum average cost per student at the whole University was $1,200 to $1,400. On January 1, 1966, the nonresident tuition fee had been raised to $500, from which it could be said in a very general way that the average subsidy to an out-of-state student was at least $700.

"No state university sets its nonresident tuition fees upon the basis of the actual cost of the education of the student in that university,"[3] the court observed, and continued: "The Board of Regents does not

[1]Newman v. Graham et al., State Board of Education, 82 Ida. 90, 349 P. 2d 716, 83 A.L.R. 2d 492 (1960).
[2]Cobbs v. State Board of Education (acting as Regents of the University of Idaho), (Dist. Ct. of Third Judicial Dist., in and for the County of Ada), Civil No. 36600 (January 16, 1967).
[3]New Hampshire enacted a statute to this effect in 1969, two years after this opinion was written.

IDAHO

Appropriations for Annual Operating Expenses of Higher Education in Idaho, Alternate Fiscal Years, 1959-60 through 1969-70 (in thousands of dollars)

Institutions	Year 1959-60	Year 1961-62	Year 1963-64	Year 1965-66	Year 1967-68	Year 1969-70
U of Idaho						
Agricultural research		4,890	5,617	7,362	9,165	10,700
Agriculture Extension		943	1,050	1,275	1,478	1,576
Applied research		702	775	891	980	1,030
Pure seed		25	52	27	67	100
Bureau of Mines			77	141	68	36
Special research		62	67	67		180
Supplemental		10				
Subtotal, U of Idaho		6,632	7,638	9,763	11,759	13,623
Idaho State University		2,814	3,471	4,567	5,851	8,475
From voca'l ed approp		412	257	520	349	
Supplemental		43				
Subtotal, Idaho St U		3,269	3,728	5,087	6,200	8,475
Lewis-Clark Normal Sch		240	251	437	605	1,056
From voca'l ed approp					124	
Subtotal, L-C Normal Sch		240	251	437	729	1,056
Boise State College[1]					250[1]	4,905
Area Voc-Tech Schs operated by public Junior Colls					290	487

Exec Dir of Higher Educ					
St aid to Jr Colls				37	50
Contin'g Educ Program				750	700
Medical Edn Study Comm				61	68
				25	
WICHE[2]					
Edn Comm of the States	154	175	200	275	275
				14	8
Total	8,799[3]	11,768	15,490	20,351	29,862[5]
Less cutback of 4.8%[6]	11,203				

[1] Boise College, hitherto a local public junior college, became Boise State College January 1, 1969. The appropriation is for the period from *January 1, 1969 to June 30, 1969* (hence not to be included in total for first year of the biennium).

[2] Western Interstate Commission for Higher Education.

[3] This sum covers *state-wide* appropriations.

[4] Appropriation of $138,025 for the Bureau of Mines, treated as an enterprise of the University of Idaho, brings the total to $20,275,000 approximately (for the biennium).

[5] Includes $113,000 for educational television and $100,000 for nuclear-oriented research.

[6] Governor's executive order, approved by the state board of examiners, a state accounting and fiscal agency.

attempt to set nonresident tuition fees upon a basis of costs per student
or any other cost basis. It does use its best collective judgment to
arrive at a figure which it believes will attract high-quality
nonresident students to the University of Idaho. . . , (It) believes that a
substantial percentage of a college student body should come from
outside of the state and that this is essential to prevent a university
from becoming provincial in outlook, and that nonresident students
are necessary to attract a good faculty."

The benefits derived from the admission of Idaho students to other
state universities on a somewhat informal reciprocal basis, and the
benefits to Idaho universities received from the attendance of
nonresident students, thought the court, were indubitably public
benefits, and "the public benefit derived from paying a substantial
part of the cost of educating nonresident students is an intangible thing
which cannot be established in dollars and cents." Such a problem of
educational policy was within the discretion of the Board of Regents,
and the court would not undertake to interpose its own judgment in
such a matter.

For the foregoing cool breezes of sensible doctrine we are indebted
to Idaho courts. There is further discussion of the classification of
resident and nonresident students in the sketch of Iowa, *infra*. Changes
in the treatment of this and related problems are evidently in the
offing.

By mid-1967 Idaho's population only slightly exceeded 700,000,
having gained less than 6 per cent since 1960. Over the period 1960-1969,
total appropriations of state tax funds for annual operating expenses of
higher education increased only slightly more than 134 per cent—a
rate of gain far less than the nation-wide weighted average of 261 per
cent for the same period.

During most of the decade Idaho had two public junior colleges, at
Boise and Cour d'Alene; but in 1967 Boise College was authorized to
become a four-year institution, and the process was begun. What
practically amounts to a "token" scheme of state aid to local public
junior colleges is embodied in statutes providing that 50 per cent of the
net collections of state liquor taxes shall be allocated to the counties;
and that 50 per cent of this money apportioned to any county embracing all or any part of a junior college district shall be distributed to
the junior college district.

The Board of Regents of the University of Idaho (except in its
legislatively created role as Trustees of Idaho State University) has a
high degree of constitutional autonomy, like that of Michigan, Minnesota, and California, as expounded at least twice in decisions of the
supreme court of Idaho.[4] As elsewhere, various state fiscal officers,

---

[4] *State ex rel. Black* v. *State Board of Education*, 33 Idaho 415, 196 P. 201
(1921); and *Dreps* v. *Board of Regents of University of Idaho*, (Ida.), 139 P. 2d
467 (1943).

ignorant of the law or contemptuous of it, have tried from time to time to overstep the bounds established by the constitution and the courts; and occasionally there may have been actual practice of unconstitutional administrative procedures. Even the attorney general has at times seemed a little confused about the matter; but the constitutional independence of the Board of Regents is there for all to see, in the constitution itself and in the supreme court decisions.

ILLINOIS

Public higher education was tardy in its beginning in this state which stretches from the latitude of Buffalo and Boston to that of southern Kentucky and Virginia. The oldest institution dates from 1857—Illinois State University (formerly for many years styled Illinois State Normal University) at the centrally located town of Normal, adjacent to the city of Bloomington.

A dozen years later the University of Illinois had its beginnings at Champaign-Urbana as the Illinois Agricultural and Industrial College. In time a group of four regionally located institutions for the education of teachers emerged: Southern, at Carbondale; Eastern, at Charleston; Western, at Macomb; and Northern, at De Kalb, in addition to the original one at Normal. These were known as normal schools, later as teachers colleges, then as state colleges, and finally as universities.

An eloquent and persuasive Illinois advocate of the land-grant college idea, Jonathan Baldwin Turner, had much to do with the inception of the University of Illinois; and some historians seem inclined to credit him with nation-wide influence in the early development of the Morrill Land-Grant Act of 1862, perhaps equal to that of the renowned Senator Justin S. Morrill of Vermont himself. The land-grant institutions had many difficulties in their early years, and the University of Illinois was no exception; but it has long since become one of the galaxy of great state universities in the Middle West.

Up to 1917 each of the Illinois state institutions had its own board of trustees. (The Illinois State Normal University was governed by a body called the State Board of Education, though this body apparently had no other duties to justify its name, and in fact had been created in 1857 for the sole purpose of governing the normal university.) The legislature of 1913 set up a "Committee on Efficiency and Economy," of four Senate and four House members, which employed as its staff director John A. Fairlie, a professor of political science at the University of Illinois. His report, released in 1915, recommended a drastic reorganization and consolidation of state agencies into 10 major departments. No legislative action was taken until the incoming of Governor Frank O. Lowden's administration in 1917. Probably not at all unaware of the patronage advantages of a sweeping reshuffling of state agencies, the new governor and legislature proceeded promptly to implement the Fairlie report in large part.

One of the new major departments was a peculiar structure designated the Department of Registration and Education, headed by an appointed director who would be nominally superior to the constitutionally elective state superintendent of public instruction. The governing body of the State Normal University was abolished, and since that time Illinois has had no State Board of Education.[1] All institutional boards of trustees except that of the University of Illinois were abolished, and the governance of the four regional institutions, as well as that of the Normal University, was vested in a newly-created board styled at first the normal school board (later to become state college board, and eventually, in 1965, Board of Governors of State Colleges and Universities). The normal school board was within the Department of Registration and Education; the board of trustees of the University of Illinois was independent of any department, as it had always been.

For 32 years this structure remained essentially unchanged. In 1949 the legislature removed Southern Illinois State Teachers College from the jurisdiction of the State Teachers College Board and gave it its own institutional board of trustees. A study recommending this had been made by a survey team. Immediately thereafter the author had the benefit of first-hand acquaintance with the institution, while serving with Arthur J. Klein, then dean of the college of education at the Ohio State University and Harvey H. Davis, provost of the University of Iowa, as consultants in the drafting of by-laws for the new independent board of trustees.

This change was followed by the almost miraculous development of the Carbondale institution (now Southern Illinois University), to become one of the top 20 major state universities in the nation within the ensuing 20 years, measured by enrollment, volume of financial support, eminence of faculty leaders, diversity of programs, and expansion of physical facilities. During the 'Sixties it became an "integrated dual university" by developing a new large campus at Edwardsville to serve the long educationally-deprived people of East St. Louis and other populous "spill-over" satellites of St. Louis located on the Illinois side of the Mississippi River, as well as others in southwestern Illinois.

The Carbondale campus is located centrally among the 40

---

[1] Since 1949, however, Illinois has had a statutory Advisory Commission on School Problems, composed of some members of each house of the legislature and some other leading citizens. With the aid of a part-time study director, this Commission has made a good record of deliberating upon the most pressing issues and for each biennium has presented a report with recommendations, of which a considerable number have been enacted by the legislature. Thus the Commission performs at least one of the most important functions of a State Board of Education.

southernmost counties of the state—a large area which had almost no other facilities for higher education during the period of the startling growth and improvement of Southern Illinois University. It probably affords the nation's most outstanding example of a large cosmopolitan public university developing swiftly to fill the vacuum of university services and higher educational leadership in a large region (the southern one-third of the state). (There are also adjacent parts of western Kentucky and southeastern Missouri that are far from any great university center. Like any large university, Southern Illinois now receives many students from Chicago and other metropolitan centers, and from many other states and foreign countries.) The local flavor is that of the handful of more or less depressed rural counties near the confluence of the Ohio and Mississippi rivers, having no urban concentrations of much size, and bearing for a century or more the ribald nickname of "Egypt."

Another reform advocated by the presidents of the five institutions for the education of teachers, and often by superintendents of public instruction, more or less continuously from 1917 through the 1940's, was removal of the teachers college board from the tight fiscal control of the Department of Registration and Education, and a loosening of the restraints placed on it by the Department of Finance and the Department of Public Works, under the highly centralized "Administrative Code" of 1917. At last the legislature of 1951, acting in part upon the suggestions of John Dale Russell in a state-wide survey of 1945, and in part in response to the urgings of the Joint Alumni Council of the five institutions, removed the board from many of the restrictions complained of. A documented and somewhat detailed story of this bit of evolution was written by Joseph T. Marsh, of the department of journalism at Northern Illinois University. [2]

Since 1950 the state-wide system of public higher education in Illinois has been under frequent if not continuous study. [3] Among the results was the creation of a statutory Commission of Higher Education in 1957, invested with mild coordinative duties. There was recurrent pressure in each succeeding legislature for a "unified" state-wide control, and this led to a situation in the 1959 session in which the Commission was directed by the legislature to produce a plan for a "unified administration" to be presented to the next regular session.

---

[2] Joseph T. Marsh, *A History of Teacher Education at Northern Illinois University.* Doctoral dissertation completed at Indiana University, 1969. 252 pp. typed. See especially pp. 156-166.

[3] The history since 1913 is recounted in some detail in a doctoral dissertation by Robert Marsh, "Coordination of State Higher Education in Illinois," completed at Illinois State University at Normal in 1967.

The Commission rejected the idea of abolishing the existing governing boards and creating one state-wide governing board. Instead it recommended a state board of higher education which would govern no institution or group of institutions, but would have "coordinating" functions, mainly advisory, but with authority to approve or disapprove each proposed addition of a new institution, department, or major program of instruction. The statute enacted by the 1961 legislature was of that general tenor, and, much influenced by the widely publicized "California master plan" which had been partly enacted in California's Donahoe Act of 1960, also charged the new board with the duty of developing a "master plan" for Illinois.

The Illinois State Chamber of Commerce had brought to its annual meeting in Chicago, October 21, 1960, as a guest speaker, John R. Richards, who was then serving as Chancellor of the Oregon system of higher education, under the State Board of Higher Education. This is a single overall *governing board* which had been in existence for three decades. Richards, speaking on "The Unified Board of Higher Education—What It Is, How It Works," candidly recommended a "permissive form of coordination":

"Your institutions (in Illinois) have grown to great size and prestige. Coordination among them is developing and must develop further. But severe coordination, shifting existing bases for authority, can jeopardize the future of these universities, perhaps shaking them to their very foundations. Illinois cannot afford to gamble in this matter. It cannot afford dispirited institutions not having sufficient authority over their own programs to move forward constructively. Immersion of great universities in a welter of bureaucratic controls, particularly if administered out of the state capital, could very well drown aspirations long held and until now properly effectuated. . . . In summary then I would say that a permissive form of coordination is indicated for Illinois rather than a severely authoritarian system centralized in any one man or in any one board."[4]

Richards' wise and moderate words were probably influential in helping to save Illinois from a drastic measure which might have abolished the governing boards and created an upheaval which could have depressed the morale of the universities for a generation.

The act of 1961 provided that the board of higher education should be composed of the chairman and one additional member of each of the three governing boards then existing, plus the state superintendent of public instruction, plus eight citizens appointed by the governor and senate, of whom not more than one should have had any connection as board member, employee, alumnus, or other representative of any one

---

[4]Quoted from press release of Oregon State System of Higher Education, Box 5175, Eugene, Oregon.

university or college in the state. This last provision, perhaps in-nocently intended to prevent any one institution from dominating the proceedings, has some toxic side-effects. It automatically tends to maximize the probability of *private college* overrepresentation, because the private institutions are so much more numerous than the public ones, although by 1968 they had little more than one-third of the total of students in the state.

In this matter of private college representation, the time-lag of one or two generations between college graduation and the period of service on the board later in life also has a powerful tendency to overweight the private college influence on the board, not only in Illinois but in practically every state having such a board, because in most states from one to two generations ago the balance was the reverse of what it is now, and *two*-thirds of college students were in the private sector. Thus in many states, if not in all, a majority of the leading citizens today are alumni of private colleges, tied to *alma mater* by gossamer threads of affection stemming from family tradition, religious faith, enthusiasm for athletics, the bonds of marriage or those of intimate friendships, and many others. Thus the appointing authority, whether unwittingly or not, is very likely to load the board with members having private college backgrounds.

To say that the private sector should be included in state-wide planning, and that it should be explicitly represented on the board, is all very well; but it is naïve to overlook the fact that such authority as the board possesses—permissive, persuasive, or coercive—is intended to be directed mainly toward the *public* universities and colleges. In fact, any thought of state coercion regarding the instructional programs of reputable *private* institutions is totally repugnant, con-trary to legal tradition, and not to be countenanced except when used negatively as an exercise of police power to extirpate fraudulent "diploma mills."

It would also be unrealistic to deny that, much as we may regret and deplore it, there are indeed real or imagined conflicts of interest between the private and public sectors in higher education. The denominational colleges no longer thunder against the "Godless state universities" as they once did, but many private college partisans bitterly resent the fact that state universities and colleges charge only low tuition fees or none at all, and would do anything in their power to force fees upward, as well as to induce the state to appropriate tax money to hire students to attend private colleges by means of "tuition scholarships."

The astounding spectacle of representatives (overt or covert) of *private* colleges of a generation ago dominating the deliberations of a state board charged with planning a state-wide system of *public* higher education for the final quarter of the twentieth century can be seen in more than a few states; and the same tends to be true of some legislatures and legislative committees engaged in policy-making for public higher education.

This factor has had a good deal to do with the restrictive measures directed at the state universities by the Illinois Board of Higher Education in the form of "master plan" recommendations, such as the recommendation that freshman and sophomore enrollments at all the state universities be "frozen" as of 1970, and that uniform minimum standards of admission be imposed upon all the eight campuses. These types of coercion would severely limit the freedom of choice of many able Illinois prospective students, and their application would effect a narrowing of educational opportunity by closing some of the options previously available.

This factor is also behind the mushrooming of the state scholarship system, which had reached an appropriation of a little over $10 million for the biennium 1965-67—a reasonable level of about $5 million a year for a state as populous as Illinois—, but was jumped to approximately $31 million for biennium 1967-69. At least 65 per cent of the awards go to students in private colleges, and the scheme is primarily for the purpose of indirectly funneling tax funds into their coffers. One of its principal effects is to enable high-fee private colleges to escalate their fees still further without losing students.

Within reasonable quantitative limits, such a scholarship system may be looked on with favor, for it enlarges the freedom of choice of some impecunious but capable students who greatly prefer a private college for reasons of their own, such as religious atmosphere, family sentiment, or social prestige. But this is a special program not in the main stream of state support of higher education, and should not expand erratically or endlessly. In 1967-69 no state except New York and Pennsylvania (in the northeastern private college stronghold) had a scholarship system on a scale anything like that of Illinois.

Parenthetically (and relevantly) it should be noted that by 1968 a consensus had developed among all the principal nation-wide associations of leaders in higher education, favoring the beginning of a program of *direct appropriations* of *federal funds*, to be distributed to *all reputable institutions* of higher education, public and private, annually to support a portion of their regular operating expenses. *Direct* support of institutions is sharply distinguishable from side-door support through scholarships. It would come most appropriately from the federal government, not only because of the huge federal tax resources, but also because at the federal level there is only the comparatively mild inhibition of tax support of private institutions provided by the "establishment of religion" clause of the First Amendment; whereas more than 40 states have in their constitutions outright prohibitions of state tax appropriations to private or sectarian

ILLINOIS

Appropriations for Annual Operating Expenses of Higher Education in Illinois, Alternate Fiscal Years, 1959-60 through 1969-70 (in thousands of dollars)

Institutions	Year 1959-60	Year 1961-62	Year 1963-64	Year 1965-66	Year 1967-68	Year 1969-70
U of Illinois[1]						
Urbana-Champaign	55,905	64,936	76,791	98,080	125,719	152,144
Medical Ctr (Chicago)					77,374	83,130
Chicago Circle					27,106	34,296
Tuberculosis Inst					21,040	30,122
Unassigned				101	198	
Gen University, incl. Exten. Div.						4,597
Subtotal, U of Illinois	55,905	64,936	76,791	98,181	125,719	152,144
Southern Ill University[2]	15,183	20,228	27,097	37,878	51,153	75,477
Educational Television				200		
Subtotal, Southern Ill U	15,183	20,228	27,097	38,078	51,153	75,477
Bd of Regents and Insts						
Northern Illinois U					25,027	31,910
Illinois State U					18,185	25,093
Sangamon State U						1,528
T C Bd and Insts	17,051	105[3]	120[3]			
Northern Illinois U		7,315	10,505	16,249		
Illinois State U		7,113	9,791	13,161		
Western Illinois U		3,945	5,647	8,097	13,279	16,453
Eastern Illinois U		4,148	5,331	7,997	11,219	14,444
Northeastern Ill Coll[4]					6,335	8,544
Chicago State College[5]		2,593	3,350	5,000	6,958	7,586
Governors State U						266
Subtotal, State U's & Colls[6]	17,051	25,219	34,744	50,504	81,003	105,824

State Scholarships	2,485	2,588	5,175		15,472	27,905
Guaranteed student loans			257		4,500	2,400
Board of Higher Education	75	75	150		323	1,718
Board of Regents[7]					150	263
Board of Governors (TC Bd)[8]					264	334
U Civil Service	90	90	145			
U Retirement System	7	24	134			
State aid to Jr Colls		6,759	11,450		22,536	37,982
State Jr Coll Board[9]			150		150	281
Total	88,139	113,043	148,170	204,403	301,136	405,077[10]

[1] All campuses, chiefly Urbana and Chicago.
[2] All campuses, chiefly Carbondale and Edwardsville.
[3] This sum is for the Teachers College Board.
[4] Formerly Chicago Teachers College North.
[5] Formerly Chicago Teachers College South.
[6] This sum is exclusive of appropriations for Southern Illinois University, and for the University of Illinois.

[7] New board (July 1, 1967) to govern Northern Illinois University and Illinois State University; later Sangamon State University also
[8] Former Teachers College Board, renamed in 1965, now governing the five institutions last-named in the tabulation of seven under "TC Bd and Insts," above.
[9] Board of eight members appointed by the governor, plus the Superintendent of Public Instruction as chairman, created by act of 1965.
[10] Includes $750,000 for East St. Louis State Junior College.

institutions. [5]

Nevertheless, in the late 'Sixties there were efforts by private college interests in Illinois to obtain direct appropriations of state tax funds to private institutions; but they did not seem to import much promise of success.

In state tax appropriations for annual operating expenses of higher education in 1968, the position of Illinois among the states can be glimpsed from three simple measures: (1) by magnitude of the total appropriations, Illinois ranked third (after California and New York); (2) by average state tax cost *per citizen*, it ranked twenty-first, with $27.58; and (3) by ratio of state tax cost to total personal income, it ranked thirty-eighth (with state tax cost only 0.69 per cent of total personal income). Thus while Illinois is investing as much or more *per citizen* in annual operating expenses of higher education than three-fifths of the other states, the bite into total personal income is less than it is in three-fourths of the other states. These relationships are more or less replicated in a few other of the most populous, prosperous, and heavily industrialized states, such as California, Michigan, and New York. Translated into the vernacular, this seems to mean that they are doing moderately well in tax support of higher education, but that they have ample resources with which to do much better.

A landmark in the financing of university physical plants was the proposal by the 1959 legislature and approval by the electors in 1960 of a bond issue of $195 million for capital improvements at the six state universities. This provided $95½ million for the University of Illinois, about equally divided between the projected new institution at Chicago Circle on the one hand and the Urbana main campus and Chicago professional school campuses on the other; $53¼ million for Southern Illinois University, split about equally between the new Edwardsville campus and the older campus at Carbondale; $15½ million for Northern Illinois University; $12 million for Illinois State University; $8 million for Western Illinois University; and $7½ million for Eastern Illinois University.

In 1961 the legislature created the Illinois Building Authority, [6] a distinctive type of public corporation empowered to borrow without creating debts against the state and free from the requirements of the debt referendum section of the state constitution. This Authority is empowered to finance any and all state buildings, including buildings on the state university campuses; and the constitutionality of its

---

[5] The wording and scope of these prohibitory clauses varies among the different states. In some instances it applies to all nonpublic universities and colleges, in others only to church-connected institutions.

[6] *Illinois Revised Statutes*, Chapter 127, Paragraph 213.1.

creation and operation has been upheld by the state supreme court.[7] The Authority is empowered not only to finance state buildings, but also to plan and erect them. This latter power has apparently not been exercised on university campuses. Planning and contract-letting and supervising of architectural work and construction of university buildings should be a function of the university governing board, not that of some other agency.

The universities repay the Authority a sum each year sufficient to amortize the indebtedness. In the case of non-income-producing buildings this money is derived from legislative appropriations, but nevertheless the whole transaction is consistently held to create no debt against the state and not to conflict with any provision of the constitution.

Unique features of the Illinois state system of public higher education are the University Retirement System and the University Civil Service System, both of which are personnel agencies whose purview embraces all the state universities and colleges, but no other state institutions or departments. They are distinct and separate from the State Employees' Retirement System and the State Civil Service. The University Civil Service relates only to nonacademic employees.

There have been times when both the legislature and the courts took petty views of the proper responsibilities of the university boards of trustees; but the differences in the tenor of two Illinois supreme court decisions of 1943 and 1957 respectively indicate a good deal of improvement in that respect during the intervening period of about a decade and a half in the mid-twentieth century.

In 1942 the distinguished jurist, Sveinbjorn Johnson, had been serving for several years at the University of Illinois as professor of law and university counsel. Early in that year the state attorney general asserted to the board of trustees that he had the legal right to appoint the university counsel. The trustees rebuffed him, whereupon he wrote to Johnson, purporting to "accept his resignation" which had not been tendered, and at the same time instructed the Auditor of Public Accounts not to issue salary warrants to Johnson. The trustees sued for a writ of *mandamus* to compel the Auditor to issue the warrants. The writ was denied on the narrowly technical ground that no specific authority for payment of "counsel" appeared in the itemized state appropriation act for the biennium; and the board of trustees could make no expenditure except out of a fund duly appropriated for that purpose.[8]

---

[7] *Electrical Contractors' Association of City of Chicago* v. *Illinois Building Authority*, 33 Ill. 2d 587, 213 N.E. 2d 761 (1966).

[8] *People ex rel. Board of Trustees of University of Illinois* v. *Barrett*, 382 Ill. 321, 46 N.E. 2d 951 (1943).

After this black-letter disposition of the fiscal aspect, the court dealt with the broader issue, however, and held that the University of Illinois is a public corporation having a legal identity of its own, and is not required to use the attorney general as its sole legal representative; and issued a writ to compel the attorney general to withdraw from a current Cook County case in which he had attempted to substitute himself for Judge Johnson as university counsel.

Fourteen years later the same court took a much more enlightened view of the fiscal relations between the legislature and the university trustees. The University of Illinois had obtained in 1953 a license to operate a television broadcasting station. Some of the necessary equipment was received as a gift, which was supplemented by an expenditure of $24,000 authorized by the trustees, and the station went on the air in 1955. Commercial television interests, which had opposed university television in arguments before the legislature and the board of trustees, brought a taxpayers' suit to enjoin the board from constructing and operating a broadcasting station, chiefly on the ground that it was not specifically authorized by statute and not expressly provided for in a line-item appropriation.

This evoked from Justice House, who wrote the opinion of the court, some cogent expressions:

"The General Assembly cannot be expected to allocate funds to each of the myriad activities of the University and thereby practically substitute itself for the Board of Trustees in the management thereof. . . ."

"The Board of Trustees has, by the statute creating the University, the power and authority to do everything necessary in the management, operating, and administration of the University, including any necessary or incidental powers in the furtherance of the corporate purposes. . . .

"The impracticality of detailing funds for the many activities and functions of the University in the Appropriation Act is readily apparent. If, as plaintiff's counsel argues, a $24,000 annual expenditure out of a biennial appropriation in excess of $82 million is required, then practically every proposed expenditure would have to be itemized. Television cannot be singled out for special treatment merely because it is relatively new. It is one of the many activities incident to the management and operation of the University included in the single objective of maintaining higher learning." [9]

After elaborate exertions involving the appointment of numerous advisory committees and specialized study committees, the Board of Higher Education issued a *Provisional Master Plan* dated March 1964

---

[9] *Turkovich* v. *Board of Trustees of University of Illinois*, 11 Ill. 2d 460, 43 N.E. 2d 229 (1957).

and *A Master Plan* bearing date of July 1964.[10] This document, sometimes hastily assumed to be the law of the land by naïve educators and other citizens, is no more than a series of *recommendations* addressed chiefly to the legislature, and only such parts of it as are enacted by the legislature have the force of law. As in the earlier case of California, only scattered small parts of it have been so enacted; the remaining parts are continuing recommendations until modified or abandoned by the Board, and they may have some influence not only on the legislature, but on educators and citizens in general.

As a preamble, this document proposes that diversity among institutions ought to be preserved and enhanced, "thus providing a range of choice for the student and opportunity for experimentation by the institution"; and that flexibility and adaptability must be watchwords. Are these principles to be observed or platitudes to be ignored? It is very difficult in many instances to reach an appropriate point of compromise between these principles and the opposite forces mindlessly demanding uniformity. In this same document, although the Board is already authorized by law to make recommendations regarding admissions policies, it asks for coercive power to fix uniform admissions practices for all the universities. It also asks for a number of other accretions of power to itself, all tending to transfer important responsibilities of the institutional governing boards to the statehouse, and tending toward bureaucratization of the state-wide system. This is the tendency of state-wide statutory "coordinating boards" wherever they exist.

In its projections of future state tax support over the ensuing three bienniums, the Board accepted the estimates of the Illinois Revenue Commission—the "highs" being $370 million for 1965-67, $505 million for 1967-69, and $575 million for 1969-71. Actual appropriations of state tax funds for operating expenses of higher education for the first two of those bienniums were respectively $408,806,000 and $602,272,000. At this writing the appropriations for 1969-71 have not yet been made; but the estimate of $575 million seems likely to be far below the mark, in view of the fact that it was already exceeded by the actual appropriation for the *preceding* biennium.[11]

Another example of timid undershooting on the part of the Board and its staff was provided when a departing executive director delivered as his swan song an explosion of prophecy, speaking to the junior college conference at Rockford, October 24, 1968. He is reported

---

[10]*A Master Plan for Higher Education in Illinois.* Springfield: Illinois Board of Higher Education, 1964. 72 pp.

[11] The actual total appropriation of state tax funds for the *one fiscal year* 1969-70 was $405 million.

to have said, "It seems improbable that higher education can continue to get an increasing proportion of the country's total economic output." On the contrary it is highly likely that tax support of higher education will continue to increase faster than the rate of general economic growth for at least another decade, or until 1980. All indications point to another doubling of enrollments in public institutions within 10 to 12 years. Continued mild inflation and other factors will cause the required public investment per year to increase faster than enrollments. The investment per student per year will rise. This means that while enrollments are doubling, total financial support will be tripled or more. In 1969 we are approximately at the mid-point of a 20-year period of unprecedented expansion and improvement of higher education. This is no time to become faint and fearful. The economy will not be destroyed, nor the public frightened out of its senses, when the share of the gross national product allocated to annual operating expenses of higher education gradually goes up to 3 per cent. This will in fact be a spectacularly productive investment.

In the expansion of higher educational facilities the Illinois Board of Higher Education has a somewhat bolder record. Upon the recommendation of the Board, the 1967 legislature created a new Board of Regents to govern Northern Illinois University and Illinois State University, taking these two institutions out of the jurisdiction of the Board of Governors of State Colleges and Universities (former teachers college board). By 1967 these two had outstripped the other two (Western and Eastern) in size and apparent growth potential, in a manner faintly reminiscent of the earlier near-miraculous development of Southern Illinois University. Northern is in the hugely populous northeastern region of the state, only 70 miles from Chicago; and Illinois State is centrally located and has the further advantage of more than a century of history as the state's principal institution of this type.

These two state universities already have doctoral programs in some departments, and the policy is to encourage them to develop advanced graduate work in many of the arts and science departments, one of the aims being to produce a larger supply of prospective college teachers. In addition to their historic roles in the education of public school teachers and administrators, these two universities governed by the Board of Regents are to become full-fledged "liberal arts universities," including advanced graduate as well as undergraduate departments in the arts and sciences.

The Chicago Teachers College, a local institution which had been substantially subsidized by the state for some years, was fully taken over by the state, becoming Chicago State College. More recently one of its two campuses has been given the name and identity of Northeastern Illinois State College. Both the new state colleges are governed by the Board of Governors of State Colleges and Universities.

The 1967 legislature also provided for the establishment of two new *senior colleges* (three-year institutions open only to third-, fourth-, and fifth-year students), one to be located in the Chicago area and one at Springfield, the state capital; and authorized the Board of Higher Education to assign the governance of each of these two institutions to one of the four existing governing boards. The Board later announced that the new institution at the south periphery of Chicago would go to the Board of Governors of State Colleges and Universities, and the one at Springfield (now named Sangamon State University) would be governed by the Board of Regents.

The Trustees of the University of Illinois made a case for including the Springfield institution within their jurisdiction, because the Urbana campus of the University of Illinois, for nearly a century the principal university of the state, necessarily maintains many instructional, research, and service activities at the state capital. No refutation of this can be made. The real motive for assigning the Springfield institution to the new Board of Regents is said to have been an idea of creating a "balance of power" among the four governing boards—a species of "divide and conquer" tactic which would "prevent the University of Illinois from becoming too powerful." If this is the case, it is somewhat less than commendable.

A new junior college statute is also in effect, looking toward the development of a complete state-wide system of two-year community colleges, generously state-aided and under the general oversight of a recently-created state-wide Community College Board. (This, one will note, is the fifth major board now in the state-wide picture of higher education in Illinois, without counting the Board of Higher Education. A staff member has said the Illinois scene is now a "system of systems.")

The community college statute contemplates the eventual embracing of the thirty-odd existing two-year colleges, and of numerous others to be established in the future, within a system of "first class" junior colleges, for which one of the prerequisites will be the maintenance of a satisfactory technical wing in each such college. (The well-known tendency is for the liberal or general or "college parallel" wing to overshadow or practically blot out the technical and vocational wing.) Coercion is applied by making the state subsidy meager unless and until the college meets the requirements established by the state for "first class" status, and generous for those so qualifying.[12]

---

[12] The constitutionality of the new Junior College Act was contested in the courts, and sustained by the state supreme court in *People* v. *Francis*, (Ill.), 239 N.E. 2d 129 (1968).

If all Illinois' "system of systems" can avoid too large an element of rigidity and arbitrary coercion, maintain flexibility, increase the devolution of decision-making to each institution, and expand the freedom of choices open to individuals, it may have a fruitful future. This will involve the maintenance and constant improvement of a *modus vivendi* between the Board of Higher Education and the several institutional governing boards and presidents.

An event of historic importance was the enactment by the 1969 legislature of a 2½ per cent tax on personal incomes and a 4 per cent tax on the net incomes of corporations, effective August 1, 1969. The state supreme court promptly let it be known that this act would not be interpreted as in conflict with the state constitution. The added revenue estimated to accrue from this source was more than $800 million per year.

An Illinois Constitutional Convention whose members were elected in November 1969 was expected to place emphasis on the modernizing of the Revenue Article of the constitution, as well as other parts of that document.

INDIANA

During the first half century of its statehood, the Hoosier state had only one state institution of higher education—Indiana University at Bloomington—placed in that southerly region of the state in 1820 because in its northern half hostile Indians were feared and white settlements were few and small. The "younger sister" state university, Purdue, was begun in 1869 in a more northerly part of the state, at West Lafayette, as the state's land-grant college under the Morrill Act.

Thus Indiana is one of the 20 states having today two large state universities of long-standing, located at a distance from each other in different parts of the state, the older being a "separate" state university and the younger being the "separate" land-grant university. A similar situation exists in the adjoining state of Michigan, but not in the adjacent states of Illinois, Kentucky, and Ohio, where in each case the largest state university and the land-grant university are one and the same institution.

Indiana University has no schools or colleges of agriculture, veterinary medicine, or engineering, while Purdue has all these but has no school or college of law or of human medicine. Both universities have long since become large cosmopolitan institutions, but the contrast between their respective scope and flavor is rather more marked than is usual in such cases.

There are two other institutions having the teacher-education background, but by 1968 having progressed far toward the size and diversity of offerings then becoming general among the leading multipurpose "regional state universities," and already having been given the designation in 1965: Indiana State University at Terre Haute and Ball State University at Muncie. The former, founded in 1865 as a state normal school, is much the older of the two; but the latter, owing its inception in 1918 to the benefactions and public spirit of the Ball brothers (nationally-famous manufacturers of glass fruit jars in Muncie), is the larger of the two, and somewhat farther along the road of diversification. When in 1967 the legislature decided that there should be a state school of architecture, it designated Ball State as the location; and Ball State is already a strong contender for a school of medicine, if and when the legislature decides to establish and finance one, in addition to the large Indiana University School of Medicine in Indianapolis.

131

For a few years both Indiana State and Ball State were governed by a state normal school board (which had governed Indiana State alone, prior to the establishment of Ball State), but Ball State was eventually given its own board, so that each of Indiana's four major state universities is governed by its own separate board of trustees. At least up to 1970 there had never been any species of state-wide "coordinating board" superimposed upon public higher education in Indiana.

Yet, Indiana was known nation-wide for a high degree of voluntary cooperation among its four state institutions, a high degree of public confidence in them, and generally good relations between governors and legislatures and the four institutions. Naturally there had been some fiscal competition (as well as football rivalry) between Indiana University and Purdue. Often beneficent legislatures disposed of this by appropriating nearly the same sums to each of these two universities; but in 1949, partly at the instance of President Herman B Wells of Indiana University, the legislature added a clause to the appropriation act directing the four institutions to cooperate in producing joint budget askings for the next biennial session, based on comparative unit costs of instruction for different programs and at different levels.

An impression of how President Wells regarded this may be had from a quotation from his *State of the University* address for the year 1950: "For the past 25 years our institution and Purdue have been allocated funds for operations and buildings in equal amounts. This formula may have had merit in the beginning. . . . In recent years, however, the system has been inequitable and intolerable. The two institutions have different specialized functions, different enrollment structures, and so on. To give each exactly the same amount regardless of need is unfair to the students and staff of both institutions and to the taxpayers."

Accordingly the presidents of the four institutions took the legislature's request seriously and acted upon it. They and selected members of their fiscal staffs devised and developed methods of making comparative cost analyses which were constantly kept up to date and improved, and used as the basis for joint biennial requests for appropriations of state tax funds for the next two decades. This was accomplished without any statutory or other formal structure at all, wholly voluntarily by a loosely-composed group of representatives from the four institutions, who met at frequent intervals for consultation and who worked industriously at the job in their home offices. There was no formal organization, no officers, no compulsion. For convenience, the group was sometimes referred to as the quadripartite interinstitutional study committee. Below the echelon of the presidents, some of the leading participants were John Evans and

Donald H. Clark of Indiana University, John W. Hicks and Wesley Arden of Purdue, and the assistants to the presidents at the other two institutions.

For nearly 20 years the scheme gained nation-wide visibility, and representatives of state governments and of public higher education in other states frequently visited Indiana to study its operation and consult regarding it, as an example of voluntary state-wide coordination. Some doctrinaire partisans of coercion, who profess to believe nothing can be accomplished without "knocking heads together" have made much of the fact that the request of the 1949 Indiana legislature was couched in mandatory terms. They overlook the fact that the idea did not originate in an angry or recriminative legislature, as the words might seem to imply, but had already taken form in the minds of President Herman B Wells of Indiana University and the other presidents and fiscal officers. The legislature itself, by and large, has always maintained a benevolent attitude toward public higher education in Indiana.

It has always been agreed that the detailed cost-studies are solely for the purpose of disclosing facts about recent operations, and not to control the expenditure by any institution of the appropriated funds. The cost-studies can be criticized as a basis for appropriations because they do not take account of the frequent needs for wholly novel programs and services. This criticism is valid against any strictly objective studies of past performance. The remedy is that the interinstitutional committee, engaged in months and years of cooperative cost-studies, were conditioned to consider fairly and frequently agree upon necessary innovations, such as various new programs at Indiana University, a new school of veterinary medicine at Purdue, and many new elements at each of the other two institutions necessary to their transmutation from single-purpose teachers colleges to multipurpose regional universities, in which they have already moved a long way.

In 1965, with the incoming of a new governor who seemed to have become somewhat disenchanted with the fiscal administration of higher education, perhaps partly because of an earlier not altogether happy experience as a member of one of the large university governing boards, a commercial management-consulting firm was employed to study the matter, and recommended that the practices of the past 20 years be not depended upon exclusively in formulating the joint askings for appropriations of state tax funds for higher education in 1967. Accordingly the four universities were instructed to submit two sets of requests for biennium 1967-69; of which one would cover only minimum essentials, and the other include substantial additional sums regarded as highly desirable but not indispensable.

This was after the manner of the "A" budget and "B" budget practice familiar to students of budget-making, and sometimes previously used in some other states. The result was a total of appropriations somewhat below the level of the "minimum essential" askings, but nonetheless representing a gain of some 40 per cent over the preceding biennium—a denouement that could be "lived with" despite the gains in enrollments and rising costs.

It was in 1969, after a change of political complexion of the state government which brought in a new governor who had campaigned on promises of "no new or additional taxes," that state tax support of higher education in Indiana suffered a real setback. The governor threatened to veto any appropriations that would require new revenues. The Speaker of the House of Representatives (of the same political party as the governor) led an open revolt to obtain enactment of reasonable and necessary increases in the very low sales tax rate and personal income tax rate (each of which stood at 2 per cent—lowest in the nation); but failure of the Senate to agree in detail, and final failure to reach agreement in conference committee, led to final failure to enact any significant tax legislation at all in the 1969 session.

Total appropriations for operating expenses of higher education were only about 16 per cent more than for the preceding biennium. The boards of trustees of each of the four state universities were faced with the immediate necessity of drastically raising student fees if they were to avert cutbacks in their programs. The board of trustees of Purdue University announced that as of September, 1969, a fee for an academic year for regular in-state students, previously $400, would be $700. At Indiana University at Bloomington the same fee went to $650. Fees for nonresidents of the state, already high, were drastically raised.

These events triggered some peaceful protest demonstrations on each of the big campuses, and a "march" of 3,000 state university students who held an orderly assembly on a plaza in front of state offices in Indianapolis (from which the governor absented himself). This produced no change in the situation. Perhaps after a year or more has passed it will be possible to ascertain some of the effects of the tactics of reducing appropriations and raising student fees. In 1969 the governor stoutly maintained that he would not call a special session to consider the matter; but a year and a half was yet to elapse before the regular session of 1971. Occasionally the governor seemed to suggest that a repetition of the executive and legislative actions of 1969 should take place in 1971, to move the state closer to the goal of full payment of the costs of higher education by the students. It does not seem probable that this will occur.

At the end of the Second World War, Indiana's public and private colleges and universities (numbering 30 to 35) organized the Indiana Conference of Higher Education, a voluntary association for the purpose of stimulating all types of institutions jointly to develop their resources sufficiently to accommodate the greatly increased needs and demands for higher educational facilities that were certain to present themselves during the ensuing decades.[1] One of its announced goals was the hope that the private institutions collectively might continue indefinitely to enroll about half of the student population of the state—an aim that soon proved to be impracticable, but which nevertheless had value in encouraging the private colleges to prepare for expansion. It was true in 1969 that something approaching half of the *undergraduate* students *on-campus* (excluding the regional campuses) were in private colleges; but the private institutions had comparatively few graduate students and commuters.

Two useful state-wide studies were made by and for the Conference during the 'Fifties, surveying potential enrollments 1955 to 1972, and needs and resources over the same period.[2] The 1961 legislature created a Post-High School Education Study Commission which included 2 members of each House and 13 other citizens widely representative of educational institutions and organizations, as well as of the state chamber of commerce and the principal state labor organization. Among other recommendations, this group advised that:

"For the immediate future, additional needs for publicly-supported collegiate level education in Indiana be met by community campuses and extension centers of the existing state institutions, and that to meet these needs the extension system be expanded and developed as appropriate and that additional state funds be made available for this development as needed";[3] and "where appropriate with respect to numbers of qualified students, program needs, and geographical location, one or more of these campuses or centers be developed into a four-year undergraduate institution and when such institution matures the General Assembly grant it independent status."

There was also a recommendation that "permissive legislation be enacted so that a community, after a referendum by the voters, could establish a local community college"; but such legislation was not enacted; and throughout the decade Indiana's policy of increasing the geographic dispersion of higher educational opportunity chiefly by

---

[1] A detailed history of the Conference: Raleigh W. Holmstedt, *The Indiana Conference of Higher Education, 1945-1965*. Bloomington: Indiana University School of Education Bulletin, Vol. 4, No. 1 (1967). 100 pp. offset.

[2] N. M. Parkhurst and Betty Suddarth, *Potential Enrollment for Indiana Colleges and Universities, 1955 to 1972*. Bloomington: Indiana Conference of Higher Education, 1955. 103 pp. mimeo.; and Wendell W. Wright and others, *A Survey of Needs and Resources: The Capital, Operating, Personnel, and Curriculum Needs of Higher Education in Indiana*. Bloomington: *Ibid.*, 1957. 68 pp. mimeo.

[3] John W. Hicks and others, *Report of the Post-High School Education Study Commission*. Indianapolis: Governor's Office, November, 1962. 56 pp.

INDIANA

Appropriations for Annual Operating Expenses of Higher Education in Indiana, Alternate Fiscal Years, 1959-60 through 1969-70 (in thousands of dollars)

Institutions	Year 1959-60	Year 1961-62	Year 1963-64	Year 1965-66	Year 1967-68	Year 1969-70
Indiana University						
Main campus[1]		27,076	30,729	38,931	47,785	54,152[2]
Regional campuses[3]				908	5,913	7,562
Hospital intern prog[4]					1,250	675
U telecom system					300	1,113
Psychiatric research					400	400
Herron School of Art[5]					187	
Mentally retarded clinic					75	75
Pub health training					40	40
Dept of Toxicology					35	30
Subtotal, Indiana U		27,076	30,729	39,839	55,985	64,047
Purdue University						
Main campus		22,937	28,153	33,346	39,184	41,215
Regional campuses[6]				707	6,647	8,441
County ag agents					867	956
Animal Diagnostic Lab[7]					231	290
Ag products utilization					90	90
Ag marketing research					50	50
Bangs disease testing					30	50
Johnson grass erad					15	15
Subtotal, Purdue U		22,937	28,153	34,053	47,114	51,090[8]

Ball State University	4,802	6,577	8,695	13,769	16,284
Indiana State Univ					
Main campus	3,501	5,407	7,378	12,942	15,037
Regional campuses				248	1,021
Subtotal, I S U	3,501	5,407	7,378	13,190	16,058
Vincennes University[9]		113	140	370	500
Ind Voc-Tech Coll[10]				2,200	3,000
Total	55,316	70,979	90,105	132,628	154,313[11]

[1]Bloomington and Indianapolis.

[2]Includes $13,803,000 for the Medical Center and other units in Indianapolis, set out for the first time as Indianapolis Campus; also $825,000 for medical education planning.

[3]Eight, located at Fort Wayne, Gary-East Chicago, Jeffersonville, Kokomo South Bend-Mishawaka, Downtown Indianapolis, Richmond, and Vincennes, the latter two being "centers" operated in conjunction with Earlham College and Vincennes University respectively.

[4]Program for more medical internships within the state of Indiana.

[5]An Indianapolis institution acquired by Indiana University in 1967.

[6]Four, located at Fort Wayne, Hammond, Indianapolis, and Michigan City. The regional campuses of Indiana University and Purdue University in Fort Wayne occupy jointly a new college plant and work in close cooperation, though retaining their identities.

[7]Located near Jasper, Indiana.

[8]Includes $3,000 for Legislative Conference for High School Students.

[9]A private corporation dating from 1806, now operating a junior college largely supported by the state and by Knox County. Under an act of 1955 the state matches the proceeds of a county levy (currently $120,000 per year) and for the biennium 1967-69 appropriated additional tax moneys to bring the total of state support up to the sums shown.

[10]A public corporation of state-wide purview, authorized to provide vocational-technical education by various means, including establishing new schools or contracting with existing schools.

[11]Includes $180,000 for guaranteed loan program, and $3,154,000 for state scholarships.

developing regional campuses of the state universities continued.

To provide added facilities for vocational-technical education, the recommendation was that the legislature should create "the Indiana School for Practical Education"—a public corporation of state-wide purview, authorized to make available vocational-technical training by various means, including establishing new schools at appropriate places, or contracting with existing public or private institutions. This was implemented by the 1963 legislature, and the new corporation was given the more attractive name of "Indiana Vocational-Technical College," soon popularly abbreviated to "Ivy Tech."

During the ensuing six years the organization appeared to be unduly slow in starting a program of any significant volume; and it was accused, rightly or wrongly, of spending too much of its modest resources on a top-heavy central administrative staff. In 1969 the incoming governor, by using his powers of appointment and removal, reshuffled the board of trustees and staff. Ivy Tech received an appropriation of $6 million for the biennium 1969-71, having requested some $41 million. The superintendent of public instruction was reported to have declared that Ivy Tech was not doing anything that could not be done equally well by public school districts or by existing institutions of higher education.

Meantime Indiana University and Purdue University were operating two-year programs in various technician-level occupations at their several regional campuses,[4] including at least five programs of two calendar years leading to the state examination for Registered Nurses. By 1969 four of these regional campuses in cities of substantial size had begun to offer four-year programs leading to bachelors' degrees in response to local demand, as foreseen by the Study Commission in 1962; and Indiana University had taken steps to recognize the importance of the regional campuses by loosening its unitary control of them by initiating a species of federal Indiana University System in which the president and his all-University staff would be at the main campus at Bloomington, while each of the component units (the main campus, the Indianapolis professional school campus, and the regional campuses) would have a local executive known as chancellor, and would have more local autonomy than under the former unitary plan.

---

[4] Purdue University had four regional campuses, at Fort Wayne, Hammond, Indianapolis, and Michigan City. The regional campuses of Indiana University and Purdue University in Fort Wayne occupied jointly a new college plant, with their facilities equally available to students (with interchangeability of credits), but retaining their respective identities.

Indiana University had six regional campuses, at Fort Wayne, Gary-East Chicago, Jeffersonville, Kokomo, Downtown Indianapolis, and South Bend-Mishawaka, plus two "cooperative university centers" operated in conjunction with Earlham College and Vincennes University respectively.

The 1965 legislature was the first to make separate appropriations for the regional campuses (collectively) to Indiana University and Purdue University. The 1967 legislature increased these amounts about sixfold. The 1969 legislature increased them again, but not so drastically, so the totals for regional campuses of each of the two large universities for the biennium 1969-71 were of the order of $17 million to $18 million. For the first time, the professional school units of Indiana University in Indianapolis were given a *separate* appropriation of approximately $30 million for the biennium.

At the same time, the *main campuses* of Indiana University and Purdue received something of the order of $1 million *less* for operating expenses for fiscal year 1969-70 than had been allotted to them for the preceding fiscal year, 1968-69. This was a factor causing the drastic raising of fees for academic year 1969-70, as above mentioned. It was also typical of a widespread tendency to fear that main campuses can become "too big" and that state tax support should be increasingly dispersed to smaller state universities and colleges, university branches, or community colleges. Carried to an extreme, this trend could be damaging, because expansion and improvement in public higher education must necessarily be vertical as well as horizontal. Irreparable loss could come from cutting down the great centers of learning that the large state universities have become and are becoming.

Geographic spreading of facilities is desirable and inevitable; but building higher the peaks of achievement must not be neglected. This applies especially to the graduate and professional schools of the big state universities, which are often the one place in the state where comparable work is being done; but it does not necessarily follow that the undergraduate population of these state universities should be "frozen" or reduced. Eighteen-year-old citizens who have the money, the brains, the maturity, and the desire to attend a great university cannot be "deflected" to lesser institutions without loss to themselves and to the state.

The benefits gained by a bright and reasonably mature-for-his-age freshman being a member of a great "city of intellect" with enormous libraries and laboratories, internationally-distinguished professors, brilliant advanced graduate and professional students, and the immense variety of intellectual and artistic resources that characterize a great cosmopolitan university should not be denied arbitrarily to any worthy young man or woman who has his heart set on them. The top state universities of the Middle West and the West Coast ought not to be vaguely "feared," distrusted, and sniped at—they are new tools for the advancement of civilization, and are on their way constantly to new achievements. They merit unprecedented public support, and they deserve to be emulated in many other states as population increases.

Let the excellence and the numbers of large public universities increase.

Indiana's 1967 legislature created a "State Policy Commission on Post High School Education" of 28 members, almost wholly lay citizens with a small sprinkling of private college presidents, and including only one woman member. It employed Earl J. McGrath and William J. Haggerty (both from New York at the time) as director and associate director of studies, and delivered its report to the governor and each member of the legislature in December, 1968.[5]

This report presented apparently sound but conservative estimates of total enrollments in Indiana through 1985, showing that the figure almost exactly doubled from 1955 (73,000) to 1965 (144,000); that the steep rise will continue unabated until 1976, when it will have been almost exactly doubled again (285,000); and that it will continue upward to a peak in 1982 (323,000), after which it may decline somewhat.

Aside from the foregoing, the report was concentrated almost wholly upon reorganization. First, a Board of Regents of nine lay citizens appointed by the governor for terms of four years, and directed to appoint a chancellor and staff, would be placed at the apex of a highly-centralized state-wide system. (Existing boards of trustees would not be abolished, but their authority would be substantially diminished by making them subservient to the Board of Regents in fiscal matters, both as to appropriated funds before and after appropriation, and as to income from nontax sources; and by removing entirely from their governance all units except their own main campuses. Regional campuses would be severed from the parent institutions and given boards of trustees of limited powers, subject to the Board of Regents.)

Second, limping Ivy Tech would be expanded and developed into a state-wide network of locally-based comprehensive community colleges. Ivy Tech's board of trustees would become a state community college board, subject to the authority of the Board of Regents. The scheme can be hastily but accurately summarized by saying it would not make the Board of Regents a single exclusive *governing board*, yet it would apparently concentrate in the Board of Regents more power than is now wielded by any state-wide non-governing *coordinating board* in any state, with the exception of the Oklahoma Regents for Higher Education (see Oklahoma, *infra* herein). The plan, embodied in a bill introduced in the 1969 legislature, failed of passage, and no measure of any kind within this species was

---

5 *An Indiana Pattern for Higher Education*. Report of the State Policy Commission on Post High School Education. Indianapolis: Governor's Office, December, 1968. 110 pp.

enacted. Thus in 1969 Indiana's system of public higher education escaped the shock of being pulled up by the roots and replanted.

Voluntary cooperation at the initiative of various institutions and groups of institutions continued, and began to take some intriguing forms. Two may be briefly mentioned: (1) The city of Richmond near the eastern border of Indiana, seat of Earlham College, an old and respected private liberal arts college, for years had been the scene of amicable cooperative instructional work by Indiana University and Earlham, for the benefit of the people of that city of substantial size. More recently it became apparent that both Purdue University and Ball State University could offer some unique additions to the "educational mix" available in Richmond. Now at least four institutions are collaborating, under the wise and restrained chairmanship of Earlham's president, in offering a wide variety of instructional opportunities that Earlham alone could not and would not want to provide, and that in all probability could not be equaled until after many years by any locally-based public community college. Besides, considering the present state of local public finance in cities and counties throughout the land, it would seem unrealistic to suppose that Indiana's counties and cities are about to assume the responsibility of creating and supporting public junior colleges. If this were to be accomplished, it would undoubtedly have to be done with a heavy exercise of state initiative and with a large infusion of state tax funds—probably at least more than half the capital and operating costs.

The second example is concerned chiefly with medical education. For the biennium 1967-69 Indiana University received an appropriation of $2½ million for a hospital intern program intended to make it possible and desirable for many graduates of its medical college to serve internships in Indiana hospitals. (More than half were going to internships outside the state.) This would require agreements with the best hospitals in several Indiana cities, and facilities for quick and constant communication between them and the medical college in Indianapolis. For this latter requirement there was also an appropriation of $600,000 for the biennium to begin the development of a "university telecommunications system," which also promised to facilitate an enlargement of the capacity and output of the medical college by embracing the four state university main campuses (and eventually some of the reputable private colleges) where some of the preclinical medical students could receive some of their instruction in basic sciences before proceeding to the medical college in Indianapolis, thus relieving the pressure of numbers there and in effect making room for somewhat larger numbers of advanced students and M.D. graduates each year.

The whole system would also offer important possibilities for the graduate training of local practitioners, especially when fully equipped to transmit lectures and demonstrations by television, with facilities for two-way communication.

This is an oversimplified sketch of the incipient "Indiana Plan for Medical Education." Appropriations to continue development of all its aspects, including the intern resident program, appear to have been about $5¼ million for biennium 1969-71.

Higher education in Indiana goes forward. It does not always appear to be symmetrical, segmented, stratified, circumscribed, and centralized; but it is lively, inventive, and creative—and these are characteristics to be sought and prized.

IOWA

Three senior institutions of higher education of long standing exist in this state: the University of Iowa at Iowa City (formerly styled, during most of its history, as the State University of Iowa), established in 1847; Iowa State University at Ames (known during much of its history as the Iowa State College of Agriculture) founded in 1855, but not opened for instruction until 1868, after it had been designated the Morrill Act land-grant institution; and the University of Northern Iowa at Cedar Falls (recently renamed), the institution formerly concentrated wholly upon the education of teachers, and known successively as state normal school, state teachers college, and state college, begun in 1876. Thus the youngest of the three is nearly a century old.

For nearly half a century recurring efforts have been made to plan and launch a state-wide system of junior colleges in Iowa, with only partial success. Several successive plans resulted in virtual failure, leaving in their wake only a handful of surviving two-year institutions with varying degrees of precariousness as to enrollments and financing, and often of doubtful quality.

The most recent effort is toward the establishment of "area community colleges," each of which will embrace a federally-aided "area vocational school" as well as a comprehensive junior college, substantially state-aided. This seems to offer the best promise of success yet observed. Previous failures and modest partial achievements have no doubt been caused in part by nonexistent or scanty state or federal support. Most of Iowa's counties have been too sparse in population and too small in wealth to support a comprehensive junior college of economic size with exclusively local resources; and the problem of forming multicounty junior college districts has proved to be formidable.

As recently as the biennium 1963-65 the total of state aid for operating expenses of local public junior colleges was reported as only $1,627,000 for the biennium — equivalent to substantially less than $1 million for either of the two fiscal years. For the next two bienniums (1965-67 and 1967-69) this appears to have been raised to about $4 million and about $12 million respectively. This latter placed Iowa near the median among the 30 states appropriating state tax funds as state aid for the annual operating expenses of local public junior colleges.

For 60 years the three senior state institutions have been governed by a single board with office in the statehouse, known during half a century as the State Board of Education (though it had no jurisdiction over the elementary and secondary schools, except for certain state schools for the handicapped). However, it was recently given the more appropriate name of State Board of Regents. Its structure exhibits at least one unique feature. In addition to the nine members of the board itself, the board is directed to appoint a "Finance Committee" of three members who are *not members of the board*; and this Finance Committee triumvirate is a species of multiple executive agency charged, as its name would indicate, with controlling the expenditures of higher education. Its members are full-time salaried officers, though not at salaries approaching those of state university presidents, and they have not been expected or required to be experienced in the administration of higher education.

The "watchdog of the treasury" idea has often been altogether too dominant in Iowa. Despite the continuous existence of the single governing board for three institutions and its full-time paid triumvirate "Finance Committee" on the job the year round, for considerable periods of their history the state universities have suffered the indignity of having one or more permanent resident employees of the central state fiscal offices (not responsible to the Board of Regents) planted on their campuses. The net effect of the activities of these functionaries was generally less than zero — it was negative, because it entailed a good deal of useless additional paperwork and needless harassment for busy university administrators and fiscal and clerical staff members of the institutions.

An important service has been performed by Professor Edward Rutkowski of the University of Northern Iowa in his scholarly and well-documented paper sketching the history of the Iowa system of higher education during this century.[1] Only a few of the highlights can be indicated here. Even in the 1890's, and throughout the first decade of the present century, an obsession with "duplication" among Iowa's three state institutions of higher education grew and grew, especially in the financial "power structure." In 1904 a legislative committee recommended that all engineering studies at the state university at Iowa City be transferred to the agricultural college at Ames. Later in the same session the legislature appropriated a special fund of $208,000 for the further development of engineering at the university. Still in the same session, a bill to abolish the three institutional governing boards (boards of regents of each institution) and to create a single state-wide

---

[1]Edward Rutkowski, "The Iowa Experiment with an Integrated System of Higher Education." Paper presented October 26, 1968, at Loyola University, Chicago, Illinois, for the meeting of the Midwest History of Education Society.

board was passed in the senate but defeated in the house of representatives; and both houses passed a concurrent resolution to create a bipartisan committee of three members of each house to investigate public higher education and report to the next session.

That committee turned in to the 1906 session a 200-page report, widely known in Iowa as the "Whipple Report," recommending that entire control of the state institutions be placed in one board. It alleged that undergraduate courses in various liberal arts departments were offered at all three schools; that the high school preparatory departments of the university and the agricultural college were duplicative of each other; that the state normal school had become a miniature university, duplicating much of the work of the State University of Iowa. The implementing bill was again defeated, and again in the 1907 session; but passed in the session of 1909.

Newspaper comment was divided on the issue. President MacLean of the state university cautiously said he would "cooperate with the board in a great experiment." President Storm of the state college of agriculture was outspokenly opposed to the idea, and within a year resigned because of it. The legendary Homer Seerley, president of the state teachers college for 42 years, was reserved at first, but soon began to voice opposition.

By 1912 the new "State Board of Education" got around to instructing its Finance Committee to study the situation and formulate a plan for meat-axing the three institutions to bring them into a "unified working relationship under unified control." In essence the Committee decided that Iowa should not have three institutions, but one consisting of three scattered fragments. All engineering should go to the agricultural college. The state teachers college was to be restricted to the training of rural and elementary school teachers, and all its courses in liberal arts and education above the sophomore level were to be discontinued. All high school teachers and school administrators were to be educated at the state university. All courses in general science, liberal arts, and home economics were to be transferred to the university. These proposals, says Rutkowski, "had a distinct economic and business flavor," and were characterized as "Iowa's contribution to business efficiency in education."

The plan was next submitted to seven eminent nationally-known educators of the time, including the president of the Carnegie Foundation, the presidents of the University of Missouri and of the University of Wisconsin, the dean of Teachers College, Columbia University, and a specialist from the U.S. Office of Education. Among these, only the redoubtable Andrew Draper, Commissioner of Education of the State of New York, had the wisdom and courage to say the plan would not work.

Thus fortified, the Iowa Board formally adopted the plan in October 1912, with six members voting the affirmative, one negative, and

IOWA

Appropriations for Annual Operating Expenses of Higher Education in Iowa, Alternate Fiscal Years, 1959-60 through 1969-70 (in thousands of dollars)

Institutions	Year 1959-60	Year 1961-62	Year 1963-64	Year 1965-66	Year 1967-68	Year 1969-70
University of Iowa	18,850	13,600	16,333	20,953	28,530	32,537
University Hospital		5,900	6,803	7,620	8,617	8,700
Psychopathic Hosp		1,000	1,424	1,652	1,897	2,043
Hospital School		634	830	1,010	1,175	1,350
Bacteriological Lab		363	432	519	627	727
Lakeside Laboratory		4	4	8		
State Sanatorium					1,453	1,549
Subtotal, U of Iowa	18,850	21,501	25,828	31,764	42,299	46,906
Iowa State University	11,890	9,495	12,219	16,279	22,536	25,634
Agric Exper Station		2,349	2,625	2,916	3,599	3,825
Coop Agric Exten		1,566	1,850	2,048	2,698	3,000
Subtotal, Iowa St U	11,890	13,410	16,694	21,243	28,833	32,459
U of Northern Iowa[1]	3,490	3,914	4,835	6,170	8,536	9,759
State Bd of Regents[2]			90	106		110
St aid to Jr Colls			813	2,000	6,000	9,700
Total	34,745	38,914	48,261	61,284	85,773	101,597[3]

[1]Formerly State Teachers College.

[2]Also governs Iowa Braille and Sight Saving School and Iowa School for the Deaf; which in the aggregate receive roughly half a million dollars annually.

[3]Includes $2,250,000 for private college student tuition grants, $267,000 for state scholarships, and $150,000 for medical student tuition loans.

two absent. It was to go into effect in September, 1913. Fortunately it was wholly rescinded by the Board April 3, 1913, in abject "obedience to the request of the General Assembly" the minutes say; but it seems doubtful that there was any formal request, and unquestionable that there was near-unanimous opposition to the plan, of which the Board members had become painfully aware. Only a month earlier, in their March 1913 meeting, the Board had adamantly ordered that the plan be printed in the catalogs of each institution, and had brusquely denied President Seerley's request for one year's delay. The newly-appointed President Bowman of the State University of Iowa, though conciliatory about the plan at first, had quickly become an opponent and resigned within the year, chiefly because of it. Controversy over the plan had been a state-wide election issue in the fall of 1912, and it was the chief bone of contention in the legislative session of 1913. The Board had concocted, considered, and adopted it without consulting the presidents, faculty members, students, or alumni of any of the institutions, and had underestimated the sentiments of the general public and of the members of the legislature.

These maneuverings, viewed in the light of more than half a century of subsequent development of higher education in Iowa, have a strongly farcical flavor. Happily Iowa now has three distinguished state universities, and not three fragmentary institutions. Again and again, in 1915, 1925, 1939, and 1950, surveys of public higher education in Iowa were conducted by panels of experts led by P. P. Claxton, S. P. Capen, the Brookings Institution, again S. P. Capen, and George D. Strayer. In succession these reports progressively softened the harshly business-oriented idea that university presidents, faculties, students, and alumni merited only suspicion and surveillance. Capen recommended that all the presidents be invited to attend all meetings of the Board, and not kept sitting on a bench in the anteroom until called in individually at the whim of the Board.

Rutkowski says the Strayer report (1950) "called for more institutional cooperation, and also recommended that coordination of efforts be made on a voluntary rather than a compulsory basis." It suggested, he says, "that the Board solicit the assistance of committees composed of interinstitutional faculty members to work on the major problems." Your author had some part in the writing of those recommendations, and would like to report that it was found that counterpart departments in science, engineering, education, and a few other fields in the different institutions had a regularly established custom of keeping well-informed of each other's aims, resources, and principal projects by correspondence and telephone communication and by informal meetings at frequent intervals, sometimes arranged at a mid-point between the institutions so as to be equally convenient for all. "Duplication" has lost most of its significance except at the advanced graduate levels; and the desirable cooperation is best achieved by the professors and advanced students who know what they are doing rather than by absentee political or fiscal "watchdogs" who have little or no understanding of what the departments of instruction and research are trying to accomplish.

The excellent but unpublicized voluntary cooperation just described was apparently going on merrily without the knowledge of the Board; and so it was that the Strayer survey team in 1950 recommended that the Board should formally recognize, praise it, and "legitimize" it by setting up a small interinstitutional committee of high-echelon administrative officers to encourage it. The incident is but another illustration of absence of adequate communication between the Board and its own men and women in the vanguard of instruction and research. Any real "coordination" will be accomplished by these latter on their own initiative, and the difficulty is to keep the Board aware of what is going on, in a manner such that its members can comprehend it as fully as a layman can understand advanced university teaching and investigation.

Several conclusions plainly flow from Iowa's experience of a century: (1) A large university is so complex and diverse an organism that it is next to impossible for a board of laymen to keep abreast of its problems and progress; but where one board governs one university, it has some chance of understanding and using the expertise of the president, deans, department heads, and faculty members whom it appoints. In no event should one board undertake to govern more than one institution. (2) It is possible for one board or council to perform a coordinative, *liaison*, and public information function for several institutions. This is very different from governing or managing the institutions. The functions just mentioned are best accomplished by fostering and facilitating voluntary interinstitutional cooperation, and by sponsoring state-wide studies that are advisory to the governor, the legislature, the institutions, and the public, and that carry no harsh coercive force. (3) In the composition of a state-wide coordinative board or council, it is a grave error to exclude the institutional presidents, who because of their usual qualifications and the nature of their jobs are superior to all other persons in their knowledge of the institutions and their potentialities.[2]

The Iowa experience also demonstrates that one board governing a whole state system is an inept and unsuitable form of organization, such as has also been demonstrated in Florida, South Dakota, and a few other states which have had such an organization for more than

---

[2] The wording of this paragraph, as of other parts of this story, is the author's; and is not to be attributed to Professor Rutkowski except when directly quoted.

half a century; that it is difficult to change such a structure by statute; but that a lay board in such a position is so nearly helpless in the face of its task that voluntary cooperation and the development of institutions in keeping with the opportunities and demands of the times go on apace, so that board members of intelligence and good will gradually come to understand that the best function of the board is to encourage these developments in the public interest. This is a far cry from the parsimonious and restrictive motives which originally played principal parts in bringing such boards into existence.

In general and over the long haul, Iowa has a tradition and a record of good support for public higher education. Each of its three institutions is among the national leaders of its type. But since 1960 the tendency has been to fall rapidly behind other, more populous, industrialized and urbanized states, in the rate of growth of state support. Iowa has only 2¾ million people, and for 10 years its population has been almost exactly "stationary." There are no huge cities, and the industries continue in large part to be those based on agricultural production (meat-packing, manufacture of breakfast cereals, and the like).

Thus Iowa's rate of gain in appropriations of state tax funds for annual operating expenses of higher education over nine years (1960-1969) was only 147½ per cent, falling far short of the 50-state average of 261 per cent. Only eight states had lower rates of gain, and seven of these were in the northwestern quadrant of the continental United States, extending in a contiguous bloc westward from Iowa to Oregon.

In fiscal year 1968, Iowa's tax investment in operating expenses of higher education was $31.25 per citizen, ranking fourteenth among the states. The ratio of state tax investment per citizen to average per capita personal income was 0.93 per cent, ranking eighteenth among the states. In fiscal 1967, Iowa's total of state and local taxes per capita was $328.04, ranking twelfth. The same total *per $1,000 of personal income was* $109.36, ranking *twenty-second.* These few figures seem to indicate that if Iowa is determined to maintain and advance the tradition of a superior state system of higher education, it has considerable room in which to move upward its state tax support before maximum effort will have been approached.

KANSAS

Senior state institutions, more numerous, more widely distributed geographically, and more in accord with concentrations of population than in the somewhat more populous state of Iowa, for example, mark the condition of public higher education in Kansas. The three types of major institutions, as in many states, are present in the shape of the University of Kansas at Lawrence (with Medical Center at Kansas City, Kansas), Kansas State University (the Morrill Act land-grant institution) at the town of Manhattan, and Kansas State Teachers College at Emporia. These date respectively from 1856, 1863, and 1863. The latter two conferred their first baccalaureate degrees in 1867; the former, not until 1873, because it had not begun operation until several years after the date of its charter.

Two other state colleges, dating respectively from 1901 and 1903, are at Fort Hays (in the westerly part of the state) and Pittsburg (in the southeast, near the Missouri border). The oil industry has brought a concentration of population in the south central region, around the cities of Wichita and Hutchinson, and in response the state took over the municipal University of Wichita and made it Wichita State University in 1964. The state also subsidizes the municipal Washburn University of Topeka with modest sums per credit-hour granted, and likewise the several local public junior colleges.

The principal source of state revenue is a general sales tax of 3 per cent, which produced 35 per cent of all state tax collections in 1966. In the 1960 legislative session the governor made an ill-advised attempt to have the sales tax rate, then at 2½ per cent, reduced to 1½ per cent, which fortunately failed.

In the 1963 session an effort was made to secure the enactment of a 1 per cent severance tax on the extraction of petroleum, which would have produced about $5 million of revenue annually—sufficient to finance the take-over and operation of Wichita University by the state; but no severance tax was enacted. It would seem that the people of the state have not only an indefeasible right, but also an inescapable duty, to provide that the removal of irreplaceable natural resources shall be subject to suitable taxation.

Kansas also has personal and corporate income taxes, but at relatively low rates. It was shown that in 1961 the difference between what Kansas collected from these two sources and what would have been possible if both had been levied at the average rate per $1,000 of

personal income (among the states having such taxes) was more than
$35 million—substantially more than the total of Kansas' ap-
propriations of state tax funds for operating expenses of higher
education for that year.[1]

As to state-wide structure for higher education, Kansas was one of
the small handful of sparsely populated western states that made the
serious mistake, during the second decade of this century, of
abolishing the institutional governing boards and subjecting the institutions to the tender mercies of a salaried "Board of Administration" which also governed the state schools for the handicapped, and numerous other penal, correctional, and eleemosynary
institutions. All these states, including Kansas, have long since
corrected that error, though Iowa and Kansas have continued to
charge their state-wide Boards of Regents not only with the governance of all their state institutions of higher education, but also with
responsibility for several state schools for the handicapped. These
latter almost always consume a disproportionate amount of the time of
the Board which is already overloaded with the superhuman task of
managing several large universities and colleges; hence the advancement of higher education suffers.

It was in 1925 that the Kansas State Board of Administration
suddenly met its Waterloo as oligarchic ruler of all higher education
after having been placed in control in 1913. In 1925 it issued an order
summarily dismissing the chancellor of the University of Kansas,
without stating cause. Chancellor Ernest H. Lindley sued for an injunction to restrain the enforcement of the order, contending that (1)
he was removable only for cause, and (2) that his allegation of malice,
oppression, and caprice entitled him to be heard as a petitioner for
court intervention in his behalf. The majority of the Kansas supreme
court denied, on dubious grounds, both of his contentions; but a
vigorous and convincing dissenting opinion was entered by Justice
Dawson, who declared the court should take cognizance of "notorious
matters of current history" in the political situation as going far to
prove the allegation of malice and caprice.[2] He quoted several
Kansas decisions in support of the proposition that an administrative
board cannot be the final judge of the reasonableness of its own actions, and that an averment of malice calls for judicial investigation.
He also argued against the policy of the majority view: "Not only may
the chancellor be truculently dismissed without a moment's notice, but
a hooligan can be installed in his stead . . . and every professor, every

---

[1] Page 40 of James W. Martin's *Revenue Potentials of the States.*
Washington: National Education Association, Committee on Educational
Finance, April 1964. 49 pp. litho.
[2] *Lindley* v. *Davis et al..* 117 Kan. 558, 231 Pac. 1026 (1925).

instructor, every janitor, can be discharged with equal expedition." The arbitrary dismissal of Chancellor Lindley was closely followed by the enactment of a statute removing the five state institutions of higher education from the jurisdiction of the State Board of Administration and placing them under the newly-created Kansas State Board of Regents. The new board promptly reappointed Chancellor Lindley, and he continued as the respected head of the University of Kansas for long thereafter.

Prior to 1913 the Kansas institutions were governed by separate Boards of Regents, each of which was a corporate entity, as is usual; but the Kansas supreme court has twice held that the act of 1913 abolishing these boards destroyed their corporate existence (if they had ever had it), and made them mere noncorporate instrumentalities. The Board of Administration, given full control of all the institutions in 1913, was not a corporation, nor was the Board of Regents which succeeded it in 1925. Hence the precedent is that the whole state system of higher education is only a noncorporate department of the state government, quite contrary to the legal theory prevailing in most of the other states. Iowa and North Dakota seem to be other states in which the state universities and colleges are held to have no corporate existence.

Late in 1959 the Kansas Legislative Council released its own review and recommendations regarding the report of a comprehensive survey of education at all levels in the state that had recently been completed. One quotation from the Legislative Council's recommendations follows: "Kansas makes no distinction between higher educational institutions and other state departments and agencies insofar as state financial administration is concerned. In contrast, the constitutions of certain states make the university independent in such matters as budgetary, personnel, and purchasing procedure. We would be inclined to favor a provision authorizing the educational institutions to make direct purchases of scientific and technical supplies and equipment for experimentation, research, and teaching."

This indicated a disposition at least somewhat favorable to freeing public higher education from the grip of the state bureaucracy. There was a nation-wide surge of this kind of recognition in 1960, as witness, for further example, the report of the Governor's Committee on Higher Education in New York State, which, among several items having the same general tendency, urged that the State University be given the option of making purchases without going through the central state purchasing agency.[3]

---

[3]Marion B. Folsom, John W. Gardner, and Henry T. Heald (Chairman), *Meeting the Increasing Demand for Higher Education in New York State.* Albany: Board of Regents, State Education Department, 1960. 74 pp.

The Kansas Legislative Council flatly rejected the idea of merging the separate retirement system for faculty members of state educational institutions with the separate plans for other state employees, and urged the legislature to establish a TIAA-type plan for college faculties, in order to reduce excessive turnover and attract talent from outside the state.[4] The Council recommended state aid for local public junior colleges, not on the high school formula basis, but on a credit-hour basis, suggesting $6 per credit-hour taught.

The 1961 legislature appropriated $605,000 as state aid for operating expenses of junior colleges and municipal universities for fiscal year 1961-62. Of this, $280,000 was for the two municipal universities, on the basis of $3 per credit-hour for each student who was a resident of Kansas. This represented approximately one-eighth of the "educational and general" costs of serving the average student at the municipal universities. At first the rate for junior colleges was $3 per credit-hour, but in 1965 the practice of adding to this a dollar-for-dollar matching of fees paid by students was begun; and in 1968 the rate became $8 per credit-hour. In 1964 Wichita University became a state institution, and in 1967 the rate for the Washburn University of Topeka became $4.50 per credit-hour. For fiscal year 1968-69 the appropriation to Washburn was $486,000; and for the junior colleges it was $2,333,000.

After having had at least nine survey reports since 1922, on higher education, Kansas received yet another one in November 1962, by a panel of nationally-distinguished educators headed by Alvin C. Eurich, vice president of the Ford Foundation and director of the Fund for the Advancement of Education.[5] Something of the tenor of the report may be savored from a quotation from Walter Lippman which it carried on page 5: "I do not mean we are doing a little too little. I mean we are doing much too little. . . . Our education effort . . . has not been raised to the plateau of the age we live in."

The report was unrealistically overoptimistic, however, about the sources of additional income. It repeatedly said, "The money requirements can be financed by allocating to higher education a small percentage of the increase in the state's gross personal income and productivity," pointing out that the personal income of the people of Kansas had increased 60 per cent during the preceding 10 years.

---

[4] The Teachers Insurance and Annuity Association, stemming from a benefaction of Andrew Carnegie near the turn of the century, operates a highly satisfactory contributory system in which some hundreds of the better universities and colleges participate. Each individual policyholder has his own contract with the TIAA, and loses nothing when he moves to another institution or another state.

[5] Alvin C. Eurich and survey team, *Kansas Plans for the Next Generation*. Topeka: State Board of Regents, 1962. 54 pp.

KANSAS

Appropriations for Annual Operating Expenses of Higher Education in Kansas, Alternate Fiscal Years, 1959-60 through 1969-70 (in thousands of dollars)

Institutions	Year 1959-60	Year 1961-62	Year 1963-64	Year 1965-66	Year 1967-68	Year 1969-70
U of Kansas	8,677	9,631	11,512	13,818	16,244	21,550
Medical Ctr	3,007	3,834	5,755	5,496	6,156	8,723
Subtotal, U of Kas	11,684	13,465	17,267	19,314	22,400	30,273
Kansas St Univ[1]	7,688	9,203	11,620	13,541	16,124	21,258
Wichita St U[2]				4,150	5,994	8,850
Kas S T C (Emporia)	2,124	2,729	3,595	3,935	4,814	6,114
Kas St Coll (Pittsburg)	2,130	2,618	3,170	3,523	4,336	5,493
Ft Hays Kas St Coll	1,519	1,832	2,271	2,770	3,295	4,183
Dental students[3]				48	15	
St aid to Municipal U Washburn U of Topeka[4]				318	430	697
St aid to Jr Colls[5]			466	1,000	1,595	2,650
Total	25,145	29,847	38,390	48,598	59,003	79,721[6]

[1] Includes experiment stations and agricultural extension service.

[2] An "associate" of the University of Kansas. Formerly a municipal institution.

[3] Having no dental school, Kansas makes payments on behalf of Kansas students studying dentistry in other states. This program is now in its final year prior to the beginning of the operation of a new interstate agreement (1968-69).

[4] At the rate of $3 per credit-hour enrolled October 15 for lower division; $5 for upper division.

[5] State aid to local public junior colleges is in two forms: (1) $3 per credit hour, and (2) dollar-for-dollar matching of student fees. For fiscal year 1967-68 the sums available for these two purposes are respectively $870,000 and $725,000.

[6] This total includes $203,000 appropriated for the Board of Regents, the state-wide governing board.

Undertaking to speak of three additional sources, the report then mentions such comparative "flea-bites" as "putting the auxiliary enterprises on a more nearly self-supporting basis" and making "moderate increases in tuition rates," and speaks of taxation as something to be "held to a minimum," suggesting first that more of the costs should be charged to the students in the form of higher rates for room, board, and tuition. This is repugnant to Kansas tradition, and more appropriate to the eighteenth century than the twentieth. In concluding, however, the report made a sound statement: "Financing higher education in Kansas is a problem of policy, not of resources," implying that the means are present if the will is strong. It also indicates that increases in costs must be much more than proportional to increases in enrollment, because of rising faculty salaries and rising costs of instructional and research equipment, as well as the necessity of adding competent teaching and research personnel.

Aware of the urgency of making Wichita University a state institution, and sensing very compulsive "establishment" opposition to the creation of a third state university, the survey team recommended that Wichita become a sort of joint regional campus of the two older state universities, and be managed by a board composed chiefly of five administrative officers of each of the two. The legislature of 1963 rejected this structure, and provided instead that Wichita State University be designated an "associate" of the University of Kansas, with its president to be nominated by the chancellor of the University of Kansas and its budgets to be reviewed by him before transmission to the State Board of Regents.

Wichita State University by statute began July 1, 1964. The state became owner of 34 buildings on 140 acres of campus, estimated to be worth $15 to $18 million, with about 6,000 students and available room for about 2,500 more. Its $3,660,000 of outstanding general obligation bonds were to be paid by continuing the 5-mill levy on property within the city of Wichita, whose proceeds had previously supplied 44 per cent of the institution's annual operating expenses. Its $7 million of outstanding "revenue bonds" (financing dormitories and other income-producing buildings) would continue to be self-liquidating. Details of the statute providing for the transfer to the state are set forth in Citizens' Pamphlet No. 33 of the Governmental Research Center at the University of Kansas. [6]

The 1965 legislature enacted tax measures estimated to produce about $45 million a year in new revenues. The sales tax was raised to 3 per cent from the former 2½ per cent. The income tax rates were

---

[6] James T. McDonald, *Decisions of the 1963 Kansas Legislature.* Lawrence: University of Kansas, Governmental Research Center, 1964. 158 pp.

slightly increased. Additional taxes were placed on liquor and cigarettes.

Over the decade of the 'Sixties, however, Kansas has accomplished only comparatively modest rates of increase in annual appropriations of state tax funds for operating expenses of higher education. For the nine years 1960-1969 the gain was only 176 per cent, as compared with the weighted national average of 261 per cent.

Kansas had fewer than 2 1/3 million people as of July 1, 1968, but had a population gain of about 9 per cent since 1960. In 1968 its state tax investment *per citizen* for operating expenses of higher education was $30.42, ranking fifteenth among the states. The ratio of state tax investment to total personal income was 0.91, ranking twenty-first. By these admittedly fragmentary measures, Kansas' "effort" appeared to be somewhat less than its comparative capability in state tax support of annual operating expenses of higher education.

KENTUCKY

Coming tardily into the scene of public higher education, this commonwealth, though a member of the Union since 1792, had no state university or college until 1865, when a small Morrill Act land-grant instructional unit was begun as a department of the private denominational college then known as Kentucky University. In fact, nothing resembling a state university existed until 1878, when the connection was severed and the Morrill Act institution was given a chance to start from scratch on a new site, by donation of land and buildings from the city of Lexington and the county of Fayette. Not until 1899 did it receive the official name of "State University"; and not until 1916 its present style of "University of Kentucky."

Next to be founded was the institution now named Kentucky State College, in 1886. First conceived as an agricultural, industrial, and normal school for Negroes, it had become by 1960 chiefly a liberal arts college with considerable emphasis on the education of teachers. Desegregated since 1954 (as were the other state institutions of higher education), at first it attracted only a handful of white students, and by 1962 its total enrollment scarcely reached 700. At that time only 7 per cent of Kentucky's population were Negroes. The college was the target of some grumbling because 30 to 35 per cent of its students resided outside the state.

A combination of these and other factors brought about a number of ill-considered proposals in the public press, such as that (1) the college should be decapitated and made a two-year junior college, (2) it should be made a branch of the University of Kentucky, (3) it should be abolished and its plant turned over to an adjacent state institution for the handicapped, or (4) it should be made strictly a vocational institute, offering only short-term occupational instruction.

In the face of this popgun barrage, the progressive Governor Bert Combs invited the author to assemble three educators from outside Kentucky, including one Negro, to visit the college and the state and prepare a report with recommendations regarding the future of Kentucky State College. This was done. [1]

---

[1]M. M. Chambers, Thomas G. Pullen, Jr., and Broadus E. Sawyer, *The Future of Kentucky State College.* Frankfort: Kentucky Council for Public Higher Education, 1962. 40 pp. mimeo.

In brief, the advice was that Kentucky State College should be continued as a four-year college of liberal arts, plus specified other programs, making it a multipurpose institution, with four main functions in view: (1) an optional facility for the education of qualified Negroes from all parts of the commonwealth until desegregation becomes actual and complete; (2) part-time education of employees of the state government in Frankfort and vicinity, at senior college and junior college levels; (3) provision of community college opportunities for the high school graduates and adults of Frankfort and its seven-county region who would not otherwise be able to obtain any formal education beyond high school; and (4) provision of occupational, technical, and subprofessional courses, adapted to the changing needs of industries and businesses of the region, and tending directly to further its economic development.

Three years later a state-wide "long-range study of higher education in Kentucky" was made by the Kentucky Commission on Higher Education at the request of Governor Edward T. Breathitt. The author was again chairman of the survey team. The report was completed early in 1966.[2] It was found that Kentucky State College had doubled its enrollment and had taken effective steps to implement the recommendations of the 1962 study. In 1969 the enrollment was over 1,600 students. The 1966 report remarked: "It is easy to envision a four-year school of business and public administration as a major coordinate division of Kentucky State College, in addition to its college of liberal arts, its division of teacher education, and its two-year college offerings. . . . It is very difficult to envision the capital city, with its own county and adjacent counties, without such a multipurpose institution of higher education."

In addition to the state university and the state college mentioned in the foregoing paragraphs, Kentucky has four regional state universities, physically quite evenly distributed along the east-west axis which is the state's most impressive dimension. These, too, came late upon the scene as public normal schools, though some of them had antecedents as private schools or academies. The two larger ones began as state normal schools in 1906; and the two at the eastern and western extremities (though not so named, but named respectively for the towns in which they are located) were started as state normal schools in 1922. All four, having become successively state teachers' colleges and multipurpose state colleges, were ripe in 1966 to become regional state universities; and a recommendation to that effect by the

---

[2] M. M. Chambers, chairman, and members of the survey team and staff, *Higher Education in Kentucky, 1965-1975: A Program of Growth and Development.* Frankfort: Kentucky Commission on Higher Education, 1966. 421 pp. litho.

Survey Team was readily adopted by the Commission and quickly enacted by the legislature.

A few opponents of the change were quick to sniff that the name does not make a university, but professed to be unable to recognize that the institutions were in fact already "emerging universities"; that they were entering a decade of redoubled enrollments and complexity of programs; and that a university is not made overnight, but is developed over a long period of years during which the high general aims must be visible. The elevation of morale which students and faculty gain from the name "university" is itself a powerful factor in uplifting the viability and quality of the institution. The name also has considerable cash value in negotiations for the recruiting of superior new faculty members, of which many will be needed as the rapid expansion goes on. Besides, it is almost nation-wide public policy that a state of 3 million people or more needs the relatively new genus of "regional state universities," in addition to its one or more "principal" or "central" state universities.

Each of Kentucky's state institutions of higher education has its own governing board. For many years the board of trustees of the University of Kentucky was almost unique in having two members of the faculty who sat with the right to speak but not to vote; but currently this practice has become somewhat more common nationally. The Kentucky legislature of 1968 also provided for at least one student and one faculty representative on each of the governing boards. The Kentucky Council on Public Higher Education is a "coordinating" body dating from 1934, antedating almost all others of that type (though Oregon is known to have had a largely futile "Board of Higher Curricula" as early as 1906).

The motive behind the Kentucky Council in its early years seems to have been mixed: to approach a certain uniformity of standards among the four state teachers colleges, and "equity" in the distribution of state funds to them. The Depression stringency kept their support extremely meager. They were probably saved from worse restrictive measures, however, by the fact that the Council itself was composed wholly of representatives of the institutions, plus the superintendent of public instruction: the president and one member of the board of regents of each of the five state colleges, with a somewhat larger representation from the University of Kentucky, including its president, its dean of the college of education, and three members of its board of trustees.

At first, and until the 'Sixties, the University and the Council largely ignored each other. The Council's attention was mostly concentrated on the state colleges. During the late 'Fifties the Council developed close ties with the state budget office, in studies encompassing the whole of state-wide higher education; and gradually as the years pass the University and the Council pay more attention to

KENTUCKY

Appropriations for Annual Operating Expenses of Higher Education in Kentucky, Alternate Fiscal Years, 1959-60 through 1969-70 (in thousands of dollars)

Institutions	Year 1959-60	Year 1961-62	Year 1963-64	Year 1965-66	Year 1967-68	Year 1969-70
U of Kentucky		15,450	20,356	30,553	41,909	51,706[1]
Western Kentucky U		2,058	2,848	5,011	6,940	11,703
Eastern Kentucky U		2,049	2,690	4,660	7,030	10,578
Murray State U		1,899	2,472	3,654	5,197	8,152
Morehead St U		1,533	2,138	3,046	4,255	7,290
Kentucky St Coll		829	869[2]	1,350	1,748	2,586
U of Louisville[3]				900	1,012	3,100
Council on Pub H E[4]		671[5]	791[5]	334	354	363
Total	14,954	24,490	32,164	49,507	68,445[6]	95,478

[1] Includes all units of the University (Medical Center, Agricultural Experiment Station, Agricultural Extension Service), and a network of 12 community colleges, all of which are branches of the University.

[2] Annual appropriations of approximately $200,000 were also made to the Lincoln Institute in Shelby County, which served as a practice school for prospective teachers enrolled in Kentucky State College. This practice has been discontinued.

[3] This university is a state-subsidized municipal institution. House Resolution 91, adopted by the 1968 legislature, authorizes it to become a state institution and requests the board of trustees of the University of Louisville and the Board of Trustees of the University of Kentucky to develop a plan of affiliation for the two universities.

[4] The Council is a statutory state-wide agency. The appropriations to it cover not only its administrative expenses, but also the costs of small state-wide programs for musical education and for occupational qualification development, as well as the sums that the Commonwealth of Kentucky pays for its participation in the program of the Southern Regional Educational Board, and certain other student exchange programs.

[5] These appropriations include $500,000 annually for the contract program of medical education and research at the University of Louisville School of Medicine.

[6] Upon reports from the state departments of revenue and finance that revenue receipts were falling below the estimates upon which the appropriations had been based, the governor announced a reduction of about $24 million in the appropriations for 1967-68, distributed in such manner that most of the various state departments were cut about 10 per cent, and public higher education lost about 8 per cent. The total of $68,445,000 shown here is as reduced by the governor's order in November 1967, from the original $74,371,000 appropriation of February 1966.

each other, though even yet in a crunch the University tends to deal directly with the governor and the leaders in the legislature. The Council gradually improves in its performance of research and public information functions.

In 1962 a statute added three lay or "public" members to the Council, which had theretofore been composed wholly of representatives of the several institutions, as already noted. In 1965 the issue of whether the Council should be reconstituted as a wholly "lay" body with no institutional representatives became prominent. The question split both the survey team (with the chairman entering a minority report against the proposal of a wholly lay Council, while the other two members recommended it), and the Commission of Higher Education, which was about evenly divided. This resulted in a recommendation by the Commission of a compromise, which was enacted by the legislature: the Council would be reconstituted to consist of nine lay members plus the presidents of each of the institutions as *ex officio* members with the right to speak but not to vote. The Commission recommended this compromise measure by the narrowly divided vote of 8 to 7. Its merit is that, though the only voting members of the Council are now nine laymen, the presidents of the six institutions have the right to be present and participate in the deliberations at all sessions.

Kentucky enacted a 3 per cent general sales tax in 1960, chiefly to finance the payment of a "soldiers' bonus" which required no more than one-third the amount of money thus produced. The remainder of the added revenue made possible substantial gains in state support of local public schools, and of public higher education. Since that year the commonwealth has made remarkable strides, achieving a gain of more than 450 per cent between 1960 and 1969 in state tax support of higher education. Only Hawaii and three states of the Northeast made higher rates of gain.

One comparison serves to illustrate Kentucky's rise. In 1960 the population of Nebraska was somewhat less than half that of Kentucky, but Nebraska's appropriation of state tax funds for annual operating expenses of higher education ($15,217,000) exceeded Kentucky's $14,954,000. By 1969 each state had had only small increases of population, and the ratio between them continued about the same; but Kentucky's appropriation was $74,371,000 as compared with Nebraska's $33,348,000. (Nebraska's percentage gain over the period was only a little over 118 per cent.) These changes, however, merely served to bring these two states' appropriations into closer correspondence with their respective populations; and in 1968 their respective state tax investments *per citizen* for operating expenses of higher education were not far apart—Kentucky's being $25.99 and Nebraska's $23.38, ranking twenty-seventh and thirty-fifth among the

50 states. Kentucky's very rapid gains had not yet brought the commonwealth up to the nation-wide average by this measure.

Upon the recommendation of Governor Louie B. Nunn, the 1968 legislature raised the general sales tax rate to 5 per cent (from the former 3 per cent which had prevailed since 1960). There is reason to expect that the added revenue will enable the commonwealth to continue commendable progress in state support of higher education.

Another act of 1968 created a new four-year state college, to be located within the three northernmost counties, in which the largest city is Covington, just across the Ohio River from Cincinnati. These three counties form a compact area embracing approximately a quarter of a million residents, and are thus much in need of a full-fledged state college, notwithstanding the oft-repeated mindless remark that their people have only to cross the river to reach the large and reputable University of Cincinnati. This fails to mention that a minimum of about $1,000 or more in annual fees is required of nonresidents of Ohio who attend the University of Cincinnati—a matter of substantial consequence. The governor appointed a Board of Regents for the new state college early in 1968, and selection of a site and early steps in the organization of the institution were begun. This was another of the recommendations of the survey report completed in 1966.

Kentucky has 15 so-called "community colleges" (two-year) which are in fact branches of the University of Kentucky, without local operating support. Two additional ones were authorized in 1968, but not financed. A few were started in the 1930's by local school boards, notably those at Paducah and Ashland, substantial cities at opposite ends of the state. The Paducah Junior College operated with increasing success for 34 years under local control and support (1932-1966), finally erecting a new plant on a new site in the 1960's. In 1966 the state took it over and made it a branch of the University of Kentucky, partly because of a state-wide craze for "systems uniformity," but perhaps more largely because the Paducah power structure was unable or unwilling to continue local tax support on a sufficient scale.

The Ashland public school district has maintained a 7-cent local property levy since 1937 to provide physical facilities for the Ashland Community College. This is by agreement with the University of Kentucky, which furnishes all instruction and operation. A recent version of the agreement (1957, as supplemented in 1964) commits the school district to purchase a large new site on which a nonprofit corporation created for the purpose will borrow money and construct buildings, to be turned over to the University as each building is completed. Meantime the district is to use its 7-cent levy to pay annual rentals to the nonprofit corporation until the cost of the land and buildings is amortized. A Kentucky Court of Appeals decision of 1966 declared that these arrangements were lawful and within the powers of the school district, and that the 7-cent levy was not invalid. [3]

Kentucky's other "community colleges" are of much more recent origin and without local tax bases. The counties and towns are generally small, and expansion of public junior colleges on local tax bases is probably impracticable, as it has been found to be in Minnesota, Washington, and Colorado.

The four regional state universities and Kentucky State College are authorized by an act of 1966 to establish and operate community college programs at their respective campuses. (Such a program at Eastern Kentucky University bears the name of Richmond College.) This is a very desirable provision because towns and counties of the size of those in which these institutions are located unquestionably need local two-year college services, but are scarcely sufficiently populous to justify the establishment of a community college as a separate institution, whether locally supported and controlled or as a branch of the distant state university. The practicable way is for the regional state university (or the state college) to provide the service. This is in marked contrast with the California practice, which virtually prohibits the four-year and five-year state colleges from offering two-year community college programs.

The University of Louisville, long a municipal institution but only scantily supported by the city of Louisville and the county of Jefferson, and increasingly subsidized by the state in recent years, was made a state institution by an act of 1970, effective July 1. The act provides for minority representation of the city and county on the new board of trustees, as long as city and county financial support is maintained up to a specified level.

---

[3] *Montague* v. *Board of Education of Ashland Independent School District,* (Ky.), 402 S.W. 2d 94 (1966).

LOUISIANA

Among all the 50 states, only one has a system of law deriving from the Continental Civil Code rather than the English common law, and styles its principal local subdivisions *parishes* rather than counties. This is Louisiana.

Another idiosyncrasy is that the institution in New Orleans, first chartered as the Medical College of Louisiana in 1834, then made a unit of the old University of Louisiana (a state-controlled institution now defunct) in 1847, was operated under state control until 1884, when, after receiving a large gift from the philanthropist, Paul Tulane, in 1882, it was turned over to the Administrators of the Tulane Educational Fund and has been a private university since that time, under the official name of the Tulane University of Louisiana.

Public higher education consists almost wholly of two systems, each under a governing board named in the state constitution, but not invested with the constitutional independence elsewhere described for the state universities in Michigan, Minnesota, California, and some other states.

The Board of Supervisors of the Louisiana State University and Agricultural and Mechanical College had become by 1969 the head of a system embracing the main campus at Baton Rouge, a large branch campus in New Orleans, the Medical Center in New Orleans, including the Dental School in New Orleans (recently acquired from the private Loyola University), three relatively new small branch campuses at Alexandria, Eunice, and Shreveport, and an incipient new branch Medical Center at Shreveport.

Other institutions are governed by the State Board of Education. These include Southern University and Agricultural and Mechanical College (attended predominantly by Negroes), with its main campus at Baton Rouge, a large branch in New Orleans, and a smaller branch in Shreveport; and eight other regional state institutions, of which the largest was named, in 1960, University of Southwestern Louisiana (at Lafayette).

Besides, there is a large locally-administered, principally state-financed public junior college (Isaac Delgado College) in New Orleans.

Most of the regional institutions date from within the present century, and most of them did not confer baccalaureate degrees before the 'Twenties. In 1934 and 1938, by separate legislative acts passed by two-thirds vote of both houses, the Ouachita Parish Junior College at Monroe and the Calcasieu Parish Junior College at Lake Charles were made branches of Louisiana State University. In 1950 several acts renamed them Northeast Louisiana State College and McNeese State College, made them four-year colleges, and transferred them to the governance of the State Board of Education. These acts were passed by less than two-thirds vote, though the state constitution required such a vote for the creation of any state educational institution not in existence in 1921. When challenged in the state supreme court, the acts of 1950 were sustained on the ground that they established no new state institutions.[1]

A state-wide survey made during the 'Fifties convincingly recommended the development of local public junior colleges; but it seems that this type of institution was not yet to take root permanently in Louisiana soil. Instead, the older state institutions offering two-year programs became four-year colleges under the State Board of Education; and two parish junior colleges (as noted) became, first, branches of Louisiana State University, and then, a dozen years later, four-year regional colleges under the State Board of Education.

Graduate programs at colleges under the State Board of Education were initiated by legislative act in 1954. Since that time, the board has authorized graduate programs at all institutions under its governance except Grambling College and the New Orleans and Shreveport branches of Southern University.

In 1967 the Board of Education approved doctoral programs at five colleges under its jurisdiction. The main campus at LSU, the New Orleans branch, and the Medical Center also offer graduate programs through the doctoral level.

In 1968 there had been for more than 20 years some agitation in favor of some sort of amalgamation or "coordination" of the two systems. This reached a raucous height during the middle 'Sixties. Proposed constitutional amendments were defeated in successive legislatures, but finally in 1968 an amendment authorizing an agency of liaison, planning, and coordination passed the legislature and was approved by popular vote later that year. This is the Louisiana Coordinating Council for Higher Education, composed of 15 members: one representative of each of the two "big boards," and 13 other lay members appointed by the governor. It is directed to approve or disapprove the establishment of new institutions or degree programs, and to develop an ongoing state-wide plan for higher education.

The legislature of 1946 directed the governor to appoint a "Special Educational Committee" of eight members to study the entire educational system at all levels. This was done, and the Committee

---

[1]*Jones* v. *State Board of Education*, 219 La. 630, 53 So. 2d 792 (1951).

LOUISIANA

Appropriations for Annual Operating Expenses of Higher Education in Louisiana, Alternate Fiscal Years, 1959-60 through 1969-70 (in thousands of dollars)

Institutions	Year 1959-60	Year 1961-62	Year 1963-64	Year 1965-66	Year 1967-68	Year 1969-70
Louisiana State U[1]	20,194	23,532	27,566	33,873	44,106	48,252
Southern University[2]	4,207[3]	4,208	5,368	6,665	8,748	9,172
U of Southwestern La	4,101	4,394	4,909	6,374	8,026	8,025
La Polytech Inst	3,347	3,571	3,866	5,143	6,555	6,781
Northeastern St Coll	1,762	2,108	2,424	3,751	4,929	5,424
Northwestern St Coll	2,837	2,738	3,053	4,090	5,239	5,306
Southeastern St Coll	1,854	1,971	2,553	4,131	4,747	4,642
Grambling College	2,185	2,393	2,615	3,514	3,983	4,637
McNeese St Coll	1,862	1,937	2,274	2,855	3,880	3,901
Nicholls St Coll	627	870	1,219	1,922	2,910	3,213
Delgado Jr Coll						1,344
Confederate Mem'l Nsg Sch (Shreveport)						196
Total	42,976[4]	48,318	55,847	72,318	93,123	101,244[5]

[1] Includes main campus at Baton Rouge; New Orleans campus; medical school at New Orleans; medical center at Shreveport; and branch campuses at Alexandria, Eunice, and Shreveport.

[2] Includes Baton Rouge campus; New Orleans campus; and a branch campus at Shreveport.

[3] Includes $455,000 for new branch at New Orleans.

[4] An additional $1,435,000 would become available for teachers' salaries in institutions of higher education if mineral lease revenues met expectations. These revenues were not budgeted because they were coming to be regarded as nonrecurring and too hazardous a base for budgeting.

[5] Includes $141,000 for the new Coordinating Council for Higher Education and $121,000 for the Higher Education Assistance Commission.

reported in May, 1948, recommending the state colleges be taken away from the State Board of Education and placed under a new "Board of Control of State Colleges and Special Schools"; and that the three "big boards" should then form voluntarily a State Coordinating Council on Education, composed of two members from each board. The 1948 legislature did not create the proposed third governing board, but created the Coordinating Council, as proposed, between the two existing boards, with the director of higher education in the state department of education to act as its chairman, *ex officio*.

However, a later study reported in 1955: "The Coordinating Council . . . is not functioning at the present time." It went on to mention that: "The Presidents' Council meets on call of the State Superintendent to discuss problems which he wishes to place before it. The Presidents at times suggest items for discussion by the Council."[2] Another report of 1958 was harsher: "The present advisory coordinating council has been authorized since 1949, and during this period has proved to be totally ineffective, and the reconstitution of such an advisory group will not solve the problem."[3]

The 1955 report had recommended (but to no avail) that the Coordinating Council be reconstituted and given a staff secretariat responsible to it alone. The 1958 report, as previously quoted, placed no confidence in this proposal, but instead recommended creation of "A Board of Regents for all institutions of higher education, to serve as the *governing board* for the state colleges and as a *coordinating council* for these state colleges and Louisiana State University, thus unifying the administration of higher education."

Notable was the further recommendation that "All funds for higher education should be appropriated to the Board of Regents for allocation to the institutions of higher learning, and appropriations directly to a specific institution of higher learning should be prohibited." (Compare Oklahoma, *infra* herein.) A proposed constitutional amendment and a wordy proposed implementing statute were included with the report of the Joint Legislative Committee, but eventually all came to naught.

For fiscal year 1959-60 Louisiana was already appropriating more than $40 million of state tax funds for annual operating expenses of higher education. The state ranked eleventh among the 50, as measured merely by the magnitude of the annual support. This was a high position, well above parity with the state's total population, which was then only 3¼ million. From 1960 to mid-1968 the population gained 14½ per cent (substantially more than the national average gain of

---

[2] *Report of the Louisiana Commission on Higher Education* (1955), quoted at p. 5 of the *Report of the Joint Legislative Committee*, cited below.

[3] *Special Report of the Joint Legislative Committee on Higher Education.* Baton Rouge: Governor's Office, April, 1958. 29 pp. litho. (Senator Rex. C. McCullough, chairman).

11½ per cent); but over the same period the gain in annual operating support of higher education from state tax funds was markedly slow.

The total rose to $99 million for fiscal year 1968-69, an increase of 124½ per cent over the preceding nine years, as compared with the weighted average nation-wide gain of 261 per cent for the same period. Measured by rate of gain, Louisiana ranked forty-second among the states. No state of equal population showed slower gains. Measured by simple magnitude of annual appropriations, Louisiana dropped from eleventh place in 1959-60 to seventeenth place in 1968-69. Even this, however, is a comparatively high rank, considering the size and resources of the state—Louisiana ranked nineteenth in total population in 1968. Additional support for this latter view is visible when it is noticed that Louisiana's state tax investment per citizen in annual operating expenses of higher education in 1968 was $27.17 (ranking twenty-second); the ratio of this sum to average personal income was 1.02 per cent (ranking fourteenth); and the total of state and local tax collections per $1,000 of personal income for fiscal year 1966-67 was $116—well above the national average of $105.50.

The annually revised map showing what type of tax produces the largest amount of revenue in each of the 50 states, which is circulated by Commerce Clearing House, Inc., and widely reproduced in the press, has for several years shown Louisiana to be unique as the only state getting more revenue from *severance taxes* than from any other type of tax. In 1968, 32 states were deriving their largest revenues from general sales or gross income taxes and 15 had net income taxes as their leading source. Two states were getting more from state gasoline taxes than from any other type: Oklahoma, because the state sales, income, and severance taxes were all at low rates and not very productive; and New Hampshire, because the state had neither a sales tax nor an income tax other than an inconsequential levy on personal income from interest and dividends only. Louisiana alone had severance taxes as the biggest source. Taxes on the extraction of minerals, oil, gas, timber, and other resources were apparently equitably fixed and efficiently administered.

Louisiana also had a general sales tax and personal and corporate income taxes, but all at low rates. If these were brought up to average, the total of revenues would be substantially increased.

It has been reported that Louisiana's appropriation of $99 million for annual operating expenses of higher education in fiscal year 1968-69 was $11.08 per $1,000 of personal income; that the amount per student at four-year institutions only (in 1967) was $1,098; and that the ratio of the appropriation to the total of state tax collections (in 1967) was 12.6 per cent; also it was shown that all these figures were distinctly higher than the average among 16 southern states. [4]

---

[4] Page 7 in E. F. Schietinger, *Fact Book on Higher Education in the South, 1968*. Atlanta: Southern Regional Education Board, 1968. 74 pp.

Relations between the public higher educational institutions and the non-educational central fiscal and administrative agencies in Louisiana apparently leave a good deal to be desired. The brief selected quotations which follow are from a competently prepared and recent publication of the Southern Association of Colleges and Schools, the regional accrediting agency functioning in 11 states of the South. [5]

As to the sensitive area of academic personnel management: "Louisiana's approach is perhaps the unique one. There is no central review of detailed salary budgets; but a detailed budget, once adopted by the institution and approved by the Division of Administration and the Legislative Budget Committee, can be changed only with position-by-position approval of the central budget officials. Approval is not always granted."

Nonacademic employees are "treated as state employees, and their salaries are established through central position review processes. In addition, promotions and position reclassifications are handled by the state personnel agency."

As to allotment of appropriated funds, in the case of higher education most states use the allotment system merely as a mechanical device to authorize the expenditure of appropriations. However, Louisiana (and Florida and North Carolina) "subdivide appropriations and otherwise involve central agencies in the process of continually revising higher education operating budgets. This often interferes with and always delays academic decisions." In Louisiana (and the two other states named) "higher education appropriations are allotted by several categories, and permission must be obtained from the budget agency to make transfers from one category to another. . . . Considerable paperwork is involved and complaints result."

Moreover: "Policies are in effect which result in denial of some types of proposed transfers. The continual budget revision processes involve the central agency in decisions concerning the use of unanticipated fee income, the disposition of salary moneys not used because of vacant positions, and other interim decisions. These issues, as well as the transfer of funds, are points of controversy and greatly reduce the flexibility of academic administration."

Summing up: "A common characteristic of a considerable amount of budgetary control is the continual, regular confrontation of budget officers and higher educators and a steady flow of paperwork throughout the year as budget revisions and salary adjustments are submitted for approval by state agencies. As a result, relatively in-

---

[5] *Higher Education and Financial Control by State Governments in Southern Association States.* Atlanta: Southern Association of Colleges and Schools, March 1968. 20 pp. unpaginated.

significant matters consume an almost overwhelming amount of time." And: "The reams of paper and level of friction associated with the review of individual positions, the transfer of funds among major budget categories, the classification and pay plans for academic and related positions, and similar processes of traditional budget control systems seriously reduce effective communications between state government and higher education, and should be eliminated."

MAINE

With a population of a little less than 1 million, and an estimated gain of only 1 per cent from 1960 to 1968, this northernmost and easternmost New England state made spectacular gains in state support of operating expenses of higher education over that period. The nine-year gain 1960-1969 was more than 432 per cent—nearly twice the nation-wide weighted average among the 50 states (261 per cent).

In common with the other northeastern states, the rapid gain was in part due to a low start. The total appropriation for fiscal year 1959-60 ($3,356,000) was more than doubled by 1961-62 ($7,238,000), and more than doubled again by 1967-68 ($18,167,000). Thus it was more than quintupled within the first seven years of the 1960's. Only five states, all northeastern except Hawaii and Kentucky, showed higher rates of gain.

A special session of the legislature in 1967 raised Maine's general sales tax to 4½ per cent from the former 4 per cent. The state had no personal or corporate income tax. In 1968 Maine continued to stand very low among the states as to state tax investment per citizen for annual operating expenses of higher education ($18.50, ranking forty-fourth) and as to ratio of state tax investment to total personal income (0.65, ranking forty-third). Moreover, its total of state and local tax collections for fiscal year 1966-67 stood at $106.27 per $1,000 of personal income, less than $1 above the average among the states. The legislature of 1969 enacted wholly new personal and corporation income taxes, the personal income tax to be graduated from 1 per cent to 6 per cent, with a personal exemption of $1,000. Estimated additional revenue was expected to be about $25 million per year.

Maine has long had a state university which is also the Morrill land-grant college; and five tiny state normal schools, recently become state colleges—among the smallest of their kind in the nation. In 1957 the University, with its main campus at Orono, acquired a branch campus in Portland, the state's principal city and seaport, by absorbing a private junior college there; and in 1961 it also took over the small private institution known as Portland University, consisting of a law school and a school of business administration. This law school was approved by the Maine Board of Bar Examiners and had statutory authority to confer LL.B. degrees.

Half a century ago the University of Maine had operated a law school for about 20 years around the turn of the century, but it had been

171

MAINE

Appropriations for Annual Operating Expenses of Higher Education in Maine, Alternate Fiscal Years, 1959-60 through 1969-70 (in thousands of dollars)

Institutions	Year 1959-60	Year 1961-62	Year 1963-64	Year 1965-66	Year 1967-68	Year 1969-70
U of Maine	4,477	4,211	5,453	7,670	10,646	22,264[1]
State Colleges:						
Gorham		796	955	1,416	1,848	2,095
Farmington		716	846	1,030	1,351	1,475
Aroostock		271	356	472	735	973
Washington		270	324	501	604	788
Fort Kent		179	242	332	425	534
Maine Maritime Acad		235	284	356	451	475[2]
Voc-Tech Institutes:						
Northern Maine[3]		216	295	376	571	
Southern Maine[4]				160	430	
Central Maine[5]			250	362	422	2,750[2]
Eastern Maine[6]					375	
Presque I Voc Sch		250				
Schools of Prac Nurs'g:						
Southern Maine					59	
Northern Maine					42	
Waterville					30	
Scholarship fund[7]		50	50	50	50	
Scholarship Admin					77	
New Eng H E Compact		44	44	46	52	
Total	4,477	7,238	9,099	12,771	18,167	25,984[2]

[1] Includes all units of the University of Maine, plus the five state colleges. Their support and control was consolidated with the University in 1968.

[2] These figures are estimates.

[3] Formerly Maine Vocational-Technical Institute.

[4] Formerly Androscoggin Vocational Institute.

[5] Formerly Northeast Maine Vocational-Technical Institute.

[6] Formerly Penobscot County Vocational Institute.

[7] For state teachers colleges only.

discontinued. Thus 1961 marked the University's second entry into the field of professional legal education.

Prior to 1968 the five small state colleges were all under the governance of the State Board of Education, as also were the four vocational-technical schools. The Maine Maritime Academy was under its own Board of Trustees. The Board of Trustees of the University of Maine governed only the University. After much study and also after much controversy, the legislature of 1968 removed the state colleges from the State Board of Education and placed them under the jurisdiction of a reconstituted board of trustees of the University of Maine, with all six institutions to be known thenceforth as the University of Maine. The vocational-technical colleges were left under the State Board of Education, and the Maritime Academy continued with its own board of trustees. The new board of trustees of the University of Maine was to have a chancellor and staff as its executive arm, with the chancellor not to be concurrently the head of any of the institutions.

This sweeping reorganization, reminiscent of similar strokes in a few other states from 30 to 70 years ago, resembles the move made by the even smaller state of New Hampshire in 1966, when it expanded the board of trustees of that university and gave it jurisdiction also over the state's two minuscule state colleges at Keene and Plymouth, and thus revived a plan of governance which had been moribund for 20 years, since New York created its agglomerate State University of New York with 30 institutions under a single governing board, in 1948. New Hampshire and Maine are adjacent to each other; both are only a short distance from upstate New York; and all share, in part, the ancient New England tradition that public institutions of higher education are second-rate and that their institutional autonomy and freedom and flexibility and morale as living organisms cannot be of much consequence. Time, and the quality of the governance issuing from the newly-consolidated boards, will tell whether these drastic changes can be justified in the long run.

Note that Maine joined in the trend toward removing the state colleges from the State Board of Education, which is observable in several other states within the past decade. State colleges are no longer "normal schools" and properly appendages of the state department of public instruction, as they were once regarded. They are now recognized as belonging to the state college and university complexes—a great gain.

Some New England judges have been quite slow to grasp the concept of the state university as it has long been understood in other parts of the country. For example, as recently as 1909 and 1911 the Supreme Judicial Court of Maine solemnly declared the University of Maine was a private corporation (to reinforce its decisions justifying local taxation of fraternity houses located on university land). This weird view was challenged and convincingly refuted by Professor Clarence W. Peabody in the *Maine Law Review*, Vol. 13: 187-197 (June 1920).[1]

In December 1969 the new Board of Trustees of the University of Maine announced its intent to detach the Portland units from the jurisdiction of the Orono campus and consolidate them with Gorham State College to form a new unit to be styled "the University of Maine, Portland-Gorham," which would also be developed as a center of graduate studies.

The other four state colleges would continue as four-year campuses of the University, chiefly for the education of teachers; but two of them (Aroostook and Farmington) would add "strong liberal arts programs towards eventually granting a liberal arts degree." All would be encouraged to add some one- and two-year programs (lower division) fitting the needs of their respective regions. The Board also expected to develop two-year community colleges in centers of population having no institutions of higher education, the first such campuses to be at Bangor and Augusta.

The University at Orono would continue as the flagship and exemplar, providing leadership and assistance in the development of the other campuses, "because of its resources in faculty and equipment, experience and tradition."

---

[1] *Orono* v. *Sigma Alpha Epsilon*, 105 Maine 214, 74 A. 19 (1909); and *Orono* v. *Kappa Sigma Society*, 108 Maine 320, 80 A. 831 (1911).

MARYLAND

With 3¾ million people in 1968, Maryland had gained more than 21 per cent since 1960. Only six states showed larger percentage gains in population—Nevada (59 per cent), Arizona (28 per cent), Florida (24½ per cent), Hawaii (23 per cent), Alaska (22½ per cent), and California (22 per cent).

Maryland's percentage gain in state appropriations for higher education did not, however, keep pace with the average among the 50 states (234½ per cent as against 261 per cent). By that measure Maryland ranked only twenty-sixth, while ranking seventh in rate of population gain.

In 1968 the state had a 3 per cent general sales tax (the modest average rate, only half that of its adjacent neighbor, Pennsylvania). Prior to 1967 the state income tax had been at the flat rate of 3 per cent. The legislature of that year replaced this with a graduated levy of 2 to 5 per cent, intended to produce $184 million of additional state revenue during its first year, as well as a separate $98 million for distribution to Baltimore City and the 23 counties of Maryland. A determined attempt was made to defeat this measure by popular referendum, and a supposedly successful drive collected some 28,000 such petitions. However, in 1968 the Court of Appeals upheld the tax statute by holding that the affidavits on the referendum petitions were erroneous and defective, and did not comply with the referendum requirements of the state constitution.

The 1969 legislature raised the rate of the general sales tax to 4 per cent from the former 3 per cent.

In fiscal year 1966-67 Maryland's total state and local tax collections were $103.35 per $1,000 of personal income—about $2 less than the nation-wide average. In 1968 the state tax cost per citizen for annual operating expenses of higher education was $18.50 (ranking forty-fourth). Its ratio of state tax cost to total personal income was 0.58 (ranking forty-fifth). Clearly it would seem Maryland has considerable latitude within which to improve its state support of higher education.

Maryland's complement of state institutions includes the University of Maryland (an early private institution in Baltimore, later combined with the land-grant college at College Park, and eventually made the state university with main campus at College

Park, a cluster of professional schools in Baltimore, now having a four-year degree-granting branch campus at Catonsville, and a division at Princess Anne known as Maryland State College and predominantly attended by Negroes). There are six state colleges, including Morgan State College, an institution predominantly for Negroes, existing as a private institution in Baltimore from 1867 to 1939, thereafter as a state college of liberal arts and teacher-education, now including master's degree programs primarily for elementary and secondary school teachers; three state colleges, at Towson, Frostburg, and Salisbury; and two lesser-developed state colleges predominantly attended by Negroes, Bowie State College at Bowie and Coppin State College in Baltimore.

In February 1960 a report on suitable organization, development, and governance of this rather diverse and complex system was issued by a body known as the Governor's Commission to Study the Problem of Expansion of the University of Maryland. [1] It recommended that the three state teachers colleges be made branches of the University of Maryland, and that it be authroized and financed to set up three other similar branches in three locations designated as the central eastern shore, southern Maryland, and the two counties of Washington and Frederick. All would emphasize teacher-education, but would have added facilities to provide A.B. and B.S. degrees in selected other curricula. This plan was said to be opposed by the redoubtable Thomas G. Pullen, Jr., long-time state superintendent of education (then senior among the chief state school officers of the 50 states), and other influential persons; and apparently it virtually came to naught.

Early in 1961 the legislature requested Governor Tawes to appoint a new Commission on the Expansion of Public Higher Education in Maryland, and it issued in June 1962 a report entitled *Public Higher Education in Maryland, 1961-1975.* [2] Staff director was Francis E. Rourke, professor of political science at the Johns Hopkins University. The report includes wise conclusions and convincing passages. It concluded that college enrollments in the state would be more than doubled by 1975, and that the major part of the increase would have to be absorbed by the public institutions. "It is true that most of the private colleges will expand, but on the whole their plans envision increases of only about 50 per cent or thereabouts; so the Commission concludes that by 1975 more than 80 per cent of Maryland's high school graduates continuing into higher education will be enrolled in the public institutions."

---

[1] *A Plan for Expanding the University of Maryland.* 1960. 44 pp.

[2] John N. Curlett, Chairman; Milton S. Eisenhower, Wilson H. Elkins, Martin D. Jenkins, Thomas G. Pullen, Jr., and others, with Francis E. Rourke, Director. *Public Higher Education in Maryland, 1961-1975.* Baltimore: June 1962. 69 pp. (Mimeo. version, same date, 138 pp.)

Viewing this future, the Commission says: "There are those who argue for a more restrictive policy on admissions as a method of meeting the rising demand for higher education. But the Commission is convinced that as many qualified young people as possible should actually be encouraged to obtain the advanced technical or academic training they will need to find career opportunities in our society. Both the economic development of Maryland and even our survival as a nation may ultimately depend upon a successful effort to upgrade the skills of our population."

Recommended was a tripartite plan of organization: (1) the University of Maryland under its own Board of Regents, as before; (2) the 6 state colleges all to be governed by a new Board of Trustees of the State Colleges; and (3) the two-year community colleges, already 12 and soon to be increased in number, to continue under the general oversight of the State Board of Education.

It is noteworthy that Morgan State College (predominantly Negro) was the only one of the six state colleges in position to make any serious claim to being a developed liberal arts college; and its president, Martin D. Jenkins, argued cogently that it would suffer if placed under a governing board responsible for five other institutions of different types and in widely different stages of development. As a result, the implementing statute was written to provide that Morgan State College should continue under its own board of trustees until such time as at least three of the other five state colleges should have become accredited as liberal arts colleges. Morgan State College came under the jurisdiction of the Board of Trustees of the State Colleges July 1, 1967. In 1963 both Morgan State College and St. Mary's College were outside the purview of the board of trustees, and the State Board of Education had general supervisory authority over the community colleges. In 1968, the General Assembly set up the State Board for Community Colleges and empowered it to fulfill the role for community colleges previously held by the State Department of Education. It offered these institutions the option of having local governing boards independent of the county school board. The result is that the community colleges are governed at the state level by the State Board for Community Colleges and at the local level by their respective community or regional boards.

St. Mary's College of Maryland, which was formerly a two-year junior college for women, in the fall of 1967 became a coeducational full four-year, liberal arts college having the role and scope of the state colleges with its own board of trustees.

The Commission's principal recommendation regarding institutional programs was for "the conversion of each of the state teachers colleges into a full-fledged liberal arts institution, providing general undergraduate instruction as well as the traditional teacher-education program."

MARYLAND

Appropriations for Annual Operating Expenses of Higher Education in Maryland, Alternate Fiscal Years, 1959-60 through 1969-70 (in thousands of dollars)

Institutions	Year 1959-60	Year 1961-62	Year 1963-64	Year 1965-66	Year 1967-68	Year 1969-70
U of Maryland (incl med units)		20,461	24,696	33,678	45,510	57,675
State colleges:						
Towson		1,528	2,072	2,819	4,912	6,730
Morgan		1,908	2,308	3,126	3,737	4,686
Frostburg		914	1,425	1,787	2,458	3,672
Salisbury		522	683	912	1,290	1,644
Coppin		468	580	763	1,151	1,529
Bowie		505	660	801	1,144	2,271
St Mary's Coll of Md[1]		229	243	352	757	953
For matching NDEA		120	66			
Subtotal, Md St Colls		6,194	8,037	10,660	15,349	21,585
State Scholarship Bd				706	77	3,471
H E Loan Corp				93	295	686
Bd of Trustees of St Colls				78	117	218
Adv Council for H E				77	166	224
State aid to Jr Colls				2,096	4,708	7,845

Private institutions:					
Johns Hopkins U	210	210	310	248	
Hood College[2]	100	100	181	158	
Washington Coll	100	100	113	157	
Western Md Coll[3]	100	100	132	142	
St John's Coll	80	80	118	111	
St Joseph's Coll[4,5]				104	
C of Notre Dame of Md[4,5]				102	
Mt St Agnes College[5]				90	
Mt St Mary's College[5]				86	
Loyola College[5]				93	
Peabody Institute	35	35	42	44	
Maryland Institute	25	25	33	43	
Subtotal, Priv Insts	650	650	929	1,378	
Total	23,818[6]	27,304	33,383[7]	48,217	67,700	92,132[8]

[1] A state institution, not to be confused with the 11 county and local junior colleges.

[2] The Maryland Court of Appeals sustained a 1966 appropriation to this tenuously church-related college, for capital improvement, as against the contention that it violated the "establishment of religion" clause of the First Amendment to the U.S. Constitution; the U.S. Supreme Court declined to review the case.

[3] A 1966 appropriation to this Methodist church-connected college for capital improvement was held unconstitutional in the above decision.

[4] In the above decision, 1966 appropriations to these two Roman Catholic colleges, for capital improvements, were held unconstitutional.

[5] These five Roman Catholic colleges were added to the list of private colleges receiving small tax-fund subsidies for operating expenses in 1967. No appropriations were made to private institutions in 1968 or 1969.

[6] This appropriation is for the entire state.

[7] Appropriations of $150,000 to the Board of Trustees of State Colleges, and $25,000 to the Advisory Council for Higher Education bring the total to $33,558,000.

[8] Includes $428,000 for computer center.

At the apex of the state-wide system the Commission urged placing an Advisory Council for Higher Education composed of three representative members of each of the three major boards mentioned previously, plus a few ranking professional educators representative of the three components. A legislative act of 1963 adopted and enacted this feature, as well as nearly all other recommendations of the Commission; but in 1964 the composition of the Advisory Council was drastically changed by abolishing it and creating a new agency of the same name, composed of nine members to serve for overlapping terms of six years, "no two of whom shall have attended the same institution of higher learning," and all to be appointed by the governor with the advice and consent of the senate.

It was reported that the governor had become adamantly opposed to the principle of representation recommended by the Commission and adopted by the 1963 legislature. Two immediate results of the change were obvious: it gave the governor opportunity to appoint the whole Council, and almost certainly it gave the private college interests a larger voice. The author, when invited to consult with members of the Commission in 1962, had recommended the structure approved by the Commission and enacted by the legislature in 1963, and takes a dim view of the drastic change of 1964, though he passes no judgment on the motives of the then governor.

A 1968 amendment, effective July 1, 1968, substituted "Maryland" for "Advisory" and substituted 13 members for 9 members. The amendment also provided that the four members added to the Council in 1968 by the governor include one representative of the University of Maryland, nominated by the Board of Regents of the University of Maryland, one representative of the state colleges nominated by the Board of Trustees of the State Colleges, one member of the state board responsible for community colleges and one representative of the several private institutions of higher education in the state.

Additional paragraphs of the eminently well-reasoned report of the Commission in 1962 merit preservation: "While higher education is a cost to the state, it is also an investment—perhaps the most important investment any state makes. Unless Maryland is prepared to support a system of public higher education capable of providing genuine intellectual enrichment, it wastes not only money, but resources much more precious—the minds and energies of its young people. . . .

"Of all the functions which the state undertakes to perform, education is the most important, since the level of achievement in all other areas of activity ultimately depends upon the success of our educational effort. In this report the Commission has tried to spell out its conviction that while the level of investment in higher education will continue to rise, the rate of return will continue to grow also. And it is a return that will enrich not only the student and the state, but the national and international communities of which we are all a part."

Finally: "The money Maryland puts into higher education is thus spent neither to satisfy the ambitions of the student, nor to gratify the pride and ambition of parents. It is an investment the community makes in its own behalf."

Maryland apparently has no state constitutional inhibitions against direct appropriations of state tax funds to private or denominational colleges or universities. It has a considerable history of such appropriations, though they have usually been comparatively small, few in number, and often intermittent. Some of the history was traced by Chief Justice Marbury of the Maryland Court of Appeals when the court sustained the constitutionality of a $1½ million issue of state bonds directed by an act of 1951, with the proceeds to go to the Johns Hopkins University.[3]

The constitutions of some 41 states continue to forbid the direct appropriation of state tax funds to nonpublic or sectarian institutions. Pennsylvania, however, makes such appropriations to selected non-denominational institutions on a considerable scale. This was also authorized by New York in 1968, but not funded in that year. However, $20 million was appropriated for the purpose in 1969. Thus, in both of these states, state tax money can go directly only to nonsectarian institutions.

It was in 1966 that this issue, after the legislature had made modest appropriations for capital outlays to four private colleges (one Methodist, two Roman Catholic, and one having a tenuous relation to another Protestant denomination), was contested in Maryland. The question was the application of the clause of the First Amendment to the Constitution of the United States which declares that "Congress shall make no law respecting an establishment of religion, or prohibiting the free exercise thereof." The same words also restrain the states since the adoption of the Fourteenth Amendment. Were these four colleges "establishments of religion"?

Three justices of the Court of Appeals, Hammond, Horney, and Marbury (a minority), believed they were not. Justice Hammond wrote: "I think that the four grants under consideration were made pursuant to long-established practice to further a secular public purpose and that any aid or benefit flowing from them to religion would be slight, vague and purely incidental." But that was the dissenting opinion which did not prevail except in the matter of the fourth college.

Four justices (the majority, led by Chief Justice Prescott) decided, after examining the evidence as to the various religious

---

[3]*Johns Hopkins University et al.* v. *Williams*, 199 Md. 382, 86 A. 2d 892 (1952).

connections of each of the colleges and their degree of religious control, that the first three were sufficiently dominated by their respective churches to make a direct state appropriation to them amount to a violation of the United States Constitution. As to the fourth, it was adjudged to be so little connected to the church as to justify the opposite conclusion. Thus, the whole court agreed that the appropriation to Hood College was valid; and the majority of the court held that the other three were unconstitutional. [4]

Both parties attempted to appeal to the United States Supreme Court, but that tribunal declined to review the case. Thus it stood as the law in Maryland.

The legislature of 1967, apparently in disregard or defiance of the foregoing Court of Appeals decision, made small appropriations for annual operating expenses to 12 private and denominational universities and colleges, including the Johns Hopkins University, all 4 of the colleges involved in the litigation just sketched, and 3 additional Catholic colleges that had not been subsidized before. The sums ranged from $43,000 to $248,000, and the total for the year was $1,378,000. No appropriations of this kind were made by the 1968 legislature for fiscal year 1968-69.

An act of 1965 increased the state's contribution for operating expenses of local public community-junior colleges to $300 per student per year, from the previous figure of $225 per student. A companion act also formalized the doctrine, prevalent in New York since 1948, but now becoming a bit tired and archaic, that in general the operating funds of public junior colleges should come one-third from the state, one-third from the local taxing district, and one-third from the students as student fees.

Saint Mary's College of Maryland was a state junior college, not to be confused with the local public junior colleges or with any private college, Roman Catholic or otherwise. Since 1967 it has been a four-year coeducational state college of liberal arts, having its own separate board of trustees.

---

[4] *Horace Mann League* v. *Board of Public Works of Maryland*, (Court of Appeals, June 2, 1966). *Certiorari* denied by U. S. Supreme Court, 35 U. S. Law Week 3174 (November 15, 1966).

MASSACHUSETTS

Though a populous commonwealth (nearly 5½ million people in mid-1968), the Old Bay State is a comparative lightweight in state tax support of operating expenses of higher education. For fiscal year 1968-69 the appropriation ($69,097,000) was almost the same as that of Kansas ($69,108,000) which has much less than half the population (2 1/3 million); and less than half that of Indiana ($144,715,000) which has fewer people than Massachusetts. Other such examples abound. Compare Massachusetts with Illinois ($301,136,000); the ratio of population is one to two, but the ratio of dollars is less than one to four.

These disparities are explained in part, but in much smaller part than is commonly supposed, by the fact that perhaps 70 per cent of all students beyond high school in Massachusetts are in private institutions—a higher percentage than in any other state. But we cannot step from that fact to the smug conclusion that the young people of Massachusetts have all the higher educational opportunities they need or want, with imperial Harvard and half a dozen other private universities, and a dozen or more distinguished private colleges. Many of these institutions are not only high-fee and highly selective in admissions, but also take care to maintain a nation-wide and international clientele, giving preference to applicants from distant states and seeing to it that their student places are not monopolized by local residents of Massachusetts.

Not only do the well-endowed private universities and colleges draw high proportions of their students from outside the state, but also much of their financial support in the form of fees and gifts comes from sources external to the state. These circumstances do not allow us to conclude that the people of Massachusetts are providing adequate support, if not through taxation then through gifts and fees, for the higher education of the young people of their own state. It is not so simple as that. No one doubts the right of the private universities and colleges to do as just sketched—and indeed they are an asset to the nation and make themselves an economic asset to their state by so doing—but they do not provide higher educational opportunities for many Massachusetts students and prospective students. As everywhere, the bulk of that duty falls upon the tax-supported low-fee public universities, colleges, and junior colleges. (The fees even in the public universities, however, are higher in the Northeast than anywhere else in the nation.)

The University of Massachusetts—with main campus at Amherst, a branch campus in Boston, and the state's first public medical college now a-building at Worcester—was for many years only a small state agricultural college; but within approximately a quarter of a century it has become a thriving state university. It still possesses only two-thirds of the title of "land-grant college" of Massachusetts, with one-third of the proceeds of the Morrill Act continuing to go to the private Massachusetts Institute of Technology in Cambridge.

The nine state colleges, some of which were among the earliest of state normal schools, functioning more than a century ago, have long been kept in a chronic condition of financial anemia. (The Massachusetts College of Art in Boston is also in a sense one of them, making 10 in all).

The small handful of technological institutes, long a distinctive feature of the Massachusetts scene, have recently shaken down to two principal ones at Lowell and North Dartmouth, both of which offer four- and five-year degrees, with the former offering the doctorate in physics. Both apparently maintain a substantial infusion of the liberal arts.

The explosion of the decade was the development of a dozen "regional community colleges" which are in fact state-supported two-year colleges. The fuse began to burn in 1957, in the administration of Governor Foster Furcolo, who was fortunately easily persuaded that here was a development that was long overdue.

First reverting a few years, we may note that immediately after World War II the state had opened and operated a large and lively two-year branch in unused parts of the vast military establishment at Fort Devens, to provide "G.I. education" for the crush of veterans of the armed services who could not be accommodated in sufficient numbers at the main campus of the University of Massachusetts or at the other state institutions. In 1950, when the "veterans' bulge" was showing signs of tapering off, the question of whether the Fort Devens branch should be continued and made a permanent institution, or whether its discontinuance should be planned, was seriously raised. As a result, Arthur J. Klein of Ohio State University, Algo D. Henderson of the New York State Education Department, and the author were engaged to make a study and report on that question.

Readily foreseeing a growing and permanent need and demand for one or more two-year public low-fee colleges in Massachusetts, the team, after finding that the hastily organized and extemporized Fort Devens branch had done and was doing an excellent job, with high morale of students and faculty in the face of many difficulties, recommended that it be kept continuously in operation and made a permanent institution. Notwithstanding, a traditionally sluggish and

bureaucratic state administration managed virtually to squelch the report, and to accomplish the abolition of the institution within a short time.
Seven years later the situation was radically different. In 1957 Governor Furcolo had established a joint legislative-executive agency known as the Special Commission on Audit of State Needs, and one of its first assignments was to examine and report on the needs of the commonwealth in higher education, especially with reference to public junior colleges. Its first report was published in March 1958, recommending that the governor and the legislature (1) expand the facilities of all existing public institutions, and (2) establish a new Board of Regional Community Colleges, which would plan for 8 to 12 regional community colleges, so located as to be within commuting-distance of the homes of about 98 per cent of the population; then establish and operate such colleges.[1]
The governor embodied these ideas in a special message in July, and the legislature substantially adopted them in October. By December 1958 the governor had appointed the 15 members of the Board, and the legislature had voted $1 million for initial planning and development of the system of regional community colleges. Ten years later the Board was operating 12 two-year colleges, to which the legislature appropriated $7,881,000 for annual operating expenses for fiscal year 1968-69. This was about 11½ per cent of the total state-wide appropriation for annual operating expenses of all higher education. It was equal to nearly half the total appropriation to the 10 state colleges, and approached a ratio of one to four with the total appropriation to the University of Massachusetts. Eight of the 12 regional community colleges were provided with more than half a million dollars each. Their second decade bids fair to be as expansive as their first.
Some of the impetus toward development of the community college system was contributed by John Powers Mallan, a professor of political science who was executive secretary of the Special Commission on Audit of State Needs. A paper delivered by him in April 1959 at the American Assembly Conference on State Problems, at Tufts University, cogently summarized the foregoing story and marshaled additional data in support of public higher educational expansion in the Bay State. [2]
The University of Massachusetts (and the other state institutions of higher education) has been especially unfortunate for many years in being subject to much detailed interference from state fiscal and

---

[1]*Needs in Massachusetts Higher Education with Special Reference to Community Colleges.* Boston: Special Commission on Audit of State Needs, 1958. 87 pp. (Legislative Printers' version, 118 pp.)
[2]John Powers Mallan, "Massachusetts Needs in Education." Reproduced in *Grapevine*, pp. 75-78 and 81-84, November and December 1959.

MASSACHUSETTS

Appropriations for Annual Operating Expenses of Higher Education in Massachusetts, Alternate Fiscal Years,
1959-60 through 1969-70 (in thousands of dollars)

Institutions	Year 1959-60	Year 1961-62	Year 1963-64[1]	Year 1965-66	Year 1967-68	Year 1969-70
U of Massachusetts (incl Amherst & Boston)	9,261	11,393		18,148[2]	29,362[3]	39,754
State Colleges:						
Boston	5,526	943		1,782	2,955	4,063
Salem		768		1,121	2,232	3,129
Bridgewater		1,286		1,212	2,117	2,855
Fitchburg		966		868	1,433	2,033
Worcester		640		764	1,305	1,912
Framingham		831		685	1,138	1,791
Westfield		449		592	1,217	1,894
Lowell		448		546	1,096	1,827
North Adams		346		355	754	872
Mass Coll of Art		373		355	531	640
Mass Maritime Acad	455	514		357	496	517
Bd of Trustees, st colls					468	344
Subtotal, State Colleges	5,981	7,564		8,637	15,742	21,877
Technological Institutes:						
Lowell Tech Inst		1,584		1,882	3,438	4,905
Southeastern Mass Tech				1,446	2,742	3,472
Bradford Durfee C of T		478				
New Bedford Inst of T		490				
Subtotal, Tech Insts	2,139	2,552		3,328	6,180	8,377

Community Colleges:						
Massachusetts Bay	192	399			924	1,134
Holyoke		262			602	1,157
Springfield Tech Inst					1,000[4]	1,269
Massasoit					545	966
Quinsigamond		233			672	835
Northern Essex	78	229			611	892
North Shore		97			534	962
Bristol					377	885
Berkshire	147	212			452	665
Cape Cod	79	196			406	579
Mt Wachusett		129			379	610
Greenfield		152			350	577
Bd of Reg Comm Colls					257	485
Subtotal, Comm Colls	496	1,909			7,109[5]	11,016
Bd of Higher Educ					953	4,254
Total	17,381[6]	22,006[6]	19,874	32,022	59,346	85,278

[1] No report for this year.

[2] In Boston is a two-year branch campus, opened in 1965. Also included in the appropriation is $100,000 for the employment of a dean and other personnel to formulate and establish the educational program of the University of Massachusetts Medical School in Worcester, which is currently in the planning stages.

[3] Includes Amherst, branch at Boston, medical college at Worcester.

[4] A new institution created by the 1967 legislature.

[5] The 12 "regional community colleges" are in fact two-year state colleges.

[6] All figures for 1959-60 and 1961-62 represent total institutional budgets. The net state tax-fund appropriations for those fiscal years were $12,167,000 and $15,281,000.

administrative functionaries. The situation was somewhat relieved by the enactment of the so-called "University Freedom Act" in 1956, which had been strenuously advocated by President Jean Paul Mather. The University continued, however, in the astounding strait jacket of a state-prescribed salary scale rigidly administered from the statehouse in such manner that the maximum salary that could be offered a full professor in 1959 was said to be some $8,100. After the legislature of 1959 refused to modify that handicap (though Governor Furcolo advocated a loosening of the chains), President Mather announced his resignation as of June 30, 1960.

With his departure the issue did not die. The 1961 legislature created a Special Commission on the Budgetary Powers of the University of Massachusetts, which reported early in 1962, recommending some further reforms. The legislature enacted, effective July 1, 1962, "An Act relative to the administration of the University of Massachusetts, granting certain powers of self-management." Perhaps the outstanding feature of this measure was: "The trustees shall have complete authority with respect to the election or appointment of the professional staff including terms, conditions and periods of employment, compensation, promotion, classification and reclassification, transfer, demotion, and dismissal within funds available by appropriation of the general court or from other sources. . . .

"In establishing the classification, title and salary plan for the professional staff of the University, the trustees shall give recognition to the need to establish and maintain appropriate academic ranks and titles as may be appropriate for higher education in order to provide for outstanding scholars, scientists and teachers."

Another significant feature was: "The trustees shall have complete authority in determining the University's travel policy. Such power shall include the right to determine who among University personnel should travel within and without the commonwealth at state expense and where such personnel shall travel."

Further: "The trustees may, without prior approval and within limits of appropriations, engage designers, lecturers, students, other professional personnel, and non-employee services, at such rates and for such periods of time as they may determine necessary for the operation of the University."

And a further concession: "Notwithstanding any other provision of law to the contrary, the trustees or officers of the University designated by them shall have the authority to make any purchase or purchases in the amount of $500 or less, and to purchase without limitation of amount: library books and periodicals, educational and scientific supplies and equipment, printing and binding, emergency repairs and replacement parts, and perishable items, without recourse to any other state board, bureau, department or commission. . . ."

These are forward steps, but it must not be supposed that they establish any really comprehensive autonomy for the University of Massachusetts. The overorganized state bureaucracy is like an octopus—cut yourself free from two or three tentacles and you are constricted by half a dozen others. In discussing the comprehensive problem, the Commission preparing the *Report*[3] from which the foregoing legislation sprang, made convincing comments:

"We have attempted to give the trustees authority commensurate with their responsibility and then trust them to do the best job possible with the funds available. It is this Commission's opinion that to do otherwise will deny the State of Massachusetts a really 'first class' University.

"The time has arrived . . . to provide the University with the necessary authority for self-management in proportion to the requirements and responsibilities for educating many young people, for providing broad professional and liberal training, for serving as a major research and service center for the State, and for serving as the capstone of public higher education in the Commonwealth."

Much wisdom is evidenced also in another paragraph: "The effect of the Massachusetts budgetary control system is such that decisions on the allocation of the appropriations are subject to the approval of agencies which are not responsible for University management. . . . Imprudent intervention of state agencies can quickly penetrate to educational policy. Teaching and research simply cannot be measured in customary fiscal terms."

The fever for "coordination" of state-wide public higher education became irresistible in Massachusetts in the Spring of 1962, when the legislature created a Commission to study all levels of education in the commonwealth, and directed it to report not later than December 1963. In 1963 the reporting date had to be extended to December 1964. Benjamin C. Willis, general superintendent of schools in Chicago, was appointed executive director of the Commission and was reputedly paid $30,000 a year for his services while concurrently occupying his $48,000-a-year job in Chicago. (This would insure a thoroughly establishment-oriented report.)

When at last the lithoprinted 70-page *Summary Report*[4] was issued at the end of 1964, it included about a dozen pages prescribing a "master plan" structure for higher education which was in part

---

[3] *Report* of the Special Commission on Budgetary Powers of the University of Massachusetts. Boston: Legislative Printers, January 24, 1962. 54 pp. (House Document No. 3350.)

[4] *Quality Education for Massachusetts: An Investment in the People of the Commonwealth.* Boston: Summary Report of the Special Commission Relative to Improving and Extending Educational Facilities in the Commonwealth, 1964. 70 pp. litho.

enacted by the legislature in 1965, providing for a State Board of Higher Education of 11 members, 4 of whom would be chosen by and from the membership of (1) the trustees of the University of Massachusetts, (2) the board of trustees of the state colleges,[5] (3) the board of regional community colleges, and (4) the board of trustees of one of the two state technological institutes, alternately (these four to serve for terms of one year; and seven other members appointed by the governor for terms of five years). Of these gubernatorial appointees, one must be a member of the governing board of a private institution of higher education in the state, one must be affiliated with the state AFL-CIO, and at least two must be women.

There was also created an Advisory Commission to the Board of Higher Education, consisting of eight persons: the presidents of the University and of the two technological institutes, the executive officers of the State Board of Regional Community Colleges and of one of the state colleges (chosen annually by majority vote of all the state college presidents), the Commissioner of Education, the director of the Advisory Council on Education, and the president of a private college or university in the state (appointed by the governor for a term of five years). The members of the commission attend all meetings of the Board, "except when it meets in executive session."

Seemingly commendable features of the structure of the Board of Higher Education include (1) the representation of the governing boards of the institutions and segments within the public sector (though it is obvious that the University is underrepresented and the technological institutes overrepresented); and (2) as to the Advisory Commission, the fact that all members are active educational administrators, and that they are expected to be present at least at all ordinary meetings of the Board of Higher Education. All this is much better than a wholly lay board meeting with one executive. Why? Because it places in the Board-room the collective knowledge and expertise of half a dozen current presidents of institutions within the system—and this knowledge and expertise is quite unlikely to be matched by that of anyone else in the room.

It is well, too, that the Board of Higher Education is not to supplant any institutional governing board; it is distinctly only a "coordinating" board, empowered in somewhat vague and inconclusive language to review institutional budget askings, to suggest or approve additions of new instructional units (but not of "courses" within broad instructional programs), and to perform statistical and public information services. Even with the vague and redundant definition of

---

[5] An act of 1963 had removed the state colleges from the status of a Division within the Department of Education and had indulged in the shadow-boxing of placing this Division under a board of trustees of the state colleges, this board to consist of the same persons as the state board of education.

its duties, as yet, its bark is probably worse than its bite, and it may not do much restrictive harm. A great deal depends on the wisdom and persuasiveness of its chancellor and small staff.

In November 1966 the electors of the Commonwealth approved by a vote of three to one the retention of the new 3 per cent limited general sales tax which had gone into effect April 1 of that year, and the sales tax now seems to be a permanent part of the state's revenue system. Food, clothing, drugs, fuel, and some other basic necessities are exempted. Within recent years two attempts to amend the state constitution to permit the levying of a graduated state income tax have been heavily defeated at the polls, though proposed by two different legislatures. Flat-rate individual and corporate income taxes have been a reliable standby, however. Effective July 1, 1968, the rate for individuals was raised to 4 per cent from the former 3.075 per cent, and that for corporations went to 7½ per cent from the former 6¾ per cent. Also the former deduction of 100 per cent of federal income tax payments from state taxable incomes was reduced to 50 per cent. The changes were enacted by a Democratic legislature as urged by a Republican governor, and thus have an air of bipartisan consensus.

The 1969 legislature enacted a miscellaneous package of tax increases estimated to produce $100 million of additional revenue annually. The principal item was a 14 per cent surtax on present rates on racing interests, restaurant meals, liquors, hotel and motel rooms, and deeds, as well as banks and insurance companies, utilities, and business corporations.

Massachusetts is at the absolute bottom of the list of 50 states as to state tax investment per citizen for operating expenses of higher education ($12.80 in 1968), and as to the ratio of state tax investment in operating higher education to total personal income (0.33½ per cent in 1968); but this circumstance is partially explained in the first paragraphs of this story; set against it is Massachusetts' reported gain of 468 per cent in total annual appropriations for higher educational operating expenses over 9 years, 1960-1969—fourth highest rate of gain among all the states. Calvin Coolidge's slogan "Have faith in Massachusetts!" rings across half a century!

MICHIGAN

Famed for public interest in and support of public higher education, this state had three major state universities throughout the decade 1960-1970: the University of Michigan at Ann Arbor, Michigan State University at East Lansing, and Wayne State University in Detroit—the last-named having been metamorphosed from municipal institution to state university during a three-year transition period ending in 1959.

In a technical sense, at least, it could be said that no other state had so many major state universities; but by the end of the decade it was unmistakably apparent that the University of California, already with at least two of its nine widely-separated campuses in the class of "major" universities, would soon have one or more others in that category. Similarly, the multicampus State University of New York, while having only one unit currently classifiable as a "major" university, bade fair to have at least two others in the early future. Illinois had two major state universities, and would eventually have others.

In 1960 Michigan had six other four- and five-year state institutions, and during the ensuing decade established three others, as well as three outlying campuses attached in one way or another to a parent institution. The state's population (7,823,000 in 1960) had increased to an estimated 8,740,000 by July 1, 1968—the increase of nearly 12 per cent being a little above the national average rate of 11½ per cent. Automobile manufacturing, centered in Detroit, Flint, Lansing, and other cities, prospered and grew.

Starting from a relatively high point in earlier years, state tax support of higher education in Michigan was notably laggard during much of the decade 1960-1970 in comparison with other states. The rate of gain in annual appropriations for the nine years 1960-1969 was only 174½ per cent, as against the national average of 261 per cent. By this measure Michigan ranked thirty-eighth among the states—at the bottom of the third quartile. Ranked by the total of dollars appropriated for fiscal year 1960 ($95,599,000), Michigan was second only to California ($188,604,000). But by 1968 Michigan ($262,424,000) had dropped to fifth place, behind California ($637,788,000), New York ($482,986,000), Illinois ($301,136,000), and Pennsylvania ($264,693,000) with Texas ($259,425,000) as a close sixth.

These changes are partly explained by differences in growth of population, and partly by the Northeastern awakening of the 1960's as well as other factors; but the fact is conspicuous that Michigan lost position rapidly. During the decade public higher education in Michigan suffered at least two distinct slumps of austerity. The gain in appropriations for fiscal 1961-62 over the preceding year was less than 1 per cent; and for 1967-68 over 1966-67 the gain was less than 5 per cent. During the five years intervening between these two dips, the rate of gain was 115 per cent.

Some of the difficulty stemmed from the fact that for 14 consecutive years, throughout the six successive terms of Governor G. Mennen Williams and that of his one-term successor, the executive branch was controlled by one major political party and the legislative branch was dominated by the other; and an extraordinary habit of partisan deadlock was developed. For example, the governors unceasingly advocated a graduated state income tax, while the legislature as regularly defeated any bill to levy such a tax, even after it had been urgently recommended by a Tax Study Committee including some members of both houses and of both parties. This impasse was due to the malapportionment of legislative districts that then prevailed in Michigan and many other states, the rectification of which was only barely begun by the epochal United States Supreme Court decision in March 1962 in the case of *Baker* v. *Tennessee*, ushering in a decade of nation-wide reapportionment activities.

Michigan's constitutional convention of 1961-62, heavily conservative in tone with regard to many matters, wrote into its draft a prohibition of any graduated income tax, though not closing the door to a flat-rate income tax; and this draft became the new Constitution which went into effect in 1963. Meantime Governor George Romney came into office, and from the beginning actively urged the enactment of personal and corporate income taxes of the type permitted by the constitution; but it was not until the session of 1967 that the legislature was finally brought to levy a flat-rate tax of 2.6 per cent on personal incomes and 5.6 per cent on corporation net incomes. Along with this, in the "package" recommended by the governor, were some increases in cigarette and liquor taxes, and some provisions for slight reductions in property taxes and the abolition of the "business activities" tax. The new package was expected to bring in additional revenue of about $270 million annually.

The year 1958 in Michigan was memorable not only for the appearance of the Legislative Tax Study Committee report already mentioned, but also for the report of a two-year study of the organization and financing of higher education in the state, completed by John Dale Russell and a small staff,[1] for another legislative study

[1]John Dale Russell and others, *Higher Education in Michigan*. Lansing: Governor's Office, 1948. 200 pp.

committee. Russell recommended that each of the nine state institutions of higher education then existing, and such others as might be established later, should be given a status of constitutional independence from other branches of government, similar to the constitutional autonomy enjoyed by the University of Michigan since 1850, Michigan State University since 1908, and presumably to be given to Wayne State University in 1959. This advice was adopted by the constitutional convention in 1962, and so the new state charter of 1963 confers autonomy on every state university or college in Michigan. (A constitutional amendment to provide this status for Wayne State University had previously been adopted at the polls in 1959.)

The Russell Report embodied many other recommendations, few of which were implemented immediately by the legislature; and, whether rightly or wrongly, the report was much resented by representatives of the three large universities who believed that in its efforts to be informative about unit costs of operation in the different institutions (such as costs of instruction per student per year) it did not emphasize sufficiently the necessarily large differences in unit costs in different types of programs of instruction, and especially the unavoidably high unit costs in advanced graduate and graduate professional programs as contrasted with undergraduate and lower division instruction. Thus it was accused of a tendency to "reduce all to a level of mediocrity." It is highly unlikely that this was actually Russell's intent; but this does not change the fact that some of his critics interpreted the report in that manner.

For more than a century the people of Michigan have cherished their constitutionally autonomous University at Ann Arbor, which early became spoken of as "the Harvard of the West," and which is today perhaps about on a par with Berkeley as one of the two most eminent state universities in the United States, insofar as these matters can be estimated by various measures of quality of faculty and students, scope and excellence of advanced graduate and professional offerings, and other elements relevant to the making of a world-renowned center of higher learning.

Founded in 1817 as the "Catholepistemiad (or University) of Michigania" the then small institution remained in Detroit for 20 years, and was moved to its present main campus in Ann Arbor in 1837. It continued as a creature of the legislature (and suffered much from erratic legislative interference) until the basis of its constitutional autonomy was written as a clause of the Constitution of 1850: "The Board of Regents shall have general supervision of the University, and the direction and control of all expenditures from the University interest fund."

A series of decisions of the Michigan supreme court, from 1869 to the present, have defined and confirmed the intent of this provision unmistakably. Perhaps the most lucid enunciation is a paragraph from a landmark decision of 1896: "The Board of Regents and the legislature derive their power from the same supreme authority, namely, the constitution. Insofar as the powers of each are defined by that instrument, limitations are imposed, and a direct power conferred upon one necessarily excludes its existence in the other, in the absence of language showing the contrary intent. . . . They are separate and distinct constitutional bodies, with the powers of the regents defined. By no rule of construction can it be held that either can encroach upon or exercise the powers conferred upon the other." [2]

As to what this means to the fiscal management and academic development of a state university, to avoid repetition here we suggest a reading of the appropriate paragraphs in the story of California, *supra* herein.

In 1947 the then President Alexander G. Ruthven called a meeting of the presidents of the other state colleges to discuss matters of common interest and to take a state-wide view of higher education. Thereafter such meetings were held at intervals, and the voluntary organization known as the Michigan Council of State College Presidents came into being. Although at first it maintained no central office or permanent staff, nevertheless it had by 1955 completed and, published, with the temporary assistance of collaborating professors, two significant state-wide studies, relating respectively to future enrollment trends and to the future economic growth of the state.

In 1956 five other state-wide survey reports were published, dealing respectively with teacher-supply and demand, pharmacy, forestry, music, and extension education. In the latter part of 1959 the Council employed a full-time coordinator of studies, Bruce K. Nelson, and opened an office at Ypsilanti. At the beginning of the next academic year Nelson was recalled to his post as vice president of Eastern Michigan University, after having visited several other states to observe their practices in fiscal and educational coordination, and worked with the nine Michigan institutions toward evolving acceptable and reasonably comparable methods of accounting, reporting, budgeting and fiscal analysis, adapted to the particular characteristics of the Michigan scene. During the next year committees of the Council continued the work of that nature.

July 1, 1961, the author was plucked from the University of Michigan Center for the Study of Higher Education and instructed to establish an office in Lansing as the Council's first full-time executive director, and served there until August 31, 1962. The office has continued to function continuously to the present; and though not widely publicized outside of Michigan, the Council of State College Presidents

---

[2] *Sterling* v. *Regents of University of Michigan.* 110 Mich. 369, 68 N.W. 253, 34 L.R.A. 150 (1896).

MICHIGAN

Appropriations for Annual Operating Expenses of Higher Education in Michigan, Alternate Fiscal Years, 1959-60 through 1969-70 (in thousands of dollars)

Institutions	Year 1959-60	Year 1961-62	Year 1963-64	Year 1965-66	Year 1967-68	Year 1969-70
U of Michigan[1]	33,367	35,377	38,225	50,355	59,161	67,317
Michigan State U						
East Lansing	27,870	29,677	32,260	36,672	45,004	54,086
Oakland U[2]				2,499	4,385	6,248
Ag Exp Station				3,499	4,077	5,017
Ag Exten Serv				2,584	3,283	4,040
Subtotal, Michigan State U	27,870	29,677	32,260	46,254	56,749	69,391
Wayne State U	14,794	15,582	17,123	25,484	33,556	41,835
Western Mich U	4,440	5,086	5,952	10,928	14,879	18,234
Eastern Mich U	2,924	3,203	3,733	6,638	10,300	14,698
Central Mich U	2,658	2,904	3,475	5,261	7,578	10,786
Mich Technolog'l U[3]						
Houghton	2,940	3,141	3,527	5,464	5,990	7,889
Sault Ste Marie[4]					1,037	1,484[4]
Inst Mineral Rsch					286	
Inst Wood Rsch					131	
Ford Forestry Ctr					125	
Subtotal, Mich Technolog'l U	2,940	3,141	3,527	5,464	7,569	7,889
Ferris State College	1,773	2,090	2,646	4,431	6,784	9,096
Northern Michigan U	1,213	1,374	1,832	3,296	5,122	6,988
Grand Valley St Coll			558	1,618	1,985	3,059
Saginaw Valley St Coll					505	1,469

Computer network[5]					
Inst of Gerontology[7]				200	175[6]
State scholarships				200	
Salary improvements			4,900[9]	8,150[8]	12,500
State aid to Jr Colls				18,831	40,696
Total	91,979	98,434	109,332	164,830	231,567	305,861
Amended Total				176,380[10]		

[1]All campuses, chiefly at Ann Arbor, Flint, and Dearborn.

[2]Campus at Rochester, Michigan. An institution about five years old, chiefly a liberal arts college, governed by the Michigan State University Board of Trustees.

[3]Formerly Michigan College of Mining and Technology.

[4]Lake Superior State College, not a unit of Michigan Technological University after July 1, 1969.

[5]To the three largest universities, jointly.

[6]Only the unused balances from appropriations of two prior years were reappropriated, on condition that federal matching funds be obtained not later than February 1, 1970.

[7]To the University of Michigan and Wayne State University, jointly.

[8]The sum includes $5,250,000 for "state competitive scholarships"; $2,700,000 for "tuition grants to students attending private colleges"; and $200,000 for "scholarships for special education teachers."

[9]This total was actually allotted to the 10 institutions, in amounts ranging from $80,000 to $1,200,000. For the six smaller universities and colleges (exclusive of Grand Valley State College), funds for faculty retirement were appropriated directly to the institutions for the first time, in amounts ranging from $255,000 to $935,000. This circumstance causes the total increases over previous years to be slightly exaggerated.

[10]Including state aid to junior colleges, and state scholarships.

continues to be a constructive factor in the ongoing development of public higher education in Michigan.

As already noted, the Constitution of 1963 provides that each of Michigan's state institutions of higher education shall have its own governing board [3] and each is constitutionally independent. Hence the legislature cannot create any power-laden "super-board" to dictate their policies or exercise any coercive control over them. In the constitutional convention of 1961-62 a considerable faction of the delegates were in favor of either a single consolidated state-wide governing board for all public higher education, or some type of all-powerful "coordinating board" superimposed over the institutional governing boards. This faction was not strong enough to win the day, as against the Michigan tradition of institutional autonomy, especially as exemplified in the illustrious history and current eminence of the University of Michigan. The principle of voluntary state-wide coordination clearly won. [4]

The former three-member State Board of Education which had governed all four of the state institutions having teacher-education antecedents, was abolished. Each of the four institutions was given its own governing board. As a conciliatory concession to the would-be centralizers, a clause of the Constitution specified that the new eight-member State Board of Education should be a "coordinating agency" for all public education from kindergarten through graduate school. Obviously, under a constitution which also gives each state university and college constitutional autonomy, any "coordinating" of higher education done by this agency must be only advisory, and its execution must be voluntary, as it should be.

The "coordinative" function of the Michigan State Board of Education has been considerably overpublicized by advocates of coercion who would like to believe it will develop de facto if not de jure powers of compulsion, and who find it difficult to grasp the thought of any possible virtue in the voluntary principle. Within the bureaucracy of the state department of public instruction (headed by the State Board of Education), a division of higher education has been established, and thus far the Board seems to have functioned in conformity with the Constitution in an acceptable manner.

---

[3] Exception: Oakland University, founded as a child of Michigan State University, continues to be governed by that University's Board of Trustees.

[4] Without asserting any claim of influence, it may be remarked that the author's booklet, Voluntary Statewide Coordination in Public Higher Education (now out of print but available in many libraries), appeared in print early in 1961, and complimentary copies were placed in the hands of all delegates to the constitutional convention, and of thousands of alumni of the University of Michigan. The 83-page document described voluntary practices in a dozen states, and made a brief favorable exposition of the voluntary principle.

When faced, for example, with a demand in 1965 that the 20-year-old Sault Sainte Marie branch of Michigan Technological University should become a separate four-year degree-granting institution, the State Board of Education, in preparation for the formulation of its own recommendations, first set up an *ad hoc* Advisory Committee composed of prominent citizens, including some of conservative tendency as well as a labor leader and a Negro educator in Detroit, and one consultant from outside Michigan (the author, then resident in Kentucky). This Advisory Committee had the staff assistance of the head of the Junior College Administrative Training Program jointly operated by the three major universities.

After several deliberative meetings and a staff report during 1965-66, the Committee recommended that the desired development at Sault Sainte Marie should be encouraged and provided for by the state; and this recommendation in substance was adopted by the State Board of Education and given a predominantly favorable reception in the legislature and by the Board of Control of Michigan Technological University. By 1967 the allocation of annual operating funds for the institution at Sault Sainte Marie exceeded $1 million, and has increased annually since. It was developing as a four-year institution. Full and final official confirmation of its separate status, and the establishment of its own constitutionally-independent governing board, awaited anticipated favorable action of the Board of Control of Michigan Technological University and of the legislature. This had taken place by 1969. The new institution is styled Lake Superior State College. It was announced August 1, 1968, that the North Central Association of Colleges and Secondary Schools had accredited it as an operationally separate four-year college.

The foregoing case is in many respects not comparable with any other in any state. The town of Sault Sainte Marie has only about 25,000 people, though it is just across the river from the Canadian city of the same name that is twice as large. The whole eastern half of Michigan's Northern Peninsula, which is its hinterland, is sparsely populated and of very modest economic pretensions. From a strictly conventional viewpoint, there is no adequate base for a tax-supported four-year college. Some conservative members of the Advisory Committee took pains to demonstrate this in great detail. This is outweighed by broader considerations: a wealthy state owes its young people in a remote and economically undeveloped region opportunities for higher education without leaving that region, even if this must be at a comparatively high cost per student per year and partly at the expense of the whole state, including its heavily populated and prosperous regions.

Equally important is the fact that a college is an economic asset to the region for the long future. It will "help to keep the region's young people at home" and attract others from a distance. (The author predicted in 1966 that as soon as Lake Superior State College at Sault Sainte Marie is fully established as a four-year state college, it will have at least 1,000 students from the city of Detroit alone, who will come for a hundred reasons.) Then there is also the exciting and mind-stretching possibility of the eventual development here of a truly international institution, perhaps involving the State of Michigan and the Province of Ontario equally in its support, with the concurrence of their respective federal governments.

Earlier in the decade Michigan's legislature had established the new Grand Valley State College near Grand Rapids, where the presence of the city and eight surrounding counties populated by roughly a quarter of a million people amply justified it from every standpoint. More recently the legislature established the new Saginaw Valley State College, adjacent to the large public junior college known as Delta College, at "University Center" near the three cities of Saginaw, Midland, and Bay City, to serve another compact area having at least 200,000 people, where the need for a four-year state college was completely manifest.

Necessary expansions of the Michigan system have also been obtained in other ways. The story of Michigan State University's School of Medicine must not be omitted. Developing its own idiosyncratic character among the leading land-grant institutions of the nation, Michigan State almost from the beginning was notably strong in the biological sciences, but somewhat less outstanding in the physical sciences and engineering. Thus it would probably be said with accuracy that the leading school of engineering in Michigan is not at East Lansing, but at Ann Arbor.

For many years President John A. Hannah continued to stress the development of superior biological science departments at Michigan State. At least as far back as the late 1950's he foresaw the eventual necessity of a third medical school in Michigan, and began to take steps, openly and without secrecy, toward Michigan State's ultimate meeting of that need. In 1962 he brought in a highly competent biological scientist to be dean of the new Division of Biological Sciences. At least as often as once a year some step of that nature was taken and announced in the daily press, so that few citizens or legislators could be unaware of it.

There were obstacles. Some argued that the city of Lansing and its surrounding counties, with perhaps 200,000 people, were not populous enough to provide clinical patients. Besides, other cities such as Flint and Grand Rapids wanted the medical school if there was to be one, entirely overlooking the fact that a medical school should be in conjunction with a large university. Perhaps the most stubborn opposition was from the deans of the two existing medical schools—the full-sized and highly-developed University of Michigan Medical School at Ann Arbor and the Wayne State University Medical School in Detroit. The latter, though it had been in existence in one guise or another for nearly a century, was substantially short of the accepted maximum size (about 200 students in each of the four classes.)

Both argued against the need for a third medical school. Ann Arbor claimed first priority on available state funds, asserting that large capital funds promised it by a legislature of a decade ago had never been fully forthcoming, entirely ignoring the fact that one legislature cannot obligate its successors except by contract. Detroit insisted that Wayne State's medical school should be brought up to full size and fully equipped for maximum output as a first step. The conservative dean of an East Coast medical school, employed independently to make recommendations on medical education in Michigan as a part of the Russell Report of 1958, had advised against a third medical school. It was also argued from some quarters that a two-year pre-clinical medical school would be unwise because it would be unlikely that its graduates would find any places in four-year medical schools in which to take their next two clinical years.

Nevertheless, during the years following 1962, development went on quietly but openly at Michigan State. Presently the Division of Biological Sciences gave birth to an Institute of Biology and Human Medicine, which was a less remote precursor of a two-year School of Medicine. By 1968 the latter was a *fait accompli*, and within a few years was virtually certain to become a full-fledged four-year school of medicine, much needed in the state of Michigan. Moreover, it was a component of a major university, as a school of medicine should be; and its geographic position near the capital city in a central part of the populous portion of the state was good. The appropriation act for fiscal year 1969-70 included a sum for planning for the third and fourth years of the new medical school.

The foregoing story illustrates how a large university is an organism which grows and changes its form to meet the exigencies of its environment, and not a lifeless mechanism which has to have new mechanical attachments added to it by artisans from the outside. Other different but similar illustrations have been cited in Illinois and Oregon. They could be found in every state. They belie the necessity, the effectiveness, and even the possibility of subjecting the development of state universities and other public higher educational facilities wholly to bureaucratic planning centralized in a state agency.

Further clarification of the somewhat anomalous position of the Michigan State Board of Education is available in the March 1965 report of a large Citizens' Committee on Higher Education which had been appointed in 1963 by Governor George Romney.[5] After speaking

---

5 Page 1V-5 of *Report of Michigan Citizens' Committee on Higher Education*, March 12, 1965. Issued from 709 South Westnedge Avenue, Kalamazoo, Michigan.

of voluntary coordination, the document says: "A second way is for the legislature to assign the institutions their respective roles by law. The Michigan Constitution has rejected this way, and this Committee would reject it.[6]

"It is believed that the system used in Michigan should retain the flexibility that now exists and encourage diversity and initiative more than can be the case when institutional roles are fixed by law.

"A third way is to have an all-powerful state board of education whose coordinating orders have the effect of law. This, of course, is rejected by the Michigan Constitution, and it has never worked long in a state whose educational system has become at all complex."[7]

Since 1965 the State Board of Education has prepared, with the aid of six "Study and Advisory Committees" and the staff of the Division of Higher Education, various fragmentary and preliminary versions of an over-all state-wide plan for higher education.[8] A good deal of this work is valuable, at least from the standpoint of disseminating public information; and future successive efforts may become more valuable as the staff gains knowledge and expertise, especially if it keeps firmly in mind that it is only advisory and no more—advisory to the governor, the legislature, the institutional governing boards, and the public.

Under this type of state-level structure Michigan has, as the experience from 1965 to 1970 tends to show, a viable, flexible, and adaptable system of public higher education (which indeed it has always had, and which in actual composition and operation rather markedly resembles the California system, but without its regrettable over-organization, over-centralization, and rigidity). Michigan has no single Board of Regents trying in desperation to function as the sole governing board of nine widely scattered university campuses. It has no single board of trustees and chancellor struggling with the impossible task of governing, from the state capital, 19 state colleges of which half are larger than most state universities. It has, indeed, no spate of large regional state universities chafing under the name of "state college" and asking vainly for a modest state funding of research work, and compelled to submit faculty personnel problems to a state personnel board (Civil Service Commission) as the California state colleges do.

The University of Michigan is wisely selective in freshman admissions, but not under any legislative mandate or with any adamantly prescribed cut-off point. In short, Michigan has never

---

[6] Observe that this is the opposite of the idea of the California master plan.
[7] For evidence supporting this last statement, compare the story of the North Carolina State Board of Higher Education, *infra*.
[8] See *State Plan for Higher Education in Michigan, provisional*. Lansing: Michigan Department of Education, September 1968. 98 pp. litho.

made the error of writing any part of a "master plan" into the statutes of the state. Complex and fluid as the Michigan picture may appear, it is one in which there is latitude for institutional initiative, and in which the desirable "coordination" that develops rests on the principle of voluntary assent. Let no one mistakenly suppose that Michigan public higher education is either governed or coercively "coordinated" by a statehouse bureaucracy. It cannot happen in Michigan under the Constitution of 1963.

By 1968 Michigan had 28 local public two-year community colleges, each based on a local taxing district but receiving state aid for annual operating expenses on a uniform basis of about $350 per student per year, so that the total appropriation for that purpose for 1967-68 was nearly $19 million, and for 1968-69, more than $24½ million. A dozen of these community colleges were established between 1958 and 1968, in part at least as a result of John Dale Russell's recommendation in his 1958 *Report* that the state should have 23 more of these, ably supported by data showing that in counties having no institution of education beyond high school, college attendance among eligible residents of appropriate age was invariably relatively low. This is proof of the impression that the public two-year college, open to all at low fees or no fees, is in good part of benefit to those who would otherwise get no education beyond high school at all.

In their recognition of this fact, as well as in the fact of each having one of the world's greatest state universities, and in the fact of having about 85 per cent of their college students in public institutions, Michigan and California resemble each other.

MINNESOTA

Like most states of the northern tier, this state has a tradition of good, generously supported public higher education. Accustomed in recent years to rely heavily on state income taxes, the 1959 legislature was urged by Governor Orville Freeman to enact an increase of 1 per cent in all brackets of the graduated personal income tax, and to adopt a withholding system. A reactionary senate blocked these measures throughout the regular session, but a 48-day special session ending July 1, 1959, raised the personal income taxes by one-half of 1 per cent in all brackets, and increased the corporation income tax rate to 9.3 per cent from the former 7.3 per cent.

The withholding measure was not enacted, but two years later the 1961 legislature made it law. Similar statutes had previously been enacted in 25 states, and the Minnesota house of representatives had passed the measure in three successive prior biennial sessions.

In 1963 the legislative interim study group known as the Committee for Study of Tax Resources and Economy of Minnesota began to consider the possibility of a general sales tax, but it was not until 1967 that Minnesota became the forty-fourth state to adopt such a measure (when the legislature enacted a 3 per cent general sales tax over Governor LeVander's veto). It became effective August 1, 1967, and was expected to produce $160 million a year in additional revenue.

Called a "selective sales tax" by some commentators, it was actually general in application but with some important exemptions. It applied to most retail purchases except food, clothing, drugs, gasoline, and services. It covered liquor and beer, and restaurant meals except meals served at school or college cafeterias or church gatherings.

The 1969 legislature, contemplating recently increased rates on corporate, individual, and bank income taxes and severance taxes that would have expired in that year, extended them for two years and raised the rates on cigarettes and alcoholic beverages.

Retail sales taxes are heavy and speedy producers of revenue. It is probably not merely coincidence that Minnesota's appropriations for annual operating expenses of higher education were only modest from 1960 to 1967—achieving barely a doubling within the seven years—, but made a gain of 45 per cent over the next two fiscal years. Even with that spurt, however, the nine-year rate of gain from 1960 to 1969 was only 190½ per cent—substantially less than the national average of 261 per cent.

The state tax investment per citizen in Minnesota for annual operating expenses of higher education in fiscal year 1968 was $28.88, ranking eighteenth among the 50 states. The ratio of this state tax investment to total personal income was 0.88 per cent, ranking twenty-third. These figures indicate that the support of public higher education in Minnesota had by no means reached a point of hardship. Minnesota's population as of July 1, 1968 (3,646,000), had increased a little less than 7 per cent since 1960.

The University of Minnesota, with main campuses in Minneapolis and St. Paul and branch campuses at Duluth, Morris, and Crookston, is one of the largest and most respected state universities in the United States. Its Board of Regents is a constitutionally independent corporation, after the manner of the Regents of the University of Michigan and the Regents of the University of California. These three are the top triad of great constitutionally autonomous state universities.

Incorporated by the Territorial Assembly in 1851, the University's name, location, and corporate existence were expressly confirmed in the state constitution of 1858, and the existing powers of the Regents given the dignity of constitutional provisions: "All the rights, immunities, franchises and endowments heretofore granted or conferred are hereby perpetuated unto the said university." Little attention seems to have been paid to this clause until 1928. From time to time the legislature invaded the province of the regents.

When a state administrative reorganization act of 1925 purported to subject all expenditures of university funds to the approval of a newly-created State Commission of Administration and Finance, and that agency disallowed, solely on the ground of policy, an expenditure by the Board of Regents for a preliminary survey of the feasibility of installing a plan of group insurance for its faculty members and other employees, the Regents obtained from the state supreme court a writ of mandamus to compel the state auditor to approve the voucher and issue his warrant for its payment. Mr. Justice Stone, for the full court, declared that the Constitution plainly placed the control of the university in the Regents, beyond the power of the legislature to infringe upon or transfer. Therefore the pertinent part of the Act of 1925 was unconstitutional and invalid. [1]

The court added an acrid comment on overzealous efforts to attain complete centralization in state fiscal administration: "The tendency to sacrifice established principles of constitutional government in order to secure centralized control and high efficiency in administration may easily be carried so far as to endanger the very foundations upon which our system of government rests. . . . It is in

---

[1] *State* v. *Chase*, 175 Minn. 259, 220 N.W. 951 (1928).

MINNESOTA

Appropriations for Annual Operating Expenses of Higher Education in Minnesota, Alternate Fiscal Years, 1959-60 through 1969-70 (in thousands of dollars)

Institutions	Year 1959-60	Year 1961-62	Year 1963-64	Year 1965-66	Year 1967-68	Year 1969-70
U of Minnesota[1]	31,044	27,911	30,138	38,500	51,801	66,936
Morris Branch			474	600		740
Crookston Ag & Tech				60		
U Hospitals		4,141	4,506	4,660	4,311	1,613
Gen Ag Extension		740	798	950	1,614	2,500
Gen Ag Research		525	580	800	1,070	1,996
Psychopathic Hosp		700	746	831	1,005	1,191
Rehabilitation Ctr		459	484	810	990	1,171
Child Psychiatric Hosp			290	318	381	451
Multiple Sclerosis		55	63	111	134	
Spec Research & Misc		1,711	1,229	1,338	1,705	
Fac & Staff Ins[2]					1,425	
NDEA Student Loans				122	218	253
TV feasibility study				150		
Subtotal, U of Minnesota	31,044	36,242	39,307	49,251	65,108	81,309[3]
State colleges:[4]	5,814					
Mankato		2,659	2,826	4,195	5,807	8,679
St Cloud		1,891	2,285	2,913	4,976	7,124
Moorhead		1,163	1,362	1,735	2,874	4,352
Bemidji		1,104	1,228	1,667	2,710	4,122
Winona		916	1,010	1,374	2,353	3,328
Southwest (Marshall)				100	2,066	3,241
St Coll Board		83	56	113	230	
St Coll Bd contingent					400	500
NDEA student loans				175	252	267
Supplemental retirement					2,980	
Doctoral Prog Study				200	250	
Enrollment contingent						
Southwest contingent				25		
General research					10	25

State Junior Colleges:						
St aid to Jr Colls			1,607			12,138
St Jr Coll Board[5]				2,940	6,947	
Contingent				250	200	
Fac & Staff Ins					135	
Supplemen'l retirement					77	
NDEA student loans				33	18	
Subtotal, State Jr Colls			1,607	3,223	7,378	12,138
Higher Edn Coord Comm[6]		21			196	311
Interinstitutional TV			28	60		360
State scholarships					350	575
Total	36,858	44,069	49,710	65,211	95,034	128,278[7]

[1] Including campuses in Minneapolis, St. Paul, Duluth, and elsewhere.

[2] The sums are approximations. Exact amounts cannot be ascertained until after the end of the fiscal period.

[3] Includes: $1,000,000 for "educational equipment"; $500,000 for "libraries"; $2,892,000 for "other special appropriations"; $32,000 for community service; and $34,000 for a new Waseca Technical College.

[4] The sums are approximations. Funds are allocated quarterly by the State College Board. These approximations also include estimated amounts for faculty and employee insurance.

[5] The state agency in charge of a state-wide network of 18 junior colleges, now deriving their tax support for operating expenses wholly from the state.

[6] Formerly designated Liaison and Facilities Commission for Higher Education.

[7] Includes: $200,000 for "student grants-in-aid"; $125,000 for nursing scholarships; and $700,000 for "planning medical education."

such fashion that the friends of free government may sap its foundations by measures they intend for its benefit."

Again in 1931 the court applied the same principle in denying an injunction to prevent the University from proceeding with its own plan to finance and erect a self-liquidating dormitory without prior legislative approval.[2] Subsequently the court was called upon to resolve a controversy resulting from conflicting opinions of successive attorneys general as to whether the Regents should continue to be appointed by the governor, as for some years prior to 1928, or should thenceforth be named by the legislature in joint session, as prescribed in the Territorial Charter of the University. The decision was that the original method must be restored, as being a part of "the whole matter of university administration" which is placed by the constitution in a sphere not subject to change by the legislative or executive branches.[3]

Minnesota has five state colleges (with normal school antecedents), at Mankato, St. Cloud, Moorhead, Bemidji, and Winona; a sixth, at Duluth, became a branch of the University of Minnesota in 1947. In 1965 a new Southwest Minnesota State College was authorized, and was in operation by 1967, making six in all. Control of all these is tightly centralized in one State College Board at the state capital.

Up to 1963 Minnesota had developed 11 local public junior colleges, receiving state aid for annual operating expenses in the amount of $300 per student per year. In that year a statute was enacted, offering, on the part of the state, to relieve the local districts of the tax support and control of these colleges, with the consent of their local boards, and convert them to state junior colleges, governed by a State Junior College Board. The local boards hastened to accept this invitation, and on August 1, 1964, the State Junior College Board formally took over the governance of the state system of junior colleges. Successive statutes authorized the number of junior colleges to be increased to 15, then to 17; and by 1968, 18 state junior colleges were in existence.

As is noted elsewhere, this shifting of public junior college support and control from local taxing districts to the state has subsequently occurred in somewhat similar forms in Colorado and Washington. Is this an incipient trend likely to continue? Will public junior colleges in all or most of the states eventually become state institutions, with no local tax support or control? The great difficulties currently experienced by cities, counties, school districts, and other local subdivisions in obtaining sufficient revenues to support their own services make this shift seem a possibility.

---

[2] *Fanning* v. *Regents*, 183 Minn. 222, 236 N.W. 217 (1931).
[3] *State ex rel. Peterson* v. *Quinlivan*, (Minn.), 268 N.W. 858 (1936).
The foregoing three decisions were all cited with approval in *State ex rel. Sholes* v. *University of Minnesota*, (Minn.), 54 N.W. 2d 122 (1952).

The Liaison Committee on Higher Education in Minnesota was a voluntary coordinating agency set up in 1959 at the request of the 1959 legislature, by the Regents of the University of Minnesota, the State College Board, and the State Board of Education. In its first biennial report, for 1959-60, a comprehensive and informative document containing much detailed data, it included among its 20 recommendations: "The Liaison Committee affirms its belief in the principle of state support of higher education as a major investment in its own economy. The state should provide, at the lowest possible cost to the student, higher educational opportunity for all capable youth in Minnesota, regardless of the student's economic status."[4]

Subsequent reports for the next two bienniums[5] were also informative, one feature being that considerable attention was given to the fact that the location of several public institutions of higher education at or near both sides of the boundary lines causes a substantial amount of student in-migration and out-migration to the adjacent states of Wisconsin, Iowa, and the two Dakotas, and that such students face the barriers of nonresident fees. The outstanding disparity appeared to be between the nearly 1,400 Minnesota students going to North Dakota in the fall of 1961, as compared with only about 450 North Dakota students coming to Minnesota. A variety of complex interstate arrangements could be devised to minimize the hardships involved; but the simplest solution, which also has other reasons to commend it, would be the abolition of differential fees against nonresidents.[6]

In 1967 the Liaison Committee was reconstituted and renamed the Minnesota Higher Education Coordinating Commission, with 18 members comprising two representatives of each of the four state boards concerned with public higher education, two representatives of the private colleges, and one citizen from each of the state's eight Congressional districts. Its duties are exclusively advisory, including the making of studies, recommendations, and comprehensive plans.

Its first report was a brief statement of major principles, in which it said: "Every high school graduate who has reasonable capacity to profit from further education should be actively encouraged to enter an appropriate program of post-secondary education, and every effort should be made to remove barriers to post-secondary education. This is a matter of urgency."[7] The Commission is now producing a series

---

[4]*Report of the Liaison Committee on Higher Education in Minnesota, 1959-60.* St. Paul: The Committee, 1961. 50 pp. mimeo.

[5]*Ibid.* for 1961-63, 16 pp. letterpress; and 1963-65, 35 pp. mimeo.

[6]Howard R. Bowen, then president of the University of Iowa, wrote in 1968: "These differentials are as improper as tariffs on the movement of commodities over state lines, specifically prohibited by the Constitution."

[7]*A Philosophy for Minnesota Higher Education.* St. Paul: The Commission, March 1968. 16 pp.

of *Planning Reports.*

One characteristic of the Minnesota state-wide system merits emphasis. The admissions policies and practices do not create a hierarchy of institutions based on "intellectual stratification." (Compare the California master plan of 1960.) The University of Minnesota, though it necessarily has to be selective regarding admissions to many of its advanced programs, continues to admit and provide suitable facilities and opportunities for all who are qualified for college-level study. It maintains its University College and its General College, both for the purpose, in different ways, of fulfilling its responsibility to serve students with different abilities and widely differing interests.

This conception of the state university as a large, complex, and resourceful center of learning, available not only to a selected elite, but to all classes and types of persons able to use it for the benefit of the state and of themselves, is worthy of pondering.

MISSISSIPPI

For a generation or more, repeated studies, reports, and rankings of the states have placed Mississippi and South Carolina at the bottom of the list by almost any measure of ability to provide improved support for elementary and secondary education. Again and again we have been told that these states have the highest ratios of population of school-age to total population and the lowest personal incomes; that their "effort" in the support of education, as measured by the ratio of state tax investment to total personal incomes, is high—about as high as it can be expected to go until the limiting conditions change.

With respect to public higher education, these general impressions need to be modified. In 1968 Mississippi's state tax investment per citizen in annual operating expenses of higher education was $20.62, ranking forty-second—ahead of Tennessee, Maine, Alabama, Ohio, South Carolina, New Hampshire, New Jersey, and Massachusetts, in that order.

The ratio of this state tax investment to the total personal income in Mississippi was, indeed, higher in the scale—but it was only 0.97, ranking seventeenth. All the 16 states outranking Mississippi were north of the Ohio River (1) or west of the Mississippi (13), except West Virginia and Kentucky. This seems to refute the idea that the greatest proportional effort in state tax support of higher education was in Mississippi, or indeed generally in the southeastern states. It was in fact largely in certain trans-Mississippi states, and especially several in the northwestern quadrant of the Continental United States, with Montana, North Dakota, and Washington heading the list.

Mississippi's nine-year rate of gain in annual appropriations for operating expenses for higher education, 1959-1968, was a little more than 216 per cent, ranking thirty-first by that measure—above the median of the third quartile of states. All the 19 states showing slower rates of gain than Mississippi were west of the "Father of the Waters" except Alabama, Michigan, West Virginia, and New Hampshire—the conspicuous laggard of New England which resolutely resisted any of the prime essentials of a present-day state revenue system.

In James W. Martin's *Revenue Potentials of the States*, Mississippi is shown to have had in 1959 nearly 59 per cent of its families with incomes of $3,000 a year or less—the highest percentage

MISSISSIPPI

Appropriations for Annual Operating Expenses of Higher Education in Mississippi, Alternate Fiscal Years, 1959-60 through 1969-70 (in thousands of dollars)

Institutions	Year 1959-60	Year 1961-62	Year 1963-64	Year 1965-66	Year 1967-68	Year 1969-70
U of Mississippi		2,500	2,577	3,358	4,093	5,132
School of Medicine		1,275	1,400	1,829	2,000	2,515
Teaching Hospital		1,500	1,740	2,063	2,205	2,505
U Ctr & Org Research					500	500
School of Nursing		200	200	207	257	290
Pharmaceutical Research				75	90	257
Subtotal, U of Miss		5,475	5,917	7,532	9,145	11,199
Mississippi State U		2,600	2,618	3,937	5,493	6,095
Ag Exten Service		1,399	1,400	1,495	1,700	2,266
Ag Experiment Sta		1,094	1,094	1,217	1,350	1,807
Chem regulatory		132	152	172	200	211
Forest products					84	144
Foundation herds		17	17	30	17	20
Subtotal, Miss St U		5,242	5,181	6,851	8,844	10,501
U of Southern Miss		1,700	1,845	2,640	3,614	4,767
School of Nursing					100	157
Subtotal, U of So Miss		1,700	1,845	2,640	3,714	4,924
Jackson State College		625	890	1,139	1,636	2,287
Miss St C for Women		750	852	1,242	1,661	1,837
Delta State College		575	661	908	1,326	1,804
Alcorn A & M College		550	668	939	1,327	1,626
Miss Valley St College		550	579	752	1,284	1,498
Rsch & Development Ctr[1]		80	110	250	1,115	1,449
Gulf Coast Research Lab				210	325	375

Technical institutes						2,350
State scholarships	327	277	384		474	706
Educational television			100	100		33
Regional education	225	200	200	208	200	200
Bd Trustees of Insts H L	100	230	175		175	190
State aid to Jr Colls	2,147	2,463	2,850		5,000	6,185
Total	15,118	18,347	19,873	26,005	36,359	47,804

[1] The Mississippi Research and Development Center is not a degree-granting institution, but its program is intimately related to those of the universities.

NOTE: The Mississippi legislature convenes biennially in even-numbered years. A lump sum (somewhat more than half of the total) is appropriated for the undivided biennium, to be allocated to the institutions by the Board of Trustees of State Institutions of Higher Learning. Other sums are appropriated by the legislature directly to the medical units; the services of agricultural experimentation and extension; and other agencies of research and service as indicated. For purposes of comparability with institutions in other states, it was necessary to place the sums appropriated to these latter agencies adjacent to the sums allocated by the Board to the different institutions to which the agencies normally appertain. Thus half the biennial appropriation to a given agency was added to the sum allocated to the institution for a fiscal year. It is to be understood, then, that the figures in this table are not absolutely exact, but are reasonably close approximations.

of any state [1] (the next ranking state being Arkansas, with more than 55 per cent). Yet in the same tabulation Mississippi's percentage gain in personal income from 1957 to 1961 is shown to have been 27.9— seventh highest rate of gain among the states, being exceeded only by Arizona (43.5), Florida (42.4), Hawaii (40.7), Nevada (39.0), California (28.1), and Colorado (28.1).

Mississippi's total population as of July 1, 1968, was estimated to be 2,342,000 showing a gain of only 7½ per cent over 1960. For many years the population was more than half Black, but the proportion was considerably reduced by heavy out-migration to northern cities. During the early 'Sixties the state provided the locale of at least two momentous court decisions intimately affecting the future of higher education.

In 1960 the state supreme court made a unanimous declaration, in the words of its opinion written by Justice Holmes, that a prosperous farmer, divorced and the father of an 18-year-old daughter living with her mother, could properly be ordered to pay $90 per month toward the college expenses of his daughter at the University of Mississippi. "We hold," said Justice Holmes, "that where the minor child is worthy of and qualified for a college education and shows an aptitude therefor it is the primary duty of the father, if in reason financially able to do so, to provide funds for the college education of his minor child in the custody of the mother, where the mother and father are divorced and living apart. . . .

"A contrary view may have been justified in former times when the needs of the family, and of society, and of government were less exacting than they are today. . . ." Elaborating, he continued: "It is a duty which the parent not only owes to his child, but to the state as well, since the stability of our government must depend upon a well-equipped, a well-trained, and well-educated citizenship. We can see no good reason why this duty should not extend to a college education." [2]

Nation-wide and world-wide publicity attended the admission of James Meredith, a Negro student transferring from Jackson State College to the University of Mississippi in September 1962, under an injunctive order of the United States Court of Appeals which the United States Supreme Court declined to review. [3] Thus the University of Mississippi became another deep-southern state university to admit qualified Negro students under federal judicial mandate.

---

[1] James W. Martin, *Revenue Potentials of the States.* Washington: National Education Association, 1964. 49 pp. litho.

[2] *Pass* v. *Pass*, 238 Miss. 449, 118 So. 2d 769 (1960). Commented upon in *University of Pennsylvania Law Review 109*: 130-134 (November 1960).

[3] *Meredith* v. *Fair*, (U.S.C.A.), 305 F. 2d 341 and 305 F. 2d 343 (1962); stays dissolved by Mr. Justice Hugo L. Black, 371 U.S. 828, 83 S. Ct. 10, 9 L.Ed. 2d 66 (1962); and *certiorari* denied, 371 U.S. 828, 83 S. Ct. 49, 9 L.Ed. 2d 66 (1962).

The state-wide network of state-aided local public junior colleges dates from much earlier than the beginning of the present decade (1960) and is in fact one of the earliest of such state-wide systems. The state was covered by 13 junior college districts and there was a handful of other overlapping districts, mostly small, intended for exclusively Negro junior colleges. A legislative education study committee reporting in 1961 recommended that the State Junior College Commission, a supervisory and regulatory body, should be supplanted by a new State Junior College Board, with the whole system more centralized than before; and that the "college transfer" programs of the junior colleges, though necessary and desirable, should be regarded as fulfilling only one of several functions of the junior colleges, and should be supplemented by an immediate and heavily emphasized upbuilding of the other functions: vocational and technical education of duration of two years or less, and educational programs for adults. [4]

The annual amounts of state tax support for operating expenses of the junior colleges moved from $1,638,000 for fiscal year 1959-60 to $2,850,000 for 1964-65 in a fairly steady progression, and then took a steeper path to $6,183,000 for 1968-69. In that year Mississippi ranked sixteenth among the states by that measure. In 1959-60 it had ranked eighth. The drop in rank is not of much significance, however, because over the period of nine years state-aided junior college systems were begun or rapidly developed in several other states, and the nation-wide total of state appropriations to aid annual operation of junior colleges increased nearly fivefold.

The University of Mississippi at Oxford (with Medical Center at Jackson), Mississippi State University at State College, and the other state colleges offering programs of four or five years' duration have all been governed by a single board at the state capital bearing the ponderous title of Board of Trustees of State Institutions of Higher Learning since 1932. This had been preceded by a somewhat similar centralized scheme as early as 1912; and in the dark days of the Great Depression it was reconstituted and tightened in its present form.

There have been occasional minor changes in the composition of the Board. In 1967 it was composed of 12 members appointed by the governor with the advice and consent of the senate for terms of 12 years. One must be from each congressional district, one from each state supreme court district, and two from the state at large. There is one additional member, known as the Trustee for the La Bauve Fund, who must be a resident of De Soto County, who is appointed by the governor alone for a term of four years, and who may vote only on

---

[4]*Public Education in Mississippi.* Report of Mississippi Legislative Education Study Committee. Jackson: Governor's Office, December 1961. 151 pp.

matters pertaining to the University of Mississippi. This is in pursuance of the condition, agreed to many years ago when the La Bauve family made a large gift to the University, that there would always be one member of the board of trustees with particular interest in the expenditure of the resulting income.

MISSOURI

The author, writing in June 1959 of this state's appropriations for annual operating expenses of higher education, said, "The annual rate of increase is about ten per cent. Maintenance of this rate would double the operating funds in eight years, and triple them in eleven years. Something of this order, or better, will probably be needed." This feeble prediction fell far short. Actually Missouri's appropriations were doubled within six years, tripled within seven years, and multiplied four and a half times within nine years.

Missouri's rate of gain over the nine years 1960-1969 was 355½ per cent, placing it, by that measure, eleventh among the 50 states. As gauged simply by the mere magnitude of the appropriations, Missouri rose from twentieth place among the states in 1959-60 to twelfth place in 1968-69. There were good reasons for this sea change.

The two large cities, St. Louis and Kansas City, located on the eastern and western boundaries of the state, had no state university campuses until after 1960. St. Louis for many years maintained two comparatively small teachers colleges (consolidated into one in 1956), but these were municipal institutions of the local school district. The Harris Teachers College, continuing in that status, received a state subsidy of $665,000 for fiscal year 1967-68; this was raised to $1,157,000 for 1968-69. It was not until the early 'Sixties that the public junior college district of St. Louis City and County was belatedly formed, but within a few years it had established and was operating three large public junior college campuses.

Kansas City had for many years a public junior college, which continues in reconstituted and enlarged form. There had also existed for some years a Kansas City Teachers College (now defunct), which had been a degree-granting institution during its later years, but was always a small municipal enterprise of the local Board of Education. The facilities just described were never anywhere near sufficient to meet the needs of either of the two large cities for public university education.

Over many years prolonged efforts were made to establish and operate a private university in Kansas City, but the institution which emerged, known as the University of Kansas City, was hardly more than barely viable, financially or academically. [1] On the other hand,

---

[1]A touch of the early history is provided in *First National Bank of Kansas City* v. *University of Kansas City*, (Mo.), 245 S.W. 2d 124 (1952).

217

in St. Louis two highly reputable and well-financed private universities had long flourished: St. Louis University (Roman Catholic) and Washington University (nonsectarian). The presence and prestige of these two excellent institutions, though they were of only modest size, were selective in admissions, charged high student fees, and on no account could hope or pretend to fulfill the needs of the great city for university facilities, nevertheless tended to lull the people of the city and the state into overlooking this urban need until the awakening of the 'Sixties.

The University of Missouri, which dated from 1839 and was located at the comparatively small city of Columbia in somewhat bucolic surroundings and a bit remote from the main lines of travel and transportation, felt no especial kinship with, or obligation to, the large cities during the first century of its existence. It was at once the "principal" state university and the land-grant institution of the state. As early as 1870 the University of Missouri School of Mines was established at the town of Rolla, and it later became an important technological institution, as have the early state schools of mines in some other states.

As recently as 1916, however, the Board of Curators of the University of Missouri was ordered by the state supreme court to establish at the school at Rolla degree programs in mine engineering, metallurgy, mechanical engineering, electrical engineering, chemical engineering, civil engineering, and general science, in conformity with a state statute enacted in 1915. The Curators resisted, arguing the Constitution of 1875 vested the governance of the University in the Board of Curators, and commanded the legislature to aid and maintain the state university as then established, in all its departments. Establishment of the specified degree programs at Rolla, they said, would attract so many students away from the college of agriculture at Columbia as to disestablish it and destroy it, in violation of the constitutional command to aid and maintain it.

The court dismissed this argument as merely conjectural, and held that the legislature was free to command the addition of new departments.[2] This interpretation was in harmony with an opinion of the same court nearly half a century earlier.[3] This earlier decision, however, was not wholly relevant as a precedent, because it was prior to the adoption of a new Constitution of Missouri in 1875. Note also that the Missouri legislature in later years has developed a custom of restraining itself from interfering in the details of the governance of the state institutions of higher education; and the state supreme court has taken similar views.

---

[2] State ex rel. Heimberger v. Board of Curators of University of Missouri, 268 Mo. 598, 188 S.W. 128 (1916).

[3] Head v. Curators of University of Missouri, 47 Mo. 220 (1871); affirmed, (U.S.S.Ct.), 19 Wall. 526, 22 L.Ed. 160 (1874).

For example, the state treasury was not permitted to capture the insurance indemnity paid to a state college Board of Regents for a building destroyed by fire;[4] and the University of Missouri was allowed to issue dormitory bonds and construct necessary student housing on its own initiative and without statutory authorization by the legislature.[5] Similarly, the University's issuing of bonds to finance a self-liquidating parking facility was recently sustained by the state supreme court.[6]

There are five Missouri state colleges of long standing (Central, Northeast, Southeast, Southwest, Northwest). Each is governed by its own Board of Regents, which has a greater degree of autonomy than is common for institutions of this type in most other states, with the notable exception of Michigan. The Missouri state colleges were among the earliest in the nation to develop full-fledged degree programs in liberal arts alongside their degree programs in teacher-education. The 1967 legislature made provision for the planning of two new state colleges, to be known as Missouri Southern College and Missouri Western College, and to be at first two-year senior colleges, admitting no students below the third year.

In 1961 all the six public junior colleges in Missouri were operated by city school districts. In that year the legislature enacted the first state-wide junior college act, authorizing public junior colleges to be organized by combinations of contiguous school districts under specified conditions, and giving the State Board of Education considerable responsiblity in supervising their development. This act also provided state aid for annual operating expenses at the rate of $200 for each·30 semester hours of credit completed. The 1965 legislature increased this to $240 for each 24 semester credit hours, not computed on the preceding year's enrollments, but on the ensuing year's *projected* enrollments. An act of 1967 again raised this sum to $320, not to exceed one-half the total annual operating cost of the junior college district.

In 1960 Governor James T. Blair, Jr., took the initiative in forming a voluntary Coordinating Council on Higher Education, composed of the presidents of the state university and the state colleges, and the chairmen of their respective governing boards. Within a few years this body evolved and was metamorphosed into a permanent statutory Missouri Commission on Higher Education of 10 members, all appointed by the governor for six-year terms. Six of the 10 are laymen, appointed with the advice and consent of the senate. Of these six, not

---

[4] *State ex rel. Thompson, State Treasurer* v. *Regents of Northeast Missouri State Teachers College*, 305 Mo. 57, 264 S.W. 698 (1924).

[5] *Curators of University of Missouri* v. *McReynolds*, (Mo.), 193 S.W. 2d 611 (1946).

[6] *State ex rel. Curators of University of Missouri* v. *Neill*, (Mo.), 397 S.W 2d 666 (1966).

MISSOURI

Appropriations for Annual Operating Expenses of Higher Education in Missouri, Alternate Fiscal Years, 1959-60 through 1969-70 (in thousands of dollars)

Institutions	Year 1959-60	Year 1961-62	Year 1963-64	Year 1965-66	Year 1967-68	Year 1969-70
U of Missouri[1]						
Columbia Campus	8,744	10,738	14,175	40,565[2]	22,239	
Medical Center	4,009[3]	5,798[3]	5,899[3]		9,461[3]	
Ag Exper Station	1,091	1,289	1,736		3,400	
Ag Extension Serv	1,166	1,487	1,968			
School of Mines	1,719	2,052	2,947			
Subtotal, U of Mo (Columbia Campus)	16,729	21,366	26,727		35,100	45,611
Kansas City Campus			2,900		7,424	11,101
Rolla Campus					5,999	8,823
St Louis Campus			342		3,209	5,412
Space Tech Ctr			125			
U-wide progs & serv					7,534	8,756
Subtotal, U of Missouri (all units)	16,729	21,366	30,094	40,565	59,266	80,702
State colleges:						
Central Missouri	1,578	2,480	2,990	5,078	7,721	9,944
Southeast Missouri	1,357	1,781	2,478	3,376	4,930	6,299
Southwest Missouri	1,518	1,934	2,359	3,245	4,964	6,950
Northeast Missouri	1,331	1,748	2,129	2,910	3,688	4,778
Northwest Missouri	1,165	1,245	1,636	2,153	2,765	4,350
Missouri Southern (new)[4]					442[4]	1,528
Missouri Western (new)[4]					40[4]	615
Subtotal, State Colls	6,949	9,189	11,593	16,762	24,550	34,464
Lincoln University	1,062	1,223	1,320	1,487	2,122	2,588
Harris Teachers Coll[5]					665	1,000

State aid to Jr Colls				3,354	6,331[6]	8,733
Total	24,744	31,779	43,007[7]	62,168	92,934	127,487

[1]The appropriation is lump-sum to the University of Missouri, and the allocations are to be regarded as somewhat flexible, and not to be taken as precisely the amounts to be expended by each component, but as approximations.

[2]This amount includes Columbia, Rolla, Kansas City, and St. Louis campuses.

[3]This includes School of Medicine, University Hospital, School of Nursing, Crippled Children, etc.

[4]Institution expected to become a new state college for students in the third, fourth, and fifth years beyond high school.

[5]Locally supported teachers college in St. Louis, state-aided.

[6]State aid to local public schools and junior colleges was increased to $320 per student per year up to a maximum of 50 per cent of total operating cost, by an act of 1967. The previous figure was $240 per student per year.

[7]This total is exclusive of $3,376,000 appropriated for state aid for operating expenses of local public junior colleges.

more than three may be of the same political party, no two shall be from the same Congressional district, not more than two shall be graduates of the same college within the state of Missouri, none shall be active as a professional educator or as a member of the governing board of any institution of higher education in the state.

The remaining four members must be (1) the president of the University of Missouri, (2) the president of one of the five state colleges or of Lincoln University, (3) the chief administrator of a public junior college in Missouri, and (4) the president of a private college or university in the state.

The statute also provides for a large Advisory Council to the Commission on Higher Education, to be appointed by the Commission itself. It is composed in such a way as to enlist the participation of larger numbers of higher educational administrators and members of governing boards than the restricted membership of the Commission itself permits.

It includes: (1) the chairmen of the governing boards of the University of Missouri, Lincoln University, and the Missouri state colleges; (2) the president of Lincoln University (unless he is serving as a member of the Commission); (3) the presidents of the state colleges (except one who may be serving as a member of the Commission); (4) the chancellor of the Rolla campus and the heads of other campuses of the University of Missouri geographically distinct from the main campus and having a full-time equivalent enrollment of 3,000 or more; and (5) the State Commissioner of Education.

There is provision for additional members of the Advisory Council "provided that none shall be serving the same colleges or universities as that served by any other member of the Commission or the Advisory Council." These may include: (1) A chairman or member of the governing board of a public junior college within the state; (2) the chief administrator of a public junior college; (3) two chairmen or members of governing boards of private colleges or universities in Missouri; (4) two presidents of private colleges or universities; and (5) "one member, who is over 50 years of age, and who is not associated directly or indirectly with the administration or alumni association of any institution in the state, who shall represent the taxpayer and shall be referred to as the public member." Thus the Advisory Council comprises 25 members or thereabouts.

The duties of the Commission appear to be wholly advisory, with the responsibility only of making studies and recommendations to the governor, the legislature, the governing boards, and the public regarding the annual budget requests, the addition of new schools or departments, and the initiation and modification of a "coordinated plan" for state-wide public higher education. The statute involved no abolition of any governing board. The apparent aim is *liaison*, voluntary cooperation where palatable and possible, continuous research on the state-wide scene, and public information. These are all commendable.

It was in 1963 that the legislature determined, upon recommendation of the Board of Curators and with the consent of the board of trustees of the private University of Kansas City, to take over that institution and develop it as a large campus of the University of Missouri, under the governance of the Board of Curators. (The board of trustees continued its corporate existence as custodian of certain private trusts for the University, and as a private fund-raising agency.) The legislature also authorized the Board of Curators to develop a major university campus in St. Louis. Thus, Missouri's two large cities, never before supplied with public university facilities, were each to have a major campus of the University of Missouri. This was an epochal step. The University became a four-campus institution. By 1965 these developments were well under way, and from then on the appropriations for operating expenses of higher education increased at a rate approximating 50 per cent every two years. Universities are not made overnight, but Missouri is on the way, in the early stages, toward eventually having four-in-one; and four is none too many for a state of 4,627,000 people in 1968, with growth of more than 7 per cent since 1960. Note that the decade has also brought new state colleges and additional public junior colleges. Can Missouri afford all this?

In 1968 Missouri's state tax investment per citizen in the annual operating expenses of higher education was $24.59, ranking thirty-first among the 50 states. The ratio of this state tax investment to total personal income in Missouri was 0.77, ranking thirty-second. In fiscal year 1967 Missouri's total state and local tax revenue per capita was $260.27—well below both the United States average of $309.51 and the median state figure of $296.42. Missouri's state and local tax revenue per $1,000 of personal income was $93.18—much below the national average of $105.50. It would seem that the state will be able to sustain the momentum of state tax support of higher education and other essential public services for some years without hardship.

A special session of the legislature in 1969 increased the maximum rate of the graduated personal income tax to 6 per cent from the former 4 per cent, effective January 1, 1970, and raised the corporation income tax to 5 per cent from the former 2 per cent. The changes were expected to bring in $113 million of added revenues over 18 months. These acts were, however, subjected to a popular referendum April 7, 1970, and defeated. Other measures will be necessary.

MONTANA

With fewer than 700,000 people in 1968, and a gain of only about 2½ per cent since 1960, this mountain state would scarcely be expected to make any spectacular exhibit. It has the dubious honor of providing one of the rare instances wherein a state's appropriations of state tax funds for operating expenses of higher education declined at one point during the decade 1960-1970. The difference between these appropriations for biennium 1959-61 and biennium 1961-63 showed a loss of $570,000 for each of the two fiscal years, a decline of nearly 5½ per cent.

Montana State College at Bozeman (now Montana State University) bore most of the loss, while a few of the other state institutions gained slightly. Montana State College continued, however, to be the largest and best-supported among all the state institutions, exceeding somewhat the Montana State University at Missoula (now the University of Montana), as had been the case for many years.

As early as 1913 Montana placed all the state institutions of higher education under the State Board of Education, with only small and powerless local advisory boards for each one. This structure has continued to the present. It has had a bumpy history with respect to the maintenance of a central executive office for higher education. The existence of any such office has been discontinuous. More than once, after having provided by statute for a chancellor or executive secretary, the legislature has in some subsequent session simply failed to appropriate any money for the purpose and allowed the office to disappear for lack of support. During such a hiatus any attention given to higher education apparently became an additional part-time duty for some member of the staff of the chief state school officer. The Board of Education "serves as the Board of Regents of the University of Montana." Before the shuffling of institutional names already mentioned all the institutions collectively were styled the University of Montana; but the collectivity is now known as the Montana University System and is a corporate entity.

A study of the system was made and reported in 1958 by G. Homer Durham (then vice president of the University of Utah, later president of Arizona State University) under the joint auspices of the Montana Legislative Council and a temporary Governor's Committee on

Education Beyond the High School. [1] The report stressed heavily several recommended means of improving the coordinative efficacy of the central office, took a rather astringently restrictive view of expansion of the programs of the six institutions (opposing the offering of liberal arts degree programs at the state teachers colleges, and deploring the incipient idea of a medical school at either of the major state institutions), but wisely recognized the fact that some instructional departments often show very high unit-costs for valid reasons, and should not be made victims of misapplied cost studies. (Poultry science in an agricultural college is only one example.)

In mid-1968 Montana's state tax investment per citizen in annual operating expenses of higher education was $35.65, standing in sixth place among the states; and the ratio of this state tax investment to total personal income was 1.23 per cent—the highest in any state at that time. The disparity between Montana's high standing in these two respects and its very low rate of gain in appropriations over the nine-year period 1960-1969 may be explained in part by the large geographical area of the state, its sparse, widely-dispersed, and slowly growing population, and the resulting necessity of maintaining six widely-separated state colleges and universities. (There are also two local public junior colleges receiving some state aid.)

Montana continues to be one of the comparatively few states retaining a state-wide property tax levy for partial support of the state universities and colleges. It is in the form of a constitutional provision permitting the legislature to levy up to 6 mills per dollar of assessed valuation of all property in the state at the beginning of each biennium. It is subject to popular referendum every 10 years. In 1958 the vote to continue it for 10 years was by a margin of only 5,249 votes; but in 1968 it won by a margin of 38,230 votes, carrying 53 of the state's 56 counties.

The state has personal and corporate income taxes, at rates classified as "moderate" or about average; but in 1968 it continued to be one of the six small states having no general sales tax. The 1969 legislature increased rates on personal incomes above $10,000 to 8 to 11 per cent, from the former 8 to 10 per cent, and raised the corporation income tax to 6¼ per cent from the former 5½ per cent.

---

[1] G. Homer Durham, *The Administration of Higher Education in Montana.* Helena: Montana Legislative Council, 1958. 153 pp.

MONTANA

Appropriations for Annual Operating Expenses of Higher Education in Montana, Alternate Fiscal Years, 1959-60 through 1969-70 (in thousands of dollars)

Institutions	Year 1959-60	Year 1961-62	Year 1963-64	Year 1965-66	Year 1967-68	Year 1969-70
U of Montana[1]	4,001	3,643	4,285	4,645	6,760	8,335
Montana State U[2]	6,037	3,629	4,221	4,869	7,025	8,745
Ag Exper Sta		687	998	1,287	1,500	1,865
Ag Exten Serv		255	352	399	500	660
Subtotal, Mont St U	6,037	4,571	5,571	6,555	9,025	11,270
Coll of Min Sci & Tech[3]	609	386	451	520	1,045	1,275
Bur of Mines & Geol		106	136	183	58	50
Subtotal, Montana Coll of Min Sci & Tech	609	492	587	703	1,103	1,325
Eastern Mont Coll	1,187	1,034	1,165	1,246	2,220	2,950
Northern Mont Coll	703	513	636	828	1,210	1,510
Western Mont Coll	480	351	446	521	790	940
Executive Secretary		56	84	91	65	70
NDEA loan funds					30	35
WICHE				142	16	16
WICHE student payments					147	239
Board of Education				19	19	25
Total	13,018	10,660	12,772	14,749	21,375	26,715
Less	-1,788[4]					
Total (net)	11,230					

[1]Formerly Montana State University.
[2]Formerly Montana State College.
[3]Formerly Montana School of Mines.
[4]This $1,788,000 was appropriated for capital outlays; not operating funds.

NEBRASKA

The history of higher education in Nebraska is characterized by peaks and valleys. The University of Nebraska had the first organized graduate program west of the Mississippi, and was one of the early members of the prestigious Association of American Universities. Thereafter decades of drought and depression retarded progress somewhat from the middle 'Thirties to about 1965. The 1967 legislature provided for important steps toward a modern state revenue system.

Use of a state-wide property tax for state governmental revenue, anachronistically depended upon up to that time, had just been prohibited by a popular referendum. A state income tax, enacted in 1965 and scheduled to become effective in 1967, had also been defeated by referendum. The state had never had a general sales tax. The 40-member senate (the one-house legislature) not only had been slow to enact modern revenue measures, but had manifestly been unable to carry the electorate with it after adopting a necessary reform.

The 1967 legislature enacted for the first time a general sales and use tax at the rate of 2½ per cent, broad in coverage with few exemptions, to be effective May 1, 1967, and expected to produce from $50 to $65 million a year. The same session also enacted a personal and corporate income tax and a corporation franchise tax, effective January 1, 1968.

The sales tax act by its own terms specified that the rate would drop to 2 per cent January 1, 1969; and this occurred, even though Governor Norbert T. Tiemann urgently requested that the 2½ per cent rate be continued to July 1, 1969, by a special session which convened in December 1968. His argument was that figures on the first year's operation of the act, not then available, might very well turn out to necessitate some other action, and thus bring about two changes in the rate within a single year—a confusing and inconvenient circumstance; but his request was ignored.

The income tax act was admirable for its attention to simplicity and economy of its administration, and for its adjustability to changing conditions. The rate, initially defined simply as 10 per cent of the individual's obligation under the federal income tax law, was not fixed permanently by the legislature, but was directed to be fixed annually by the State Tax Commission, so as to produce sufficient revenue to fill the gap between the state's estimated income from all

NEBRASKA

Appropriations for Annual Operating Expenses of Higher Education in Nebraska, Alternate Fiscal Years, 1959-60 through 1969-70 (in thousands of dollars)

Institutions	Year 1959-60	Year 1961-62	Year 1963-64	Year 1965-66	Year 1967-68	Year 1969-70
U of Nebraska	12,500[1]	14,000	15,739	17,566	15,148	20,241
Medical Ctr	148[2]				4,926	8,271
Ag Exp Sta					3,144	3,631
Ag Exten Serv					1,845	2,438
Genl exten & pub serv					545	714
Conservation & survey					235	263
Omaha University[3]					1,504	4,883
Subtotal, U of Neb	12,648	14,000	15,739	17,566	27,319	40,733[4]
State colleges:						
Kearney	2,550	3,077	1,090	1,793	2,264	2,951
Wayne			848	1,054	1,315	1,481
Chadron			618	859	1,082	1,373
Peru			519	621	573	897
Subtotal, St Colls	2,550	3,077	3,075	4,327	5,235	6,703
Normal School Board	19					
State aid to Jr Colls					693	950
Total	15,217	17,077	18,814	21,894	33,248	48,386

[1]All appropriations are "plus reappropriations of unexpended balances as of June 30, 1959."

[2]The sum appropriated for operating expenses is for "care and treatment of indigent and needy patients at University of Nebraska Hospital." The sums appropriated to the hospital also include anticipated receipts collected during the biennium, and therefore are estimates.

[3]The sum appropriated was conditional upon approval of the voters of the city of Omaha of the merger of the Municipal University of Omaha with the University of Nebraska, as voted by the 1967 legislature. It was approved by the voters of Omaha.

[4]Includes $290,000 for School of Technical Agriculture.

other sources and the total of its budgeted expenditures. In 1969 it was set at 13 per cent for 1970.

The principle of determining the needs of a governmental unit for a fiscal period, and then fixing the tax rate to fit those necessities, is widely practiced in many states by local subdivisions in levying their local property taxes; but the application of this principle in fixing state tax rates is rare. Much more prevalent has been the inverted custom of first estimating the revenue and then cutting the cloth of appropriations to fit, giving distinctly second priority to the total justified needs of the state agencies and institutions. If Nebraska is leading a revolution in this respect, more power to Nebraska!

The 1959 legislature enacted, to be effective from that year through 1964, a tax of one-fourth mill per dollar on the grand assessment roll of all taxable real property in the state, the proceeds to go into a fund to be known as the University of Nebraska College of Medicine and University Hospital Building Fund.

In January 1961 a survey of higher education in Nebraska was reported, having been made under auspices of the Legislative Council by Lyman A. Glenny, then associate professor of government at Sacramento State College in California. Most of the staff work was done by local talent in the Nebraska institutions. Glenny essayed a projection of total operating costs (from state funds) of all the public institutions in 1970, at that time 10 years in the future. He cautioned that his estimate was probably conservative, as indeed it had already proved to be by 1967. The estimate for 1970 was $29½ million. The actual appropriation of state tax funds for each of the fiscal years 1967-68 and 1968-69 was $33¼ million; and close scrutiny of the basis of Glenny's 1970 figure indicates that these latter figures would go up to about $36 million if made accurately comparable.

The report commended the practice of the legislature in making lump-sum appropriations to the institutions, and the practice of the state auditor in restraining himself from overstepping his lawful functions—that is, he properly scrutinized expenditures only on the ground of their legality and the sufficiency of funds, and did not question their expediency or wisdom. Thus he avoided interference in educational policy.

Rightly the report was critical of the practice of requiring the institutions to submit their biennial budget requests on antiquated "object" forms, largely meaningless in higher educational administration.[1] The University of Nebraska and the other institutions had long since adopted the scheme of accounting and budgeting, expertly developed by committees of leading college and university business officers under the encouragement of the American Council on

[1]Lyman A. Glenny, *The Nebraska Study of Higher Education*. Lincoln: The Legislative Council, January 1961. 109 pp.

Education, and published in successively revised manuals, beginning in 1935. The two-volume edition current during the early 'Sixties had been published in 1952 and 1955. (An up-dated one-volume version was published in 1968.[2]) Budgets prepared in the manner suggested by these guides are meaningful and useful in the management of an institution of higher education; the ancient "object" forms are not, except in an extremely limited sense. Thus the University of Nebraska necessarily had the annoyance and expense of maintaining two accounting systems. The Nebraska legislature now no longer requires, through its own review procedures, the laborious necessity of double bookkeeping on the part of the institutions.

Considering the matter of state-wide "coordination" of higher education in Nebraska, the 1961 report sensibly and candidly recommended, "Coordination of these institutions should continue to be the responsibility of the legislature. No central board for coordination is necessary." Apparently no action was attempted until the 1967 legislature considered a bill to create a statutory Coordinating Council. Provision would have been made for this Council to be partly composed of members of the legislature; and the bill was eventually withdrawn because of constitutional barriers to dual office-holding. This must have been in the last analysis largely a matter of semantics—because there could be no barrier to having a legislative committee for the legislative function of weighing questions of coordination and finance. Such a committee could very well have a small permanent professional staff to provide it with studies and recommendations. But this would short-cut the idea of having a governor-appointed "coordinating board" in the executive branch, with statutory powers of coercion over the institutions, which was and continues to be (though perhaps with declining prevalence) the acme of the "conventional wisdom" and the rumbling bandwagon propelled by a strong faction in almost all legislatures.

The author has briefly proposed in print that adding a new layer of bureaucracy in the executive branch be avoided by making instead a direct channel of communication and reporting from the institutions to a joint legislative committee which will in any event have the legislative responsibility of recommending appropriations.[3] There is a good deal to be said for the thought that even in the largest and most populous states the central agency of research, planning, and public information could very well be the small permanent staff of a joint legislative interim committee rather than a proliferating bureau in the

---

[2] George E. Van Dyke (Ed.), *College and University Business Administration*, Revised edition. Washington: American Council on Education, 1968. 311 pp.
[3] M. M. Chambers, *Higher Education: Who Pays? Who Gains?* Danville, Illinois: The Interstate Printers & Publishers, Inc., 1968. 303 pp. (Chapter 26, Statewide "Coordination" in Public Higher Education.)

executive branch, headed by an ambitious "big executive" type armed with statutory license to "throw his weight around," needlessly harassing the institutions and annually reaching out for more staff and more arbitrary power. The choice between these alternatives has intimate bearings upon the maximum productivity of each tax dollar.

The 1969 legislature proposed a constitutional amendment, to be submitted to the electorate in 1970, which would abolish the existing institutional governing boards and create a single, elected Board of Trustees for Higher Education in Nebraska.

Probably the most significant recent development in the organization of Nebraska higher education was the bringing of the former Municipal University of Omaha into the state system as a part of the University of Nebraska. With the University of Omaha's over 11,000 students, and an excellent physical plant—though much in need of expansion—located in the state's only large city (400,000), the merger brings total enrollments in the University of Nebraska to well over 31,000 students and makes it among the 30 largest universities in the nation. State appropriations for the University rose to over $81 million for the 1969-71 biennium, a 48 per cent increase over the previous biennium—and four and a half times greater than the 1965 operating budget rate. In 1965 the legislature set in motion a major capital building program for all state institutions, which, though not fully funded in the succeeding bienniums, has resulted in about $65 million in academic construction at the state's institutions of higher learning since 1965.

Junior college development has lagged in the state with its small population and large geographic areas. But the legislature has moved into a state aid program and there is now some advocacy of full state support of this level of education beyond high school.

NEVADA

As of July 1, 1968, this state, with only 450,000 people dispersed over a vast area, continued to be among the half dozen least populous, although it had a population gain of about 59 per cent since 1960.

The University of Nevada System consists of four divisions: University of Nevada, Reno; University of Nevada, Las Vegas; Desert Research Institute; and the Community College Division. The fourth division was added by the legislature and the Board of Regents in 1969 and presently operates Elko Community College. Planning for community colleges at Reno and Las Vegas is under way.

The University of Nevada is governed by a Board of Regents whose 11 members are elected from three geographical districts. The division heads (presidents of the two universities and directors of the Desert Research Institute and the Community College Division) report to a chancellor and through the chancellor to the Board of Regents.

The Board of Regents is one of some seven state university governing boards whose members are elected by popular vote (boards of the three major state universities in Michigan and of one principal state university in Illinois, Nebraska, and Colorado). Decisions of the Nevada supreme court have established that the Regents of the University of Nevada have constitutional autonomy after the manner of the state universities of Michigan, Minnesota, California, Idaho, and a handful of other states.

Article XI of the Nevada Constitution, dating from 1864, is the source. It seems, however, that the tenor and intent of the autonomy clause were more or less ignored for several decades, if not forgotten or wholly misinterpreted unofficially. It was a decision of 1948 that affirmatively settled the matter.[1]

A legislative act of 1947 had purported to create an "Advisory Board of Regents," of not more than seven members, to be nominated by the Board of Regents itself and appointed by the governor. These "advisory regents" would have "all the rights and privileges, including travel and incidental expenses, of the elected Regents but shall not have a determining vote on any matter properly under the control of the elected Board of Regents."

---

[1] *King* v. *Board of Regents of University of Nevada,* (Nev.), 200 P. 2d 221 (1948).

The majority of the supreme court declared, in a scholarly 12,000-word opinion: "It was the intention of the framers of the constitution to vest exclusive executive and administrative control of the university in a board of regents to be elected by the people; and the act creating the advisory board would change, alter or modify its constitutional powers and functions and cannot find its justification in the power of the legislature to define the duties of the elected board."

In the course of the opinion attention was given to the leading cases on the constitutional independence of state institutions of higher education in Michigan, Minnesota, Idaho, and Oklahoma. A paragraph by Justice Horace Badt does much to clarify a popular misconception regarding the relation between a state legislature and a constitutionally autonomous state university: "Respondent insists that the unquestioned right of the legislature to appropriate the required funds for maintaining the university indicates that the elected board of regents was not vested by the constitution with exclusive and plenary control. However, the two processes are distinct. The power of the legislature to provide the requisite money and to limit and decrease the amount considered necessary by the regents is entirely a different function from the administration and control of the university itself."

In the early 'Sixties the University found itself again chafing under acts of the legislature purporting to subject it to control by various non-educational state administrative and fiscal authorities, one particularly galling instance being an act delegating to a State Planning Board the exclusive power to furnish engineering and architectural services to all state agencies constructing any buildings, "the money for which is appropriated by the legislature." The Planning Board was to have "final authority as to approval of architecture . . . supervision or inspection of construction or major repairs."

In 1963 the attorney general rendered an opinion: "The Board of Regents of the University of Nevada is not within the purview of (the foregoing act); even if the money is appropriated by the legislature, the delegation of powers to the State Planning Board being in derogation of powers conferred on the Board of Regents by the Constitution." [2]

During the same year a thorough and convincing study and report, confirming the autonomy of the University of Nevada by an analysis of the *King* decision and a traverse of the legal history of the matter, was made by Frank C. Newman, dean of the school of law at the University of California at Berkeley. [3]

---

[2] State of Nevada, Department of Attorney General, *Opinion No. 70*, September 12, 1963.

[3] Frank C. Newman, *The Legal Position of the University of Nevada as an Agency of the State of Nevada*. Reno: University of Nevada Press, 1963. 59 pp.

NEVADA

Appropriations for Annual Operating Expenses of Higher Education in Nevada, Alternate Fiscal Years, 1959-60 through 1969-70 (in thousands of dollars)

Institutions	Year 1959-60	Year 1961-62	Year 1963-64	Year 1965-66	Year 1967-68	Year 1969-70
U of Nevada[1]	3,636	4,863	6,042	7,114	6,101	7,589
Reno campus[1]						
Nevada Tech Inst					346	265
Library books					406	
Las Vegas campus[1]					1,971	3,348
NSU Tech Inst					272	265
Library books					359	
Football					15	
Research & Exten					1,767	2,130[2]
General Administration					536	314
Total	3,636	4,863	6,042	7,114	11,773	14,778[3]

[1] One university, with main campus at Reno and branch campus at Las Vegas. The Las Vegas campus bears the name of Nevada Southern University.

[2] Includes: $840,000 for "research and public service"; $708,000 for Agricultural Experiment Station; and $582,000 for agricultural extension service.

[3] Includes: $250,000 for classified salary increases; $401,000 for Computing Center; $25,000 for NDEA loans matching funds; $26,000 for Pahrump Valley; and $150,000 for Elko Community College, a new unit, university-controlled.

NEW HAMPSHIRE

Once one of the smallest in population, this state had an estimated 702,000 people as of July 1, 1968, having had a growth of more than 15½ per cent since 1960. During that period it rose from forty-fifth place among the states to forty-second, overtaking Montana and each of the two Dakotas. Despite the vigorous uptrend in population, New Hampshire's rate of increase in state tax appropriations for operating expenses of higher education over the nine years 1960-1969 was sluggish (a little over 157 per cent as against a nation-wide weighted average of 261 per cent); and in the ranking of the states in order of the magnitude of their total appropriations for that purpose, New Hampshire was shaken down from forty-fifth ($3,973,000) for fiscal year 1959-60 to fiftieth ($10,221,000) for fiscal year 1968-69. Thus in 1968 New Hampshire stood in the anchor place as to tax support of higher education, but in forty-second place (above eight other states) as to total population.

This anomaly is probably in large part due to the conspicuous paucity of state tax legislation throughout the whole period. New Hampshire had neither a general sales tax nor an income tax (except a negligible personal tax on income from dividends only, not touching salaries and wages). Thus the central elements of a modern state tax system were absent. In fiscal year 1966-67 New Hampshire's state tax receipts for state purposes only ($66,200,000) were smaller than those of any other state except Alaska ($58,200,000) and Wyoming ($55,300,000), with each of these two states having a total population of less than half that of New Hampshire.

New Hampshire's total tax receipts for both state and local purposes, per $1,000 of personal income, stood at $92.77. In only four states was this figure smaller: the populous and prosperous states of Texas ($91.08), Illinois ($85.29), Ohio ($82.23), and Connecticut ($91.47). Forty-five states were above New Hampshire's figure. The three highest were Hawaii ($134.97), Wyoming ($131.97), and New York ($131.85).

In 1968 New Hampshire's state tax investment per citizen in the annual operating expenses of higher education was $14.64—third from lowest among the 50 states. The ratio of this investment to total personal income was 0.45—third from lowest. The highest states by each of these measures were Alaska ($42.80), and Montana (1.23)—in each case nearly three times as high as the New Hampshire figure.

NEW HAMPSHIRE

Appropriations for Annual Operating Expenses of Higher Education in New Hampshire, Alternate Fiscal Years, 1959-60 through 1969-70 (in thousands of dollars)

Institutions	Year 1959-60	Year 1961-62	Year 1963-64	Year 1965-66	Year 1967-68	Year 1969-70
U of New Hampshire	3,244	4,020	4,359	7,325[1]	9,190[1]	10,224[1]
Keene State College	393	385	443			
Plymouth State Coll	332	308	344			
Coord Bd of Adv Edn and Accreditation				10	11	
Unallocated		4				
Total	3,969	4,717	5,146	7,335	9,201	10,585[2]

[1]This figure includes the Durham campus, and the state colleges at Keene and Plymouth. Support and control of the two state colleges were consolidated under a reconstituted University Board of Trustees in 1965.

[2]Includes: $250,000 for educational TV and $111,000 for "extension in counties."

It could be added that the adjacent state of Vermont, with a population only about 60 per cent as large as that of New Hampshire, appropriated more money for operating expenses of higher education than did New Hampshire, for the fiscal years 1967-68 and 1968-69.[1]

All the foregoing juggling of figures does not prove conclusively that New Hampshire has been remiss in state tax support of higher education; there are many other variable factors that have not been brought into the picture—but it certainly does not tend to indicate that the state has extraordinarily strained its resources for that purpose. This inference carries no disparagement of the quality of the work of the University, for quality can presumably be maintained by a policy of highly-selective admissions; but apparently expansion must be slow in relation to nation-wide and regional norms.

New Hampshire's complement of institutions embraces the University at Durham (with a Merrimack Valley Branch in the Manchester area, authorized in 1969); two state colleges at Keene and Plymouth; and four small vocational and technical schools (these latter governed by the State Board of Education). For many years the University had its own board of trustees, and the two state colleges (teachers' colleges until 1963) were governed by the State Board of Education. The legislature of 1963 created an enlarged Board of Trustees of the University of New Hampshire (of 22 members, including the presidents of the University and the two state colleges as voting members) and charged it with governing all three institutions, making the two state colleges in effect branches of the University.

The picture is therefore one of a state university with two branch colleges (often called regional campuses in other states), rather than one of a state-wide system consolidated under one governing board; especially since the state vocational-technical schools were not included in the jurisdiction of the reconstituted board of trustees, but remained under the State Board of Education. This view becomes all the more convincing when it is observed that there is no separate central office for the three institutions under the board of trustees other than that of the president of the University of New Hampshire, who is the principal executive officer of the board and hence of the three institutions, now combined.

The three institutions are physically separated by no great distances, and their combined enrollment (about 12,500 in the fall of 1967) is no larger than that of many single-campus state universities. The legislature of 1963 rejected a recommendation of the establishment of local public comprehensive junior colleges in the state.

---

[1]This statement is based on reports which include the Vermont Technical College in the Vermont totals, but do not include the New Hampshire Vocational Schools in the New Hampshire totals. However, omission of the Vermont Technical College would not change the relative positions of the two states for the biennium 1967-69.

NEW JERSEY

The Middle Atlantic states had prominent parts in the "Northeastern revolution" in state support of higher education during the decade 1960-1970. New York and Pennsylvania made phenomenal rates of gain. New Jersey's rate of gain was somewhat less, but much above the national weighted average over the nine years 1960-1969—332¼ per cent as against the nation-wide average of 261 per cent.

In both New York and Pennsylvania the private universities and colleges received substantial fractions of the increased annual tax support. In New Jersey their fraction was only indirect, through scholarships and other student aids, and its magnitude was relatively small. Details of the New York and Pennsylvania scenes appear on later pages. Observe here New Jersey.

As to population, only seven states are larger, but New Jersey has more than a million and a half persons less than the smallest of those, and nearly a million persons more than its own runner-up (estimates as of July 1, 1968: Michigan, 8,740,000; New Jersey, 7,078,000; Florida, 6,160,000). It may also be helpful to notice that New Jersey, though small in geographical extent, has almost as many people as all the eight vast mountain states of the West.

It was as recently as 1956 that Rutgers, the State University of New Jersey, became unequivocally and unmistakably a state institution.[1] A private corporation since its founding in 1766, it had been a sort of "mother hen" for the state-supported College of Agriculture since 1864. The relationship between the private corporation styled the Trustees of Rutgers College in New Jersey and the State College of Agriculture and its allied units was generally analogous to that of Cornell University in New York to the "contract colleges" adjacent to its campus (see New York, *infra*). In 1917 the New Jersey legislature gave the name of "State University of New Jersey" to the state-supported units at Rutgers, but this in no way impaired the private character of Rutgers University.

The state also maintained a different type of contractual relationship (for purchase of educational services) with the Trustees of Schools for Industrial Education at Newark, the board which con-

---

[1]For details see *Trustees of Rutgers College in New Jersey* v. *Richman*, 41 N.J. Super. 259, 125 A. 2d 10 (1956).

trolled the Newark College of Engineering. By the middle 'Twenties there was considerable dissatisfaction with this rather chaotic and rudimentary way of managing the state's interests in higher education, and in 1929, after a study of the whole situation had been made and reported, a statute was enacted, creating a new Board of Regents, composed of the Commissioner of Education and seven other members appointed by the governor, to be a permanent body having general oversight of all state-supported higher education except what was under the jurisdiction of the State Board of Education (chiefly the six state teachers colleges and normal schools).

The Board of Regents was to have surveillance over the Trustees of Rutgers College as to their administration of the state-supported units; power to contract for purchase of educational services with any and all private institutions of higher education when deemed in the best interests of the state; and responsibility for all state property used for higher educational purposes at the state-supported units at Rutgers and at any private educational institutions. Another board of longstanding—the Board of Visitors of the State Agricultural College— also had concurrent oversight of the Trustees of Rutgers College as to their management of the state-supported units at Rutgers University, and the Visitors, consisting of 21 members, one from each county of the state, were also exclusively in control of the Agricultural Experiment Station. The statute of 1929 made no change in the status and authority of the Visitors; hence the scene continued to appear complex.

Eventually the statute creating the Regents was repealed, and an act of 1956 was the last step in the metamorphosis of all elements of Rutgers University into "Rutgers, the State University of New Jersey"—the name it has borne since that year. The statute sets up a new Board of Governors for this newest of state universities, composed of eleven members: six appointed by the governor and five chosen by the Board of Trustees of Rutgers College, which was continued in existence as a corporate body, with a general advisory relationship to the new Board of Governors, and also charged with the control of all properties, funds, and trusts vested in it as of August 31, 1956 (except those originating from state or federal sources), and private gifts received thereafter, if so designated. It has sole power to invest the funds under its control; to turn over the income annually to the Board of Governors to be used in maintaining a university of high standards; and to withhold these funds, subject to adjudication by the courts of the state, if and when it believes they are or will be used to defeat the intent of maintaining "an essentially self-governing university of high standards."

In brief, the 200-year-old private corporation lives on, receives private gifts, and invests the endowment funds which have come or will come from private sources. It is also authorized, whenever a new president of the University must be chosen, to ratify or reject the choice of the Board of Governors.

It will be noticed that the statute of 1956 speaks of "an essentially self-governing university." This explains in part why, though the New Jersey state government is notorious for its penchant for symmetrical organization and overcentralization in the executive branch, Rutgers, the State University, actually has a considerable degree of freedom from the restraints emanating from central non-educational administrative and fiscal agencies in many other states; and indeed, from just such restraints which bear down upon the six state colleges in New Jersey itself. This will soon appear.

An important document was the report of the Governor's Committee on New Jersey Higher Education (appointed by Governor Hughes in 1963 and reporting in November 1964). [2] Said this Committee: "The program in higher education now maintained by the state of New Jersey is gravely inadequate to meet the needs of its citizens and satisfy the demands of a rapidly growing industrial state. The state-supported institutions are badly undernourished; the variety of their educational curriculums is critically insufficient; there is too little opportunity for professional study; and provisions for specialization in advanced fields of knowledge are severely limited."

Deploring the form of organization under which the State Board of Education and the Commissioner of Education exercised detailed control over the state colleges, the Committee continued: "New Jersey can well profit from the experience of industry, as well as of other states that have recently reorganized their educational systems, in recognizing that there are times when greater decentralization of control is essential for effective results."

Under the scheme then prevailing a college president could make no appointments without the approval of the Commissioner of Education *and* the State Board of Education. He was hamstrung by rigidly low salary schedules and by rigid line-item budgeting under which transfers of funds from one item to another—in the natural course of events bound to become highly desirable from time to time— were so hedged about by red tape as to be practically impossible.

Faculty recruiting was severely handicapped by the fact that the state college presidents were not permitted to use the common practice of paying the travel expenses of a candidate invited to the campus for an interview.

Rutgers, the State University, was exempt from the practice of line-item appropriations, as was also the Newark College of Engineering; but, incredibly, Rutgers was operating with salary schedules "on a par with those of the six state colleges," as dictated by the State Board of Education. Impossible? Yes; but Rutgers had ob-

---

[2] *A Report Prepared by the Governor's Committee on New Jersey Higher Education.* Trenton, N.J.: Governor's Office, November 1964, 45 pp.

tained only a few special exceptions (fighting through miles of red tape for each one) to attract professors of sufficient competence in certain academic areas, and for a few special positions in the Law School, the School of Engineering, and the Medical School then being organized.

Showing that populous New Jersey should then be producing about 640 Ph.D.'s annually, but actually turned out less than half that number in 1964, the Governor's Committee urged a great expansion of upper-division and graduate facilities at the State University and at the Newark College of Engineering, emphasizing that "The salary schedule at Rutgers University, especially for members of the graduate faculty, must be made competitive with the salary scales that are common at other great universities."

Touching the perennial problem of New Jersey's too-heavy "exportation" of students to colleges in other states, the Committee pointed out that in the fall of 1963 the *net* out-migration of New Jersey students was the astounding number of 56,503—by far the largest excess of out-migrants over in-migrants ever reported by any state. New York, with a population about three times that of New Jersey, was second with a net out-migration of 36,283 students. Commenting caustically, the Committee said, "New Jersey has depended too long on other states to carry too many of its educational burdens. This dependency has never been right nor just."

As to the state-level structure for higher education, the Governor's Committee recommended that the state colleges be taken from the jurisdiction of the State Board of Education and placed under a new Board of Trustees for State Colleges; and that at the apex of the state-wide system there be an Advisory Council on Higher Education, having no powers of mandate or coercion, but authorized to make recommendations. The Committee took cognizance of the possibility that the New Jersey Constitution, with its intense preoccupation with tidy symmetrical organization of the administrative branch, might be interpreted as prohibiting the changes in the structure proposed. Evidently somewhat fearful of an adverse decision on that question, the Committee undertook to provide in part for that contingency by recommending that in the event of such a decision a new and separate State Department of Higher Education be created, with "the actual administrative controls and regulation of the individual institutions and groupings therein to be *held to an absolute minimum*."

The upshot was that the legislature of 1966 enacted a statute effective July 1, 1967, setting up a State Department of Higher Education as one of the major branches of the executive branch of the state government. This Department is headed by a Board of Higher Education of 15 members: nine residents of the state, of whom two must be women, appointed by the governor with the consent of the senate for overlapping terms of six years; and six others, identified as follows:

NEW JERSEY

Appropriations for Annual Operating Expenses of Higher Education in New Jersey, Alternate Fiscal Years, 1959-60 through 1969-70 (in thousands of dollars)

Institutions	Year 1959-60	Year 1961-62	Year 1963-64	Year 1965-66	Year 1967-68	Year 1969-70
Rutgers, St U of NJ[1]	21,982	15,398	19,560	21,678	33,697	47,320
State colleges:						
Montclair		2,322	3,158	3,859	4,135	5,680
Trenton		2,448	3,619	4,066	3,712	5,643
Newark		1,721	2,342	3,103	3,404	4,859
Paterson		1,654	2,237	2,765	3,175	4,919
Glassboro		1,836	2,954	3,587	3,393	4,507
Jersey City		1,424	2,353	2,730	3,124	4,609
Subtotal, St Colls		11,405	16,663	20,110	20,943	30,517[2]
N J Coll of Med & Dent[3]		1,488	1,997	2,328	4,005	8,009
Newark Coll of Engrg					3,949	5,880
State-wide pay raises			1,600			3,300
Office of the Chancellor					281	727
Scholarships & loans				4,834	7,089	9,197
Ed'l Opportunity Fund						4,000
St aid to Schs of Nurs'g						1,700
St aid to Jr Colls				1,700	13,255	15,600
Mercer Co College[4]				177	539	
Union Co Jr Coll						
Total	21,982	28,391	39,820	50,826	83,758	126,250

[1]All units of the University, including Agricultural Experiment Station and Agricultural Extension Service.

[2]Includes $150,000 for each of two new state colleges (to be located respectively in the northern and southern parts of the state)

[3]In Newark. Acquired from Seton Hall University, a private institution, in 1965, and subsequently moved from Jersey City to Newark.

[4]Formerly Trenton Junior College.

The chairman of the Board of Governors of Rutgers, the State University; the chairman of the Board of Trustees of Newark College of Engineering; the chairman of the Council of State Colleges; the chairman of the Council of County Colleges (junior colleges); the president of the State Board of Education; and one representative of the private colleges and universities, designated by their state-wide association with the approval of the governor.

The principal administrator for the Department is the chancellor, appointed by the Board with the consent of the governor, for a term of five years. He need not necessarily be a resident of New Jersey.

Each of the six state colleges has its own board of trustees of nine members appointed by the Board of Higher Education with approval of the governor. At least two of the members of each board of trustees must be women, not more than three may reside in any one county, and there must be bi-partisan representation. The advisory Council of State Colleges consists of the presidents and chairmen of the boards of each of the six state colleges, plus the chancellor as a nonvoting member. The statute declares: "The Legislature hereby finds that it is in the best interest of the State that the state colleges shall be and continue to be given a high degree of self-government"; but subsequent events, soon to be noted, seem to indicate that at least up to 1969 this generalization was honored chiefly in the breach. A knowledgeable local observer has said the entanglements of the state colleges with non-educational fiscal and personnel agencies of the state were made somewhat less complex by the new act, "because they can now approach those agencies directly without going through either the State Board of Education or the State Board of Higher Education." However, they are within the jurisdiction of the Department of Higher Education, and it continues problematic as to whether this will ultimately bring any loosening of the restrictions on their autonomy.

Very little was done toward freeing the colleges from the incubus of tightly centralized and detailed fiscal control by non-educational fiscal agencies of the state. At the same time the colleges were mandated to expand quickly and develop programs in the arts and sciences and other suitable programs desired by eligible prospective students, in addition to their traditional programs for the professional education of teachers. This challenge should be accompanied by a degree of freedom and flexibility to accomplish the aim.

The situation was regarded as intolerable by many members of the college boards of trustees, and by most, if not all, of the college presidents. These individuals said the college presidency was an "errand-boy's job" which would not attract and hold men of stature. Some members of the boards of trustees said they felt powerless if all important decisions had to await approval from the statehouse, and under such conditions their positions and responsibilities had no attraction for able civic-minded citizens.

Accordingly, at the initiative of the New Jersey Education Association a remedial bill—a "State College Autonomy Bill"—was drafted and introduced in the 1968 legislature by Senators White, Hauser, and Tanzman. It was moved to second reading before the end of the session, and Senator White introduced a version of it (S-256) in the 1969 session and pressed for its passage with the aid of several of his colleagues. Its content was similar in general nature to that of the "Autonomy Acts" enacted in earlier years in Delaware and Massachusetts (which see, *supra*). The measure was enacted in somewhat modified form.

Basically, the new legislation provides for a decentralization of authority and decision-making to the boards of trustees and administrators of the state colleges in four specified areas, namely: personnel, budget execution, contracting, and purchasing. The law permits the colleges to transfer funds among general accounts (thus breaking away from the traditional line-item approach), set their own salaries within broad state guidelines, hire their own architects, and retain more of the fees which they collect (previously fees were designated for the general state treasury). The law was strongly supported by the college presidents, the New Jersey Education Association, and other faculty and alumni groups.

Now to the history of state financing of the expansion of very inadequate physical plants for public higher education in New Jersey. The legislature of 1959 proposed a bond issue of $67 million for university and college buildings, and this was approved by the electorate in November of that year. Nearly half the proceeds were allocated to Rutgers, the State University, with the remainder distributed among the Newark College of Engineering and the six state teachers colleges. Four years later, in November 1963, a $750 million bond issue that would have provided $275 million for capital improvements for higher education, was defeated at the polls. In November 1964, a state bond issue of $40 million, wholly for public higher education, and mainly for classroom buildings and other instructional facilities, which the legislature had proposed as a stop-gap to meet immediately pressing needs, was approved by the voters. Again in 1968 a state bond issue of $990 million, including $230 million for construction on the state university and college campuses, was overwhelmingly approved at the polls.

Meantime, on May 13, 1968, the State Board of Higher Education made a special report to the legislature recommending that the state should invest half a billion dollars in physical facilities for public higher education by 1975. It estimated that $302 million would be necessary to finance additional space for 83,000 more undergraduates than were presently enrolled. For academic facilities for additional graduate students, $10½ million would be needed. Forty-one million would be necessary for expanded medical and dental school facilities. Two new state colleges, presumably to be built from scratch, were proposed to be located in Bergen County and Atlantic County.

The fairly rapid gains in appropriations of state tax funds for operating expenses of higher education were not achieved without some tax reforms. At long last the legislature enacted a 3 per cent general sales tax which became effective in 1966 and was producing $250 million a year by 1968. In January 1966 Governor Richard J. Hughes was urging the legislature to enact a graduated personal income tax at rates from 1 per cent to 5 per cent.[3] The immediate response was not favorable; but in 1968 an organization known as the New Jersey Economic Policy Council published an estimate that this tax would produce $268 million the first year, and $284 million the second year, if enacted.

Thus it appeared that New Jersey was perhaps approaching the stage where it would have both a general sales tax and graduated state income taxes, enabling it to abandon its traditional practice of too-heavy reliance on local property taxes for the support of essential public services.

In 1962 the legislature enacted an elaborate statute authorizing and regulating the establishment of two-year colleges, to be known as "county colleges" in any county, but leaving the initiative with the "Board of Chosen Freeholders" (usually called *county commissioners* in other states) and also allowing their initiative to be defeated by popular referendum under certain circumstances. As a result, a few years were required to get the ball rolling. (Prior to 1962 the state had been lightly subsidizing a local public junior college at Trenton.) The 1962 statute provided for state aid of only $200 per student per year for annual operating expenses, or one-third of the total, whichever was less. In subsequent years the subsidy was increased to $300, in accord with an original intent that the state should provide about one-third of the operating expenses. It was also stated that the intent was for the state to supply about one-half of the capital outlay funds for the county colleges. The scheme is modelled closely after the New York practice in subsidizing community-junior colleges. New Jersey's appropriation for these purposes for fiscal year 1964-65 was $1,700,000, and had reached $7,686,000 by fiscal year 1968-69.

At about the same time that a new medical school was being planned and organized as a unit of Rutgers, the State University, at New Brunswick, there came also an offer from the Seton Hall College of Medicine and Dentistry, in Jersey City (a private institution operating as an outlying enterprise of Seton Hall University, the Roman Catholic university having its main campus at South Orange), then in financial straits, offering to sell its assets to the state for $4

---

[3]New Jersey then had a corporation income tax, at the rate of 4¼ per cent.

million, plus an operating subsidy of $300,000 for the period from January 1, 1965, to June 30, 1965. The legislature of 1965 authorized the purchase, and changed the name to New Jersey College of Medicine and Dentistry.[4]

A joint legislative committee was also created to continue the study of the immediate and long range needs of New Jersey for medical and dental education. At that moment the state had two public medical schools (at New Brunswick and Jersey City[5]), the one being only newly begun and the other in dire need of rehabilitation and expansion. It seemed probable that the state would develop both of these two public medical schools. This was a modest expectation, because a state of more than seven million people manifestly needs facilities equal to those of *three* full-fledged and full-size medical schools, with allied schools of various paramedical occupations and professions.

Late in 1966 the Board of Trustees of the New Jersey College of Medicine and Dentistry (then in Jersey City) decided to relocate it in downtown Newark, a city of more than half a million people. Negotiations had established that the city would provide a large site cleared as a result of urban renewal operations in a deteriorated part of the central city. When strenuous remonstrances came from some activist Negro residents of the area, the size of the site was reduced somewhat from its original over-ample dimensions, leaving it of sufficient size for its purposes.

Plans indicate that the large Newark City Hospital will be adjacent or nearby, and the state will also probably locate a large facility for mental health care in the immediate vicinity. Moreover, the medical college will be a component of a growing academic complex that already includes the Newark Campus of Rutgers, and the Newark College of Engineering. The vision is that Newark will eventually have a great comprehensive and cosmopolitan state university center in what was once a deteriorated "central city."

New Jersey is on the way toward adequate facilities for public higher education. It has a long way to go. It will be able to finance the effort. In 1968 the state's investment of state tax funds per citizen in annual operating expense of higher education was $13.57. The ratio of this state tax investment to total personal income was 0.34½ per cent. By both of these measures the state ranked forty-ninth. On both scales the state at the bottom—Massachusetts—was only a fraction below

---

[4]For disposition of a bequest to the private institution, which was ready to be paid over a few days after the transfer to the state, see *Montclair National Bank and Trust Company* v. *Seton Hall College of Medicine and Dentistry,* 90 N.J. Super. 419, 217 A. 2d 897 (1966)

[5]For inklings of the location of the Seton Hall College of Medicine and Dentistry in rented quarters in Jersey City, see *Robbins* v. *Jersey City,* 23 N. J. 229, 128 A. 2d 673 (1957).

New Jersey. In that year the percentage of Massachusetts students in public institutions in Massachusetts may have been as low as 30 to 35 per cent. The percentage of New Jersey students in public institutions in New Jersey was certainly more than 50 and may have been more than 55 per cent.

In fiscal year 1966-67, New Jersey's total state and local tax collections per $1,000 of personal income were $92.83, well below the national average of $105.50, and far below those of New York, which were $131.85. New Jersey has the resources.

NEW MEXICO

A leading citizen of this state recently made an encapsulated characterization of it as "a state with a high percentage of school-aged children in the total population, a low per capita income, a high welfare expenditure, and a large area to be covered by highways."[1] These features have bearings on the need and possibility of developing public higher education.

The population had reached 1,015,000 by July 1, 1968, after a modest gain of somewhat less than 7 per cent since 1960. Thus New Mexico "graduated" from the "less than a million" class, leaving 13 other states below that mark. The rate of increase over the eight years, however, had been less than that of any of the adjacent states: Colorado, 17 per cent; Oklahoma, 8 per cent; Texas, 14½ per cent; Arizona, 28 per cent; and Utah, 16 per cent.

New Mexico has seven state institutions of higher education, including the principal state university, the separate land-grant university, a school of mines, a military institute, and three regional institutions having normal school antecedents but now styled universities. The state constitution provides that each of these shall be governed by a Board of Regents and directs the legislature to provide for the composition and powers of such a Board for each institution. Members of these boards are appointed by the governor with the consent of the senate for overlapping terms of six years, and are removable only by an original proceeding in the state supreme court, on grounds of "incompetence, neglect of duty, or malfeasance in office."

Prior to 1951 any central direction of the state-wide system that took place was by the state general fiscal office known as the State Board of Finance, or by action of the governor and the legislature in making appropriations. In 1951 a statute was enacted creating a State Board of Educational Finance, to be concerned exclusively with state-wide higher education, to study and review the programs of each of the institutions, and to adjust and correlate their periodic budget

---

[1] Mrs. Irene S. Mills of Los Alamos, formerly president of the New Mexico School Boards Association, "ECS Commissioners Speak Out." *Compact* 3: No. 1, 23-24 (February, 1969).

requests. Its position is hence in part that of an intermediary between the institutions and the State Board of Finance. The 1951 statute stipulates that "the board (of educational finance) shall be concerned with the adequate financing of said institutions and with the equitable distribution of available funds among them. The board shall receive, adjust, and approve the budgets submitted by the several institutions prior to the submission of said budgets to the budget officers of the state and shall exercise such other powers as may hereafter be granted it by law."

Subsequent legislatures added other responsibilities, including those of allocating the proceeds of state bond issues for capital improvements among the several institutions; promulgating an official definition of legal residence in the state for use by the institutions in charging in-state and out-of-state student fees; and approving or disapproving requests for out-of-state travel money by officers and employees of the institutions. Also, any new graduate programs must be approved by the Board before they are begun, and likewise any expenditures for acquisition of real property or construction of buildings.

In most of the foregoing matters the Board is required to have the concurrence of the State Board of Finance, so that in effect it appears to be a subordinate advisory body for that Board. It also appears that these same provisions have not been enacted as separate statutes under their own captions or as amendments to existing statutes, but have merely been added as "riders" to successive biennial appropriation acts. Where that is the case, any such provision expires at the end of the fiscal period covered by the appropriation act, and disappears without the necessity of any repeal or amendment. It may, of course, be continued by again including it in the appropriation act for the next ensuing fiscal period.

The Board of Educational Finance consists of eleven members; one from each of the eleven judicial districts in the state, appointed by the governor for terms of six years. Not more than six members may be of the same political party. It is usually rated, possibly erroneously, as one of the more powerful or "harsh approach" coordinating boards. This may be due in part to the fact that it was created early in the 'Fifties, before the rush of "soft approach" coordinating boards and councils set up in several other states during the middle and late 'Fifties; and also to the fact that during the first several years of its operation its executive officer (then known as chancellor; now as executive secretary) was the energetic and indefatigable John Dale Russell, unquestionably one of the nation's most knowledgeable higher educational statesmen.

An event of 1961 was the legislature's authorization of the establishment of a two-year medical college at the University of New Mexico. The medical school opened its doors in 1964; and the

NEW MEXICO

Appropriations for Annual Operating Expenses of Higher Education in New Mexico, Alternate Fiscal Years, 1959-60 through 1969-70 (in thousands of dollars)

Institutions	Year 1959-60[1]	Year 1961-62	Year 1963-64	Year 1965-66	Year 1967-68	Year 1969-70
U of New Mexico		4,831[2]	6,085[3]	8,784[4]	12,853[5]	15,566
New Mexico St U		3,664[6]	4,632[7]	6,475[8]	8,564[9]	10,847
Eastern N M U		1,432	1,829	2,452	3,103	3,919
N M Highlands U		1,119	1,265	1,431	1,623	2,061
N M Inst Min & Tech		951[10]	1,021[11]	1,280[12]	1,476[13]	1,825
Western N M Univ		820[14]	969[15]	1,112[16]	1,320	1,481
N M Military Inst		186[17]	159[18]	100[19]	[20]	172
WICHE				15[21]	15[22]	15
Total	11,165	13,002	15,960[23]	21,649	28,954	36,126[24]

[1] This is a state-wide total.

[2] Includes $135,000 for Western Interstate Commission for Higher Education and a supplementary dental student exchange program.

[3] Includes $150,000 for the WICHE Student Exchange Program and a supplementary dental student exchange program. In addition the Board of Educational Finance received $15,000 for WICHE.

[4] Includes $195,000 for WICHE student exchange program and a supplementary dental student exchange program.

[5] Includes Medical School. Includes $155,000 for WICHE student exchange program and a supplementary dental student exchange program.

[6] Includes $160,000 for the State Department of Agriculture, administered by New Mexico State University.

[7] Includes $183,430 for administering the State Department of Agriculture.

[8] Includes $200,000 for administering the State Department of Agriculture.

[9] Includes $230,000 for administering the State Department of Agriculture.

[10] Includes $328,000 for the State Bureau of Mining and Mineral Resources, of which $100,000 comes from federal mineral leasing funds and is appropriated at the state's discretion.

[11] Includes $265,000 for the State Bureau of Mining and Mineral Resources, of which $100,000 comes from federal mineral leasing funds and is appropriated at the state's discretion.

[12] Includes $400,000 for the State Bureau of Mining and Mineral Resources.

[13] Includes $473,000 for the State Bureau of Mining and Mineral Resources.

[14] Includes $35,000 for administration of the state school bus safety program.

[15] Includes $35,000 for administering the state school bus safety program.

[16] Includes $39,000 for administering the state school bus safety program.

[17] The appropriation is for the entire program for grades 10 through 14. About 42 per cent of the students are at college level (grades 13 and 14).

[18] Only about 40 per cent of the students are at college level, 60 per cent being in grades 11 and 12. The appropriation is for the whole program.

[19] Only about 40 per cent of the students are at college level, 60 per cent being in grades 10 through 12. The appropriation is for the whole program.

[20] Accumulated balances and other incomes were such that no appropriation was made for 1967-68. Three-fifths of the students are in grades 10 through 12, and two-fifths at college level. In prior years the state appropriation has been for the support of the entire program.

[21] This is the state's flat payment in support of WICHE, and is in addition to the $195,000 mentioned in footnote 4.

[22] This is the state's flat payment for the support of the Western Interstate Commission for Higher Education, and is in addition to the $155,000 mentioned in footnote 5.

[23] Includes $36,388 appropriated to four institutions for state planning research.

[24] Includes $240,000 as state aid to local public junior colleges.

development of a full-fledged four-year medical college was authorized by the legislature of 1966 in time for the first class of students who completed the two-year course to continue their studies toward the degree of M.D. at the same institution without interruption, and graduate in 1968. Thus at the time when the state's population was reaching the one million mark, it had a new four-year medical college in actual operation—a matter of congratulation. [2]

The Board of Educational Finance mounted a comprehensive study of public higher education in the state, results of which were reported in October 1964.[3] The 50 explicit recommendations seem to have been rather trite and wordy, with little tendency to press for significant changes; but the report is valuable for its projections of enrollments and operating expenditures to 1975, though they are modest and conservative. Total operating expenses (including much more than state tax-fund appropriations) of $42 million in 1962-63 were projected as $58 million in 1965-66, as $78 million in 1970-71, and as $109 million in 1975-76—less than tripling over a period of 12 years. This is a rate of gain almost surely short of the mark, but nevertheless serving a purpose by alerting interested citizens to the fact of inescapable ongoing increase.

"By 1975 the student enrollment will be two and one-half times the 1961 enrollment," said the *Report*, "and the cost will have increased by nearly three times during that same period." Further, "The Commissioners recognize that the total higher education program brings economic growth as well as being a dynamic source of our cultural and social enrichment. Through our higher educational programs we cultivate our human resources and expand our human capital. Because the dividend can be so great, we must not only support higher education but be absolutely certain our product is good."

The legislature in 1969 raised the rate of New Mexico's general sales tax to 4 per cent from the former 3 per cent. It also stepped up the corporation income tax to 5 per cent from the former 3 per cent.

---

[2] An expansive view holds that there should be at least one medical college or comprehensive center of medical education for each unit of one million peopie. This is based on the customary dictum that a medical college should not be larger than 200 students in each of the four classes. For some other ideas on decentralization of medical education by the use of modern communications, see Indiana, *supra*.

[3] *New Mexico Commission on Statewide Higher Education Problems, Final Report.* Santa Fe: State Board of Educational Finance, 1964. 164 pp.

NEW YORK

Public higher education in the Empire State is conveniently thought of as two "academic states"—the State University of New York, and the City University of New York, the latter being much older than the former. Observe for a moment the two lines of history.

A free public academy was opened in New York City in 1847. This came to be the City College of New York, which has long had its principal campus at Convent Avenue and 139th Street in Manhattan. For generations it was the ladder of hope for many thousands of the great city's high school graduates in families of intellectual ambition but limited financial resources.

Hunter College, a municipal college for women which became coeducational in 1964, originated as the Female Normal and High School in 1870, received its present name in 1914, and in 1929 was placed, along with City College, under the governance of the Board of Higher Education of the City of New York. By 1969 this Board governed a total of nine municipal colleges, including: Brooklyn College (1930), Queens College (1937), Richmond College (1965), John Jay College of Criminal Justice (1965), York College (1967), Bernard M. Baruch School of Business and Public Administration (separated from City College in 1968), and Herbert H. Lehman College (separated from Hunter College in 1968). There were also six municipal junior colleges (named Borough of Manhattan, Bronx, Kingsborough, New York City, Queensborough, and Staten Island) and four additional junior colleges planned.

In 1961 all colleges and junior colleges then governed by the City Board of Higher Education, and such others as might be established in the future, were declared units of the City University of New York, newly created, governed by the Board of Higher Education. One of the objects of this scheme was to facilitate the development of advanced graduate studies. The senior colleges were already providing master's degree programs. The City University was given a chancellor and staff, and the expansion of doctoral programs was begun.

Always since 1847, all units of what is now the City University have been tuition-free for full-time regular undergraduate students. In recent years the Board of Higher Education has successfully resisted pressure from the governor's office in Albany to charge at least $400 per academic year to all students, as the units of the State University of New York were required to do by a statute first enacted in 1963. The City University charges tuition fees to students other than regular full-time undergraduates, and hence has a substantial income from student fees, because large parts of its total enrollment consist of graduate, special, and part-time students.

Primarily supported from city tax funds, the University has received subsidies from the state for many years, at first comparatively small, but increasing rapidly during the decade 1960-1970, from something of the order of $10 million in 1959-60 to some $80 million for 1968-69 (for annual operating expenses only). At the end of the decade the annual contribution of the state for operating expenses was approximately equal to that of the city; but this does not alter the fact that the University is a municipal institution, primarily city-supported and governed by the City Board of Higher Education. Its constituency, including perhaps nine million people, comes near being as large in population as all the rest of the state of New York; and it is larger than any of the 50 states except half a dozen at the top.

Because this present story is intended to include all higher educational agencies receiving annual appropriations of state tax funds, the City University of New York must be given important notice, though it is not a state university. In other parts of the nation municipal universities, never numerous, had by 1969 all but disappeared by way of becoming state institutions: Wayne University, Wichita University, Omaha University, and the three municipal universities in Ohio. (Akron and Toledo became state institutions, and the University of Cincinnati became "state-affiliated.")

The City University of New York, in contrast, grew swiftly, added new campuses, and bade fair to continue as a great municipal institution, state-subsidized, but retaining its city support and city control. It constituted almost half of the total public higher educational enterprise in New York State. Being a century older in origin (1847) than its counterpart, the State University of New York (1948), it has a somewhat different niche in the state governmental structure. For example, a statute of long standing (Education Law, Section 6202) made the city colleges "a part of the public school system," and from this it follows that the State Commissioner of Education has jurisdiction of appeals in disputes within the City University, as declared by a landmark decision of the Court of Appeals in 1942. [1] The Commissioner has no such jurisdiction relative to disputes within the State University of New York. [2]

The Commissioner is chief executive officer of the august body known as the Board of Regents of the University of the State of New

---

[1] *Board of Higher Education of the City of New York* v. *Cole,* 288 N. Y. 607, 42 N.E. 2d 609 (1942).

[2] *Application of Bowen,* 17 A.D. 2d 12, 230 N.Y.S. 2d 578 (1962).

York and State Board of Education,[3] and as such he bears the ponderous title of President of the University of the State of New York. The "University of the State of New York," as is generally understood, is simply an all-embracing designation for all formal education at all levels, private and public. Hence the Board of Regents and its Commissioner properly have much of their attention pre-empted by policy-forming for elementary and secondary education. In the field of higher education, until a decade or two ago, the Regents have usually been largely preoccupied by their solicitude for private colleges and universities, on the more or less overt and taken-for-granted theory that private higher education was the central and major part of the whole enterprise and should dominate the state-wide scene, while the public sector should be allowed to develop only grudgingly and solely to fill in some necessary educational services rejected or neglected by the private institutions.

Prior to 1948 public higher education in New York State could be characterized as "a limping and apologetic enterprise."[4] There was no state university. The state colleges of Agriculture, Home Economics, Veterinary Medicine, and Industrial and Labor Relations were on state-owned campuses adjacent to Cornell University, and their administration was entrusted by law to the Board of Trustees of Cornell University, a private corporation. The same was true of the Agricultural Experiment Station, located at the town of Geneva. The State School of Ceramics, offering both undergraduate and graduate programs through the doctoral degree, was in similar relationship to Alfred University, a private liberal arts college. The State School of Forestry, adjacent to the private Syracuse University, was governed by its own board of trustees.

There were 11 small single-purpose state teachers colleges, most of which had started as two-year normal schools in 1866. The one at Albany had begun in 1844, and was thus among the earliest normal schools in the nation. Some were established as late as the 'Eighties. They had virtually impotent local boards, and were in fact governed from the statehouse by the State Education Department.

There were no public junior colleges or two-year technical schools. There were no public medical colleges. Such public colleges as existed

---

[3] Existing in one form or another since 1784, the Board of Regents has in recent decades been composed of about 13 to 15 members, one elected each year by the legislature, for a term of 13 to 15 years, the long and overlapping terms insuring a degree of continuity.

[4] These words were applied in the context of 1960 in the report of the Governor's Committee on Higher Education, the members of which were Henry T. Heald, then president of the Ford Foundation; Marion B. Folsom, former Cabinet member; and John W. Gardner, then president of Carnegie Corporation of New York.

were, as already noted, generally governed by private corporations or by the State Education Department. In all cases they were tightly controlled financially by the State Department of Finance at Albany, and, in their construction enterprises, by the State Department of Public Works. Their programs of instruction, research, and public service were not expanded sufficiently to supply the great new demands for public higher education of the post-War period. This brought on the revolution of 1948, in which the state began to awaken after a century and a half of dormancy regarding public higher education.

After state-wide studies in which many qualified persons from other states participated, the legislature of 1948 created the Board of Trustees of the State University of New York, composed of 15 members appointed by the governor for terms of 10 years, and with its chairman and vice-chairman designated by the governor, to be the governing board of all the state colleges, and to be concerned with the development of a state-wide system of public institutions of capacity and quality to fit the needs of the future.

This amounted to placing an intermediary board between the Board of Regents and the state institutions, and relieving the Regents of much of their thinly-spread responsibility in that field. The board of trustees is nominally subordinate to the Board of Regents, and its major policies and plans must be submitted to the Regents for approval; but in fact this seems to tend to be a rather perfunctory matter, and the board of trustees functions for practical purposes as a nearly-autonomous governing board, to the extent that is possible under New York's incredible maze of fiscal controls. In the language of the statute the board of trustees is "within the State Education Department," but in many respects it is actually apart from it. The relationship was known to be anomalous when it was first created in 1948, and it continues to be anomalous in the judgment of most observers. In 1948 Governor Thomas E. Dewey was determined to have the board of trustees look to the governor rather than to the Regents, and he was in considerable part successful, though neither the wording of the statute nor the practice under it is wholly unequivocal.

The relationships of the "contract colleges" at Cornell University and Alfred University were essentially not disturbed, and continued as before. All institutions were left in the toils of the central fiscal control bureaucracy. The board of trustees and its staff came into the picture as an added layer. The city colleges in New York City (to become the City University in 1961) and their Board of Higher Education were not within the purview of the act.

Although the board of trustees had an executive officer and staff from the beginning in 1948 (the executive was called president until late in the 1960's, when the title was changed to chancellor), it did not really hit its stride in fostering public higher education befitting the nation's most populous state until more than a decade later. During that first decade there was generally too-rapid a turnover in the president's office, and an apparent inability of the trustees to agree on major policies and plans. For example, when one president, backed by eminent scholarly authority from other states, argued that the conglomeration of colleges called the "State University" would never be a university in fact until the state developed at least one campus as a large center of learning with a great advanced graduate school and at least some graduate-professional schools, at first a majority of the board disagreed with him strenuously, and he was soon forced out; but scarcely two years had elapsed after his departure before the board adopted a plan for not one, but *two* advanced graduate University Centers, and this was soon expanded to *four*. Action in accord with this plan began in the early 1960's, and had made good progress by 1969, but had yet a long way to go.

State acquisition of the private University of Buffalo in 1962 brought in a "ready-made" university center of considerable size and passable repute, with undergraduate, graduate, and professional faculties already "in business." Starting with an appropriation of $5,775,000 for operating expenses for fiscal year 1962-63, the annual appropriations of state tax funds to the "State University of New York at Buffalo" zoomed to $49,834,000 for fiscal year 1968-69. In that year it appeared that only about 14 other comparable public universities in the nation got larger sums of state tax funds for annual operating expenses.[5] Thus it might be said that, even though the university at Buffalo had not yet had time to convalesce fully from the throes of its change from private to public, nevertheless in 1969 the state of New York at long last had, or was about to have, one top-echelon state university.

The other three "State University Centers"—at Albany, Stony Brook, and Binghamton—were developing, but at not quite so swift a pace. Each grew out of smaller antecedents (Albany from the state college of education, dating from 1844; Binghamton from the relatively young state college of liberal arts named Harpur College; and Stony Brook from the stones and the brook[6]). All three of these bade fair to become major state universities of distinctive excellence within another decade.

---

[5] To arrive at this ranking, eight multicampus "megaversities" were first eliminated as not comparable. Among these was the multicampus State University of New York itself. No more than approximate comparability is possible, even after eliminating the 8, because several of the 14 remaining were multicampus, but had a large percentage of their students on one main campus.

[6] Actually it began in 1957 at Oyster Bay as a new State University College of Science and Engineering, was renamed Long Island Center in 1960, and was moved to Stony Brook in 1962.

Preceding the foregoing by a dozen years, the board of trustees had moved promptly in 1950 to merge two private medical colleges of long standing into the State University of New York. This was necessary because of the state's dire need for public facilities for medical education, and because of the financial straits in which these medical colleges found themselves, without ability to expand and with their ability to survive a matter of some doubt. Thus the private Long Island College of Medicine became the Downstate Medical Center of the State University of New York, and the medical college of the private University of Syracuse became the Upstate Medical Center of SUNY, both in 1950.

In the late 1940's the legislature also provided for six two-year colleges styled Agricultural and Technical Institutes as state institutions with no local tax base; and for a state-wide system of local two-year community colleges, to be established on local option with a county as the local taxing subdivision which would provide half the capital outlay and one-third of the annual operating expenses. The state would supply half the capital funds and one-third of the operating funds, and the remaining one-third was to come from student fees. This scheme has apparently had a good deal of success over two decades. Thirty-seven comprehensive local public community colleges were in operation by 1969, and four more had been approved by the board of trustees of SUNY for establishment. For fiscal 1968-69 the state appropriation for their annual operating expenses had grown to about $35 million, placing New York third among all the states by that measure, after only California and Florida.

The community colleges have their own local boards of trustees, but the central agency for their state-wide leadership is under the board of trustees of SUNY. Hence it might be said they are nominally, or to a limited extent, units of SUNY. It is often said that SUNY is composed of sixty-odd campuses; but about half of these are community colleges primarily supported and controlled by their own local taxing subdivisions. Some stirrings have been heard to the effect that these colleges should become *state* two-year colleges, as the Agricultural and Technical Institutes are. The thought may gain some credence from the fact that local public junior colleges have been taken over by the state in Minnesota, Colorado, and Washington.

The effective exercise of the taxing power inexorably moves upward to the larger units of government because of economic progress; and the smaller units such as cities, counties, school districts and junior college districts, dependent as they must be almost wholly on property taxes, have increasing difficulty in supporting their own necessary public services. This means that the state must subsidize them with increasing amounts, or assume their full tax support. There is also, of course, the additional possibility of an eventual massive federal program of annual institutional grants direct to institutions of higher education, by-passing the state governments.

All the foregoing is intended to convey a sketchy impression of two large systems of public higher education in New York: The City University of New York (CUNY), and the State University of New York (SUNY). Bits of their history, their organization, their respective relations to the city government and to the state government, and their state tax support will serve as backdrop for other features of the story. We hold in mind, too, that in 1968 New York had 143 private colleges and universities, of which 60 were nonsectarian and 83 classified as denominational. More of that further on.

Some Studies of Higher Education, 1960-1968

A landmark of the decade was the release of the report of the Governor's Committee on Higher Education in November 1960. [7]

The report frankly pointed to a well-known fact—that New York was currently exporting many "educational emigrés" to colleges and universities in other parts of the country because educational opportunity was not available to them at home. It candidly "laid on the line" the fact that New York's expenditure per capita of state and local tax dollars for current operation of higher education in 1957-58 had been only $5.41 as compared with $15.17 for California, $11.82 for Michigan, $10.29 for Iowa, $8.55 for Indiana, $8.08 for Illinois, $7.61 for Texas, $7.60 for Wisconsin, and so on.

Among the goals advocated by the Committee were two superb ones: (1) wide availability and diversity of educational opportunity for students with various intellectual capabilities and *of all income classes in the state*; and (2) a strong system of public as well as private higher education, *including strong public universities*.

Pointing to the motto on the seal of the State University of New York: "Let each become all he is capable of being," the Committee bluntly declared that public higher education in New York should "cease to be a limping and apologetic enterprise," and "achieve the spirit and style which characterize the nation's great public institutions."

Among many recommendations to implement the improvement of the public system were: transforming the 11 state colleges of education into high-grade colleges of liberal arts with appropriate departments of education; enlarging the existing community colleges; converting the 6 state technical institutes into community colleges; and building new two-year community colleges as rapidly as a minimum enrollment of 500 students could be anticipated within two years after establishment. It was also recommended that the state's

---

[7] Henry T. Heald, Chairman; Marion B. Folsom; and John W. Gardner. *Meeting the Increasing Demand for Higher Education in New York State.* Albany: State Education Department, 1960. 74 pp.

contribution to the annual operating expenses of public community colleges (then about one-third) should be increased to perhaps one-half.

The Committee touched off an instant storm of opposition from the students and faculties of the municipal colleges in New York City, and from many persons at various ranks in the vast New York City system of public schools, with its 40,000 teachers and more than one million pupils, by its recommendation that the City Colleges, which had always been tuition-free for regular full-time undergraduates, should charge $300 a year tuition fees to all students except those whose families were shown by state income tax returns to have incomes of less than $5,000 a year.

The viewpoint of the Committee was that this would make tuition fees approximately uniform for all undergraduates in all public institutions of higher education in the state.[8] The issue of whether public higher education shall or shall not be on a basis of substantial charges to students is a fundamental and important one, from the standpoint of the availability of educational facilities to qualified persons of all economic classes. The Committee said it espoused the principle of availability, but somehow was able to reconcile this with the idea of charging fees to all except those who show an extremely low family income, and at the same time stand among the top 20 per cent of their high school graduating classes. What would happen to those who were merely in the top half or top three-fourths of their classes, or whose family incomes were $5,001 instead of $4,999, the Committee did not undertake to say.

The state-wide system of competitive scholarships (Regents' Scholarships) for which New York had been known for many years should be supported by larger state appropriations, and the scholarships should be made tenable in institutions outside the state as well as within it, the Committee thought.

Another highly controversial feature of the report was the recommendation that public tax funds be paid directly to private institutions, including denominational institutions. The Committee rather sheepishly suggested that the obvious conflict with the state constitution could be obviated by paying the institutions a specified sum for each student receiving a degree, under a contract between the state and the institution rather than under an outright appropriation to the institution. Only a modest scale was proposed—about 6 per cent of

---

[8] At the time, some of the state colleges were tuition-free; but they were all required to charge a minimum of $300 by a statute effective September 1, 1963. Subsequently this was raised to $400. This was a prime element in Governor Nelson A. Rockefeller's plan to finance academic buildings by issuing bonds backed by a fund built up from student fees. The City Colleges (now the City University of New York) continued throughout the decade to be tuition-free for regular full-time undergraduates, despite strong pressure from Albany.

the total cost to the institution of educating the student, with no contemplation that this should ever rise above 10 per cent. If started in 1961-62 as indicated, its initial cost would be about $10 million a year, the Committee estimated.

Nothing was done about this recommendation until 1968, when another and quite different Governor's Commission, set up especially to revive the issue, did so. Meantime much water had been over the dam, including the Constitutional Convention of 1967 whose work turned out to be futile except for any side-effects it may have. We reserve that story for later paragraphs, and continue here with the notable report of the Governor's Committee of 1960.

On the question of top-echelon organization for public higher education, it was recommended that the historic Board of Regents of the University of the State of New York continue at the apex, with its traditional role of high-level surveillance and oversight of private and public institutions. In harmony with this role, its only added duty with respect to public higher education would be to receive, examine, and act upon a "master plan" for its development, which should be submitted at least once every three years by the board of trustees of the State University of New York. The Regents would be a species of reviewing and consenting body, while the trustees would be fully responsible for planning and its implementation.

Speaking of the relations of the board of trustees to state central administrative and fiscal agencies, the report said: "Its present powers of self-determination should be extended and clarified to bring them up to the level which is taken for granted by the great public universities of the nation." More specifically, "The State University should be granted a large degree of freedom from existing budgetary requirements for the establishment of individual positions and more leeway in shifting appropriated funds from one educational purpose to another, and in the use of non-appropriated income."

Moreover, "The State University should also be granted the right to determine what positions within its structure are 'educationally related' and hence can be established by the State University on its own initiative, rather than requiring approval of the Civil Service Commission."

Still further, the Committee believed the State University should have the option to make purchases through sources other than the State Division of Standards and Purchase; and to avoid intolerable red tape and delays, the State University should be staffed with appropriate officers of its own to handle its own architectural, engineering, and construction contracting services." [9]

---

[9] Apropos of this last recommendation: In 1962, after Governor Nelson A. Rockefeller could no longer brook the delays of four to six years between

One cannot fail to note that these recommendations would loosen the strangle hold of one of the tightest state bureaucracies in existence, over higher education; and that they are in harmony with the famous report of Milton Eisenhower's Committee on Government and Higher Education in 1959, which was based at the Johns Hopkins University.[10]

All the changes could be made by action of the legislature, and some of them merely by executive orders of the governor. Reasonable university autonomy would be more permanent and more secure if it were written into the state constitution, as it is in Michigan, Minnesota, California, and half a dozen other states (which see). As it is in New York State, little has been done other than the vigorous Governor Rockefeller's cutting of the Works Department red tape in 1962. The other needed changes could be made piecemeal, or all at once in a sweeping "Autonomy Act," as has been done in Delaware, Massachusetts (twice), and New Jersey (which see).

One more recommendation of the Heald-Folsom-Gardner Committee must be observed, though the report expressed it all too briefly and in unfortunately ambivalent and equivocal words: "Local boards of overseers" for each of the numerous institutions composing the State University of New York, "to supplant existing advisory boards, trustees, or councils," should be established. In scarcely more than a single paragraph the report referred to them as "strong local boards" available "to help govern the institution," and then listed their duties as to "make recommendations . . . , advise the president . . . , and marshal local constituency support," and then again spoke of making them "responsible for operational management."

This left it rather unclear as to whether they were to have any real discretionary authority. It had the virtue, however, of impliedly admitting that the existing practically impotent local boards were unsatisfactory, and that each institution should have the benefit of a local governing board. In the present New York system, such boards, while having a somewhat circumscribed sphere of authority as compared with institutional governing boards in other less centralized systems, could be given enough power and autonomy to attract the best citizens

---

authorization and occupancy of college buildings, occasioned by the bumbling of the Department of Public Works, he persuaded the legislature to create the new independent State University Construction Fund and to remove the construction of academic buildings from the jurisdiction of the Department of Public Works and place it under the new Fund, headed by General David W. Traub, retired Controller of the U.S. Army. This was a successful emergency stroke to expedite the large building program then beginning. For the long run, it would be better to entrust the whole function to the board of trustees of the State University. This was impliedly recommended in the *Wells Report, infra*.

[10] Committee on Government and Higher Education, *The Efficiency of Freedom*. Baltimore: Johns Hopkins Press, 1959. 44 pp., and the resource volume: Malcolm Moos and Francis E. Rourke, *The Campus and the State*. Baltimore: Johns Hopkins Press, 1959. 414 pp

NEW YORK

Appropriations for Annual Operating Expenses of Higher Education in New York, Alternate Fiscal Years, 1959-60 through 1969-70 (in thousands of dollars)

Institutions¹	Year 1959-60	Year 1961-62	Year 1963-64	Year 1965-66	Year 1967-68	Year 1969-70
State University of New York						
University Centers:						
Buffalo²	799	1,530	9,211	26,498	45,405	55,920
Stony Brook (L I)	2,276	2,712	2,837	7,150	18,641	29,648
Albany	920	1,154	4,641	8,640	18,640	28,381
Binghamton (Harpur)			3,015	5,300	9,474	15,926
Subtotal, U Ctrs	3,995	5,396	19,704	47,588	92,160	129,875
Medical Centers:						
Downstate (NYC)	3,888	4,190	5,498	11,712	17,444	25,313
Upstate (Syracuse)	2,740	3,076	3,990	12,252	16,901	21,939
Subtotal, Med Ctrs	6,628	7,266	9,488	23,964	34,345	47,252
Colls of Arts & Sciences:						
Buffalo	2,460	2,843	4,199	6,675	10,398	15,261
New Paltz	1,476	1,713	3,134	5,259	8,505	12,436
Oswego	1,990	2,319	3,656	5,580	8,549	13,509
Oneonta	1,461	1,843	2,800	4,212	7,279	11,323
Brockport	1,431	1,690	2,687	3,885	6,707	11,448
Cortland	1,864	2,188	3,346	4,615	6,924	9,585
Geneseo	1,290	1,602	2,492	3,783	6,229	10,184
Plattsburgh	1,347	1,610	2,543	4,016	6,096	9,781
Potsdam	1,383	1,614	2,498	3,500	5,903	9,298
Fredonia	1,299	1,476	2,309	3,633	5,535	8,457
Old Westbury					445	1,843
Purchase					450	959
Rome-Utica-Herkimer					100	350
Subtotal, Colls of A & S	16,001	18,898	29,664	45,158	73,120	114,434

Statutory Colleges:						
Agriculture	6,872	7,411	8,979	10,413	12,211	14,214
Home Economics	1,538	1,664	2,019	2,401	3,038	3,513
Ag Exper Station	1,417	1,571	1,925	2,123	2,537	3,093
Veterinary	1,227	1,317	1,735	1,974	2,481	3,004
Indus-Labor R	1,125	1,264	1,570	1,836	2,352	2,670
Ceramics (Alfred U)	770	872	1,100	1,266	1,680	1,956
Gen'l Services	1,563	1,627	1,915	2,113	2,589	3,214
Subtotal, Statutory Colls	13,742	14,854	18,143	20,860	25,208	31,664
Specialized Colleges:						
Forestry (Syracuse)	1,859	2,022	2,825	3,716	4,830	6,062
Maritime (NYC)	947	993	1,265	1,959	2,568	3,118
Subtotal, Spec Colls	3,576	3,887	5,190	6,941	9,078	9,180
Grad Sch of Pub Aff (Albany)[3]			219	574		
Agricultural & Technical Insts:						
(2-year colleges)						
Farmingdale	1,670	1,720	2,185	4,080	6,058	7,540
Alfred	869	1,000	1,454	2,314	4,081	6,676
Morrisville	606	652	941	1,691	2,712	4,277
Cobleskill	387	470	838	1,486	2,703	4,098
Delhi	369	471	799	1,482	2,392	4,040
Canton	451	460	699	1,186	2,137	4,028
Subtotal, Agri & Tech Colls	4,352	4,773	7,135	12,813	20,083	30,659

(Continued)

NEW YORK (Continued)

Institutions	Year 1959-60	Year 1961-62	Year 1963-64	Year 1965-66	Year 1967-68	Year 1969-70
University-wide:						
Administration	865	1,011	1,591	3,544	4,577	5,787
SUNY scholarships			1,250	1,750	2,000	1,800
All SUNY Institutions[4]			1,949	7,177	7,266	
Ctr for Internat'l Studies				150	1,128	6,139
Gen'l U-wide Programs						
Supplemental dorm operation				5,700		
Subtotal, U-wide	865	1,011	4,790	18,321	14,971	23,153[5]
Less amounts financed by fees[6]				-25,700	-23,165	-47,126
SUNY Net Total from Tax Funds				149,946	245,800	381,791[7]
Other:						
City U of N Y	11,329	24,075	29,821	40,000	58,800[8]	92,493
Scholar incentive prog	11,158	22,844	22,500	33,400	38,700	36,600
Schol'shps & fellowships			21,955	32,900	33,400	33,300
HE Assistance Corp		2,495	5,029	11,046	13,512	1,494
Community colleges[9]	3,450	5,690	9,500	16,000	29,900	44,000
Two-yr Urban Ctrs					2,800	5,886
Equal Opp Prog (NYC)						5,000
Priv Medical Colleges				430	6,300	1,410
Endowed chairs					800	1,000
Contracts with priv schs for health professions					1,200	
Subtotal, Other	25,937	55,104	88,805	133,776	185,412	243,550
Total	78,546	111,189	182,918	283,722	431,212	625,341[10]

[1] All the institutions named are components of the State University of New York.

[2] Metamorphosis from private to state ownership and control completed September 1, 1963.

[3] Operated with state subsidy by two private universities (New York and Syracuse) prior to 1961-62, and now a unit of the State University Center at Albany.

[4] For allocation to the institutions for their share of the NDEA student loan program, the nursing loan program, faculty research grants, educational communications, information processing, continuing education, the scholars-in-residence program professional recruiting, the Women's Vocational Guidance Center, the faculty senate, the university press, the admissions program, Distinguished and University Professorships, and the student work-study program.

[5] Includes $5,160,000 for professional salary increases, and $4,267,000 for upstate SEEK program for deprived college students.

[6] This amount is deducted as representing institutional income derived from non-tax sources, chiefly student fees. It is to be noted that the sums are therefore somewhat larger than they would be if they represented only *appropriations of state tax funds*.

[7] Includes $42,700,000 for fringe benefits.

[8] Excludes $3½ million for debt service on prior capital projects, and $3½ million for state support of a new capital construction fund.

[9] The community colleges are nominally a part of SUNY, but each has a local taxing district which provides one-third of its operating expense and one-half of its capital outlays.

[10] Includes $20,117,000 for aid to private institutions; $2,000,000 for Brooklyn Polytechnic Institute; and $250,000 for New York Ocean Science Laboratory.

and make them willing to assume the unpaid civic duty of membership. The advantages of having such a board for each institution need hardly be argued.

From the standpoint of the board of trustees and its staff, one big benefit of having a competent and self-respecting local governing board for each institution would be in the ability of the local boards to settle many local problems and prevent them from being escalated to the State University headquarters in Albany, where the crush tends to enlarge the bureaucracy and to introduce an increasingly stiff and far-fetched quality into the administration, while causing delays and harassing uncertainties at the points where the problems arose.

Successive presidents and the current chancellor of the State University of New York, without explicitly advocating a new kind of local governing board, have spoken often and eloquently of the desirability of as high degrees of local institutional autonomy as the limitations of the present system permit. This can include, of course, larger voices in the management of the institutions for their presidents, faculties, and students; and for their total constituencies, including parents, alumni, donors, and others. Such reforms are possible.

Four years later (early in 1965), the same recommendation regarding local boards was repeated in more forthright terms in the *Wells Report*.[11] This 65-page document was almost contemporaneous with the 1964 "master plan" of the trustees of the State University. There is little or no conflict between the two sets of recommendations, and they complement each other quite well. The *Wells Report* deals with several matters of great importance that were not touched at all in the *"master plan."*

Foremost among these is the autonomy of the University: "Give the University substantially increased powers of self-determination, easing even further the remaining restrictions of administrative flexibility and permitting its board and central staff to function as an overall policy-making, planning and coordinating agency. . . . The board and the staff can perform this essential function effectively only if they give up responsibility for the day-to-day operation of component units and are, in turn, freed from jurisdictional and policy conflicts with the Board of Regents, the state executive departments, and the Governor's office."

Dovetailing perfectly with the foregoing: "Authorize the University's Board of Trustees to establish local boards of overseers

---

[11] In the summer of 1963 the leaders of the two houses of the legislature employed Chancellor Herman B Wells of Indiana University to review the entire program of higher education in New York. Associated with him were: President John A. Perkins of the University of Delaware, Chairman G. Russell Clark of the Commercial Bank of North America, and Sidney Tickton as study director. The report was released to the press December 30, 1964.

for each unit of the State University to replace the existing advisory boards. These boards should be responsible for local operation and management."

And yet another: "Improve the relationship between the State University Construction Fund and the State University. Surely a better system can be devised than the present one, which splits responsibility between two state-supported organizations, both located in Albany." The *Wells Report* seems to be asking indirectly, "Why can not the SUNY board of trustees be trusted to supervise and operate its own building program?"

Another important recommendation of the *Wells Report* of early 1965 agrees emphatically with the Governor's Committee of 1960: "Grant the State University the option now available to the "contract colleges" (at Cornell University and Alfred University) to make purchases through sources other than the New York State Division of Standards and Purchase."

Other recommendations point toward the desirability of a climate in which the trustees will feel free to encourage variations in the programs of the different units of the University, and the creation of new programs to meet new needs; to select suitable locations for the concentration and research in rare advanced specialties; to work out forms of interinstitutional cooperation which may involve both private and public institutions; and "to enter into forms of joint partnership with industry and government to provide the advanced technical and semi-professional training and retraining already badly needed and likely to be needed increasingly in the future in the science and engineering fields, business, the health professions, and the social welfare specialties."

These latter arrangements, the *Report* indicated, will involve some ingenuity and inventiveness on both sides, and industry and government may well adopt more and more liberal policies and practices regarding leaves of absence for study, and payment of all or of a substantial part of the travel, tuition, and other costs.

The *Wells Report* looked with some enthusiasm on the likelihood of developing a really top-ranking public university in the Buffalo area, partly by means of improving the organization and relationships of the three units of the state university already located there: the State University at Buffalo (formerly the private University of Buffalo); the State University College at Buffalo (formerly the State College for Teachers); and the State University College at Fredonia about 45 miles distant. Considering the huge concentration of population in the City of Buffalo and Erie County, the evolution of a great public university appeared promising.

Setting a distant benchmark at 1985, the *Report* said the 1964 headcount total of 290,000 students in New York private institutions will increase to 500,000. The 1964 total of 260,000 in public institutions (including both the State University and the City University) will increase to one million. Thus within 20 years two-thirds of New York students beyond high school will be in public institutions. Public expenditures for higher education will be tripled by 1975, only 10 years from 1965.

Chancellor Wells and his associates did not fail to notice that the Board of Higher Education of the City of New York, governing the City University of New York, has been and is subjected to much the same administrative controls and fiscal rigidities as those that burden the State University. "We believe the degree of control by non-university officials over university operations is so great as to reduce the potential educational effectiveness of many of the City University's most capable personnel."

All the major studies of the period point to three conclusions, among others:

1. Public higher education in New York can thrive in an anomalous relationship with the Board of Regents of the University of the State of New York, if this Board ascends to the exalted status of honored sovereign who "reigns but does not rule."

2. The trustees of the State University of New York cannot function "in the spirit and style of a great public university" unless and until they are released to a very great extent from detailed restrictions and unnecessary harassments emanating from numerous non-educational administrative and fiscal departments of the state government. These controls, written into the statutes with the good intent of promoting economy and efficiency, have been shown when applied to universities to be self-defeating and productive of waste and loss.

3. Within the multicampus State University of New York, little has yet been done toward solving the crucial problem of adequate devolution of decision-making to the local units, through the creation of properly empowered local institutional governing boards and through other means, so that each institution will have a climate of local autonomy, local support, local enthusiasm, local morale running high in governing board, administration, faculty, students, and total general constituency.

Some Developments of the Late 'Sixties

It is necessary only to look at the statistical exhibit accompanying this story to see that New York State tax support for annual operating expenses gained rapidly from 1960 to 1965, and at an accelerated rate from 1966 to 1970. New York's percentage of gain over the nine years, 1960-1969, was 515 per cent—higher than that of any other state except Hawaii—meaning that appropriations made in 1968 were a little more than sixfold what they had been in 1959, nine years earlier. The great gain was due in large part to the state's comparative neglect of tax support of higher education until the middle of this century and beyond. It may also be ascribed in part to the energy and wisdom of Nelson A. Rockefeller, the only governor among the 50 states who served throughout the decade 1960-1970, and who repeatedly and consistently demonstrated keen comprehension of the role of public higher education.

The governor not only supported large expansion of public college and university tax support generally throughout the decade, but also advocated indirect state tax support of private institutions of higher education though state scholarship systems (of which the main beneficiaries are the private colleges because they are thus enabled to raise their fees without losing students). In 1968 he also publicly recommended direct annual appropriations of state tax funds to all reputable private institutions, including denominational colleges.

First the state scholarship acts. The 1961 legislature expanded the number of Regents' scholarships from 7,200 to about 17,000. It also enacted, to become operative January 1, 1962, the large-scale "scholar incentive program" which was urged by the governor. This provided for payments of $100 to $300 to students in any reputable college who were paying not less than $200 tuition fees. The governor originally intended that any student who got into a college and continued as a student could qualify, but yielded to critics who insisted that the Board of Regents should be directed to set up some narrower test of qualification. The Board developed four optional methods of qualifying, under which it was estimated that more than 80 per cent of all high school graduates would be able to become eligible for the payments.

The governor also favored a flat-sum payment of $200 to each and every beneficiary, but accepted the sliding-scale provision under which the variable amounts, averaging in general about $200, would depend on family income as shown by state income tax returns. The state appropriation for fiscal year 1962-63, the first full year of the operation of the "scholar incentive program," was approximately $24 million for it, while the enlarged Regents' scholarship and fellowship program got more than $19 million, making a total of about $43 million for both. By 1968-69 this figure had risen to $70 million, and there was another appropriation of $13½ million to the Higher Education Assistance Corporation, bringing the total annual appropriation for student aids up to $83½ million, constituting somewhat more than 17 per cent of all state tax support for operating expenses of higher education appropriated for that fiscal year.

A score of other states had relatively small systems of state tax-supported scholarships, but none approached either the absolute or proportional magnitude of New York's state-supported student aids,[12]

---

[12] A collection of data from 17 states, based on a questionnaire circulated in 1966, became available in April 1967: Josephine L. Ferguson, *Survey of State*

except Pennsylvania, whose scholarship appropriations, having been greatly increased in preceding years, aggregated about $50 million for 1968-69.

It is noteworthy that the Board of Regents, in its 1967 annual report, repeated its recommendation first made in the summer of that year, that the historic and fiercely competitive Regents' Scholarships be phased out, to be supplanted by the "scholar incentive program" which the Regents said is expected eventually to provide to "all college-capable students, according to their financial need, the full costs of graduate or undergraduate study at the colleges of their choice in New York State, including tuition and maintenance."

New York had a Constitutional Convention in session through the summer of 1967. Among many other matters, there was much debate on the question of removing or modifying Article XI, Section 3, of the Constitution of 1894: "Neither the state nor any subdivision thereof shall use its property or credit or any public money, or authorize or permit either to be used, directly or indirectly, in aid or maintenance, other than for examination or inspection, of any school or institution of learning wholly or in part under the direction or control of any religious denomination, or in which any denominational tenet or doctrine is taught, but the legislature may provide for the transportation of children to and from any school or institution of learning."

The Convention eventually removed that Section from its draft, and substituted for it a statement practically identical with the "establishment of religion" clause of the First Amendment to the United States Constitution. (See discussion of a recent interpretation of this Amendment as applied to state tax support of private colleges, by the Maryland Court of Appeals, in the story of Maryland, *supra*.) The architects of this change thought it unlikely that sectarian schools and colleges (except schools and seminaries of religion or theology) would be adjudged to be "establishments of religion," and hence the way would be opened, at least to a greater extent than formerly, for state tax support of denominational colleges and schools.

Governor Rockefeller (though not a member of the Convention) let it be known that he supported the change; and also strongly advised the Convention that its new draft of the Constitution, when submitted to popular vote in November, should be on the ballot not as "one package," requiring only a single affirmative or negative vote, but should be presented in such form as to permit separate Yes or No votes on each of its major articles. At the last moment the Convention voted down this suggestion by a narrow margin, and determined to offer the draft to the voters in "one package." In November the popular vote

---

Scholarship Programs. Association of Collegiate Registrars and Admissions Officers, 1967. 54 pp. mimeo.

was negative by more than two to one, and the Constitution of 1894 stood as before. [13]

There is a sequel to the foregoing events, as will soon appear. Meantime, two other incidents of the 1967 Constitutional Convention:

It was reported in the daily press of June 15, 1967, that Chancellor Samuel B. Gould of the State University of New York had appeared before the Education Committee of the Convention and urged that the new Constitution should contain clauses providing for autonomy of the State University and of the City University of New York. He said constitutional autonomy for the universities was necessary "as a protection against the possibility of future political or administrative interference in the conduct of their affairs." He continued: "The vigorous development of institutions of higher education is best fostered in an atmosphere of independence and freedom." (Compare with the Report of the Governor's Committee in 1960 and the *Wells Report* to the legislature in 1965 mentioned earlier in this story.)

Anthony J. Travia, President of the Convention, declared on June 25 that the time had arrived for the state to provide free public higher education for all citizens who could benefit from it; and that the Constitution should require all state institutions of higher education to be tuition-free. This proposal had strong support from delegates from New York City and elsewhere, and it appeared for a time that it might be adopted. It was immediately opposed, however, by two upstate delegates in the Convention, and by Governor Rockefeller. (Recall the governor's plan of 1961 to finance academic buildings with bonds backed by a fund built up from student tuition fees.) At this moment, when a customary periodic offering of academic building bonds was placed on the market as usual, the bond houses concertedly refused even to bid on them, and the panicky rumor spread that if the free tuition clause were adopted, college buildings under construction in many parts of the state would stand unfinished for lack of funds.[14]

Prior to the defeat of the new draft of the Constitution by popular vote in November, 1967, Governor Rockefeller (jointly with Chancellor Edgar W. Couper of the Board of Regents) had appointed a "Select Committee on the Future of Private and Independent Higher Education in New York State."[15] Its report was published in January,

---

[13]A recital in detail of the campaign against Article XI, Section 3, is available: Edd Doerr, *The Conspiracy That Failed: The Inside Story of the Campaign to Scuttle Church-State Separation in New York.* Washington: Americans United for Separation of Church and State, 1968. 186 pp., paperbound.

[14]Discussed in a little more detail in M. M. Chambers' *Higher Education: Who Pays? Who Gains?* Danville, Illinois: The Interstate Printers & Publishers, Inc., 1968. 302 pp.

[15]This was a five-man body headed by McGeorge Bundy, president of the Ford Foundation, and hence sometimes called the "Bundy Committee." The

1968, in time for the 1968 legislature.16

As might easily have been anticipated, the Committee's first finding was: "The moderate but real level of present need calls for direct assistance from New York State to private colleges and universities."

Its second finding: "Insofar as it affects four-year colleges and universities, the State Constitution should be amended to conform to the Federal model."

The third and fourth major findings recommended: ". . . the existing powers and responsibilities of the Board of Regents be reconfirmed, and reinforced by strengthening the staff of the State Department of Education"; and, "Both private institutions and the Board of Regents should take steps to develop a much stronger base of information and reporting upon which statewide educational decisions can be based."

In its appraisal of the actual current condition of the New York private colleges (60 nondenominational, 83 denominational) the Committee tried to be judicious and moderate: "We find the private colleges and universities . . . to be in better health than we or they had supposed. . . . we have found evidence of serious need, but not of impending catastrophe." It scoffed at the wild predictions of the eventual disappearance of the private institutions, and concluded that a "modest amount of public aid should assure their vigorous health for the foreseeable future." It recommended an appropriation of about $33 million for fiscal year 1969-70.

The action of the 1968 legislature on this issue was somewhat ambivalent. On the one hand, it enacted a measure authorizing subsidies of $400 per year for each bachelor's or master's degree conferred, and $2,400 for each doctoral degree conferred (based on statistics of the preceding year) for private colleges and universities, to begin with fiscal year 1969-70, but with no funding in 1968. The initial amount necessary was estimated at about $33 million.

On the other hand, it was universally understood at the time that these subsidies could be given only to qualified nonsectarian institutions unless and until the Constitution might be amended; and in the same 1968 session a bill proposing such an amendment was passed in the senate but defeated in the lower house. In preparation for the 1969 session, the governor placed $20 million in the executive budget askings for this purpose, apparently on the theory that for 1969-70 only

---

other four members were: James Bryant Conant, John A. Hannah, The Rev. Theodore M. Hesburgh, and Abram L. Sachar. Hannah, president of Michigan State University and the only public university representative, was heavily outnumbered by four private university men—Bundy and Conant from Harvard, Hesburgh from Notre Dame, and Sachar from Brandeis University.

16 *New York State and Private Higher Education.* Albany: State Education Department, 1968. 155 pp.

nonsectarian institutions could be subsidized, and that amount would be sufficient for them and in accord with the Committee's recommendation. The 1969 legislature appropriated the sum recommended by the governor.

Governor Rockefeller has often forthrightly told the legislature and the public that upward revisions of state taxes are necessary, so convincingly that they have been forthcoming. In the 1968 session one of his recommendations was a 20 per cent surtax to be added to the existing income tax rates. This was not enacted, but a less productive substitute consisting chiefly of four new high-income brackets at the top of the schedule, advocated by Speaker Anthony Travia of the Assembly, became law. It was said this would affect only about 5 per cent of the taxpayers, while the surtax would have affected all. Thus it was hailed as a "soak the rich" measure, and a victory for "little people," and its sponsor was dubbed Robin Hood.

All political leaders admitted that another revamping of the revenue system would be necessary in 1969, and suggested that the prognosis would be better than for the election year of 1968. Early in the 1969 session the governor urged that the state-wide general sales tax of 2 per cent be raised to 3 per cent, effective April 1, 1969, to produce additional revenue of $340 million a year. This measure was passed, and signed by the governor the same day it was enacted.

New York City, with nearly half the population of the whole state, and several other local subdivisions had a local sales tax of 3 per cent. Thus after April 1, 1969, a majority of the state's people were subject to aggregate sales taxes of 6 per cent—the highest rate in the nation, then prevailing in only one other state, Pennsylvania. New York also had a productive personal income tax, while Pennsylvania had none; and in general New York's total revenue system was comparatively a good one, but not quite sufficient to produce the $6.7 billion requested in the 1969-70 state budget. Estimated revenue would be $6.4 billion; and the governor took an uncharacteristic step by advocating a 5 per cent reduction, "across-the-board" in the state budget askings. Since about 65 per cent of the budgeted income goes back to the local subdivisions, this step was bitterly resisted by the cities, the local school districts, and the City University, as well as by the state departments and agencies; but it appeared inevitable, because the legislature adjourned without providing any additional major revenue measures to fill the gap.

New York's total of state and local revenues per capita in fiscal year 1966-67 was $457.84, highest among the states (California was second with $414.55); and the amount per $1,000 of personal income was $131.85—exceeded only by Hawaii's $134.79.

But in 1968 New York's state tax investment per citizen for annual operating expenses of higher education was $26.72, ranking twenty-sixth among the states, and the ratio of this investment to total personal income was 0.65 per cent—ranking forty-second. This would seem to suggest that in the immediate future some shifts in the relative support of New York's numerous state functions may be necessary in order to continue to raise higher education from its former stepchild status.

All in all, superb progress was made during the decade 1960-70. The ensuing decade will see New York develop four great university campuses to rank among the top 20 universities in the nation; build up much increased capacity in its public facilities for education in medicine and the numerous allied health professions; make its former colleges of education into multipurpose institutions; expand and improve its state-wide network of public community colleges; and become a close competitior of California in the size, diversity, excellence, and financial support of a great system of public higher education.

NORTH CAROLINA

In the Depression days of the early 'Thirties, the legislature of 1931 abolished the governing boards of this state's three principal state institutions of higher education: the University of North Carolina at Chapel Hill; the state College of Agriculture and Engineering (now North Carolina State University) at Raleigh; and the state College for Women (now coeducational and named University of North Carolina at Greensboro). A new board of trustees, modelled closely after the former board which had governed the University at Chapel Hill, was created to govern all three, thenceforth to be known as the University of North Carolina, and popularly as the "Consolidated University of North Carolina."

The board of trustees consists of 100 members, of whom at least 10 must be women, elected by the General Assembly for terms of 10 years, with the State Superintendent of Public Instruction *ex officio.* The chief executive agent is a president of the consolidated University, and each of the component units has a chancellor. In 1965 a fourth component was added—Charlotte College, renamed the University of North Carolina at Charlotte. In 1969 two additional units were added: Wilmington College and Asheville-Biltmore College.

There were in 1931 nine separate state colleges apart from the consolidated University. By 1967 the number had grown to 12 (mostly by the upward extension of two-year colleges in populous places). North Carolina has the unusual number of five state institutions of higher education originally for Negroes, and still predominantly Black; and also one state college at Pembroke which was once exclusively for Cherokee Indians.

No stroke of consolidation has been attempted for the several separate state colleges, except that in the 'Forties the seemingly rather preposterous suggestion was occasionally heard that the five Negro colleges should have their governance merged into one board and be known as the "Negro University of North Carolina." Nothing came of it. The recommendations of the State Board of Higher Education in 1968 were much more promising: the predominantly Negro colleges should receive drastically increased state tax support to enable them to upgrade and enlarge their faculties and facilities; they should provide compensatory and remedial instruction for underqualified students and bring them up to college level; and they should participate in a state-wide effort to recruit able but academically deprived students. This effort, however, was not by any means to be an exclusive responsibility of the Negro colleges: "All institutions in the state should actively recruit students, black and white, who have educational disadvantages but who appear to have the ability to do college work, and the institutions should provide remedial and compensatory education and special counseling as needed." [1]

The same report recommended that methods and practices of voluntary interinstitutional cooperation be studied continuously and applied as practicable, especially between Negro colleges and nearby campuses of other universities and colleges.

There has been no more abolition of institutional governing boards; but in 1955 the legislature created the State Board of Higher Education "to plan and coordinate" and "to allot the functions and activities of the institutions of higher education," and "determine the types of degrees which shall be granted by each of such institutions." It was also charged with the usual statistical and advisory functions, and authorized to have an executive agent to be styled director of higher education, appointed by the Board with the approval of the governor.

The composition of this Board has been tinkered with occasionally, reflecting the difference of opinion between those who believe it should consist wholly of laymen having no connection with any of the state institutions, and those who believe that at least some of the presidents and board members of the different institutions should have membership on the Board, to provide it with the professional expertise and intimate knowledge of the operations and aspirations of their own institutions as well as of the state-wide system, which would otherwise be lacking or incomplete.

The composition of the Board of Higher Education in 1967 was reported to be: Fifteen citizens of the state, *one* of whom shall be a member of the State Board of Education; *eight* of whom shall be appointed by the governor to represent the state at large, for terms of six years, subject to confirmation by the house and the senate in joint session, but none of whom shall be officers or employees of the state or trustees of any state-supported institution of higher education; *two* of whom shall be selected by the Board of Trustees of the University of North Carolina, provided no trustee member shall be a member of the General Assembly [2] ; and *four* of whom shall be selected by the boards of trustees of the senior colleges, each of which shall select one member for a term of two years so that four colleges will be

---

[1] *Planning for Higher Education in North Carolina.* Raleigh: North Carolina Board of Higher Education, November 1968. 497 pp. litho.

[2] Membership on the 100-member Board of Trustees of the University of North Carolina is not incompatible with membership in the legislature.

represented at any one time. (The governor shall select four colleges every two years to have this right, in such order of rotation as he chooses, provided the right be rotated among all the colleges equally.) The 1969 legislature added seven members: the governor as chairman, and six members of the legislature, being the chairmen of the separate senate and house committees on Appropriations, Finance, and Higher Education. This linking of influential members of the legislature may be a promising development.

During its first decade and a half the Board found its road quite rocky, because it construed too literally and too harshly the phrases of the statute defining its authority. During the first four years it was in protracted dispute with the trustees of the University of North Carolina over orders or threatened orders to reduce or discontinue various units or programs of instruction at one or another of the three component campuses of the University.

The result was an amendment to the statute in 1959 which drastically reduced the authority of the Board of Higher Education in that matter: "All institutions included in the state system of higher education shall conform to the educational function and activities assigned to them respectively, *provided*, that the Board shall not require any institution to abandon or discontinue any existing educational functions or activities, if, after notice and hearing, the institution is not in agreement with the decision of the Board, until such decision is *first recommended to and approved by the General Assembly.*"

Another sentence was also added to the first section of the statute, having the effect of softening the wording somewhat from a harshly mandatory tone to a more permissive tenor: "The Board will seek the cooperation of all the institutions of higher education and of other educational agencies in planning a system of higher education that will serve all the higher educational needs of the state and that will encourage a high standard of excellence in all institutions composing the system, each operating under the direction of its own Board of Trustees in the performance of the functions assigned to it."

The first section of the statute contained the negative mandate: "The Board shall not allot to any senior college the right to award the doctor's degree." Doctoral programs were reserved to the consolidated University, and were not for any other public institutions. The authors of this injunction were probably entirely unable to imagine that there might ever be any future time when even a small advanced graduate school of any kind or for any purpose might be desirable in the public interest, outside the consolidated University. Their intent must have been essentially restrictive, and their motive based on a deeply-felt absence of confidence in the educational expertise, practical wisdom, and devotion to the public interest of the faculties, presidents, and boards of trustees of the state colleges.

Appropriations for Annual Operating Expenses of Higher Education in North Carolina, Alternate Fiscal Years, 1959-60 through 1969-70 (in thousands of dollars)

Institutions	Year 1959-60	Year 1961-62	Year 1963-64	Year 1965-66	Year 1967-68	Year 1969-70
U of No Carolina (Consolidated)						
Chapel Hill (acad)	5,464	6,008	8,596	11,757	16,650	23,442
Health Affairs	2,541	2,917	3,804	4,415	5,359	10,250
Memorial Hosp	1,333	1,582	2,248	2,698	3,540	7,731
Psychiatric Ctr	531	599	691	732	882	1,310
Long-range planning		35	37	39		
Subtotals, Chapel Hill Campus	9,869	11,141	15,376	19,641	26,431	42,733
NC State U (acad)	5,246	6,039	7,908	10,325	13,200	19,278
Ag Exp Sta	1,977	2,369	2,744	3,320	4,171	6,610
Ag Exten Serv	2,624	2,781	3,086	3,616	4,061	5,914
Industrial Serv	95	100	106	116	236	380
Research	83	164				
WUNC-TV		243				
Subtotals, NC State U (Raleigh)	10,025	11,696	13,844	17,377	21,668	32,182
UNC (Greensboro)[1]	1,876	2,084	2,662	3,700	5,187	7,798
UNC (Charlotte)			1,213	1,487	2,169	3,632
Bd of Trustees (Consol)	174	207	354	1,041	744	1,407
Subtotal, UNC (Consol)	21,944	25,128	33,449	43,246	56,199	90,722[2]
Regional Universities:[3]						
East Carolina U	1,789	2,139	3,429	4,796	7,032	10,137
Appalachian St U	982	1,207	1,809	2,378	3,707	5,770
Ag & Tech St U	1,345	1,555	1,864	2,315	2,977	4,087
Western Carolina U	691	937	1,412	1,797	2,713	4,865
Subtotal, Reg Univs	4,807	5,838	8,514	11,286	16,429	24,859

Senior Colleges:						
No C Coll (Durham)[1][4]	1,056	1,344	1,784	2,122	2,793	3,798
Winston-Salem[5]	452	540	681	969	1,313	1,746
Pembroke[5]	210	237	476	819	1,266	1,631
Fayetteville[5]	356	431	560	830	1,005	1,270
Wilmington[6]				766	975	[6]
Asheville-Biltmore[6]				712	968	[6]
Elizabeth City[5]		441	641	791	907	1,371
NC Sch of the Arts					667	995
Subtotal, Senior Colleges	2,074	2,993	4,142	6,859	9,894	10,811
Reserve to replace support from auxiliary enterprises[7]		962	275	196		
For summer schs & other reserve		755				4,134
Board of Higher Education	66					2,120
Student aid	382				1,162	987
State Education Assistance Auth					31	53
State aid to Community Colls			388	14,586	22,837	42,230[8]
Total	29,621	35,678	46,768	76,323	106,550	175,931

[1] Formerly Women's College of North Carolina.

[2] Includes $1,590,000 for UNC at Wilmington, and $1,380,000 for UNC at Asheville, both of which became campuses of The Consolidated University July 1, 1969.

[3] These four institutions were designated as regional universities in 1967.

[4] Renamed North Carolina Central University in 1969.

[5] Renamed as state university in 1969.

[6] Became a campus of The Consolidated University in 1969.

[7] This is to restore educational income to be lost by placing auxiliary enterprises on separate accounts and allowing them to carry forward their own surpluses, if any.

[8] State support for community colleges and technical institutes.

This "wedding-cake" conception of a state system of higher education is very familiar as having been a favorite preoccupation of the survey team that wrote the California "master plan" of 1960. Doctoral programs are only for the top layer of the symmetrical cake; and any thought that as the years pass the shape of the cake may bulge here and there in unpredicted ways or heave up a new summit at some unforeseen place, seems absolutely incomprehensible. The rigid mold must hold. (In 1969 the North Carolina legislature abandoned this idea by authorizing nine institutions outside the consolidated University of North Carolina to confer all appropriate degrees, including doctoral degrees, as explained a little later in this story.)

Through the 'Sixties some bulging occurred in North Carolina, and in the legislature of 1967 an eruption took place. East Carolina College at Greenville, favorably located for a large clientele, grew swiftly, diversified, and expanded horizontally and vertically to become a multipurpose institution of more than 9,000 enrollment by 1966. Its alert and energetic president is reported to have said, "Here stands a university; why not proclaim it?" The board of trustees voted against seeking to become a fifth branch of the consolidated University, but opted for seeking recognition as a regional state university through the Board of Higher Education, the governor, and the legislature. The conservative governor declared his opposition. The overcautious Board of Higher Education ahemmed and decided an "objective study" was necessary, and brought in a team of hand-picked academicians, some from private institutions in conservative northeastern states, who stroked their beards and declared East Carolina College was "not yet ready" to be called a university or to begin preliminary spadework toward the development of advanced graduate programs. This negative recommendation was made in February 1967, near the beginning of the 1967 legislative session.

In June, however, as adjournment of the legislature drew near, political reporters said the governor and other leaders of his party recognized that a revolt among the numerous constituencies of East Carolina College was a threat to the state-wide hegemony of the party, and had something of a change of heart.

In the jockeying at the end of the session, the measure that became law created four regional state universities, which represented a new class of institution for North Carolina. These, in addition to East Carolina University at Greenville, were: North Carolina Agricultural and Technical University at Greensboro (one of the larger and better Negro land-grant institutions in any state) and two somewhat smaller but rapidly-growing former state teachers colleges in the western regions of the state: the Appalachian State University at Boone, and Western Carolina University at Cullowhee.

Perfectionists accustomed to the confines of rigid academic orthodoxy, and others unable to see that the era of universal higher education is virtually here, may sniff and say naming an institution a university does not make it a university, or that North Carolina will never need any public universities other than the Consolidated UNC; but to the author and others it seems quite plain that the development of a regional university is a matter of several decades, and that 1967 was an excellent time to begin that progression in four locations in North Carolina. Already with a population of 5,135,000, who can be sure that by the end of the century it may not have 10 million people, and urgent need for a well-developed university for each million of population? Meantime, the name "university" lifts the morale of students, faculties, and governing boards, attracts good students and faculty members, inspires confidence in the constituencies and the public at large, and has a solid cash value to all citizens and taxpayers.

There is ample reason, after calm reflection on the foregoing happenings, to believe that this was an instance where "politics in higher education" had a decidedly beneficent effect on needed expansion and upgrading of facilities. The lock of the "single state university" idea has been broken.

The legislature of 1969 continued in the spirit of expansiveness. It added the other five state colleges to the list of universities, making nine in all outside the consolidated University of North Carolina; and authorized each of the nine to confer all suitable degrees, including doctoral degrees.

Conferring of doctoral degrees is to be deferred, however, until after the completion in 1972 of a laborious study of "roles and scopes" by the State Board of Higher Education; and doctoral programs are to be approved or disapproved by that Board. In the light of 15 years of experience in North Carolina, this really means the Board can only recommend, and its decisions are affirmed or reversed by the legislature. Thus the statute of 1969 gives the nine institutions encouraging reasons to begin looking forward to appropriate doctoral programs.

Can North Carolina finance all this? Observe some smatterings of evidence: In fiscal year 1966-67, her total of state and local tax revenues per $1,000 of personal income was $99.41—six dollars less than the national average of $105.50. In 1968, her state tax investment per citizen for annual operating expenses of higher education was $22.85, ranking thirty-sixth among the states; and the ratio of that investment to total personal income was 0.86½ per cent, ranking twenty-fourth. There seems to be room for upward movement.

North Carolina has two types of institutions beyond high school offering instructional programs of two years' duration or less: local public junior colleges, and technical institutes and industrial training centers. That these two types of institutions eventually should be merged when in physical propinquity, and developed so that in the long run all will become *comprehensive* junior colleges offering both general and technical programs was one of the recommendations of a Commission on Education Beyond the High School set up by the liberal "Education Governor" Terry Sanford, reporting in 1962.[3]

The Commission thought that the state leadership for these types of institutions should continue in the State Board of Education. It proposed a plan for financing them, under which land, buildings, and plant maintenance would be locally provided; equipment, furnishings, and library acquisitions would come from state and federal funds; and annual operating expenses would come from three sources in these approximate proportions—state and federal, 65 per cent; county funds, 15 per cent; and student fees, 20 per cent.

By 1965 the total of state tax contributions to the operating funds of junior colleges and technical-vocational schools was of the order of $12 million a year, and for fiscal year 1968-69 it was $24½ million. Since many of the students in technical schools are not high school graduates, these large sums cause some overstatement of the state's total appropriations for operating expenses of education beyond high school. Governor Sanford's Commission showed that from 1953 to 1963 the state's total appropriations for annual operation of higher education varied from year to year between 7 per cent and 8 per cent of the total of state General Fund expenditures. Upward mobility was in order.

---

[3]*Education Beyond the High School.* Report of the Governor's Commission. Raleigh: Governor's Office, 1962. 133 pp.

NORTH DAKOTA

With only 627,000 people in 1968 (having had a population decline of about 0.9 per cent since 1960), and with a vast area and no large cities, North Dakota has a great acreage of fertile wheat-producing land and the marked asset of a generally industrious and frugal population, including many persons of Scandinavian extraction, noted for political progressivism and for a high respect for the values of higher education.

In 1968 the state tax investment per citizen in annual operating expenses of higher education was $32.50 (about twice that of Ohio's $16.48), ranking twelfth among the states; and the ratio of that investment to total personal income was 1.21 per cent (more than twice that of Maryland), ranking second only to that of Montana, its adjoining neighbor to the west.

The complement of institutions includes the University of North Dakota at Grand Forks and North Dakota State University at Fargo (both at the eastern boundary); four small state colleges at Dickinson, Mayville, Minot, and Valley City; and the State School of Science at Wahpeton. The former Ellendale Normal and Industrial College was made a two-year branch of the University of North Dakota in 1965, and the former State School of Forestry at Bottineau became a branch of North Dakota State University in July of 1969. The University of North Dakota also has a two-year extension center campus at Williston which is supported in part from local funds. In addition the state has two junior colleges, one at Bismarck and one at Devils Lake which are supported by local funds and a per student allocation of state funds.

In 1915 all institutional governing boards were abolished, and governance of all institutions centralized in a three-man, salaried State Board of Administration which also governed correctional and eleemosynary institutions. (Compare the story of Kansas, *infra.*) In 1938 an amendment to the Constitution changed this arrangement and set up a State Board of Higher Education of seven non-salaried members to govern all the institutions of higher education, only. They are appointed by the governor with the consent of the senate for seven-year terms. Not more than one may be an alumnus of any state-supported institution in North Dakota. None may be appointed while employed by any state institution, or for two years after terminating such employment. The Board chooses a chief executive agent known as State Commissioner of Higher Education.

NORTH DAKOTA

Appropriations for Annual Operating Expenses of Higher Education in North Dakota, Alternate Fiscal Years, 1959-60 through 1969-70 (in thousands of dollars)

Institutions	Year 1959-60	Year 1961-62	Year 1963-64	Year 1965-66	Year 1967-68	Year 1969-70
U of No Dakota	3,059	3,059	3,455	4,054	5,527	6,342
Medical Center					314	453
Ellendale Branch[1]		273	298	353	445	443
Subtotal, U of No D	3,059	3,059	3,455	4,054	6,286	7,239
No Dakota State U		2,516	2,804	3,096	4,394	5,204
Ag Experiment Sta		916	1,061	1,254	2,016	2,361
Branch Ag Exp Stas		218	220	277		
Ag Exten Serv		366	395	490	626	767
Subtotal, No D St U		4,016	4,480	5,117	7,036	8,332
Minot St Coll		897	1,034	1,137	1,537	1,656
St Sch of Sci (Wahpeton)		653	749	894	1,449	1,932
Valley City St Coll		505	580	642	907	1,047
Dickinson St Coll		377	576	617	871	1,164
Mayville St Coll		377	420	470	669	718
St Sch Forestry (Bottineau)		156	175	195	275	304
State Forest Service		69	89	93	116	106
Faculty sabbatical leaves[2]					65	
St Bd of Higher Education					94	
State aid to Jr Colls		119	360	415	581	750
Total	9,368[3]	10,505	12,219	13,989	19,888	23,249

[3]This total is a state-wide appropriation.

The powers of the Board are the usual and traditional ones appertaining to a governing board, plus the unusual explicit authority to "prescribe the books or works to be used in the several courses of instruction." (Doubtless the Board delegates this to the professors and instructors.) It also seems to have the unusual power to confer degrees without the recommendation of the faculty (but it follows the general custom of accepting faculty recommendations).

The Board is directed to adjust the budget askings of all the institutions according to its best judgment, and submit them to the state budget board and the legislature as a "unified" budget; but the legislature is directed to make separate appropriations to each institution, but "all contained in one legislative measure."

The Amendment authorizes the Board to "fix and charge fees for instruction in the professional schools and colleges and for extra studies." This seems to imply no fees for nonprofessional undergraduates. Section 148 of the Constitution provides for "a system of free public schools extending through all grades up to and including the normal and collegiate course." An act of 1965 authorized the fixing of "student facilities fees" to pay half the cost of amortizing bonds issued by the Board to finance campus buildings. The University of North Dakota fixed these fees at $7.50 per semester. The father of two sons who were students and had paid this fee joined other plaintiffs in a suit to have the act declared unconstitutional.

The North Dakota supreme court did not decide the fee issue. Instead, it found the whole act to be an unconstitutional delegation of legislative power: "In this case the Legislature has not determined the question of the necessity of any particular type of building, at any particular institution, nor laid down any rule to guide the Board in determining these questions. It has authorized the construction of facilities at some or all of the institutions. It has attempted to delegate to the Board the power to determine what facilities shall be constructed at the different institutions, and the amount, if any, to be expended at each. This, we find, is an unconstitutional delegation of legislative authority. . . . It is not necessary to pass on the other challenges to the constitutionality of the Act." Therefore the fee issue was undetermined on its own merits.[1]

The decision indicated that the North Dakota supreme court does not regard the State Board of Higher Education as having any large sphere of authority within which it is immune from control by the legislature. Contrast the powers of the Oklahoma Regents for Higher Education and the constitutional autonomy of the state universities in Michigan, California, Minnesota, and some other states.

---

[1]*Nord* v. *Guy*, (N. D.), 141 N. W. 2d 395 (1966).

OHIO

The history of public higher education in this state is a fascinating story which can be indicated here by only a few crude strokes. Ohio University (Athens) is the oldest state university in the Middle West, having been founded in 1804, and Miami University (Oxford) is not far behind (1809). These are in the southeastern and southwestern regions of the state, where the earliest settlements were made. Both are beneficiaries of federal land grants pursuant to the Ohio Company contract or similar contracts, under a policy established broadly in the famed Northwest Ordinance of 1787, three quarters of a century before the Morrill Land-Grant Act of 1862; and until 1870 these were the only state universities in Ohio.

Until after the Civil War state appropriations to these universities were few, intermittent, and extremely scanty. Their boards of trustees were coöptive after the manner of the private colleges, and they were regarded virtually as private institutions, because the idea of the tax-supported state institution of higher education had not yet evolved in the custom and law of Ohio. The words were used, but not the tune.

Then came the founding of the Ohio State University at Columbus (1870), in response to the Morrill Act. It was first named the Ohio Agricultural and Mechanical College, and ridiculed as "the college in the cornfield"; but by virtue of its central location and its presence in the state capital city it outstripped in size its older sister institutions within a generation, and soon after the turn of the century it was designated by the legislature as the *one* state university in which advanced graduate studies at the doctoral level and the accompanying research would be concentrated. It was destined to experience tremendous expansion and to become one of the constellation of nine great state universities in the Midwest popularly known as the "Big Ten"[1] —the cognomen of their football league. By 1950 this group, if measured by size, financial support, graduate school productivity, extent and quality of physical plants, eminence of leading faculty

---

[1] The nine are the University of Michigan and Michigan State University, Ohio State University, Indiana University, Purdue University, and the Universities of Wisconsin, Illinois, Minnesota, and Iowa. The tenth member of the football league is Northwestern University, a private institution.

members, or by almost any other appropriate yardstick, was superior to any other concentration of state universities anywhere in the world.

It is significant that in the late 'Fifties these 10 universities, with the aid of some modest philanthropic support, established an organ of intercommunication and interaction with regard to the development of their programs of advanced graduate studies and research in their respective highly-developed specialties, to the end that optimum opportunities should be available to student and faculty specialists, and the total of these programs in all the universities should progress in a manner to the maximum benefit of the whole region and of the nation and the world. This involves facilitated interchange of limited numbers of students and teachers, and many other cooperative enterprises. Styled the Council of Institutional Cooperation, the group also includes the University of Chicago, and therefore is sometimes informally called "The Council of Eleven." [2]

In addition, Ohio had witnessed the development of three universities under municipal sponsorship. In 1870 the General Assembly had enacted a law permitting cities of the first class to establish a university. Cincinnati responded immediately, creating the University of Cincinnati from a private institution, Cincinnati College. In 1884 the City of Toledo took over a private institution, the Toledo University of Arts and Trades, and in 1913 the City of Akron absorbed a private college, Buchtel College. By the mid-1950's the University of Cincinnati had become a large, multipurpose university with a number of professional schools and a modest graduate program. The Universities of Akron and Toledo were smaller, less well supported municipal universities with almost no graduate study beyond the master's degree.

In 1910, the population having boomed in both of the northern corners of Ohio, two state normal schools were established in Kent (northeast) and Bowling Green (northwest) respectively. Within half a century these two passed very rapidly through the evolutionary phases of normal school—teachers college—state college—state university, and grew to a size somewhat larger than that of their much older sisters in the southeast and southwest.

Meantime the state had established in 1887, in conjunction with Wilberforce University (a small private college for Negroes at Xenia) a teacher-education and technical-education program. At first a "department" of Wilberforce, this unit was administratively disentangled in 1951 and renamed Central State College, having grown to a

---

[2] During the late 'Sixties the Council had its central office at Purdue University, West Lafayette, Indiana. It is not a statutory *interstate* compact, but a voluntary *interuniversity* organization. See Stanley F. Salwak, "The Need for Cooperation and the C.I.C. Response." *Educational Record* 308-316 (Summer 1964).

size of some 1,500 students, of whom a growing percentage were white. This state college continues cooperative relationships with the adjacent Wilberforce University.

Thus the scene at mid-century included one large state university of Big Ten caliber, four lesser state universities (one in each of the four corners of the state), and one unique state college. The Ohio State University was somewhat larger in enrollment and in volume of financial support than the other five institutions combined. Evolution was continuing, however, and this ratio would not be continued indefinitely, because the relative roles of the five institutions were growing, and there were positive indications that doctoral programs would not forever be confined to the state university at Columbus.

In 1956 a survey of higher education in Ohio by the indefatigable John Dale Russell showed that Ohio was producing a small number of doctoral degrees, for a state of its large population, wealth, and college attendance rate. [3] The legislature enacted, effective in November 1959, a wordy revised section which is in fact a clear authorization for the development of advanced graduate programs by the universities at Kent and Bowling Green; and some work of this kind had already been started at Ohio University and Miami University.

The 1959 statute: "The board of trustees of Bowling Green State University and Kent State University, respectively, may create, establish, provide for, and maintain a college of liberal arts, a college of education, and a college of business administration, and include the instruction appropriate to the awarding of graduate and other degrees. On recommendation of the faculty, the Board may confer such honorary and academic degrees as are customarily conferred by colleges and universities in the United States."

While there may be some question as to whether all legislators and others concerned with the enactment of that section were fully aware of its broad implications, there can scarcely be any doubt that the words of its final clause embrace the conferring of doctoral degrees. Each of the two named universities actually offers doctoral degrees in some departments.

Ohio could be said to have been the first state (or at least very nearly the first) to provide a statutory warrant for doctoral programs, in addition to other graduate and undergraduate liberal and professional programs, in multipurpose "emerging state universities" having normal school and single-purpose teachers college antecedents. Of course there are near-exceptions, and perhaps real exceptions, to this generalization, and a lengthy pedantic discourse could be written about them. Colorado State College has conferred doctoral degrees for many years, but it is not called a university.

---

[3] John Dale Russell, *Meeting Ohio's Needs in Higher Education.* Columbus: Ohio College Association, 1956.

California has long refused to concede to its large state colleges either the name of university or the right to offer doctoral degrees independently. But in other states, particularly in the Midwest and South, it is the custom to grant both of these concessions to such of the state colleges as are flourishing and respected multipurpose institutions. Probably 30 or more such institutions were given the right to insert "state university" into their official names during or before the decade 1960-1970, following Ohio's example.

Over a long period, no doubt that practice will continue to spread, within reasonable limits, as the institutions of that type continue to grow in size and quality and move toward providing several degree programs at all levels up to and including doctoral study. For recent specific instances of this kind of evolution, one may look at Illinois, Indiana, and at least half a dozen other states.

The newly evolving state universities give rise to a bit of difficulty in the semantics of classification: To distinguish them from the relatively long-standing principal state universities and land-grant universities, shall they be called "lesser" or "emerging" or "second echelon state universities"? All these have a distasteful pejorative connotation, though each has a grain of basis in fact. Possibly a better way of expressing the distinction is to refer to them as "regional state universities" because most of them were originally located with service of a geographic region within the state in mind, and many of them proclaim evidence of this in their most recent official names. One must notice, too, that the evolution is not by any means uniform or simultaneous. Irrespective of name or location, some of the state universities with normal school antecedents will join the top 20 or 30 state universities, as Southern Illinois University has already done. The picture must be viewed as moving, not static.

Ohio's population of 10,591,000 persons in mid-1968 was not far from the figure of 10,974,000 for Illinois and 10,972,000 for Texas. Both Ohio and Illinois gained about 9 per cent since 1960. The gain in Texas for the same period was 14½ per cent. In fiscal year 1966-67 the total state and local tax revenues per $1,000 of personal income were far below the national average in each of these populous and prosperous states, Ohio's being lowest of the three: Texas, $91.08; Illinois, $85.29; Ohio, $82.23.

In 1968 Ohio's state tax investment per citizen for annual operating expense of higher education was $16.48, ranking forty-sixth among the states. The ratio of this state tax investment to total personal income was 0.48 per cent, ranking forty-seventh, with only New Hampshire, New Jersey, and Massachusetts lower.

In the past Ohio has generally been distinctly less generous in its state tax support of higher education than its neighboring states of the Midwest. Until recently the state had a relatively high percentage of its students in private and municipal institutions; but since 1960 that situation has changed very markedly, and continues to change, as a sketch of the history of the decade of 1960-1970 shows. By 1967 there were 12 universities in Ohio receiving substantial state tax support, whereas at the beginning of the decade there had been only six.

In 1961 Governor Michael V. DiSalle was faced with a parsimonious legislature dominated by the political party opposite to his own. Appropriations were made for state tax support of higher education for biennium 1961-63, specifying separate sums for each of the two fiscal years, with the total for the second year only about $1 million larger than that for the first year. This meant regression. The governor exercised his power to veto the appropriations for the second year, and called a special session for November 14, 1961, to consider the veto and possibly to make new appropriations for fiscal year 1962-63. New appropriations were made, but on a scale resulting in a gain of only about $3½ million over the preceding fiscal year—a gain of less than 7 per cent.

Early in 1961 Governor DiSalle received a report of the Interim Commission on Education Beyond the High School which had been created by the legislature of 1959. [4] This report related to the question of whether Ohio should have locally-based public two-year colleges, of which at the time it had none, or whether it should rely entirely upon further development of the university "extension centers," of which the five state universities then had a total of some 29 in various stages of viability and development; or upon some combination of these schemes.

The report of the Commission embodied something of a compromise. It contained a draft of a proposed statute which would authorize any county or combination of counties having more than 100,000 population to establish a junior college district to be governed by a board of trustees consisting of seven local residents appointed by the governor for overlapping terms of five years. The local board of trustees would be empowered to determine whether the junior college would be operated wholly by the district, or operated wholly or in part under contract with an accredited university or college.

There was at the time an urgent demand for a local public junior college in Cuyahoga County (containing Cleveland, a city of a million people). The legislature soon enacted a permissive statute, much as recommended by the Commission, and steps were begun to establish a Cuyahoga County Community College in Cleveland, and another in the neighboring lakeshore county of Lorain, in the city of Elyria. More recently a public community college has gotten under way in Dayton by means of cooperative interaction between the county and a former private institution. This does not seem to mean that Ohio intends to

---

[4] *A Proposed Policy for the State of Ohio for Community Colleges and University Branches.* Columbus: Governor's Office, 1961. 75 pp. mimeo.

substitute local two-year colleges for university branch two-year colleges. By 1968 the number of university extension centers had been somewhat reduced from the high point of about 30, but designedly to eliminate the weakest and most precarious ones and strengthen the others. It seemed probable that Ohio would continue for some time to have multiple types of immediate post-high school institutions—perhaps some twenty or more university branches, a few locally-based public community colleges in some of the larger cities, and a few technical institutes where most in demand.

An event of 1961 was the enactment of a statute which made some attempt to alleviate in part the incredibly confused maze of laws and attorney generals' opinions touching the custody and disbursement of various types of institutional nontax income—determining which sorts must go to the state treasury, and what is their destination thereafter; and which kinds are to be kept on the campus where received, and there disbursed.

A statute dating from the early years of this century, enacted as a result of the movement toward tight centralization of state financial control and abolishing the nineteenth-century abuses such as allowing some public officers to collect fees for services and keep them as their own personal property, required that institutional and departmental income be promptly deposited in the state treasury and held there until appropriated by the legislature. In 1961 this statute was Section 131.01, Revised Code of Ohio.

As in many other states, the framers of this "reform" law took no notice of any differences between the operations of a university on the one hand, and the functions of a justice of the peace or a highway engineer on the other. They were blissfully unaware of the inconveniences and actual losses such sweeping requirements could inflict on the universities and the state.

A half century of history shows gradual piecemeal modifications of the effects of Section 131.01 by a series of opinions of the attorney general ruling that receipts from dining halls and dormitory room-rents, as well as athletic fees and receipts from class plays, did not have to be paid into the state treasury; but maintaining that charges for educational services or supplies would be subject to that requirement.

In 1930 the attorney general made a series of 10 rulings in which he tried to put some semblance of order and logic into the picture; but at the end of his lengthy discourse he admitted that he was not happy with the result, but was not disposed to disturb the various opinions of his predecessors.

The net result was that after these rulings the following receipts had to be paid into the state treasury: charges to students for laboratory supplies, fees for maintenance of student health services, fees charged for extension courses, bookstore receipts, and diploma fees.

OHIO

Appropriations for Annual Operating Expenses of Higher Education in Ohio, Alternate Fiscal Years, 1959-60 through 1969-70 (in thousands of dollars)

Institutions	Year 1959-60	Year 1961-62	Year 1963-64	Year 1965-66	Year 1967-68	Year 1969-70
Ohio State U						
U Hospitals	20,766	23,832	26,674	34,134	41,617	55,047
Ag Research Ctr	3,630	3,054	4,500	5,350	6,000	7,835
Ag Exper Sta	1,849	1,065	2,163	2,868	3,950	4,558
Ag Exten Serv	1,101	1,209	1,175	1,656	2,150	2,515
Rsch & Pub Serv					1,500	
U Branches	250	380	303			
Subtotal, Ohio St U	27,596	29,540	34,727	44,008	55,217	69,955
Kent State U	4,657	5,793	6,654	8,829	15,330	19,903
Branch campuses			138[1]			
Ohio University	4,657	5,319	6,064	7,902	14,353	17,132
Branch campuses			167[1]			
Bowling Green St U	3,350	4,058	4,690	6,124	9,629	12,796
Branch campuses			47[1]			
Miami University	3,880	4,577	4,816	6,255	9,245	10,755
Branch campuses			33[1]			
U of Cincinnati[2]			446[1]	1,349	6,500	15,475
U of Akron[3]			248[1]	646	6,412	10,347
U of Toledo[3]			268[1]	745	6,176	10,338
Youngstown St U[4]					5,860	8,802
Cleveland St U[5]				1,575	5,297	8,504
Wright St U (Dayton)[6]				1,137	2,900	5,530
Central St U	1,520	1,662	1,830	2,007	2,293	3,150
Branch campuses			½[1]			
Toledo St Coll of Medicine[7]				100	700	2,300
Subtotal, 11 U's & TSC	19,913	22,474	27,564½	39,537	84,695	125,032

U Branches and Ctr[1,8-9]				2,916	4,978	9,790
Community Colleges[10]			220		4,174[11]	8,531[11]
Cuyahoga (Cleveland)				856		
Lorain County				264		
Technical Institutes[12]					888	3,030
Regents' Professorships[13]			100	150	350	
Board of Regents[13]					225	373
Total	45,661[14]	52,014	60,450	85,045	150,527	239,891[15]

[1] Sums were allocated by the Board of Regents to branch campuses, municipal universities, and community college districts out of lump appropriations for all those purposes.

[2] Municipal university, now "state-affiliated."

[3] Former municipal university, now a state university.

[4] New state university which absorbed the private Youngstown University.

[5] New state university which absorbed the private Fenn College in Cleveland.

[6] New state university, formerly a branch jointly of Ohio State University and Miami University.

[7] A state medical college in initial stage, at present not connected with any university.

[8] Includes branches of all the six long-established state institutions.

[9] There is a total of 13 permanent branches operating in 1967, attached to universities; Ohio State, 3; Kent, 4; Ohio University, 4; Miami, 1; and University of Cincinnati, 1. There will be 18 in operation in 1968. In 1967 there are also 9 smaller and less permanent "academic centers," which may later decline in number.

[10] These are two-year public colleges supported primarily by local taxing districts, but receiving state aid.

[11] Four 2-year colleges, based on counties: Cuyahoga at Cleveland, Lorain at Elyria, Lakeland at Willoughby, and Sinclair Community College at Dayton, formerly a private institution.

[12] Three institutes, based on local public school districts, at Springfield, Toledo, and Columbus.

[13] A body created by the 1963 legislature.

[14] Subsequent rectification has reduced the total, to $43,331,000.

[15] Includes $1,500,000 as subsidy for medical school of private Case-Western Reserve University; $1,500,000 for "public service"; $180,000 for special student aid; and $20,000,000 to restore to operating funds sums equal to student fees pledged for debt service.

The following receipts did not have to be paid into the state treasury: room reservation fees for dormitory space, student activity fees, receipts from dining-room services and room-rents, and receipts from plays.

Obviously these lists do not make much rhyme or reason; and they rest upon the frail reed of an opinion of the attorney general, which could be changed by any subsequent attorney general, to say nothing of a court decision or a statute.

As to fees from students for registration and tuition (no tuition fee was then charged except to out-of-state students), these were deposited in the state treasury to the credit of the state General Fund and would have been lost to the universities had not the biennial sessions of the legislature developed the habit of providing in each appropriation act that they should be appropriated to the respective institutions from which they came. The legislature also adopted the custom of establishing separate rotary accounts for receipts from fees for laboratory supplies and equipment, student health services, and extension instruction; and every two years the legislature would appropriate all in these funds to the respective universities which had collected them.

As to the important matter of receipts from research contracts, foundation grants, and private gifts—it appears that in the case of *one* university these were deposited in a state rotary account; but in the cases of the *other five* institutions these were retained in the custody of their respective governing boards. All these arrangements depended solely on the custom of the legislature, as expressed in the biennial appropriation acts, and could be changed by any future legislature, piecemeal or *in toto*.

At last, in 1955, at the advice of bond counsel who pointed out the desirability of a firmer base for the soundness of university bonds issued to finance dormitories and other self-liquidating projects (which would make such bonds more readily salable and at lower interest rates), the situation was somewhat clarified by the enactment of the following statute:

"All receipts from student fees and deposits of the state universities receiving state aid, required by law to be paid into the state treasury, shall be credited therein to special funds to be appropriately designated by the names of the respective institutions from which they are received. Such funds shall be applied to the uses and purposes of such respective institutions, and shall be used for no other purpose."

That section continued in force, and a new section effective October 2, 1961 was added to it:

"Those receipts which are required by law to be paid into the state treasury shall be limited to registration fees and non-resident tuition fees, which fees shall be credited to the Student Fee Memo accounts of the respective institutions; academic fees for the support of off-campus instruction, laboratory and course fees when so assessed and collected, and student health fees for the support of a student health service, which fees shall be credited to the designated rotary accounts of the respective institutions.

"All other fees, charges, deposits, receipts and income from all or part of the students shall be held and administered by the respective boards of trustees of the state-supported universities and colleges notwithstanding Section 131.01.

"Fees, charges, revenues or receipts, and proceeds of borrowings or sales of evidences of indebtedness, heretofore or hereafter received by said respective boards of trustees . . . shall be held and administered by said respective boards of trustees and used only for the purposes for which they are collected and received." [5]

In the context of Ohio law and custom, this was a considerable step forward toward reasonable fiscal freedom for the universities. By the standards of Michigan and other states having constitutionally independent universities, as well as other states whose legislatures have habitually respected the sphere of discretion properly belonging to university governing boards, Ohio's partial evolution as just described was less than half a loaf. In 1965, however, the legislature enacted a new statute (House Bill 307 of that session) providing that *all* student fees collected by the state-assisted universities were to be retained in the hands of the individual institutions and *not* to be deposited in the state treasury and not required to be appropriated by the legislature before being available for expenditure.

This act was sponsored by the recently-created Board of Regents and the State Department of Finance—a fact indicative of a change of climate away from the primitive idea that all institutional receipts should reach the state treasury before sundown of the day of receipt. This is one of several steps needed in many other states to restore to the state universities and colleges a reasonable degree of autonomy in the management of their own fiscal affairs, essential to the efficient accomplishment of their educational purposes.

The Period After 1963

At the general election of November 1962 a conservative and business-oriented governor, who had been for many years a city auditor, state auditor, and mayor of Columbus, was swept into office. Along with him came a legislature in which both houses were heavily dominated by conservative members of his own political party, eager to follow his wishes. In these circumstances the 1963 legislature established a Board of Regents of 11 members: 9 to be appointed by the governor and senate for terms of nine years, plus the chairmen of the

---

[5]For the thorough study from which the foregoing sketch is adapted, credit is due to John D. Millett, then president of Miami University, and since 1964, chancellor, Ohio Board of Regents.

education committees in each house of the legislature, serving *ex officio* and without vote. This was a coordinating board superimposed on all the institutional boards of trustees. Contrary to the general trend of the time, it was given powers and responsibilities somewhat beyond what would have made it a "soft approach" research and advisory body. Most of its lengthy list of statutory duties were of the study-making and advisory type, but it was empowered to approve or disapprove plans for the establishment of new universities or colleges, new degrees and degree programs, new community college districts, and new technical institutes.

In practice, a good deal of its initial authority derived from the fact that the governor immediately urged and obtained large capital appropriations for expansion of public higher education—especially in the populous northeastern region of the state (where it is fair to say the need was indeed great, and where a great deal of electoral strength was concentrated)—and, anxious for prompt action, succeeded in persuading the legislature to appropriate a large unallocated sum to that region, entrusting the allocations to the Board of Regents.

At the time it was uncertain as to whether there would be a new state university in Cleveland, and if so, whether the state would acquire an existing private college, or "start from scratch"; what the state would do about higher education in the city of Youngstown, where a private institution was struggling to survive; whether the state would start a new medical college, and if so, where; whether the state should take over the three municipal universities, or merely subsidize them on an increasing scale; and whether and where some state-supported technical institutes would be founded.

Within from three to five years these questions were answered, largely at the discretion of the Board of Regents, with the aid of its chancellor and staff, and with the concurrence and support of the governor and the legislature. John D. Millett, having been president of Miami University for 11 years, resigned and took up his duties as chancellor of the Ohio Board of Regents July 1, 1964. In mid-1969 he entered into his sixth year in that post. His eminent qualifications and his continuous tenure were of great advantage to the Board of Regents. The record of 1964-1969 was a record of progress for public higher education in Ohio; but it must also be said that the shock of the act of 1963 caused reverberations that are yet spreading, and that the uncertainties, dislocations, and losses of morale that inevitably accompany such shocks could not be wholly avoided. There is danger that the new structure may leave the way open for too much governor-domination of higher education in Ohio. In early 1969 the daily press reported that a grandiose scheme of reorganizing all higher education in Ohio into some eight geographic districts[6] —a plan which in its

---

[6] Compare with the proposed regional scheme mentioned in the California story, *supra*.

superficial aspects might seem to mean decentralization—had been proposed by the governor. If the press reports can be believed, it developed that the governor had announced this without once mentioning it to the Board of Regents, much less consulting them; whereupon one member of the Board promptly resigned.

In the legislative stampede of 1963, as had been the case in California in 1960, [7] an excellent organ of voluntary cooperation and coordination among Ohio's state universities was summarily pushed aside and ignored. This was the Ohio Inter-University Council, composed of the president, the chief business officer, and one member of the governing board of each of the six institutions. It had functioned well for nearly a quarter of a century, with gradually increasing efficacy and scope.

Its earliest and central accomplishment was the reaching of a binding consensus, for every biennium since 1940, in the preparation and presentation jointly of the biennial budget askings of the six institutions, both for capital outlays and for operating expenses. In its more mature years it became much more than a mere fiscal agency in a narrow sense, and became a forum for deliberation on various problems of the institutions such as the standards for probation and retention of marginal students, uniform reporting of enrollments, methods of encouraging the superior student, policies regarding selective admissions, plans for the support of faculty research, schemes of faculty fringe benefits, and the question of a state-wide broadcasting and telecasting network. A little more detailed sketch of the record is available in a 1961 pamphlet by the author. [8]

Desirable as it may be to involve state governors in the advancement of higher education, it is doubtful that any governor should be encouraged to regard it as his proprietary domain. The Ohio governor was also reported in 1969 as initiating a proposed scheme of greatly escalated student fees, including a demand that out-of-state residents be charged the *full cost* of their education in Ohio public institutions. This undoubtedly would be prohibitive for medical students and for most advanced graduate students in the arts and science disciplines, and would place upper-division undergraduates on a tuition fee basis higher than that of many private colleges.

Changes in fees are customarily at the discretion of institutional governing boards; and this is one of the major matters of policy that

---

[7] California's Donahoe Act of 1960 ignored the Liaison Committee of the Board of Regents of the University of California and the State Board of Education. It had a well-documented record of 15 years of successful operation. See the California story, *supra*.

[8] M. M. Chambers, *Voluntary Statewide Coordination in Public Higher Education*. Ann Arbor: University of Michigan Publications Division, 1961. 83 pp. See especially pp. 32-39 and 69-70. Out of print, but available in many libraries.

governing boards should retain. There is nearly unanimous consensus that student fees should not be set by governors, legislatures,[9] or coordinating boards. There is sometimes a temptation for an aggressive governor to make a political issue of this, especially when he has a big majority of adherents in the legislature and a state-wide coordinating board composed wholly of his own appointees.

The appearance of new public institutions of higher education in Ohio between 1963 and 1967 was rapid, as will be readily observed in the accompanying tabulation of biennial appropriations for annual operating expenses. Here there is space to recount the details of only one case: the establishing of the new Cleveland State University. The founding act (Chapter 3344, *Ohio Revised Code*) became law December 18, 1964. It provided for a board of trustees of nine members, to be appointed by the governor. Under an "Agreement of Transfer and Transition" Cleveland State University used as its beginning nucleus the faculty, staff, and facilities of Fenn College, a private institution which originated in the 1920's as an enterprise of the Cleveland Young Men's Christian Association. In the 'Thirties it had been separately incorporated, and in 1951 entirely severed from any connection with the YMCA.

The Fenn College Board of Trustees turned its plant and facilities over to the Cleveland State University, and received from the state $260,000 and the expectation that the state would enormously expand the operation, and would "continue, so far as practicable," the "cooperative program of education in engineering" with business and industrial employers.

The Fenn Board of Trustees had its charter amended to become the "Fenn Educational Foundation" and carried on as "a nonprofit corporation supporting worthy educational, literary, charitable, and scientific endeavors." The Common Pleas Court issued a declaratory judgment concerning the rights of all parties, including private donors to the college.

Noting that "Those who have been generous to Fenn in the past have the assurance that their charitable intents will be perpetuated, and, although they have no legal title or interest in any of Fenn's assets, that their donations will continue to advance the cause of education," the court said the "doctrine of deviation" in the operation of charitable trusts was applicable, and declared that the Fenn

---

[9] It must be admitted that legislatures in several states have virtually forced the raising of fees by indirection; that is, by appropriating less money than the university needs to avoid retrogressing, and broadly suggesting that the university raise its fees. This poses a dilemma for presidents and governing boards: Either cut back some of the programs or let them deteriorate and forego the initiation of any new programs, or raise fees and thereby exclude some students who lack financial resources.

trustees "had full and complete legal authority . . . and ample discretion to enter into the agreement and transfer most of their assets to the newly-created state university."[10]

The same session (December 1964) created Toledo State College of Medicine, to be a wholly new institution. By July 1, 1967, the municipal universities of Akron and Toledo had become state universities; Wright State University at Dayton had its own identity (it had been a large branch campus jointly of Ohio State and Miami Universities); and Youngstown State University had come into existence somewhat after the manner of Cleveland State University (absorbing a former private institution). The municipal University of Cincinnati continued as such, but with augmented state subsidies—a "state-affiliated university."[11]

In 1963 and 1965 state bond issues for state university and college construction aggregating $320 million were approved at popular elections; but during the years 1960-1965 the gains in appropriations for annual operating expenses were only modest. In mid-1967 the state was in a revenue crisis, because the state administration had been preoccupied with a proposed constitutional amendment which would have created an Ohio Bonding Commission authorized to borrow in amounts up to 0.75 per cent of the state's annual revenues without submitting the question to popular vote, but only with the approval of the legislature. This measure had been defeated by a two-to-one popular vote on May 2, 1967.

Pending the hoped-for adoption of the lost amendment, nothing had been done about much-needed new revenue measures. Governor James A. Rhodes adhered to his five-year-old campaign pledge of "no new taxes," and the state was in a desperate situation with regard to both capital needs and immediate operating needs. At length a new tax program to produce $180 million of additional revenue per year was enacted, effective September 1, 1967. The general sales tax was raised to 4 per cent from the former 3 per cent, and a rearrangement of the small-purchase brackets made it start with purchases of 16 cents. Its coverage was also extended to sales of beer and cigarettes, and to industrial towel and linen services, as well as to certain sales of goods to one industry by another, previously exempt on the ground that such sale was a part of the manufacturing process.

The special sales tax on cigarettes was raised to 7 cents from the former 5 cents a pack, and, with the coverage under the general sales tax just mentioned, this meant actually a tax of 8 cents. The corporation franchise tax was raised from the former 3 mills to 4 mills,

---

[10]*Fenn College et al.* v. *Nance et al.,* (Ohio Com. Pl.), 210 N.E. 2d 418 (1965).
[11]Some of this story is in *Master Plan for State Policy in Higher Education.* Columbus: Ohio Board of Regents, June 1966. 170 pp.

based on the company's net worth figured on sales inside the state of Ohio. Beginning to see a little light at the end of the tunnel, the legislature made appropriations for annual operating expenses of higher education for fiscal year 1967-68 amounting to an unprecedented gain of 77 per cent over the comparable figure for two years earlier, and boosting Ohio's eight-year gain since 1959 to 247½ per cent—well above the national average rate of gain for that period.

No income tax was enacted. The forthright President William T. Jerome of Bowling Green State University was reported to have told the Senate Finance Committee late in May 1967: "An income tax is inevitable in a state as wealthy as Ohio." His statement was and is correct.

One new act of 1967 declared that each of the state universities is a "body politic and corporate." While the terminology is archaic, it means that each university is a public corporation. To observers unlettered in the law, this might seem hardly of more than academic interest. It is, however, of potential real importance, because it may have some weight in determining the degrees of autonomy possessed by the several governing boards in various circumstances.

The matter is of special concern in Ohio because for nearly a century there had been doubts and ambivalency and recurring differences of opinion among judges and attorneys general as to whether the Ohio State University really was a corporation.[12] Apparently all doubt was removed by the act of 1967—a wholesome step.

Certainly recognition is growing that scarcely anything could be more repugnant to the nature and functions of a state university than to be regarded solely as a "branch plant" of the state administration.

The institution derives a certain identity and dignity from being designated a public corporation—a certain impression of separateness and self-control that comports much better with its nature and purpose than does the notion that it is only a noncorporate segment of an all-encompassing state bureaucracy. (Robert Frost: "The separateness of the parts is at least as important as the connections of the parts.")

The legislature of 1969 enacted tax measures estimated to produce about $90 million a year in additional revenues, principally from increased rates on cigarettes, alcoholic beverages, and on franchises and utilities. Another act authorized annual subsidies to medical school programs in reputable private institutions of higher education; and an appropriation of $1½ million each year for the biennium 1969-71 was made to the Medical School of Case-Western Reserve University. The trustees of Cleveland State University were empowered to make

---

[12] This somewhat involved story is told briefly on pages 122-124 of Edward C. Elliott and M. M. Chambers, *The Colleges and the Courts*. New York: Carnegie Foundation for the Advancement of Teaching, 1936. 562 pp.

arrangements with the concurrence of the Ohio Board of Regents, to acquire the private Cleveland-Marshall Law School.

An act intended to facilitate the financing of capital improvements at the state institutions of higher education by the issuance by the institutions of "revenue bonds" pledging student fees for payment of principal and interest was enacted. The intent is that the legislature will periodically make appropriations sufficient to restore the student fees so pledged and used, so that the institutions will actually incur no loss of operating income by their pledging of student fees; and an appropriation of $20 million for each year of the biennium 1969-71 was made for that purpose. Whether future legislatures will continue this practice is somewhat problematic, for a legislature can not bind its successors except by contract, and it is doubtful that there is anything in the act that would be construed as a contract between the state and the institutions or between the state and the bondholders. Probably the "revenue bonds" will be simply contracts between the institution and the bondholders, as is usually the case.

An appropriation of $8½ million was made for fiscal year 1971 (the second year of the biennium) for a "program of instructional grants" which is a state scholarship system for full-time undergraduate students with variable grants scaled according to family income, skewed in favor of the private colleges by setting the maximum grant at $900 a year where the tuition charged is $1,000 or more, and at $300 a year where the tuition fees are less than $1,000 a year.

The legislature set out to bind the feet of the five older state universities by placing rigid limits on fall quarter enrollments at their respective central campuses—15,000 each at Bowling Green and Miami, 20,000 each at Kent and Ohio (at Athens), and 40,000 at the Ohio State University. In further pursuance of this restrictive policy, another new statute provides that none of the universities just named shall contract for the construction of any new residence hall facilities on its central campus without the prior approval of the Ohio Board of Regents.

The renaissance of growth in total appropriations for annual operating expenses of higher education in Ohio continued. For fiscal year 1969-70 the appropriation of $240 million was a gain of nearly 60 per cent over the comparable sum of two years earlier; and the $260½ million appropriated for fiscal year 1970-71 was nearly 50 per cent larger than the total for 1968-69. If these rates of gain are maintained, Ohio may eventually catch up with such sister states as Michigan, Texas, and Illinois, and take her proper rank in state support of higher education.

OKLAHOMA

For more than a generation this state has had the unusually large number of 18 state institutions of higher education. In 1968 an additional state junior college was in process of being established in Tulsa. Total population in 1960 was 2,238,000, reached 2,518,000 by mid-1968 (a gain of 8 per cent), and was projected to 2,677,000 by 1975, making a gain of 15 per cent during 1960-1975. Over the same 15 years, college-age population was projected to gain 57 per cent.

The large number and wide distribution of public colleges and universities explains in part why in 1967 total college enrollment was 58 per cent of the state's college-age population—a percentage substantially higher than in any other southern state.

Before 1911 each institution had its own governing board, but subsequently the institutions have been grouped in various ways. The University of Oklahoma has its own Board of Regents; the Board of Regents of the Agricultural Colleges governs the Oklahoma State University (the land-grant university) and a spate of state agricultural colleges; the Board of Regents of State Colleges governs a group of institutions having teachers college origins; and a few of the small specialized schools have separate boards.

The Board of Regents of the Agricultural Colleges is a constitutionally autonomous body, that status having been fortified early by a decision of the state supreme court.[1] A statute had created a State Board of Public Affairs, to have charge of the construction, repair, and operation of all buildings owned or used by the state. Soon the inevitable controversy over whether this Board was authorized to contract for and erect buildings for the Agricultural and Mechanical College reached the state supreme court, and was decided against the Board of Public Affairs, because the power of the Board of Regents to govern the College, including the provision of its campus and buildings, was held to be clearly established in the Constitution. (This status does not apply to any other governing boards of state institutions except the Board of Regents of the Agricultural Colleges.)

This constitutional autonomy was reconfirmed by the attorney general half a century later. In 1959 a statute known as the "Oklahoma

---

[1]*Trapp, State Auditor* v. *Cook Construction Company,* 24 Okla. 850, 105 P. 667 (1909).

302

Central Purchasing Act" purported to require all state departments and institutions to procure all contractual services, supplies, materials, and equipment through the purchasing division of the State Board of Public Affairs.

At the request of the Board of Regents, on November 9, 1959, the attorney general issued an opinion declaring that insofar as this act applied to this Board of Regents, it was unconstitutional and of no effect. The act was in conflict with Sections 31 and 31a of Article 6 of the Oklahoma Constitution, under which the Agricultural and Mechanical Colleges had had constitutional independence continuously since the adoption of the Constitution in 1907.

The opinion further set out that the Board of Regents could voluntarily avail itself of the services of the state purchasing director in cases where the Board deemed this to be advantageous; but in all such cases the specifications, quantities, prices, and other features of the transaction as determined by the Board of Regents must not be subject to change by the state purchasing director. This issue is a familiar one in many states.

Meantime in 1941 the Oklahoma Constitution was amended to create a Board of Regents for Higher Education as a state-wide coordinating body—not a governing board. (Readers will have to use care not to confuse this Board of Regents with other Boards of Regents in Oklahoma that are governing boards.) The Constitution gives this Board of Regents exclusive power to allocate among all the institutions the funds appropriated by the legislature for higher education, and forbids the legislature to appropriate any funds for higher education except to this Board. Thus when the 1945 legislature made direct appropriations to the Southern Oklahoma Hospital at Ardmore (under the governance of the Board of Regents of the University of Oklahoma at Norman), the act of appropriation was clearly unconstitutional and void, and the state treasurer could not be compelled to pay claims under its authority. [2]

It seems plain, then, that the Oklahoma Board of Regents for Higher Education, with sole authority to allocate appropriated funds among the institutions, is the most power-laden of all "coordinating boards." Some of the state-wide consolidated *governing boards* (as in Georgia) have this power; most of them do not—the legislature appropriates all or nearly all the funds directly to the institutions, even though they are all under one governing board. No "coordinating board" within my knowledge (except the Oklahoma Regents) has this power, though the Ohio Board of Regents seems to have been given it temporarily and to a partial extent only (with respect to new institutions) by an act of 1963.

---

[2] *Board of Regents of University of Oklahoma et al.* v. *Childress, State Auditor,* (('la.), 170 P. 2d 1018 (1946).

OKLAHOMA

Appropriations for Annual Operating Expenses of Higher Education in Oklahoma, Alternate Fiscal Years,
1959-60 through 1969-70 (in thousands of dollars)

Institutions	Year 1959-60	Year 1961-62	Year 1963-64	Year 1965-66	Year 1967-68	Year 1969-70
U of Oklahoma		6,224	6,997	8,546	9,584	12,076
Medical Center		1,018	1,224	1,730	5,443[1]	7,163
Geol'l Survey		222	241	265	276	304
U Hospitals		2,647	2,799	3,138		
Subtotal, U of Okla		10,111	11,261	13,679	15,303	19,543
Oklahoma State U		6,281	7,066	8,568	9,533	11,613
Ag Exper Sta		1,554	1,658	1,821	2,004	2,474
Ag Exten Serv		1,648	1,714	1,840	1,965	2,448
Coll of Vet Med		351	383	460	520	694
Tech Trng Sch (Okmulgee)		761	828	959	1,063	1,512
Tech Inst (Oklahoma City)					104[2]	263
Subtotal, Okla St U		10,595	11,649	13,648	15,189	19,004
Central State Coll		1,381	1,705	2,454	2,829	3,919
Northeastern St C		1,091	1,280	1,881	2,167	2,976
Southwestern St C		844	1,014	1,530	1,774	2,309
East Central S C		763	879	1,207	1,330	1,538
Southeastern S C		707	804	1,055	1,131	1,230
Northwestern S C		577	650	911	995	1,177
Cameron St Ag Coll		419	466	682	789	1,279
Okla Coll of Lib Arts[3]		541[4]	552	629[4]	724	978
Langston University		530	563	717	767	849
Okla Panhandle S C[5]		536	586	675	722	780

State Junior Colleges:

Northeastern Okla A & M		377	433	631	703	1,044
Eastern Okla St Coll		326	354	442	494	632
Northern Okla College		269	299	409	445	562
Murray St Coll of Agric		258	280	366	394	458
Okla Military Academy		258	284	331	350	378
Connors St Coll of Agric		258	288	322	336	388
State aid to Jr Colls					200	200
SREB & Dental Edn Asstnce				208	265	85
Reserve for adjusts (unallocated)		49	107	20	150	200
Med Ctr Chaplaincy						
Special Education			15			
Regional Education		36	37	70		
Higher Education Study		75				
Total	27,014[6]	30,000	33,505	41,867	46,858	59,552[7]

[1] Includes U Hospitals.
[2] A new technical branch of Oklahoma State University.
[3] Formerly the Oklahoma College for Women.
[4] Includes $15,000 for Speech-hearing Clinic.
[5] Formerly Panhandle A & M College.
[6] This total is a state-wide appropriation.
[7] Includes $25,000 for Commission on Education.

The Oklahoma Regents for Higher Education initiated in 1961-62 an ambitious self-study of the state-wide scene, which produced a series of eight reports by the end of 1966.[3] Studies of the dropout problem were also made and published separately.[4] During these years the Board had the very great asset of a small, but thoughtful and industrious, staff headed by Chancellor E. T. Dunlap, who came to the post in 1961 from the presidency of Eastern Oklahoma Agricultural and Mechanical College at Wilburton; and John J. Coffelt, who became vice chancellor for research and planning. A 1968 report undertook to tabulate the previously published recommendations and the extent of their implementation up to that time.[5] It contains a quotable generalization:

"The planning and execution of state policy for higher education necessarily depends upon continuing, harmonious association with institutions and other constituent agencies. . . . It is imperative that such association not impose inappropriate constraints upon these institutions and agencies. The responsibility for institutional management resides with the governing board, administration, and faculty of the institution; and the coordinating agency must exercise due care that the implementation of state-level policy does not impose unnecessary restrictions or limitations which hamper the fulfillment of institutional responsibilities. Freedom of inquiry, institutional initiative, and administrative flexibility are important elements that must be protected."

There are and will continue to be, however, many difficulties in determining precisely the points where the responsibilities of the two parties should begin and end. In its commendable zeal for the im-

---

[3]No. 1: John J. Coffelt, *Organization and Plan for Self-Study of Higher Education in Oklahoma.* January 1962. 24 pp.

No. 2: John J. Coffelt, *Selecting, Retaining, and Utilizing Higher Education Facilities.* December 1962.

No. 3: Dan S. Hobbs and John J. Coffelt, *Enrollments and Projections.* February 1963.

No. 4: Charles R. Walker and John J. Coffelt, *Financing Current Operating Costs.* March 1963. 102 pp.

No. 5: Charles R. Walker and John J. Coffelt, *Physical Facilities.* December 1964.

No. 6: John J. Coffelt, *Medical Education in Oklahoma.* June 1965.

No. 7: Dan S. Hobbs, *Higher Education Opportunities and Needs in Oklahoma.* September 1965. 102 pp.

No. 8: John J. Coffelt, Dan S. Hobbs, and A. J. Brumbaugh, *Goals for Oklahoma Higher Education.* September 1966. 59 pp.

[4]Among these were: Dan S. Hobbs, *Admission and Retention of Students.* January 1962. 60 pp.; and John J. Coffelt and Dan S. Hobbs, *In and Out of College—A Longitudinal Study of the 1962 Freshman Class in Oklahoma Colleges.* October 1964. 120 pp.

[5]John J. Coffelt, *The Status and Direction of Oklahoma Higher Education.* Oklahoma City: State Capitol, May 1968. 50 pp.

provement of higher education, will the state-wide agency unwittingly invade the sphere that is properly within the discretion of the institutions? A specific example for the application of this query: Up to 1968 the Regents allocated lump sums annually to the institutions. These might be accompanied by recommendations as to how the money should be used; but the understanding among all parties was that these were merely advisory, and that the power of decision was in the respective institutional governing boards.

In early 1968 the Board obtained from the attorney general a ruling that it had the power to allocate the funds to the colleges for specific purposes, and that such allocations would be mandatory for the colleges. Thereupon the Board announced three priority uses for 1968-69, in the order named: (1) meet the 1967-68 salary average; (2) employ additional faculty members to maintain the 1967-68 faculty-student ratio; and (3) work toward reducing the faculty-student ratio. All institutions were instructed to file a report in June 1968 on how they planned to execute this priority schedule. The two state universities, the Regents reported, had an average salary of $10,658, compared with the regional average of $11,587. The senior college level was $9,161 as against the regional figure of $9,569; and the junior college average was $7,641 with a regional average of $8,484.

Leaving open the question of whether, under Oklahoma conditions, the Board is tending to infringe upon the administrative sphere of the institutions, it is possible to note here Oklahoma's paramount deficiency—parsimonious legislative appropriations, continuous since 1959. The rate of gain in appropriations of state tax funds for annual operating expenses of higher education over the nine years 1960-1969 was the lowest among all the 50 states—95½ per cent. Oklahoma was the only state that failed to double these appropriations during that period. The average gain among the 50 states was 261 per cent—an increase of more than three and one-half fold.

Oklahoma's appropriations for operating expenses of higher education for fiscal year 1968-69 ($52,858,000) were only $8.08 per $1,000 of personal income—lower than in 10 southern states, and higher than in only four southern states.[6] Oklahoma's state tax investment per citizen for annual operating expenses of higher education in 1968 was $21.37—ranking fortieth among the states. The ratio of this figure to total personal income was 0.75½ per cent—ranking thirty-third. For fiscal year 1966-67 the total of state and local tax collections per $1,000 of personal income in Oklahoma was $105.67—this figure being the median among the 50 states. If one looks at the ranking of the 50 states simply according to the magnitude of their state tax-fund appropriations for annual operating expenses of higher education over

---

[6] E. F. Schietinger, *Fact Book on Higher Education in the South, 1968.* Atlanta: Southern Regional Education Board, 1968. 74 pp.

the nine years 1960-1969, Oklahoma ranked seventeenth in 1959-60 and thirtieth in 1968-69. This was the most precipitous drop made by any state during that period.

The foregoing figures seem to suggest that (1) Oklahoma's total of state and local tax collections is not overly burdensome in relation to personal incomes, and could go up without hardship; (2) operating expenses of higher education have been in a declining priority position among the state functions for a decade as compared with the other 49 states, and should be raised. (These appropriations by all 50 states were 7.8 per cent of state tax revenues in 1959-60, and 11 per cent in 1966-67; in Oklahoma these figures were respectively 9.8 per cent and 10.4 per cent.) During a decade of unprecedented expansion of higher education as a state function, in Oklahoma higher education's proportionate share of state revenues made only negligible gains.

OREGON

Oregon has a splendid history of support of public higher education in a day that is past. As recently as 1960, with a population of only about 1¾ million, the state stood fifteenth among all the states when ranked according to the magnitude of their appropriations of state tax funds for annual operating expenses of higher education. This meant very extraordinary effort in proportion to population.

However, by 1968, although Oregon had a fairly vigorous growth of population (13½ per cent as against the national average of 11½ per cent), and then had slightly more than 2 million people, its ranking by the measure of support just mentioned had fallen from fifteenth place to twenty-sixth. No other state had so precipitous a decline, except Oklahoma, which fell from seventeenth place to thirtieth. Measured by rates of gain in appropriations for annual operating expenses of higher education over the same nine years, Oregon showed 136½ per cent, as compared with the national weighted average of 261 per cent. This gave a rank of forty-third, very definitely in the fourth quartile by that measure. In short, this was a decade of slowdown, perhaps in small part justified by Oregon's high place at its beginning.

In 1966-67 total state and local tax collections per $1,000 of personal income were $109.38, only about 3½ per cent above the United States average of $105.50. There was room for improvement without hardship. State tax support per citizen for operating expenses of higher education was, however, in the upper ranges above average in 1968 ($33.92, ranking eighth), and the ratio of this figure to total personal income was 1.03½ per cent, ranking thirteenth. This picture seemed to indicate that higher education still had a high priority claim on Oregon's state tax income, but that the magnitude of the state tax income as a whole was only about average in proportion to personal incomes.

A large factor in producing this condition was Oregon's reliance on state income taxes as the principal source of revenue, and the long-continued and obdurate resistance of the legislature and the people to a general sales tax. In 1968 Oregon, comparatively small in population though it was, was the largest of six small states which had no general sales tax. Forty-four states had adopted this productive revenue-raiser.

Oregon had productive state income taxes: Personal income tax graduated from 3 per cent to 9½ per cent in six steps, on incomes from

$500 to $8,000; and corporation income tax at 6 per cent, with 8 per cent on financial institutions. One suggestion that immediately leaps out is that the personal income tax could well have had the addition of a few higher brackets above $8,000; but the scheme as it stood was such as to cause the Advisory Commission on Intergovernmental Relations to place Oregon among the seven states rated as having "high" income taxes.[1] The other six states in this category, with the exception of Delaware, were all in the northernmost tier: Idaho, Minnesota, Wisconsin, New York, and Vermont.

In 1929 public higher education in Oregon was offered by five institutions: the University of Oregon, the Oregon State College (land-grant institution), and three state normal schools or teachers colleges. A legislative act of 1929 abolished the governing boards of these five institutions, and consolidated their governance in a newly-created State Board of Higher Education composed of nine members appointed by the governor with the consent of the senate for terms of six years. No member may be connected with any institution governed by the Board; and not more than five graduates of the Oregon state institutions, and not more than two graduates of any one such institution, may be on the Board at any one time.

The Board has the usual powers of a governing board. This means that it is responsible for the administration, management, and operation of all the institutions. This soon led to the building up of a considerable central staff under the chancellor, and a high degree of centralization. One policy of the Board seems to have been to fragment the institutions to some extent. Thus the University of Oregon at Eugene, its Medical School in Portland, and its later-acquired Dental School in the same city report to the Board as three entirely separate units. The University has no administrative connection with either of the two Schools, though each of them bears its name. This is a unique arrangement, found in no other state.

Almost immediately after the consolidation of 1929 the extension services of all the institutions (excluding the Cooperative Agricultural Extension Service of Oregon State College, designated as Oregon State University in 1961) were removed from the control of the respective institutions and placed under one central administration, now known as the Division of Continuing Education, which also reports to the Board as an independent unit.

Because all the institutions were located at considerable distances from Portland, the principal city, it was inevitable that a major state institution would have to be developed there. Portland State College (now Portland State University) began on a modest scale in 1955 and developed to a stage where it received about $7½ million of state tax

---

[1] Reported in *U. S. News & World Report,* May 1, 1967.

fund appropriations for annual operating expenses in 1968-69. Oregon Technical Institute, started in the southern Oregon town of Klamath Falls in 1947, was a two-year institution until 1965, when it was authorized by the legislature to confer bachelor's degrees.

Thus in 1969 the Board of Higher Education had 10 units reporting to it, whereas originally it had had five. The legislature adopted the custom of appropriating biennially to the Board a large lump sum for allocation among the institutions, but carried further the idea of fragmentation, by itself making direct appropriations to such services as the University Hospital, the Agricultural Experiment Station, and the Agricultural Extension Service. Such services as these cannot be fitted into any rigid formula for budgeting based on alleged unit costs computed at x dollars per credit-hour produced under the conditions of face-to-face association of teacher and student in the classroom; hence an accountant-inspired separation of their financial affairs from the institutions to which they appertain. This is a step in the largely futile effort to arrive at rigidly comparable unit costs of "student education" in different institutions—taking no account of differences in quality and diversities of environment which have important values of their own—and an unfortunate tendency to rely mindlessly on techniques of "quantifying the unquantifiable." This half-on and half-off practice of allowing a consolidated governing board to allocate appropriated funds to the institutions, while the legislature itself makes direct appropriations to some of their principal appendages, is also followed in a few other states having a single consolidated governing board, such as, for example, Mississippi.

In the early 'Sixties the Oregon Board of Higher Education let it be known that it had misgivings about the wisdom of the highly-centralizing practices of its earlier years, and declared its intent to achieve a substantial decentralization of authority to the presidents of the respective institutions. However, appropriations to the Board for its "central activities," described as "administration, budgeting, accounting, disbursing, and other centralized functions," were about $700,000 a year for biennium 1961-63, about $1 million a year for biennium 1963-65, roughly $1¼ million a year for biennium 1965-67, and $2 million a year for biennium 1967-69 (until revised to the level of $1½ million a year by a special session of the legislature in 1967 which effected a general reduction of all appropriations).

Twice within the decade the biennial appropriations for operating expenses of higher education were substantially reduced by subsequent special sessions of the legislature. After the defeat by popular referendum on October 15, 1963, of a measure that would have brought in $60 million of additional revenue by upward revision of the state income tax, a special session which convened on November 11 cut back the appropriations for biennium 1963-65 from $82 million to $77 million—a reduction of about 6 per cent. Again in October 1967 a

OREGON

Appropriations for Annual Operating Expenses of Higher Education in Oregon, Alternate Fiscal Years, 1959-60 through 1969-70 (in thousands of dollars)

Institutions	Year 1959-60	Year 1961-62	Year 1963-64[1]	Year 1965-66	Year 1967-68	Year 1969-70
U of Oregon	5,403	6,667[2]	7,405[2]	8,922	11,056	14,264
U of Ore Med Sch[3]	1,695	2,032[2]	2,237[2]	2,598	3,325	4,404
Tchng hosps & clinics	2,602[4]	2,855	2,967	3,327	4,678[5]	6,241
TB hosps	443[4]	508	957	1,053	1,023	1,417
Crip Children Div	583[4]	642	750	826		
U of Ore Dental School[3]	767	878[2]	957[2]	1,065	1,268	1,633
Subtotal, U of Oregon	11,493	13,582	15,275	17,790	21,350	27,958
Oregon State U	6,859	7,554[2]	8,592[2]	10,361	12,542	15,504
Ag Exp Station	2,245[4]	2,744	2,710	3,113	3,200	3,859
Ag Exten Serv	1,745[4]	2,046	1,941	2,358	2,465	2,880
Forest Rsch Lab					217	369
Subtotal, Ore St U	10,849	12,344	13,243	15,795	18,425	22,612
Portland St U	1,525	2,245[2,6]	2,759[2]	4,316	7,391	9,531
Oregon Coll of Edn	892	1,107[2]	1,297[2]	1,430	2,085	3,092
Southern Ore Coll	873	1,060[2]	1,258[2]	1,902	2,870	3,390
Eastern Ore Coll	687	830[2]	943[2]	1,090	1,318	1,643
Ore Tech Inst		1,252[2]	1,411[2]	1,481	1,727	2,115
Edl Television	100[4]					
Div of Contin'g Edn[7]	707	1,085[2]	1,387[2]	1,613	1,784	2,216
WICHE[8]	32	37[2]	41	48	68	114
Centralized activities[9]	597	736	958	1,150	1,605	2,490
NDEA matchg loan funds				198	261	230

State aid to Comm Colls				1,362	2,400	6,315	11,636
Total	27,759[10]	34,370	39,936	49,252	65,199	87,683[11]	

[1]Less cutbacks of about $5 million.

[2]Sums marked are allocated by the Board of Higher Education. These sums are only approximations.

[3]The medical and dental schools are administratively unconnected with the University, but bear its name.

[4]These sums were specifically appropriated by the legislature. Sums not so marked are estimated allocations by the State Board of Higher Education, out of a lump-sum appropriation.

[5]TB hospitals are included in this sum.

[6]Appropriation of $85,000 for School of Social Work is not included in this sum.

[7]State-wide general extension service is now termed as Division of Continuing Education.

[8]The Western Interstate Commission for Higher Education, the administrative body for the interstate compact among 13 westernmost states, including Alaska and Hawaii, for cooperation in the use of facilities for higher and professional education. In this case the appropriation is intended to pay one or more other states for providing education in veterinary medicine for qualified Oregon students. Oregon has no college of veterinary medicine.

[9]Administration, budgeting, accounting, disbursing, and other centralized functions carried on by the offices of the State Board of Higher Education.

[10]Subsequent rectification has increased the total in this tabulation to $28,719.

[11]Includes $211,000 for State Scholarship Commission, and $445,000 for Educational Coordinating Council, a body created and funded by the legislature to evaluate and advise regarding education at all levels from Kindergarten through graduate school.

special session, having failed to enact a general sales tax or any other substantial revenue measure, cut back the higher education operating appropriations for the ensuing biennium by a little over 3 per cent for fiscal year 1967-68 and a little over 4 per cent for fiscal year 1968-69.

In this history of fiscal frustration there is one bright ray. In the 'Twenties, Oregon was one of the pioneers in devising the "special fund" theory, under which state universities were permitted to issue so-called "revenue bonds" to finance the construction of self-liquidating buildings such as dormitories and dining halls.[2] Since such bonds command substantially higher rates of interest than state bonds backed by the "full faith and credit and taxing power of the state," Oregon amended its constitution in 1950 to permit the bonds thereafter issued to finance self-liquidating buildings to be general obligation *bonds of the state*, thus achieving a considerable saving in interest charges.

The amendment of 1950 limited the amount of state bonds for this purpose which could be outstanding at any one time, to 0.75 per cent of the *assessed value* of all taxable property in the state. Another amendment of 1960 made this read *"true cash value"* and thus approximately tripled the limit, which had already become insufficient because of the greatly expanded enrollments in all the institutions.

A further amendment approved May 28, 1968, applied the same principle to the financing of non-income-producing academic buildings, by authorizing state bonds to be issued up to a limit of three-fourths of the true cash value of all taxable property in the state, to finance "educational and general purpose buildings" at the state universities and colleges and at the local public community colleges, but not to exceed the amount of matching funds appropriated by the legislature. Apparently this meant a policy of financing academic buildings one-half by "pay-as-you-go" legislative appropriations, and one-half by state bonds. Self-liquidating nonacademic buildings were expressly excluded from the provisions of this amendment.

_____

[2] *McClain* v. *Regents of University of Oregon*, 124 Ore. 629, 265 Pac. 412 (1928).

PENNSYLVANIA

In this Middle Atlantic state the public sector of higher education consists of the Pennsylvania State University (begun as a Farmers' High School in 1855), 14 state colleges having private normal school antecedents, nearly a score of "Commonwealth campuses" of the state university, and a growing number of local public junior colleges.

The private sector includes an Ivy League university (the University of Pennsylvania, founded in 1740), two large urban universities (Temple University in Philadelphia and the University of Pittsburgh), and more than one hundred varied private institutions, mostly comparatively small and a majority being primarily undergraduate colleges of liberal arts.

Pennsylvania is the only state in the Union having a tradition of direct appropriations of state tax funds to selected private institutions on a substantial scale. [1] Although the state constitution (Article 3, Section 18) prohibits appropriations for charitable, educational, or benevolent purposes to "any denominational or sectarian institution," appropriations were made to one or more such institutions in 1881, and continued on an increasing scale until 1919, when their aggregate exceeded $2 million. Thereafter a state appropriation to the Duquesne University of the Holy Ghost in Pittsburgh was challenged, with the result that the state supreme court declared that all direct appropriations of state tax funds to denominational institutions must cease, as in violation of the constitution; but it did not interdict state appropriations to private nonsectarian institutions. [2]

Prior to 1965 the state had developed a policy of providing regular annual subsidies for operating expenses of about 15 selected private .. ~~ectarian institutions. In considerable part the rationale was that of assisting medical education. (Pennsylvania has three private universities operating medical colleges, and some five other independent private colleges of medicine and related health sciences receiving state subsidies.) The three largest private universities also

---

[1] Among a few other states making such appropriations, but on a scale so small as to be almost negligible, are Maryland (though Maryland seems to have discontinued the practice in 1968), Alabama, and Vermont. Florida subsidizes the Medical College of the private University of Miami.

[2] *Collins* v. *Kephart*, 271 Pa. 428, 117 Atl. 440 (1921).

received, in addition to their medical subsidies, substantial assistance for their "general maintenance"; and half a dozen diverse types of smaller institutions also were subsidized in smaller amounts. Of these latter, the largest was Drexel Institute of Technology, which received a little less than $1 million for fiscal year 1964-65.

The total picture of state appropriations for fiscal year 1964-65 was divided into three roughly equal parts. All together it involved about $70 million: $25 million for the Pennsylvania State University, $19½ million for the 14 state colleges, and $24½ million for 15 private institutions.

By 1965 it had been amply demonstrated that large urban private universities such as Temple University and the University of Pittsburgh, striving to serve large numbers of qualified students living in their respective metropolitan areas, could not hope to achieve that aim unless they could find some means of reducing their student fees to approximately the level of those of state universities. This was sharply pointed up by the financial near-collapse of the University of Pittsburgh in 1965, when its operating deficit had mounted to some $20 million and it became immediately necessary for the state legislature to provide a substantial interim emergency subsidy to keep the University in operation.

Released in July 1966 was a state-wide plan for higher education prepared by the State Board of Education. This envisioned three large universities—the Pennsylvania State University, Temple University, and the University of Pittsburgh—as composing the "Commonwealth Segment" of higher education in Pennsylvania. The policy, already adopted in practice, of subsidizing these three institutions (in addition to their regular ongoing annual subsidies) with sums sufficient to enable them to reduce their fees to stated levels slightly lower than those previously in effect at the Pennsylvania State University and its branch campuses, without loss of operating income, was continued by the 1966 legislature and its successors in the immediately ensuing years.

The appropriations to enable the universities to reduce fees without loss of operating income are appropriately called "tuition reduction supplements." This is Pennsylvania's way of proceeding in accord with the declared purpose of the state-wide plan: "To guarantee the availability of quality higher education at low cost to the individual student."

The three large universities involved in this scheme are given a new classification as "state-related" (to be explained in a moment). The University of Pennsylvania is no part of this plan, and continues as a "state-aided" institution, getting approximately its customary annual state subsidies, along with Lincoln University, Drexel Institute of Technology, and a dozen other smaller private institutions.

For fiscal year 1968-69 the state-wide fiscal picture had changed somewhat from the one-third for the state university, one-third for the state colleges, and one-third for the private institutions, as it was for fiscal year 1964-65. For 1968-69 the state university was getting about 30 per cent, the state colleges about 30 per cent, and the private institutions (both "state-related" and "state-aided") about 40 per cent. This was exclusive of the appropriations for student aids.

It is often loosely and erroneously said that Temple University and the University of Pittsburgh "have become state universities." Not so. They are private corporations. It is true that the statutes of 1965 and 1966 giving them the cognomen "state-related" provided that 12 of the 36 members of the governing board of each institution should thereafter be appointed by public authorities; but this did not terminate the existing corporations, nor, indeed, change their legal nature at all. The plan of enlarged state tax support is no more than another step in Pennsylvania's traditional policy of providing state tax support to selected private institutions.

Neither Temple nor Pitt has "become a state university," as the formerly private University of Buffalo became a campus of the State University of New York in 1963. The state has, however, adopted a˜ policy and practice of expanded state aid to these two large private universities in Philadelphia and Pittsburgh respectively, in order to enable them to provide good and diverse educational facilities at reasonable or low cost to the student.

It may also be worthy of note that the Pennsylvania State University is not regarded as a "state-owned" university. This is a case, apparently unique among the states, where the governing board (corporation) is sole owner of the plant and property of the public university, as is the case with most private institutions. In all other states, the state itself is the legal owner of the property of the state university, and the governing board holds it as trustee or agent for the state.

The peculiar Pennsylvania concept may have arisen in part from the fact that only 6 of the 32 members of the board of trustees of the Pennsylvania State University are chosen by public authorities—appointed by the governor with the consent of the senate. There are also 5 members ex officiis—the governor and the state secretaries of agriculture, mines, and public instruction, and the president of the University; but adding these brings the total of publicly-selected members to only 11, a minority composing only one-third of the total membership. Nine other members are elected by the alumni, and 12 are elected by delegates from county agricultural and engineering societies.

In strictest legal theory the composition of the governing board does not define the difference between a state institution and a private institution. (Often private college boards have had some members appointed by public authorities, and many state institution boards have some members elected by alumni or other nonpublic organizations.) Nor is the distinction defined by the sources of funds. Private institutions can receive state tax support where the state and federal constitutions permit it; and public institutions can and do receive private gifts, and some state universities have large endowment funds and considerable portions of their physical plants largely derived from private sources.

Ownership of the institutional property seems to be the test; and in Pennyslvania the only "state-owned" institutions of higher education are the 14 state colleges (including the recently renamed Indiana University of Pennsylvania, formerly one of the state colleges); and the Pennsylvania State University, though for all intents and purposes a public institution,[3] is classified as "state-related."[4]

In fact, says William A. Cornell, who studied the matter in 1965, "No institution of higher education in Pennsylvania was ever founded as a public institution." The 14 state colleges, now state-owned, were all founded as private normal schools and later purchased by the Commonwealth under a statute of 1911. (The local public junior colleges, established under an act of 1963, were not intended to be within the purview of Cornell's statement.)

Before shaking off these technicalities, it will be well to note that the Pennsylvania State University's status as a "state university that is non-state" has had the very salutary result of protecting it to a substantial extent from entanglement with non-educational administrative and fiscal agencies of the state, at whose hands the 14 state colleges have suffered greatly. Some notion of what this means may be had from a newspaper editorial published in the *Lock Haven Express* early in 1964. Addressing himself to the newly-created State Council of Higher Education (a panel of the reconstituted State Board of Education) the editorial writer said:

"The Council should look into the thicket of obsolete regulations, time-worn regimentation, and stultifying controls exercised by offices in Harrisburg where there is neither knowledge nor experience of educational problems.

"Three abuses of long-standing should be rectified promptly if Pennsylvania really wants to let its state colleges live up to their responsibilities:

---

[3] The phrase "for all intents and purposes" is used here because the Pennsylvania State University has long borne much the same practical relationship to the state as do the state universities in other states.

[4] Technically, it may be a private institution; if so, it is in the unique position of being a state university that is not a public university. William A. Cornell, in his *Patterns of Appropriations for Institutions of Higher Education by the General Assembly of Pennsylvania* (Edinboro, Pa.: The Author, 1966. 45 pp. mimeo), says: "The Pennsylvania State University was founded as a private institution, was designated as a land-grant institution, and operated from 1887 to this day with state aid as a private corporation in a 'state-related condition'," citing "Act of April 1, 1963, P.L. 213; and the *Legislative Record* for April 19, 1899, p. 3039."

"One of these abuses is the quaint system which forces the colleges, year after year, to follow the same rules and red tape set up to control state penitentiaries, hospitals, and other custodial institutions. . . .

"Another abuse is the concept of budget-making for the sake of budget-making. The fiscal officers of the colleges are kept busy making and remaking the budget, justifying requests, submitting new sets of forms, and trying to get the means to operate from bureaucrats who do not comprehend the special problems of an educational institution. . . .

"The third abuse is the dishonest procedure under which fees paid by students in state colleges are turned over to the state, to be included later in the college appropriations. If the state goes on an 'austerity program', reducing the funds paid back to the colleges, they may not get all the money their students have actually paid. Is that a good way for the Commonwealth of Pennsylvania to support higher education for its young people—to take some of their educational money for other state purposes?" (Compare different practices with regard to these matters in other states. See the stories of the "freedom bills" in Delaware, Massachusetts, and New Jersey; the story of central purchasing in Oklahoma; the handling of student fees and other institutional receipts in Ohio and South Dakota; and especially the position of the constitutionally autonomous state universities in Michigan, California, and Minnesota.)

The next year (1965) the Pennsylvania House of Representatives passed by a vote of 200-to-3 a bill to confer on the state colleges some measure of autonomy, but the bill died in a Senate committee. It would have authorized the college boards of trustees to purchase items costing up to $1,000 without advertising for bids (the previous limit was $300); and purchases up to $3,000, in any emergency declared by the board of trustees, would have been authorized to be made after soliciting bids from only three responsible bidders.

The state colleges would have been expressly empowered to receive, hold, and expend grants from the federal government, philanthropic foundations, or business corporations. The whole matter of authorizing and subsidizing travel, in-state and out-of-state, of state college staff members would have been placed in the hands of the institutional governing boards. (Previously out-of-state travel required the consent of the governor.)

Better than from a recital of additional petty details, the essence of the matter comes clear in a few quotations from a speech of Representative Guy A. Kistler in the House on September 1, 1965:

"Pennsylvania's state colleges need administrative and fiscal autonomy commensurate with their obligations and responsibilities if they are to become strong and effective institutions of public higher education.

"The appointment of faculty members now requires the approval of a personnel officer in the Department of Public Instruction, which results in delays and dependence on the judgment of an individual not familiar with the educational programs and professional requirements of the state colleges. These delays involve up to six weeks, which places the presidents of the state colleges in an untenable position in recruiting and employing capable faculty members in the current competitive situation.

"Presidents should have the authority to employ new faculty members under employment policies approved by the local board of trustees and within the budgetary appropriations without being required to secure approval from officers of state agencies. The presidents of the state colleges are best able to make decisions regarding professional personnel and to adjust decisions to changing circumstances resulting from the competition and dynamics of faculty employment.

"The administration of federal and foundation grants at the state colleges is being frustrated by requirements and restrictions imposed by state agencies. This is especially true because of the practice of mandating that these federal moneys be handled through the general fund of the Commonwealth. . . . The processing of these grants through state agencies results in delays in the execution of the objectives of the grants, whether they be for the purchase of instructional equipment or the financing of research projects or educational programs.

"Today the travel of employees, both in-state and out-of-state, is vitally important to the administration of any institution of higher education. College presidents must authorize attendance at professional meetings for administrators and college teachers. This applies at the state colleges the same as at other institutions of higher education. . . . The state college presidents should have the authority to administer all travel of state employees whether it be to professional meetings, or for the recruitment of professional personnel, or for the general administration of the institution."

Development and Support

The late 'Fifties and early 'Sixties saw the appearance of several state-wide studies of higher education in Pennsylvania. On February 15, 1957, Governor George M. Leader's Commission on Higher Education, appointed 18 months earlier, submitted its report.[5] This body was composed of Pennsylvania educators almost exclusively. Of the nine members, the chairman and five others were representatives

---

[5] *Higher Education in the Commonwealth: Report of the Governor's Commission on Higher Education.* Harrisburg: Governor's Office, 1967. 84 pp. litho.

of private institutions; one was from Pennsylvania State University, one from a state teachers college, and one from a private philanthropic foundation. In general, the recommendations forecast, albeit sometimes dimly, the changes that were to occur during the ensuing 10 years.

One of the supporting documents stressed that in 1951-52 Pennsylvania's colleges and universities had ranked forty-first among the states in total current income per student, and remarked that "This unfavorable position was due primarily to the low level of state government contributions." In the same year higher education in Pennsylvania ranked forty-third "in terms of dollars per capita of the state population; forty-fifth in terms of its percentage of the total income payments received by individuals in the state; and forty-sixth in terms of its percentage of the state government's total expenditures."

In mid-1968 Pennsylvania had come up to thirty-seventh place in annual state tax investment per citizen in operating expenses of higher education ($22.64); up to forty-first as to the ratio of this tax investment to total personal income (0.66½ per cent); but continued to stand at forty-sixth as to ratio of state tax investment in annual operating expenses of higher education to total state tax revenue for fiscal year 1966-67 (7.7 per cent). By this last measure, only four states were lower in rank: Connecticut (7.5), South Carolina (6.9), Delaware (6.2), and Massachusetts (4.6). As to total state and local tax revenue per $1,000 of personal income in fiscal year 1966-67, Pennsylvania was in the lowest quartile of the states, with $94.57, far below the national average of $105.50. There was much room for progress.

January 2, 1959, the Joint State Government Commission of the Pennsylvania General Assembly received from an Advisory Panel a report on higher education which was printed at the University of Pittsburgh with the aid of a gift from the Scott Paper Company. 6 The panel of six members consisted of three industrialists, two presidents of private universities, and one public school superintendent. Both the chairman and the research director were at the University of Pittsburgh.

This report was prescient in some respects, but quite reactionary in others. It said, "Our estimate of 1970 enrollment in Pennsylvania colleges and universities is 443,000, an increase over 1958 of over 158 per cent." It showed strikingly that since 1910 Pennsylvania had been steadily losing rank among the states as measured by the percentages of college-age population enrolled in institutions of higher education: Pennsylvania ranked fifteenth in 1910, twenty-third in 1930, and twenty-seventh in 1955.

---

6 *Higher Education in Pennsylvania: Analysis of Problems with Proposals.* Pittsburgh: University of Pittsburgh, 1959. 85 pp.

PENNSYLVANIA

Appropriations for Annual Operating Expenses of Higher Education in Pennsylvania, Alternate Fiscal Years, 1959-60 through 1969-70 (in thousands of dollars)

Institutions	Year 1959-60	Year 1961-62[1]	Year 1963-64	Year 1965-66[3]	Year 1967-68	Year 1969-70
Pennsylvania St U[2]	17,138	18,508	25,090	30,142[3]	44,333	69,163
Tuition supplements[4]					3,745	
Social security				1,200[5]	391	
Special research						
Retirement costs				2,800[6]		
Subtotal, Penn St U	17,138	18,508	25,090	34,142	48,469	69,163
State-owned institutions:						
Indiana U of Penn	1,395	1,823	2,151	3,050	6,024	7,786
West Chester St Coll	1,093	1,382	1,722	2,942	5,418	6,828
California St Coll	781	1,314	1,465	2,342	4,506	5,733
Clarion St Coll	498	879	1,153	1,973	4,036	5,062
Millersville St Coll	799	1,003	1,219	1,921	3,749	5,259
Slippery Rock St Coll	618	981	948	2,042	3,975	5,616
Edinboro St Coll	560	873	1,004	1,896[7]	3,016	5,553
Shippensburg St Coll	619	754	889	1,638	3,274	4,185
Bloomsburg St Coll	727	1,106	1,175	1,845	3,027	4,306
Kutztown St Coll	650	845	1,040	1,523	2,689	3,588
Mansfield St Coll	506	577	620	1,325	2,546	3,953
East Stroudsburg St Coll	610	809	990	1,480	2,391	3,867
Cheyney St Coll	401	617	775	1,142	2,015	3,386
Lock Haven St Coll	507	788	800	1,338	1,964	2,919
Emergency fund				500		
For allocation	1,525		1,040			13,000
Special state schs						
Subtotal, S o i's	11,289	13,751	16,991	26,956	48,179	81,041

State-related universities:						
Temple University[8]	2,239	3,823	6,516	11,547[9]		41,392
Genl maintenance					15,549	
Tuition reduction suppl'ts					3,310	
School of Medicine					9,202	
Subtotal, Temple Univ	2,239	3,823	6,516	11,547	28,061	41,392
U of Pittsburgh[8]	2,659	3,973	4,795	13,373[10]		37,899
Genl maintenance					8,445	
Tuition reduction supp'ts					16,200	
School of Medicine					1,750	
Library School					199	
Computer Center					678	
Nursing Program					250	
Allegheny Observatory					80	
Chair of Exp'l Med					32	
Subtotal, U of Pittsburgh	2,659	3,973	4,795	13,373	27,634	37,899
Private institutions, state-aided						
U of Pennsylvania	3,185	5,522	6,659	7,531[11]		12,000
Genl maintenance					7,775	
School of Medicine					2,005	
Sch of Vet Med					1,353	
University Museum					95	
Subtotal, U of Penn	3,185	5,522	6,659	7,531	11,228	12,000

(Continued)

PENNSYLVANIA (Continued)

Institutions	Year 1959-60	Year 1961-62[1]	Year 1963-64	Year 1965-66	Year 1967-68	Year 1969-70
Drexel Inst of Tech		405	977	1,741[12]	2,162	2,277
Drexel Library Sch					142	
Subtotal, Drexel Inst of Tech		405	977	1,741	2,305	2,277
Jefferson Medical Coll		1,808	1,929	2,165	2,362	2,487
Hahnemann Medical Coll		1,048	1,188	1,343	1,503	1,582
Phil Coll of Osteopathy		136	483	852	1,275	1,343
Woman's Medical College		488	621	736	803	846
Lincoln University		328	377	534	672	850
Phil College of Art		105	171	186	283	299
Moore College of Art		42				
Phil C of Textiles & Sci		105	80	188	199	210
Del Valley C of S & A		52	3	119	147	155
Penn Acad of Fine Arts				3		
Penn Coll of Podiatry				50	106	112
Phil Music Academy					75	75
Dickinson Sch of Law		54	70	70	95	90
Penn Coll of Optometry			63	75	79	84
Other state-aided insts[13]	10,793					
Subtotal, P I's, state-aided	10,793	10,093	12,621	15,593	21,131	22,410
Penn Higher Ed Asst'ce Agency						
Scholarships						51,411
Loan guarantees						
Administration						1,589
Matching funds						1,000
Subtotal, HEAA						54,000

State aid to Comm Colls

					1,000[14]	5,738[15]	11,400
Total	47,285[16]	50,146[16]	66,064	102,611	179,212	317,305	

[1] Sums were appropriated for 13 months.

[2] Pennsylvanians insist that this is not a state university, but "state-related" because its governing board has only a minority of its members appointed by public authorities. It is, however, for all intents and purposes the principal state university in Pennsylvania, as its name implies.

[3] Includes $1.4 million appropriated specifically to replace income foregone by reduction of student fees: $860,000 to reduce the fee at the University Park Main campus to $150 per quarter term; and $541,000 to reduce the fees at the several Commonwealth campuses to $130 per quarter term.

[4] Sums appropriated specifically to replace income foregone by reduction of student fees.

[5] From the Department of Labor and Industry.

[6] From the General State Authority.

[7] Includes a supplemental appropriation of approximately $240,000.

[8] Temple and Pitt are private corporations, with one-third of the members of their governing boards appointed by public authorities under statutes of 1965 and 1966. They are often grouped with Pennsylvania State University as "state-related," the three composing the "Commonwealth Segment" of higher education in Pennsylvania.

[9] Includes $½ million to enable Temple University to reduce student fees. The bill as originally introduced allocated $3.1 million for this purpose, but when it became apparent that enactment would not be accomplished in time to affect fees for the first semester of the current academic year, this sum was reduced by $2.6 million.

[10] This figure is an estimate of the total appropriated to date to the University of Pittsburgh. An "emergency appropriation" of $5 million was made shortly before the beginning of fiscal year 1965-66, and at the moment it is difficult to ascertain precisely the exact amounts attributable to each fiscal year.

[11] The amount in the bill passed by both houses was $7,931,000, but this was reduced by the governor by approximately $400,000.

[12] Includes $1,101,000 for general maintenance, $500,000 for graduate program, and $140,000 for Library Science.

[13] Includes certain medical schools, and industrial, agricultural, trade, and art schools.

[14] $1 million as aid for annual operating expenses. Another $1 million was appropriated for capital improvements.

[15] This figure represents state aid for *operating expenses*, and does not include an additional $3,974,325 appropriated as state aid for *capital improvements* to community colleges.

[16] Subsequent exclusion of schools below the college level reduces the total slightly.

At the same time it asserted, "Parents . . . must assume a far larger share of the costs of higher education by paying higher tuition or by going into debt, even though this may require a basic change in their values"; and "The student must assume a greater responsibility for his own education, by a willingness to pledge part of his future earnings for support of the costs of education." There was no foreknowledge that within eight years the legislature would be appropriating more than $32 million a year to three large universities to enable them to establish substantially reduced student fees.

In April 1961 Governor David L. Lawrence received the final report of his Committee on Education, including sections on higher education prepared by a special task force on that field.[7] The summarized principal recommendations were succinct:

"The legislature should take steps to guarantee that 300,000 Pennsylvania college students can be enrolled by 1970—60,000 in the state colleges, 35,000 in the Pennsylvania State University, 126,000 in the private and state-aided institutions, and 79,000 in community colleges.

"The state colleges should be converted to liberal arts colleges.

"State-aided colleges should receive increased state assistance in terms of established program goals.

"Community colleges should be established and located according to a state plan; financed by an equalization formula and student fees; and established by a school district or local government, or a combination of the two."

Other recommendations related to a proposed system of state scholarships for 5 per cent of each year's high school graduating class, and to a state-insured plan of private loans at low interest to students.

A five-member committee of the State Council on Education should be created, thought this group, with the Deputy for Higher Education in the State Department of Public Instruction as its executive agent, to have oversight of all higher education, and draft a "master plan."

An act of June 1963 reorganized, reconstituted, and renamed the State Council on Education, to create a State Board of Education of 17 members appointed by the governor and the senate, to serve overlapping terms of six years. The novel feature of the new Board was that it was to consist chiefly of two panels of seven members each, to be known respectively as the Council of Basic Education and the Council of Higher Education—the first being charged with duties appertaining to schools below the level of higher education (including area vocational schools), and the second with duties appertaining to higher education (including community colleges and technical institutes).

---

[7] *The Final Report of the Committee on Education appointed by David L. Lawrence, Governor.* Harrisburg: Governor's Office, 1961. 139 pp.

Three "members-at-large" were entitled to attend meetings of both panels. The governor was empowered to select from among the 17 members the chairman of the Board itself and the chairmen of each of the two panels. A quorum was to consist of a majority of the full Board, including at least four members of each panel; and for the adoption of policies and regulations, a recorded affirmative vote of a majority of all members of the Board was required. "The superintendent of public instruction or his designated representative" was made the chief executive officer of the Board, and policies or regulations of the Board were made binding on the Department of Public Instruction.

A substantial representation of professional educators on the Board was made possible by the provisions that "not more than two members" of either panel may be employees of any school system or any educational institution, and "at least two members" of each panel "shall have had previous experience with technical education or training."

Budget requests of the institutions of higher education were to be reviewed by the Council of Higher Education and by the full Board, and "returned to the department (of public instruction) with comments, if any, prior to their submission to the budget secretary (of the Commonwealth)."

The legislature of 1963 also appropriated $500,000 to the Department of Public Instruction for purposes of state aid to community colleges. Another major event of that year was the gift by the Milton S. Hershey Foundation of $50 million to establish and operate a medical school, hospital, and research center in Derry Township, near Harrisburg—all to be administered by Pennsylvania State University. From $20 to $25 million were to be used for construction, and the remainder for endowment to provide operating income.

At the beginning of 1964 the Pennsylvania State University also opened an off-campus center of graduate education at King of Prussia in Upper Merion Township near Philadelphia, for southeastern Pennsylvania, chiefly to meet the demand for graduate instruction for engineers and scientists employed in that populous area. The first approved programs led to masters' degrees in engineering. The first plant was a junior high school building leased from the local board of education, containing 24 classrooms and library, laboratory, and office space. Wherever there is a considerable population of professional persons wishing to pursue master's-level graduate study, the operation of off-campus graduate centers is an important service of a large university. Compare the activities of this type carried on by the University of Michigan and Michigan State University, and other state universities in other states.

Developmental happenings in subsequent years in Pennsylvania included the establishment of state-aided local public community colleges in the vicinities of Harrisburg, Philadelphia, and Pittsburgh, and considerable growth and broadening of educational opportunities in the 14 state colleges. Of these latter, the largest one, having reached an enrollment of the order of 6,000 students, and coveting the advantages of using the name "university" for an institution which is expanding and diversifying and upgrading itself rapidly in keeping with the needs and demands of the times, succeeded in 1965 in persuading the legislature to confer on it the singularly incongruous-seeming title of Indiana University of Pennsylvania. When one remembers, however, that another of its sister institutions in Pennsylvania bears the equally confusing name of California State College, the incongruity does not appear unique. Recalling, too, our tortuous and reluctant conclusion that Penn State is not a state university technically (Footnote 4, *supra*), hail the presence and name of Indiana University of Pennsylvania as negating any statement that Pennsylvania has no state university!

The new State Board of Education obtained from the consulting organization known as the Academy for Educational Development, Inc., an unpaginated report of perhaps 150 pages (mimeo) entitled *Elements of a Master Plan for Higher Education in Pennsylvania*, bearing date of December 31, 1965. This contained data and recommendations thought appropriate for consideration by the Board as it and its constituent panel (the Council of Higher Education) faced the task of developing a continuing and flexible plan for the Commonwealth. In a sense the whole matter can be summarized in the statement, "Support of higher education in Pennsylvania, as in other states, is a problem of policy, not of resources."

Hence a sketchy look at some of the principal features of the state's revenue history is pertinent. In 1953 Pennsylvania rather belatedly enacted its first general sales tax act, at the minuscule rate of 1 cent on the dollar. In 1955 this was raised to 3 cents; and in April and August of 1959 it was put up to 3½ cents and 4 cents successively. June 1, 1963, a new rate of 5 cents on the dollar became effective. This was the highest rate of any state sales tax in the nation; but the contrast with other states having the 4-cent rate was not so great as it might seem, however, because groceries, shoes, and clothing were exempted in Pennsylvania, mitigating to some extent the regressive character of the sales tax by providing some measure of relief for low-income families who had to spend all their incomes for necessities.

The calendar year 1967 was a great year for revenue improvement in the state. The governor suggested, in the hope of balancing a much-enlarged budget, that the legislature enact a "stand-by" personal income tax, to become effective only if and when the total state budget should reach or exceed $1.9 billion. This would have been only a modest 1 per cent flat-rate tax on personal adjusted net income as reported to the federal government. It would have been easily and economically administered, and nearly painless; but it was not enacted.

Later in the year (in December 1967), the legislature, having previously enacted a bill raising the net income tax on corporations to 7 per cent (from the former 6 per cent), retroactive to January 1, 1967, and to 7½ per cent beginning January 1, 1968; and also having raised the cigarette tax to 13 cents a pack from the former 8 cents, then turned to with a will and enacted virtually all the other numerous tax measures advocated by Governor Raymond P. Shafer, in a "package" intended to produce about $285 million of additional revenue per year.

Not content with this, in the middle week of December legislative leaders suddenly proposed raising the 5 per cent general sales tax to 6 per cent, and it was done. At that time Washington State had a 5-cent rate; Maine had 4½ cents; and 41 other states ranged downward as low as 2 cents, with six states having no general sales tax at all.

Among the other revenue measures enacted in December 1967 were:

1. Capital stock and franchise tax, increased to 6 mills from 5 mills, retroactive to January 1, 1967.

2. Gross receipts tax on utilities, raised to 20 mills from 14 mills, retroactive to January 1, 1967.

3. Inheritance tax on direct heirs, to 6 per cent from the former 2 per cent.

4. Annual tax on bank and trust company shares, raised to 10 mills from the former 8.

5. Tax on shares of mutual thrift institutions, raised to 7½ per cent from the former 6.

6. Excise tax on liquor at state stores, raised to 18 per cent from the former 15.

7. Sales tax exemption on restaurant foods, reduced to 10 cents from the former 50 cents. (This alone was estimated to produce $8½ million a year.)

It has been observed in many states at different times that shortly after any substantial improvement in the productivity of the state revenue system becomes effective, important advances in state support of higher education are made. This seemed to hold true in Pennsylvania. Appropriations of state tax funds for operating expenses of higher education for fiscal year 1968-69 represented unprecedented gains over previous years, with a total of $264,693,000. This placed Pennsylvania above Michigan ($262,424,000) and Texas ($259,425,000), and installed the Commonwealth in fourth place among the states, inferior only to California, New York, and Illinois.

Pennsylvania's nine-year rate of gain from 1959-60 to 1968-69 was 509 per cent—the most rapid rate of gain among all the states except those of Hawaii (525 per cent) and New York (515 per cent). This illustrates a familiar story: The Middle Atlantic and New England states were all at low points in 1960, and all made dramatic gains and spectacular progress during the ensuing decade, except New Hampshire (157¼ per cent) and Vermont (235¼ per cent).

General sales taxes and corporation income taxes were good producers of revenue for Pennsylvania. The conspicuous absence of a graduated personal income tax appeared to be the major defect in the system. The Governor's Tax Study and Revision Commission made a forthright and well-reasoned recommendation on this point in its "Final Long-Range Report" of December 1968.[8]

It recommended: "That there be enacted a state tax on personal income earned in Pennsylvania, comprised of both 'earned' and 'unearned' income including income from unincorporated business enterprises, to be levied at a uniform rate upon income taxable for federal income tax purposes."

Even if levied at a uniform rate, the Commission said, "Such a tax would be markedly progressive, primarily because personal exemptions and federal deduction would be allowed." It illustrated this by a small tabulation showing that at the rate of 1 per cent, the estimated average "bite" would be 0.36 per cent of a taxable income of $1,500, and would range steadily upward to 0.80 per cent of an income of $29,000.

A sound statement follows: "The Commission believes that the administration of a state personal income tax would be simplified and its collectibility enhanced by conforming its base to that reported on federal tax returns, and by utilizing withholding and estimated payments procedures similar to those required for federal taxes." The annual yield from such a tax in Pennsylvania, it thought, based on estimated 1969-70 taxable personal income, would be approximately $170 million for each 1 per cent rate. Indiana had in 1968 a tax of this type at the rate of 2 per cent, and Michigan a similar one at 2.6 per cent. This matter of a flat rate levied on adjusted personal income must be sharply distinguished from the different device of levying a stated percentage of what the taxpayer concurrently pays as federal income tax.

In 1968, 20 states were using the adjusted gross income as reported to the Federal Internal Revenue Service as the tax base for their own state income taxes. Of these, only Indiana and Michigan were levying a flat rate on that income. Three others were levying a stated percentage of the concurrent federal tax payment by the taxpayer: Nebraska, 10 per cent; Alaska, 16 per cent; and Vermont, 25 per cent. The other 15 states in the group were administering graduated rate scales of their own applied to the same adjusted gross income base. The extreme range among them was from 1 per cent to 14 per cent (always somewhat narrower for any particular state), with from 4 to 24 rate steps, depending on the state.

---

[8] *Final Long-Range Report of the Governor's Tax Study and Revision Commission.* Harrisburg: Commonwealth of Pennsylvania, 1968. 75 pp.

As to the "progressivity" of the proposed Pennsylvania uniform rate personal income tax, it is comparatively slight compared with the true progressivity obtainable either by adopting a progressive rate scale for the state or by simply levying a percentage of the federal income tax. Pennsylvania's Commission undoubtedly proposed the uniform rate because there was confusion and doubt as to whether any other scheme would pass the test of the state constitutional requirement that the levying of taxes must be uniform. The issue had never been decided by the state supreme court, and conservative lawyers were forever arguing about it, some of them no doubt hoping to stampede the legislature away from the idea of any kind of income tax. The Commission was not even sure that its own proposed personal income tax would survive the court test; but it urged "that every effort be made to enact such a tax, when required to meet essential revenue demands, and to test its constitutionality in the most expeditious manner."

This picture is reminiscent of the fact that three other large, populous, and industrialized states had no state income taxes: Illinois (until 1969), Ohio, and Texas. In Illinois nineteenth-century provisions in the state constitution had for years maintained a fog of uncertainty; but in 1969 the legislature enacted income taxes of 2½ per cent on persons and 4 per cent on corporations, and these measures were promptly sustained by the state supreme court. In Ohio and Texas, as also in Florida and half a dozen smaller states, the absence of state income taxes may have been due more to pious desires for a "favorable industrial climate" than to real or imaginary constitutional barriers. "Something will have to give." Big industrialized states cannot subsist through the twentieth century without state income taxes of any kind.

Pennsylvania's unique policy, begun by the legislature in 1965 and 1966, of making large appropriations of state tax funds to three large popular universities to enable them, without loss of operating funds, to reduce their student fees to stated reasonable levels, merits more than passing attention. By tying state support to fee reductions, the Commonwealth accomplishes with a single simple stroke a great gain toward placing higher educational opportunity within the financial reach of all capable prospective students. This is the exact opposite of what legislatures in many other states were doing from time to time during the decade—short-changing the state universities in their appropriations, knowing that this would force them to raise their student fees.

Nor is the Pennsylvania plan to be confused with the burgeoning, variegated, and complicated schemes of state scholarships, state and federal student loan and "guaranteed loan" schemes, all of which tend toward the eventual destruction of free or low-fee tax-supported public higher education, by overtly or covertly advancing the unconscionable theory that the full cost of higher education should eventually be paid by the student or his family.

RHODE ISLAND

In the old city of Providence and its curtilage officially known as the State of Rhode Island and Providence Plantations, for two centuries a continuing element in the higher educational scene has been Brown University (1764), now among the smaller of the eight Ivy League private universities, of which seven trace their origins to pre-Revolutionary times.

The institution now known as Rhode Island College was established in 1854 as the Rhode Island Normal School. In 1863 the state contracted with Brown University to maintain a "college or department" of agriculture and mechanic arts in return for the benefits of the Morrill Land-Grant Act of 1862. Thirty years later the legislature designated the new state college of agriculture and mechanic arts (which had been chartered in 1888) as the land-grant college of the state, and thereafter the proceeds of the Morrill Act and subsequent federal acts subsidizing the land-grant colleges were paid to it.[1] It is now the University of Rhode Island, having been so named in 1951. The state of Connecticut had somewhat similar contemporaneous experiences in the early development of a land-grant university. Until 1893 federal land-grant funds went to Yale University, and thereafter to the state agricultural college which is now the University of Connecticut. In Massachusetts the outcome was a little different.[2] A minor fraction of the land-grant proceeds continues to this day to go to the private Massachusetts Institute of Technology, but the major part goes to the University of Massachusetts (formerly the state agricultural college).

Prior to 1935 in Rhode Island the State College (now the University of Rhode Island) was governed by a separate Board of Managers. Rhode Island College was governed by the State Board of Education. Two drastic shake-ups were to take place within the next five years, due in large part to the exigencies of politics. In 1935 both the Board of Managers and the State Board of Education were abolished, and both state colleges were placed under a single 10-member Board of

---

[1]*Brown University* v. *Rhode Island College of Agriculture and Mechanic Arts,* (U.S.C.C.), 56 Fed. 55 (1893).

[2]*Yale College* v. *Sanger,* (U.S.C.C.), 62 Fed. 177 (1894); and *Massachusetts Agricultural College* v. *Marden,* 156 Mass. 150, 30 N.E. 555 (1892).

RHODE ISLAND

Appropriations for Annual Operating Expenses of Higher Education in Rhode Island, Alternate Fiscal Years, 1959-60 through 1969-70 (in thousands of dollars)

Institutions	Year 1959-60	Year 1961-62	Year 1963-64	Year 1965-66	Year 1967-68	Year 1969-70
U of Rhode Island		4,350[1]	6,066	8,015	11,601	17,903
Rhode Island College		1,477	1,897	2,626	3,956	6,606
Rhode Island Jr Coll[2]				600	1,436	2,632
Bd of Trustees of St Colls[3]				22	45	129
Subtotal, U & Colls		5,827	7,963	11,241	17,038	27,270
State scholarship system[4]				1,606	1,348	1,577
Scholarships, Bryant Coll[5]					15	15
Total	4,477[6]	5,827	7,963	12,868	18,401	28,935[7]

[1]Includes $403,147 for debt service.
[2]A state institution.
[3]Governing Board of the University and the colleges.
[4]Scholarships for 5 per cent of annual graduating classes in public and private high schools, to attend any accredited college in the United States.
[5]A private nonprofit four-year institution specializing in business training. The scholarships are for teacher-training in business subjects.
[6]This total is a state-wide appropriation.
[7]Includes $70,000 for professional nurse scholarships and $3,000 for war orphans.

Regents. Soon a committee of citizens under the chairmanship of President Henry M. Wriston of Brown University was appointed to recommend a suitable structure for the governance of public higher education and draft an appropriate statute.

Following the recommendations of this Committee, the 1939 legislature abolished the Board of Regents and substituted for it a nine-member Board of Trustees of State Colleges having substantially the same powers as a single board governing the two formerly separately-controlled state institutions. This Board, which was made subordinate to a new Board of Regents for Education (at all levels) by a statute of 1969, is composed of the Commissioner of Education *ex officio* and eight other members, six of whom are appointed by the governor for seven-year terms, and two others who must be alumni of at least 10 years' standing, one being selected by each of the two alumni associations for terms of three years. No officer of the state or any of its subdivisions, or any officer or employee of either of the state institutions, is eligible.

Aside from making possible a turnover of personnel, the chief result of the new statute of 1939 was some progress in disentangling the institutions of higher education from the non-educational administrative and fiscal agencies of the state, into whose mazes they had been deeply ensnared. The author, "borrowed" for a month from the American Council on Education, took care to write 10 subsections into the proposed statute, each one providing for a feature of fiscal and administrative autonomy for the new board of trustees. The statute was enacted verbatim by the 1939 legislature, but in subsequent years there was some tendency to amend or repeal the "autonomy clauses" one by one. Yet a good deal survived; and in 1967 a digest of the current version could report that:

"In order that the Board may control the personnel and equipment of the colleges in the interest of their educational efficiency, they are exempted from state regulations regarding the employment of personnel, and the purchase of supplies and equipment, and from the control of the state director of administration.

"The appointment, promotion, salary, tenure and dismissal of employees of the state colleges are not in any manner under the control of the personnel administrator, or of any officer or board other than the Board of Trustees."[3]

The legislature of 1959 established a state scholarship system, to provide for from $250 to $1,000 per academic year, renewable for not more than three additional years or until a four-year degree is earned, to be awarded by the Commissioner of Education to 5 per cent of each

---

[3]Page 101 of Robert L. Williams' *Legal Bases of Coordinating Boards of Higher Education in Thirty-Nine States*. Chicago: Council of State Governments, September 1967. 129 pp. (mimeo).

year's graduates of public and private high schools. These were made tenable in any accredited college or university within or without the state of Rhode Island—almost a necessity in view of the small area of the state and the small number of institutions within it. By fiscal year 1968-69 this system was receiving an annual appropriation of a little over $1½ million.

The 1959 legislature, perhaps influenced by contemporary similar activities in Massachusetts, directed the Board of Trustees of State Colleges to investigate and report on the feasibility of establishing one or more local public two-year community colleges in the state. A 30-page report was made February 12, 1960,[4] recommending that three such colleges be set up at designated points in the state; and that they be governed by the existing Board of Trustees of State Colleges, that they be administered by one president from a single office, and that they be supported by state funds and by student fees.

This rather expansive plan did not materialize; but the urgent need for a large public junior college in the metropolitan area of Providence continued, and in 1964 an item of $98,000 (later increased to $200,000 by Executive Order) for annual operating expenses of Rhode Island Junior College appeared in the appropriation act. For fiscal year 1968-69 this item was well above $1½ million. The college was a state institution (not based on a local taxing subdivision) as also are the community colleges in Massachusetts. It is the third institution to come under the governance of the Board of Trustees of State Colleges.

During the 10 years 1960-1970 Rhode Island rose from forty-fourth place to fortieth place among the states, measured simply by the total magnitude of annual appropriations of state tax funds for operating expenses of higher education; but, like all the northeastern states, it was at a relatively low point at the beginning of that period.

In fiscal year 1966-67 Rhode Island's total of state and local tax revenues per $1,000 of personal income was $97.72, much below the national average of $105.50. The state tax investment per citizen in annual operating expenses of higher education for fiscal year 1968-69 was $24.43—in thirty-second place, while the ratio of this sum to average total personal income was only 0.67—in fortieth place by that measure. There is evidence that Rhode Island could do better.

A legislative act effective July 1, 1969, created a new Board of Regents for Education, to succeed to all the powers of the State Board of Education and the Board of Trustees of State Colleges, and with authority to continue, reconstitute, or abolish them. This opened the way for many months of uncertainties and adjustments.

The 1969 legislature also enacted tax measures intended to produce $29 million a year in new revenue. Among these was a 10 per cent tax on the investment income of resident individuals.

---

[4]*Report on Community Colleges*. Providence: Board of Trustees of State Colleges, 1960. 30 pp. litho.

SOUTH CAROLINA

Comparative "effort" toward state tax support of higher education, in proportion to the resources available, can be crudely indicated by the ratio between the total state tax investment in annual operating expenses of higher education and the total of personal incomes for the same year. In South Carolina in 1968 this ratio was 0.63½ per cent, placing the state forty-fourth among the states by that measure. The state tax investment per citizen was $15.18, ranking forty-seventh.

The low ratio was in marked contrast to those of some other southern states. Arkansas and Mississippi each showed a ratio of 0.97 per cent, and ranked in sixteenth and seventeenth places among the states by that measure of "effort." The foregoing impressions tend to be corroborated by the fact that South Carolina's appropriation of state tax funds for operating expenses of higher education for fiscal year 1966-67 as a percentage of total state tax revenues (6.9 per cent)[1] was lowest among 15 states of the South; and South Carolina's total state and local tax revenues per $1,000 of personal income was $96.43—markedly below the national average of $105.50.

The 1969 legislature raised the rate of the general sales tax to 4 per cent from the former 3 per cent, and increased the rate on cigarettes to 6 cents from the former 5 cents a pack. Fractional increases were made in liquor and beer taxes. The corporation income tax was also slightly raised. The measures were effective June 1, 1969.

During the present century there was little change in South Carolina's complement of public institutions of higher education until after 1960, except the phenomenon of growing enrollments, which occurred everywhere. Within the past 10 years, however, much progress has been made in making facilities available at many places in the state, and thus accessible to commuting students of whom most would not otherwise obtain any formal education beyond high school. This was done concurrently by two methods: (1) the establishment of university extension units or branch campuses, and (2) the creation of local public two-year institutions jointly supported and controlled by the state and the local subdivision.

---

[1]Page 12 of E. F. Schietinger's *Fact Book on Higher Education in the South, 1968*. Atlanta: Southern Regional Education Board, 1969. 74 pp.

By 1968 the University of South Carolina had small branch units at Aiken, Allendale, Beaufort, Conway, Florence, Lancaster, Spartanburg, and Union. Local schools of the other type, officially named Technical Education Centers, were in operation at Greenville, Conway, Greenwood, Columbia, Sumter, and Pendleton.

Governor Ernest F. Hollings, addressing the legislature in 1961, indicated that he had a keen historical sense: "In 1950," he said, "had a legislator proposed on this House floor a $23 million capital improvement program for the next ten years, he would have been ridiculed here and probably defeated for re-election at home. But the fact remains that we spent that much at Clemson College alone between 1950 and 1960, and the facts also indicate we will spend in excess of $50 million during the next ten years for improvements at the state's institutions."

Some months earlier a joint legislative committee had been appointed "to investigate the feasibility of increasing existing facilities and erecting and maintaining two-year colleges in various locations within this state." This committee published a brief staff report in May 1961.[2] The committee members were three from the Senate and three from the House, plus three citizens appointed by the governor. One of these latter was Mr. A. L. M. Wiggins of Hartsville, who became chairman. He was reported to have said: "Our greatest need today is for a crash program to multiply educational effort, not only quantitatively but qualitatively." The governor had recently pointed out that in 1975 South Carolina would have at least 65,000 students in colleges and universities—more than twice the enrollment of 1961.

The staff report made a good case for a state-wide network of local public junior colleges. There were some minority dissents within the Committee. For example, one member was said to have feared that the establishment of tax-supported institutions would have adverse effects on the private colleges. This view has been encountered again and again in many states, but it is largely nonsense. The low-fee or tuition-free public junior college serves mainly students who would not otherwise be able to attend any college. Some of them, on completion of the two years of "college-parallel" studies, then seek to study for a degree in some four-year college; and this may well be a private college. This improves private colleges both financially and academically by "beefing up" their scanty enrollments in the upper two classes, where classes are smallest and instruction is most expensive.

---

[2]*Report of the Joint Legislative Committee Created to Study Problems of Educating on a College Level the Increasing Number of Students of College Age in South Carolina.* Columbia: South Carolina General Assembly, May 8, 1961. 14 pp.

Another member of the Committee dissented because he thought the extension centers of the University of South Carolina could better perform the functions of local two-year colleges. This dispute has also persisted in many states; and several populous and educationally important states have proceeded gaily to develop *both* types: university branches and local junior colleges. Witness Ohio and Pennsylvania, for example. It has not been shown that this dual development is extravagant or bad in any way; but some educators and others look upon it skeptically because they are compulsively obsessed with the notion that if a state has two-year colleges, they must all be units in a uniformly-centralized state-wide system. Rigidity and uniformity seem to be their prime goals. These are everywhere unworthy and inappropriate in higher education.

There is a third segment of opinion which rejects or minimizes both the university branch and the local comprehensive junior college, in favor of the "technical institute" or "terminal vocational school." These people believe all problems will be solved if a majority of each annual crop of high school graduates is quickly trained in some occupational specialty and placed in a wage-earning job as speedily as possible. They are so enamored of this idea that they want the training limited largely or wholly to the essential technical skills, without devoting much or any time or effort to general or liberal education which others think should accompany the occupational training.

The three disparate positions just mentioned can be found in every state, with the three in various degrees of ascendancy. It seems that in South Carolina, at least up to 1969, the comprehensive local public junior college had not taken root. The University of South Carolina had its outlying branches in a spate of towns; and the "technical education centers," not connected with any university, but fostered by the division of vocational education in the state department of education and aided by federal and state money for vocational education, operated in another spate of towns.

This picture was not so dark as it might seem to some doctrinaire advocates of the truly comprehensive community college. The hope of many persons, and a plausible expectation, is that eventually over the ensuing years all these institutions, whether junior colleges, university branches, or technical schools, will evolve into and become comprehensive community colleges.

In South Carolina it does not appear that two of the foregoing types of schools exist in the same town; but this situation exists in some instances in some other southern states. Where, for example, a university branch unit and a vocational-technical school exist in the same town or within a few miles of each other, probably the ideal solution is the delicate and ever-progressing dovetailing of their curricula and operations to approach as nearly as possible the circumstances in which any eligible student in the commuting area can

SOUTH CAROLINA

Appropriations for Annual Operating Expenses of Higher Education in South Carolina, Alternate Fiscal Years, 1959-60 through 1969-70 (in thousands of dollars)

Institutions	Year 1959-60	Year 1961-62	Year 1963-64	Year 1965-66	Year 1967-68	Year 1969-70
U of So Carolina		3,726	4,739	6,364	10,702	16,334[1]
Medical Coll of So C		2,522	3,023	4,048	8,898	13,354
Clemson University		3,415	4,096	4,962	7,320	11,154[2]
Winthrop College		1,519	1,925	2,412	3,126	3,968
So C State College		1,594	1,747	1,928	2,497	3,944
The Citadel		1,673	1,830	1,689	2,605	3,479
Total	12,113[3]	14,449	17,360	21,403	35,148	53,316[4]

[1] Includes $1,205,000 for regional campuses.
[2] Includes $261,000 for extension centers.
[3] This total is for state-wide appropriations.
[4] Includes $812,000 for Commission on Higher Education, and $271,000 for Southern Regional Education Board.

attend either or both, either alternatively or concurrently, to obtain the two years of education and training that best suit his individual needs and ambitions.

Questions as to whether the financial support shall be from federal and state sources, state and local sources, or solely through the budget of a state university, and whether control shall be primarily from a university governing board, a local board of trustees, or a state education department are all of less importance than the simple fact that some local facilities for education immediately beyond high school are *in situ* and available to eligible students of today. We may hope that eventually a comprehensive two-year community college will be within easy commuting distance from the home of every citizen, except in rare instances where conditions of terrain and sparsity of population render this wholly impracticable. This will not be achieved overnight. Meantime, the pragmatic policy is to start where we are and develop what we have toward the goal, with tolerance of different methods of support and control.

Governor Hollings, apparently even before he had received the staff report of the Joint Legislative Committee in 1961, appointed a new Governor's Advisory Committee on Higher Education, of seven citizens, with Mr. A. L. M. Wiggins again as chairman. This Committee reported March 6, 1962.[3] Early in the report there appeared a singularly candid confession: "In the past decade, higher education in South Carolina has not kept pace with the progress of other states in the Southern Region nor in the United States generally. This is shown by the comparatively low level of the financial support of the state's institutions of higher learning, their lack of accreditation in many subjects, the limited development of their graduate schools and their meager programs of basic and applied research."

Prominent among the recommendations were: (1) that the five extension centers of the University of South Carolina then existing (and becoming "branch campuses") should be converted into comprehensive community colleges, with increased emphasis on technical-vocational offerings and adult education, as well as their academic programs, and that five more such institutions should be contemplated in order to approach making their services available to all citizens of the state; and (2) that there be a state-level coordinating agency for all higher education created by statute: "The proposal is not for the establishment of a superboard nor for setting up an overall administrative agency. The plan proposed is for setting up a body with advisory powers only that will be charged with the duty of making continuing studies of the state's institutions of higher learning and of making recommendations that will result in greater coordination and

---

[3]*Report of the Governor's Advisory Committee on Higher Education.* Columbia, S. C.: Governor's Office, 1962. 72 pp.

cooperation of the various institutions, that will produce greater efficiency and economy in operation, and that will promote excellence in higher education in all the institutions."

This latter recommendation was implemented by the enactment of a statute by the 1962 legislature creating a State Advisory Commission on Higher Education "to be composed of seven members appointed by the governor." One section stipulated: "The Commission shall establish a Council of Presidents consisting of the presidents of the state institutions of higher learning. The Council of Presidents shall appoint a chairman and such other officers and committees as it may see fit. It shall meet at least four times a year, of which two meetings shall be held jointly with the Commission. The Council of Presidents shall establish committees consisting of qualified personnel representing the various state-supported institutions of higher learning, either upon request of the Commission or upon its own initiative, to investigate, study, and report on such subjects as: (1) academic planning, (2) business and financial coordination, and (3) library utilization and coordination."

It seems that a later statute added the chairmen of the governing boards of the respective institutions as members *ex officio* of the Commission, thus bringing its total membership up to 13; and a sentence was added which broke over the original injunction that "Nothing in this act shall be construed as clothing the Commission with any apparent or inherent powers except those of an advisory nature." The added sentence was: "No new program shall be undertaken by any state-supported institution without the approval of the Commission or the General Assembly."

The policy seems to be to move toward interinstitutional teamwork by means of studies and joint deliberations, rather than by the impracticable and often self-defeating route of overcentralized administration. Wisely, it seems, the practice is to involve in the organs of cooperation and state-wide study, not only a group of selected laymen, but also the chairmen of the governing boards, the presidents, and appropriate other members of the staffs of each of the state institutions.

An event of the 1968 legislative session was the approval by the legislature of a state bond issue of $5½ million for new construction at South Carolina State College, the institution predominantly for Negroes. This was part of a $32½ million bond issue authorized for various state purposes, including state parks, state office buildings, and the state's tri-centennial exposition in 1970. In March 1968 Negro students staged a peaceful demonstration at the Capitol and presented a petition to Governor Robert E. McNair. The governor recommended the bond issue for the college, and it was also recommended by a committee composed of Lieutenant Governor John C. West and three members of the state senate who visited the campus and inspected its facilities.

SOUTH DAKOTA

With a "stationary" population over the preceding four decades, punctuated by occasional slight declines, South Dakota lost 3½ per cent between 1960 and 1968, showing an estimated total of only 657,000 as of July 1, 1968. This helps to explain that the state's nine-year rate of gain (1960-1969) in state tax-fund appropriations for operating expenses of higher education (111 per cent) was second lowest among the 50 states.

Conditions in South Dakota bear considerable resemblance to those in the sister state of North Dakota, but many indications make it appear that North Dakota is somewhat superior in its tradition of tax support for higher education and in its proportionate effort expended for that purpose. In 1968 the state tax investments per citizen in annual operating expenses of higher education were: North Dakota, $32.50 (twelfth place); South Dakota, $26.35 (twenty-sixth place). The ratios of these investments to total personal incomes were: North Dakota, 1.21 per cent (second place); South Dakota, 0.92¼ per cent (twentieth place).

The 1969 legislature raised the rate of the general sales tax to 4 per cent from the former 3 per cent.

South Dakota public higher education suffers from statutory relationships with the state treasurer and other central fiscal officers of the state that are conspicuously unfortunate in more than one respect. For example, the state captures all student fees and other institutional receipts for the state treasury. Twenty per cent of these funds are earmarked for financing academic buildings at the institutions. Eighty per cent are commingled in the state General Fund, and thus lost to the institutions from which they originated; student fees become the equivalent of a general state tax paid only by students, but not allocated to the operation of the state colleges and universities—a concept that seems difficult to explain or condone.

The legislature of 1959 authorized a state-wide survey of higher education, which was executed by a group of staff members of the U.S. Office of Education. [1] Among more than one hundred specific recommendations was: "The Regents of Education should seek and

---

[1] Sebastian V. Martorana and others, *Higher Education in South Dakota.* Washington: U.S. Office of Education, 1960. 122 pp.

344

the legislature should enact amendments to the laws of South Dakota which govern state fiscal procedures so that approvals of expenditures are made a responsibility of the Regents of Education and a function of the executive director, thereby relieving the institutions of unwieldy and delaying fiscal controls."

Much the same point is made at another place in other words: "The Regents should be made the official and sole state agency responsible for approval and pre-audit of expenditure of moneys appropriated to implement the budget approved by the governor and the legislature." In the vernacular, higher education would be more efficient and productive in the use of available funds if fiscal strangulation from the statehouse were thrown off.

South Dakota has had the longest continuous experience of any state with the centralized system in which one board governs all the state institutions of higher education. During the late 'Eighties and early 'Nineties there was a board of trustees for each institution, and one central board with some supervisory authority over all. In 1896 this scheme was abolished. Substituted for it was the one central governing board known as the Board of Regents of Education, today governing seven institutions.

This Board is composed of seven members appointed by the governor and senate for terms of six years. No member may be a resident of any county in which any of the institutions is located. Different regions of the state must be represented, and no one political party may hold all the seats. The authority of the Board, though in a sense very broad, is restricted not only in the ways already described herein, but also in the matter of land acquisition and building construction. It is expressly prohibited from erecting any structures or maintaining or equipping buildings unless as authorized by a legislative act. A statute empowers it to provide facilities for housing and feeding students by issuing "revenue bonds" and making charges for room and board sufficient to amortize the debt within a specified time; but such projects may be undertaken only when approved by the governor and the secretary of finance.

The statute originally empowered the Board to pledge not only the inco͏͏ ͏ ͏rom the building or buildings to be financed by such a bond issue, but also "(for a period not longer than ten years) the net income of other dormitory and apartment facilities then existing at such institution." In 1956, however, when the state supreme court had to pass upon the legality of a proposed issue of revenue bonds to finance three dormitory buildings at South Dakota State College at Brookings, the ruling was that insofar as the bonds were payable only out of funds to be derived from the proposed new buildings, they created no state debt; but insofar as they were also payable out of the net income of other dormitory buildings of the college, the bonds would create a state debt; and accordingly the court restrained the Board from pledging

SOUTH DAKOTA

Appropriations for Annual Operating Expenses of Higher Education in South Dakota, Alternate Fiscal Years, 1959-60 through 1969-70 (in thousands of dollars)

Institutions	Year 1959-60	Year 1961-62	Year 1963-64	Year 1965-66	Year 1967-68	Year 1969-70
U of So Dakota	1,911	1,796	2,384	4,256	5,699	6,442
So. Dakota St U[1]	4,071	4,418	4,771	7,631		
Main campus					6,239	7,362
Ag Exper Sta					1,985	2,061
Ag Exten Serv					1,206	1,328
Subtotal, So Dakota St U	4,071	4,418	4,771	7,631	9,430	10,751
Northern St Coll	721	765	854	1,673	2,418	3,100
So Dakota Sch of Mines	774	817	1,024	1,467	2,003	2,552
Black Hills St Coll	257	363	377	1,057	1,677	2,122
Southern St Coll	201	238	367	755	1,135	1,381
Genl Beadle St Coll	205	278	356	688	1,009	1,346
Bd of Regents of Edn	31			4,344[2]	1,621[3]	122
For allocation						1,011
Total	8,173	8,675	10,133[4]	21,872	24,999[5]	28,827
Less est student fees & other instit'l receipts				-5,885	-8,000[6]	-10,600
Net Total				15,987	16,992	18,227

[1]Formerly South Dakota College of Agriculture; later, South Dakota State College.
[2]This includes $1,232,000 for deferred maintenance, $504,500 for building repairs hitherto appropriated directly to the institutions, and $1,067,500 as an operating contingency reserve; also $1 million for salary increases; and for this purpose an appropriation of $500,000 was also made for the fiscal year 1966-67.
—$76,000 for the Board's executive office, and $1,545,000 for allocation.

raise the yearly totals by roughly $350,000. The Board also governs institutions for the blind and the deaf, for which it got $445,000 for the biennium.
[5]Does not include $522,000 appropriated to the state schools for the blind and the deaf, both of which are governed by the Regents of Education.
[6]Institutional receipts are captured for the state treasury. Eighty per cent are commingled in the General Fund of the state. Twenty per cent are earmarked for financing academic buildings.

the income of existing dormitories to help finance the construction of the proposed new ones.[2]

Persons familiar with the foregoing particular point will recall that an Alabama supreme court decision in 1957 reached the same result[3]; but this was nullified by an amendment to the Alabama Constitution adopted in 1961, as construed by an Alabama supreme court decision of 1966.[4]

In 1958 the Board of Regents of Education brought upon itself considerable nation-wide notoriety when it summarily dismissed the head of the department of agronomy at South Dakota State College after he had served 15 consecutive years. When he invoked the ineptly drafted "tenure policy" then in effect as a part of the rules of the Board, the South Dakota supreme court noted that under these rules "Apparently the Board could not discharge or remove a member of the faculty for any reason if the president failed to file a complaint, or failed to recommend dismissal. . . . We believe this to be an unlawful abdication of the Board's exclusive prerogative and power." Thus the removal of the professor by direct action of the Board was sustained,[5] though later sharply criticized by learned legal scholars.[6]

---

[2] *Boe* v. *Foss*, 76 S. D. 295, 77 N. W. 2d 1 (1956).

[3] *Opinion of the Justices*, 266 Ala. 78, 93 So. 2d 923 (1957).

[4] *Pincard* v. *State Board of Education*, (Ala.), 189 So. 2d 153 (1966).

[5]*Worzella* v. *Board of Regents of Education*, 77 S. D. 447, 93 N. W. 2d 411 (1958).

[6]Especially by Clark Byse, "Academic Freedom, Tenure, and the Law: A Comment on *Worzella* v. *Board of Regents*," in *Harvard Law Review* 73: 304-322 (December 1959).

TENNESSEE

Extending a long way westward from its northeastern extremity in the Appalachians between Virginia and North Carolina to Memphis on the Mississippi River, this state is comparatively narrow from north to south, and presents a "strip" configuration. For this reason its three "grand divisions"—East Tennessee, Middle Tennessee, and West Tennessee, are often mentioned in law and custom, and appear in the nomenclature of its regional state universities (with Memphis as surrogate for West Tennessee).

Nashville, the metropolis of Middle Tennessee, has been known as "the Athens of the South" on account of the remarkable concentration of colleges and universities, private and public, in and around it. Among the private institutions are Belmont College, David Lipscomb College, Fisk University, Meharry Medical College, George Peabody College for Teachers, Trevecca College, and Vanderbilt University. The public institutions include the Tennessee Agricultural and Industrial State University (recently renamed Tennessee State University); the Nashville Center of the University of Tennessee; and two others within 40 miles or less from the city—Austin Peay State University at Clarksville, and Middle Tennessee State University at Murfreesboro.

Knoxville, in East Tennessee (the part of the state settled earliest) is the seat of the main campus of the University of Tennessee, which traces its origins to 1794. The University has its Medical Center at Memphis, and sizeable campuses at Martin and Chattanooga, the latter being the result of the state's acquisition of the formerly private University of Chattanooga in 1969. Development of a large campus at Nashville is also contemplated, but in 1968 was temporarily delayed by court actions regarding its relationship to state-wide racial desegregation of higher education, to be discussed *infra* in this story.

Six former state colleges were renamed regional state universities during the late 'Sixties in recognition of their growth and of the fact that they had already become or would soon become multipurpose institutions. These include the Tennessee State University at Nashville, predominantly for Negroes. Insofar as this institution serves black students from all parts of the state, it does not fit wholly into the concept of "regional state universities"; but it seems possible that racial desegregation may eventually and gradually diminish the relative importance of the emphasis on state-wide service to Negroes, though the complete disappearance of the need for that service cannot now be foreseen.

By all odds the largest of the regional state universities is Memphis State University, which is more than twice the size of most of the other five. East Tennessee State University at Johnson City is second largest. These two institutions are separated by 475 miles. All six regional state universities are governed by the State Board of Education.

Tennessee was tardy in developing a network of public community colleges. The first appropriation for that purpose seems to have been a token $500,000 for fiscal year 1966-67. Separate appropriations for three state "community colleges" appeared for both fiscal years of biennium 1967-69. In the appropriation act for fiscal year 1969-70 a total of six such institutions appeared, and the aggregate of appropriations was about $4¼ million. The legislature of 1969 also authorized the establishment of three additional such colleges, which would make a total of nine. All these are *state* institutions, not dependent on a local taxing district. Tennessee thus adds its weight to the tendency for public junior colleges to be or become *state* institutions, as evidenced in Georgia, Minnesota, Washington, and Colorado; not to mention the states where such colleges are predominantly branch units of parent state universities, such as Wisconsin, Indiana, Ohio, and Kentucky.

In these latter instances they are also *state* institutions, but receive both support and governance from the parent state university. The point is worth noting because the local public junior college primarily supported and controlled by a local subdivision, once thought by many to be the ideal form which would eventually cover the nation, has not proved to be practicable in a substantial number of states; and a few of the states which once had that form have changed to state support and governance for two-year colleges.

One might be tempted to raise the questions as to whether—in view of the growing financial stringency in cities, counties, school districts, and other local subdivisions, depending chiefly, as they must, on property taxes—there may not be a likelihood that the support of junior colleges may pass more and more to the states themselves, with their ability to levy and administer sales taxes, income taxes, and other components of a modern revenue system based on ability to pay much more realistically than are property taxes.

Tennessee, with an estimated 3,976,000 people in mid-1968, was very near the mythical "state of average population." Its rate of growth since 1960 was 11½ per cent, exactly the same as the national average rate for that period.

The rate of gain over the nine years 1960-1969 in appropriations for annual operating expenses of higher education was 329½ per cent—much above the national average of 261 per cent—and ranking third among the 15 southern states. In fiscal year 1966-67 Tennessee's total state and local tax collections per $1,000 of personal income were $95.72—well below the national average of $105.50. In 1968 Tennessee's state tax investment per citizen in annual operating expenses of higher education was $18.56, ranking forty-third among the states; and the ratio of that sum to total personal income was 0.72 per cent, ranking thirty-fourth. Thus no great strain was being placed on the resources of the state by the operating cost of higher education. There was leeway for improved tax support.

A conspicuous vacuum in the state revenue system was the absence of any tax on individual incomes except on interest and dividends (often called "unearned" income as distinguished from salaries and wages). This latter income was taxed at the rate of 6 per cent, except dividends for corporations having 75 per cent of their property taxable in Tennessee, in which case the tax was 4 per cent. There was a flat-rate corporation income tax at 5 per cent.

Public higher education in Tennessee seems to be relatively free from burdensome and self-defeating external fiscal controls from state administrative agencies. The legislature has also customarily refrained from excessive interference. A 1968 report of a survey of 11 southern states on this particular point says: "In summary, practices followed by the Southern states in the administration of higher education funds are characterized more by their diversity than by common features. All states use some procedural devices which relate to higher education budgets. These are rudimentary in some states and in some others, where comparatively detailed systems exist, they are not applied to colleges and universities: Mississippi is an example of the former and Tennessee of the latter." [1]

Throughout the decade there was discussion of various forms of centralization of the higher educational structure in Tennessee. The University of Tennessee system governed by its own board of trustees, and the six other institutions governed by the State Board of Education, presented to some minds a picture of "two titans" that were thought to be too competitive—"wastefully competitive" in the words of some viewers whose reasoning was probably as much *a priori* as it was based on fact—and the constant complaint on this score that was characteristic in many other states droned on and on.

A joint resolution of the legislature of 1963 directed the Legislative Council to "study the need for either a single unit to direct a program of higher education in Tennessee, or in the alternative a commission on

---

[1] *Higher Education and Financial Control by State Governments in Southern Association States.* Atlanta: Southern Association of Colleges and Schools, March 1968. 20 pp. unpaginated. Edward J. Boling and J. Jefferson Bennett were joint chairmen of the committee making this report. Robert Cornett and Joe Johnson were staff members.

public higher education which might give appropriate representation
to the Board of Trustees of the University of Tennessee, the state
Board of Education, and lay citizens of our state as well."

The resulting report, a modest 23 pages, was largely limited to
lengthy and repetitive recitals of the proposed powers and duties of
four boards which it recommended: (1) a Board of Regents of Higher
Education, which would not be a governing board, but would have
extensive supervisory powers; (2) the board of trustees of the
University of Tennessee, which would continue with its customary
powers and duties, except as limited by the board named in number 1;
(3) a new Board of Trustess of State Colleges and Universities, to
which governance of the six other state institutions would be transferred from the State Board of Education; and (4) the State Board of
Education, which would retain the state-level functions related to
junior colleges and technical institutes.[2]

Devoid of supporting data, the report employed the tired phrases
of Depression days and earlier, and blandly assumed that "wasteful
duplication" was rampant; that "too many persons are being educated
for some pursuits and too few for others"; and that since the higher
education enterprise is growing larger and more complex it must
necessarily come under more tightly-centralized control.

None of these assumptions is supportable; and they all run counter
to the priceless principle that individual freedom of choice and institutional autonomy are indispensable ingredients in making higher
education the best of public investments. Today it hardly makes sense
to assert that we shall have "too many educated people" in any
category. The great expansion of higher education and the incredibly
rapid accretion of new knowledge takes practically all point out of the
idea of "duplication" except in the levels of highest specialization; and
at those levels the advanced graduate students and professors, who
are comparatively few in number, invariably keep themselves aware
of what their counterparts in other institutions are doing, so that the
matter of unnecessary or undesirable duplication almost
automatically takes care of itself. In any event, instruction and
research in the advanced specialties cannot be effectively controlled
by a board of laymen except upon the advice of the scholars engaged
in them; and by virtue of their purpose and nature they *should not* and
cannot be effectively controlled.

The increasing size and complexity of the whole enterprise of
public higher education does not mean that freedom for individuals
and for institutions must be surrendered; instead it affords opportunity for broader freedom of choice than ever before, if we can rid
ourselves of the notion that increased size must mean increased

---

[2]*Study of the Administration of Higher Education, 1964.* Nashville: Tennessee Legislative Council, 1964, 23 pp. litho.

TENNESSEE

Appropriations for Annual Operating Expenses of Higher Education in Tennessee, Alternate Fiscal Years, 1959-60 through 1969-70 (in thousands of dollars)

Institutions	Year 1959-60	Year 1961-62	Year 1963-64	Year 1965-66	Year 1967-68	Year 1969-70
U of Tennessee (incl all campuses)		9,700	12,587	17,219	25,832	37,270[1]
Ag Exten Serv		1,400	1,660	1,910	2,185	2,503
Ag Exper Station		900	1,064	1,314	1,639	1,842
Memorial Research Ctr (Knoxville)		100	100	275	275	450
Munic Tech Serv		53	60	72	139	164
Subtotal, U of Tenn		12,153	15,171	20,790	30,070	42,229
Memphis St U		1,700	3,404	6,177	10,550	14,062
East Tenn St U		1,683	2,395	3,811	6,062	7,099
Tenn A & I St U		2,186	2,475	2,939	4,633	4,198
Tenn Technol U		1,299	1,839	2,935	4,487	5,247
Middle Tenn St U		1,228	1,921	2,893	4,756	6,146
Austin Peay S C		773	1,119	1,561	2,289	2,759
Enrollment reserve		500				
Community Colleges						
Columbia					750	1,063
Cleveland					400	1,091
Jackson					400	1,091
Additional community colls (3)						1,075
Higher Edn Commission					75	287
Total	17,022[2]	21,522	28,324	41,106	64,472	86,595[3]

[1]Includes $3,325,000 for the University of Tennessee at Martin, and $3,052,000 for the University of Tennessee at Chattanooga (the former private University of Chattanooga). Also includes medical center at Memphis and extension center at Nashville.

[2]This total is for the entire state.

[3]Includes $1,075,000 for three additional community colleges, at Dyersburg, Motlow, and Walters; also $248,000 for Southern Regional Education Board.

centralization of control. This is a *non sequitur*, contrary to modern theories and practices of business and governmental administration, and especially inappropriate in education. The perfunctory report of 1964 betrayed the sources of its outmoded assumptions by actually lifting some phrases out of earlier surveys of higher education in Tennessee dated 1934, 1946, and 1957, assuming and implying that the economy of scarcity and the necessity of parsimony had not changed since the depths of the Depression.

It conceded that progress in state-wide liaison and teamwork had been accomplished in preceding years. Two paragraphs on this point have historical value:

"Some limited success in coordination was achieved in 1961 and 1962 through the medium of a coordinating committee by executive direction of Governor Buford Ellington. The committee consisted of three representatives of the board of trustees of the University of Tennessee and three representatives of the State Board of Education. Since the committee had no statutory sanction, its authority ceased with the expiration of Governor Ellington's term.

"Some voluntary coordination is, however, achieved through the work of an informal joint committee, composed of representatives of the Department of Education and the colleges and universities, including the University of Tennessee. Too, the Presidents' Council, another informal organization, has been responsible for some coordination between the six state colleges and universities now governed by the State Board of Education."

The plan proposed in 1964 failed of enactment, and it was not until the session of 1967 that a simpler and less drastic scheme was enacted, involving the creation of a Tennessee Higher Education Commission, effective July 1, 1967. This was a "soft approach" coordinating board, composed of nine members appointed by the governor for terms of nine years (overlapping). Three members must be residents of each of the three "grand divisions" of the state—East, Middle, West. At least three must be members of the principal minority political party. No member is to be an official or employee of the state, or a trustee, officer, or employee of any public institution of higher education in Tennessee while a member of the Commission.

The duties of the Commission seem to be largely *advisory* to the governor, the legislature, and the governing boards of the institutions involved. There is seemingly unequivocal language to the effect that the Commission shall "make determinations" regarding the establishment of new institutions or programs; but in practical effect such "determinations" can hardly be more than advisory to the legislature. There is the added duty, stated with admirable simplicity, of "conducting a program of public information concerning higher education in Tennessee." Some of the enumerated functions, as worded in the statute, could be interpreted as going somewhat beyond the purely advisory function; but this can be accurately determined only in practice, and perhaps with the aid of judicial decisions in appropriate cases. There is the usual chestnut about "developing a 'master plan' for the future development of public higher education in Tennessee." While such an ongoing plan might be useful and influential, it would have no legal force except as parts of it might be enacted by the General Assembly. Good sense dictates that such a plan should be forever flexible, and should not be frozen into the statutes.

Two others of the statutory duties of the Commission: "The Commission shall review and approve or disapprove proposals for new degrees or degree programs, or new departments or divisions. *It shall, however, have no role with respect to specific courses or course content*"[3]; and, "The Commission shall study and make determinations concerning the establishment of new institutions of higher learning." Can the words "review and approve or disapprove" and "study and make determinations" mean anything more than "make recommendations"? Almost certainly not. The practice seems to be that the legislature, not the Commission, authorizes the establishment of each new institution, though perhaps on the recommendation of the Commission (in a recent instance the legislature authorized establishment of three new community colleges, *against* the contrary recommendation of the Commission); and as to new degree programs, departments, or divisions, one can be sure that if the Commission attempted to veto such an innovation, the legislature would have power to reverse that determination if it thought such action to be in the best interest of the state. Compare the story of North Carolina, *supra* herein.

Another of the statutory duties is "to develop policies and formulae or guidelines for the fair and equitable distribution and use of public funds, *recognizing institutional differences in function, services, academic programs and levels of instruction.*"[4] One must remark that the distribution of public funds should be based on studied judgments rather than solely on mathematical formulas which need to be constantly revised and which are too often used as substitutes for thought. The word "equitable" which creeps into many statutes of this type is often used as a political expression having little direct relation to the educational needs of diverse regions or the financial needs of widely diverse institutions. But such a statute may serve well if it is

---

[3]The author's underscoring indicates his view of the importance of this limiting sentence. Some comparable provisions in other states, less precisely drawn, contain no such limitation at all. This has very significant bearings on the institutions' autonomy, morale, and ability to serve the needs of their students and of their constituent regions.

[4]Here again my underscoring indicates my admiration of the wording which is often absent from statutes of this kind in other states.

wisely administered by the Commission with the aid of a knowledgeable and competent staff and with the cooperation of the several governing boards and presidents.

A new step in the course of racial desegregation of higher education was taken early in 1968 when certain citizens of Tennessee asked a federal court to enjoin the expansion of the Nashville extension center of the University of Tennessee by erecting a new building in a better location, on the ground that desegregation would not be advanced by creating an institution primarily for white students in the city which is the seat of the Tennessee State University, which is a predominantly Negro institution. Federal District Judge Frank Gray refused the injunction, but commented that the enrollment at the Tennessee State University was 99 per cent Negro, and that "nothing is being done to dismantle the dual system"; he ordered the State Board of Education and the board of trustees of the University of Tennessee to submit by April 1, 1969, a plan for complete desegregation of the state's public colleges and universities.[5]

Such a plan, in great detail, was filed with the court March 28, 1969. Among many suggested actions was "Merger of Tennessee A & I State University and the University of Tennessee Nashville Center, 'to create a regional university of substantial impact in the city and the pivotal factor in meaningful desegregation in Tennessee.'" Meantime the United States Supreme Court had affirmed without argument the refusal of an injunction in the comparable Alabama case (see the story of Alabama, *supra* herein).

The Office of Civil Rights, in the U.S. Department of Health, Education and Welfare, apparently taking a leaf from Judge Gray, almost immediately began the practice of requesting comprehensive plans for desegration of higher education from some other states.

---

[5] *Sanders* v. *Ellington*, (U.S.D.C. Tenn.), 288 F. Supp. 937 (1968).

TEXAS

Once waggishly called "the richest province in the Empire of Manhattan," Texas is itself a vast empire in its own right, with a population of nearly 11 million people in 1968, and with territorial extent larger than that of most major European nations.

Historians say that between 1813 and 1835, while Texas was still a part of Mexico, 31 church-sponsored colleges and schools were founded by the Baptist denomination alone. From 1845 to 1860, during the period from the time when the sovereign Republic of Texas joined the United States to the beginning of the War Between the States, more than one hundred such institutions were opened by various denominations and individuals. Most of these have been defunct for many years. They exhibited a variety of standards, grade levels, and titles (such as institute, academy, seminary, college, or other). Their college instruction was generally inadequate and slight by modern standards. They were typical of a pioneer stage in which small private colleges sprouted thickly on the American frontier, while the idea of tax-supported public higher education in the states had not begun to grow.[1]

The creation of public colleges and universities was in the minds of the pioneers, but did not materialize until the 'Seventies and 'Eighties. In 1839 the Congress of the Republic of Texas appropriated 50 leagues of land for the purpose of university education, and passed another measure looking toward the founding of a public university. Again the state legislature attempted, in 1858, to found a university, but nothing came of it except the dedication of 1 million acres of public land for the purpose. The Constitution of 1876 contained a mandate:

"The Legislature shall, as soon as practicable, establish, organize, and provide for the maintenance, support, and direction of a university of the first class, to be located by a vote of the people of this State and styled 'The University of Texas' for the promotion of literature, and the arts and sciences, including an agricultural and mechanical department."[2]

---

[1] One of the histories is by C. E. Evans: *The Story of Texas Schools*. Austin: Steck Company, 1955. 309 pp.

[2] The subsequent history is briefly sketched in pages 3-8 of *Public Higher Education in Texas, 1961-1971*. Report of the Texas Commission on Higher Education, March 25, 1963. Austin: Governor's Office, 1963. 99 pp.

The same Constitution relocated the one million acres which had been set aside as endowment, substituting lands farther westward; and the legislature of 1883 added another 1 million acres. (Even to this day it is difficult to place a precisely estimated value on the endowment of the University of Texas, but unquestionably it is larger than that of any other state university in the nation.) A popular election of 1881 determined that the main University would be located at Austin, and its Medical Branch at Galveston. The University was actually opened in 1883, and the Medical Branch in 1891.

Meantime the legislature of 1866 had accepted the provisions of the federal Morrill Act, and in 1871 passed legislation to establish the required land-grant college, which was implemented in 1876, by the opening of the Agricultural and Mechanical College of Texas, near the town of Bryan. In 1878 the legislature established, after the fashion of the time in the 17 southern states, a separate land-grant college for Negroes. At first this was a false start and a failure, and was closed in 1879 for want of students; but the legislature resuscitated it by converting it to a teacher-education institution, renaming it the Prairie View Normal School, and placing it under the governance of the Board of Directors of the Agricultural and Mechanical College of Texas. In 1890 it again acquired the status of a land-grant college, and in 1901 was authorized to offer full four-year college courses.

In 1879 agents of the George Peabody Fund, offering generous foundation subsidies, had persuaded the legislature to found the Sam Houston State Normal Institute at Huntsville.

The four institutions named in the foregoing paragraphs were the only state institutions of higher education in Texas until near the turn of the century. They represent the roots of the three "systems" which developed during the first half of the twentieth century: (1) the University of Texas System; (2) the Texas A & M System; and (3) the Teachers College Group, later to be more properly styled State Colleges. By 1969 several of the third group had justifiably acquired the designation of "State University."

By 1925 there were 16 state-supported colleges and universities. The seventeenth, the Texas State College for Negroes at Houston (now Texas Southern University) was created in 1947. The number was to grow to 22. Available documentation makes it possible to sketch the picture of the governing boards at two points in time: as of approximately 1935 and 1960.

In 1935 the three "system" boards exercised governance as follows:

1. The Board of Regents of the University of Texas, three units—the Main University at Austin, the Medical Branch at Galveston, and the College of Mines and Metallurgy at El Paso (now the University of Texas at El Paso).

2. The Directors of the Agricultural and Mechanical College of

Texas, four units—the A & M College of Texas at College Station (Bryan); the Prairie View Normal and Industrial College for Negroes, near Hempstead; the John Tarleton Agricultural College at Stephenville; and the North Texas Agricultural College at Arlington. The latter two were state junior colleges, later to become four-year institutions.

3. The Regents of State Teachers Colleges governed seven state teachers colleges—Stephen F. Austin at Nacogdoches, Sam Houston at Huntsville, East Texas at Commerce, West Texas at Canyon, South West at San Marcos, Sul Ross at Alpine, and North Texas at Denton.

Three other institutions had their own separate governing boards: The College of Industrial Arts for Women, (now Texas Woman's University) at Denton, Texas Technological College (now Texas Technological University) at Lubbock, and Texas College of Arts and Industries at Kingsville.[3]

Prior to 1929 Texas had an archaic and rudimentary type of State Board of Education composed wholly of a handful of state officers *ex officio*. A constitutional amendment of 1928 did away with this, and a statute of 1929 created a new State Board of Education of nine laymen appointed by the governor and approved by the senate for overlapping terms of six years.

The act of 1929 required the new Board to consider the financial needs of all state institutions of higher education and to make recommendations biennially concerning them; to make formal recommendations concerning all proposals for the establishment of new institutions; and to make careful study of the scope and purpose of the work of each higher educational institution. It was expressly provided that nothing in the act should be construed to lessen the powers of the existing governing boards. Thus the State Board of Education was without authority to impose its conclusions upon any institution concerned. In relation to higher education it was thus merely an advisory board. The position of the Texas State Board of Education as defined in the act of 1929 and that of the Michigan State Board of Education as prescribed in the Michigan Constitution of 1963 seem to be markedly similar so far as their relations to public higher education are concerned. (See the story of Michigan, *supra* herein.)

The Texas State Board of Education as just described was abolished and superseded by an elective board of 21 members by a statute of 1949. In 1955 the legislature created the Texas Commission on Higher Education, a coordinating body (superseded by a new Coordinating Board in 1965). Meantime, observe the state-wide structure as of 1960, for comparison with that of 1935, as already sketched:

---

[3]A description and graph of the state-wide structure as of 1935 appears at pages 226-228 in *State Educational-Administrative Organization*, by M. M. Chambers. Washington: American Council on Education, 1936. 283 pp.

1. The Board of Regents of the University of Texas governed five units. Added to the original three were two medical centers, at Houston and Dallas.

2. The Board of Directors of the Agricultural and Mechanical College of Texas continued to govern four units, as before.

3. The Board of Regents of State Teachers Colleges governed six institutions, having lost North Texas State College (now North Texas State University), which was given its own separate governing board in 1949.

Institutions having their own separate governing boards numbered six in 1960. [4] The former group of three had been doubled by the incoming of North Texas, as just mentioned, plus Texas Southern University (1947), and Lamar State College of Technology (1951). The number of state institutions, counted thus, was 21.

Other additions came during the 'Sixties. Midwestern University at Wichita Falls came in 1961. The University of Houston (a former municipal institution) became state-supported in 1963. The South Texas Medical School at San Antonio was added to the University of Texas System. Pan American College at Edinburgh became a state institution. Arlington State College was transferred from the A & M College System to the University System; but the A & M soon gained the newly established James Connally Technical Institute (renamed Texas State Technical Institute in 1969), and the Texas Maritime Academy.

Texas was early in the local public junior college field. From 1920 to 1928. 18 junior colleges were put into operation by independent public school districts (one was discontinued almost immediately). These were created without explicit statutory authorization, but a legislative act of 1929 provided validation, and also authorized the establishment of junior colleges in county-wide districts, multicounty districts, or union school districts, with the junior colleges to be governed by their own district-elected Boards of Regents. [5]

State aid began in 1941 at $50 per student per year, was later increased to $100, and by 1948 amounted to $882,000 for 33 junior colleges. State aid rose to an average of $243 by 1963. The total for fiscal year 1964-65 was $8,284,000. For 1966-67 it was $13,931,000; for 1968-69, $26,508,000. In this category of state appropriations Texas has in general maintained about fourth or fifth place among the states, being exceeded only by California, Florida, and New York, in that order. Washington held fourth place until the late 'Sixties when it disappeared from the list because the state assumed the full operating cost

---

[4]S. V. Martorana and E. V. Hollis, *State Boards Responsible for Higher Education*. Washington, OE-53-005, Circular No. 619: 1960. 254 pp.

[5]Kathleen Bland Smith, "Crossroads in Texas." *Junior College Journal* 35: 14-16 (December, 1964).

of the junior colleges, with an appropriation of $65½ million for biennium 1967-69.

The report of Governor John Connally's Commission on Education Beyond the High School (to be noticed again herein in another connection) recommended in 1964 that the state of Texas increase its contribution to the operating income of local public junior colleges, at an estimated cost of $22 million annually for biennium 1965-67 and $28 million annually for biennium 1967-69. The actual appropriations for those four fiscal years appear to have been about $13 million, $14 million, $23½ million, and $26½ million.

Up to about 1950 Texas was clearly second only to California in developing a state-wide junior college network; but on account of a considerable reluctance on the part of both local subdivisions and the state to finance rapid expansion, the junior college enterprise in Texas was in a comparative slump, or on a relative plateau, for some 15 years between 1950 and 1965. The number of local public junior colleges generally remained constant at 32 or 33. Enrollments grew, and financial support increased, but not at a rate sufficient to match the great strides that were being made contemporaneously in California, Florida, and New York. Since 1965 the junior college scene in Texas has been somewhat brighter.

A 1961 report of the Texas Education Agency exhibited the fact that progress had already been made toward modern forms of organization and support for the network of local public two-year colleges.[6] There were 32 such colleges, of which two were operating outlying branches of their own. Of the 32, 13 were county junior college districts having their own boards of trustees or Regents. Sixteen were independent junior college districts, of which 11 had their own governing boards exclusively, and 5 had boards elected to serve both the college and the public school district in a dual capacity. The remaining three were directly under the jurisdiction of the boards of trustees of the public school districts of which they were a part. In three, the presidency of the college and the superintendency of the public schools was a dual role. The other 29 colleges had their own presidents. The identity of the junior college was emerging.

State Revenues and the Financing of Public Higher Education

For many years Texas held out against a general sales tax. As the pressure grew greater, successive legislatures tended to increase the number and rates of selective sales taxes. For example, in 1959, after long contention over revenue measures, bills were enacted to add about $175 million of new revenue for the ensuing biennium. These

---

[6]The Public Junior Colleges of Texas for the Academic Year 1960-61. Austin: Texas Education Agency, 1961. 54 pp. mimeo.

acts, in descending order of their importance as revenue-producers, were principally the following:

New taxes on tobacco products ($80 million); increased corporation franchise taxes ($32½ million); a series of special sales taxes on specified items ($31½ million); a new severance tax on natural gas ($15½ million); liquor and wine taxes ($6¼ million); and an increased tax on radio and television sets ($6 million).

Texas stood adamantly among only three other states having no general sales taxes *and* no state income taxes—Nebraska, New Jersey, and New Hampshire.7 It might well have been said that these four states had neither of the two types of state taxes that rank first and second as revenue-producers, and constitute the dual core of a modern state revenue system. In Texas the question might also have been asked, "Can a lengthening series of selective sales taxes ever be a suitable equivalent of a general sales tax?"

In 1961 the dam broke, and the legislature enacted a 2 per cent general retail sales tax, which Governor Price Daniel allowed to become law without his signature. It covered all sales amounting to 25 cents or more, with a few exemptions such as food for home consumption. Proceeds would be about $160 million a year. Other tax measures enacted at the same session were expected to boost the total of new revenue to $177 million a year.

Seven years later, in June 1968, the general sales tax rate was raised to 3 per cent, effective October 1, 1968. At that time 24 other states had the 3 per cent rate. Fourteen states had higher rates. Only five states had lower rates (2 per cent). Six small states had no general sales taxes. Texas was far from leading the procession; and the total absence of state income taxes in Texas was glaring.

Another revenue measure of 1968 increased the corporation franchise tax, due May 1 of each year, to $2.75 from the previous $2.25 per $1,000 of capitalization. A bill to legalize the sale of liquor in drink-size bottles, and thereby get $17½ million a year in new taxes, was lost. However, the new revenue measures of 1968 taken together, including the 1 cent rise in the general sales tax, were expected to provide $176 million a year in additional revenue. It was said that one effect of the session of 1968 was to make the legislators more tax-conscious and more knowledgeable in that field than before; and it was asserted that there was a general expectation among them that provision would have to be made for at least an additional $200 million a year in tax receipts in the regular session to begin in January, 1969.

With respect to its rate of gain in total appropriations for annual operating expenses of higher education over the nine-year period 1960-

---

7New Hampshire had and now has a personal income tax only, limited to unearned income (interest and dividends received) and not applicable to salaries and wages—therefore producing only negligible proceeds.

TEXAS

Appropriations for Annual Operating Expenses of Higher Education in Texas, Alternate Fiscal Years, 1959-70 through 1969-70 (in thousands of dollars)

Institutions	Year 1959-60	Year 1961-62	Year 1963-64	Year 1965-66	Year 1967-68	Year 1969-70
U of Texas (Austin)	11,673	13,207	16,129	24,349	33,065	41,687
Med Br (Galveston)	6,410	6,824	7,329	8,982	12,415	16,369
Anderson Hosp (Houston)		5,079	5,776	6,584	10,671	10,859
SW Med Sch (Dallas)		2,247	2,640	3,329	4,665	6,584
U of T (Arlington)[1]	1,878	2,563	3,601	5,721	7,149	9,463
U of T (El Paso)[2]	2,760	1,817	2,412	3,360	4,879	7,813
Med Sch (San Antonio)[3]			4,293	524	2,041	6,467
Dental Sch (Houston)		1,592	1,687	2,494	2,884	3,949
Sch of Nurs'g (system)					250	1,150
Sch of Pub Health (Houston)					250	849
Grad Sch of Bio-med Sci (Houston)		10	12	191	417	652
Other med schools	8,230					
Subtotal, U of Texas	30,951	33,339	43,879	55,534	78,686	118,141[4]
Texas A & M U	4,800	5,663	7,020	11,089	17,085	22,979
Ag Exper Sta	1,515	2,292	2,494	3,176	4,397	5,645
Ag Exten Serv		1,772	2,008	2,720	3,785	5,051
Prairie View A & M C	1,590	1,879	2,531	2,954	3,338	4,536
J Connally Tech Inst				200	1,793[5]	
Tarleton St College	677	790	887	1,257	1,522	2,267
Texas Forest Service		898	983	1,090	1,363	1,824
Engrng Exper Station		489	627	981	1,065	1,324
Texas Maritime Acad		141	109	273	324	438
Vet'nary Med Diag Lab						253
Rodent Control Serv		352	384	393	461	529
Engrng Exten Service		177	168	172	265	366
Other[6]	1,512					
Subtotal, Texas A & M	10,094	14,453	17,211	24,305	35,398	45,212

	(1)	(2)	(3)	(4)	(5)	(6)
Texas Technological U	4,325	5,593	7,000	10,078	15,383	20,833
U of Houston	3,333	4,222	7,620	10,373	14,547	19,670
No Texas St U	1,669	2,091	5,617	7,904	11,007	13,922
East Texas St U	1,832	2,589	2,501	4,429	6,717	8,861
Sam Houston St U	1,706	2,373	3,026	4,330	5,757	7,689
Lamar S C of Tech	1,235	1,398	3,131	4,275	5,782	7,273
Stephen F. Austin St U	1,297	1,614	1,925	3,011	5,100	7,084
SW Texas St College	1,543	1,823	2,152	3,283	4,882	7,067
Texas Woman's U	1,458	1,787	2,212	3,200	4,731	6,029
Texas Arts & Inds U	1,200	1,482	1,986	2,918	3,685	5,383
West Texas State U	1,602	2,201	1,867	2,475	4,024	5,232
Texas Southern U			2,621	3,462	3,270	3,945
Pan American College				2,390	2,250	3,442
Midwestern University		759	1,554	3,113	2,881	2,855
Sul Ross State U	675	811	1,004	1,296	2,200	2,480
Angelo State U				3,396	2,084	2,574
Texas State Technical Institute						3,826
Three System Offices	424	550	435	469	901	1,672
Coordinating Bd (state-wide)				1,300	706	755
Cotton Research Committee			225	269	256	329
Regional Education	921	241	113	90	87	94
Other agencies[7]			289	470	587	511
Governor's Committee[8]			175			
Subtotal, all state insts	64,838[11]	77,873[11]	106,672	152,370	210,539[9]	304,908[10]
State aid to Jr Colls			8,256	12,931	23,550	35,138
Total	64,838[11]	77,873[11]	114,928	165,301	234,109[9]	340,046

[1]Formerly Arlington State College.
[2]Formerly Texas Western College.
[3]Formerly South Texas Medical School.
[4]Includes $550,000 for UT Dental School at San Antonio; $250,000 for UT at Permian Basin; and $250,000 for UT at San Antonio. Also $10 million to initiate UT Medical School at Houston, and $1,250,000 for UT at Dallas.
[5]This institution was later removed from the Texas A & M System, given its own governing board, and renamed Texas State Technical Institute in 1969.
[6]Includes Rodent Control, Engineering Experiment Station, Engineering Extension, and Forest Service.
[7]Includes chiefly five institutional museums, Cotton Research Committee, and county taxes on university lands.
[8]Governor's Committee on Education Beyond High School.
[9]Subsequent rectification has changed these totals to $210,921 and $234,471 respectively.
[10]Includes $10 million to initiate the Texas Technological University Medical School at Lubbock, embracing some operating expenses and some capital outlays.
[11]Omission of sums appropriated for "State aid to junior colleges" makes these totals somewhat understated.

1969, Texas, with a gain of 265¼ per cent, is nearest of all states to the national average of 261 per cent. It is between the two states having most nearly the same population—Illinois, 233½ per cent; and Ohio, 302 per cent. But for fiscal year 1968-69, the Illinois total ($301,136) was 40 million above that of Texas ($259,425); and that of Ohio ($174,136) was 75 million below Texas. Michigan ($262,424), barely above Texas. and with a generally slow rate of gain (174½ per cent over nine years), seemed likely to be surpassed soon by Texas.

In mid-1968 the average investment of state tax funds per citizen in Texas for annual operating expenses of higher education was $24.07, ranking thirty-fourth among the states. The ratio of this sum to total personal income was 0.78½ per cent, ranking thirtieth.

In the 1966-67 fiscal year, the total of state and local tax revenues in Texas per $1,000 of personal income was $91.08, as compared with a nation-wide average of $105.50. On this measure Texas ranked forty-eighth, with only two states lower—Illinois ($85.29) and Ohio ($82.23). The three big states having nearly 11 million people each were conspicuously at the bottom of the list.

As to the relations between the state legislative and administrative practices and the management of public higher education, the recent study made of 11 southern states for the Southern Association of Colleges and Schools[8] finds Texas in some unique positions. The authors note, for example, that "The (11) states vary considerably in the degree of flexibility permitted in the use of appropriated funds. Most states appropriate in broad categories, yet one state (Texas) specifies considerable detail in the appropriation laws."

More explicitly: "Appropriations range from the situation in Georgia where there is one lump-sum appropriation for the entire higher educational system, to the Texas procedure under which appropriations are made for each major function in the institution and further limited by language in the appropriation act which specifies, sometimes in detail, for what purpose the appropriation may or may not be used." Texas and Florida, we are told, are the only states (among the 11) wherein the legislature fixes student fees at the state institutions of higher education. While this practice may run counter to the principle of maximum university autonomy, and the principle that generally the legislature should not concern itself with matters of institutional administration, nevertheless it must be noted that during the past decade student fees at the Texas institutions, at least, have been among the lowest to be found anywhere in the nation—a condition much to be desired and wholly admirable in the broad view of higher education.

---

[8] *Higher Education and Financial Control by State Governments in Southern Association States.* Atlanta: Southern Association of Colleges and Schools, March, 1938. 20 pp. unpaginated.

The Southern Association report also observed that in Texas (as well as in Alabama, Kentucky, and Mississippi, and substantively, though not procedurally, in Tennessee) "decisions concerning academic positions and salaries are made entirely by individual institutions with no outside involvement except for the constraints imposed by the funds available."

State-Level Structure 1955 to 1965 and Since 1965

Apparently the advisory coordinative functions given to the State Board of Education in 1929 were not very impressively performed; and this was perhaps even more true after it was superseded in 1949 by an elective board which, with its entire staff, constituted a newly-named Texas Education Agency—despite the fact that the 1949 board expressly succeeded to all the powers and duties of its predecessor. However that may be, a moderately soft-approach coordinating body known as the Texas Commission on Higher Education was created by statute in 1955.

It turned out that this board functioned for 10 years. It had a small staff, and accomplished with reasonable success the types of work defined for it in the statute, including a good deal of difficult pioneer effort involved in initiating and encouraging studies of unit costs of instruction on a more or less comparable basis for the large and complex state-wide system of public higher education.

One apparent source of growing dissatisfaction, especially during this Commission's later years, was the fact that the public junior colleges were not within its purview, and continued under the jurisdiction of the Texas Education Agency. Junior college students, teachers, and administrators wanted to be closely identified with higher education; and the feeling grew, in Texas as well as nationwide, that a comprehensive state-wide agency for higher education of whatever nature should bear the same relation to junior colleges as to other colleges and universities. A notion developed in other quarters, too, that the Commission did not have enough "teeth" or sufficient coercive powers to accomplish the desirable degree of coordination needed in a system as far-flung and diverse as that of Texas.

This latter view was not universally held, but in the administration of Governor John Connally it was pushed. The idea came to the fore that the Commission should be abolished and supplanted by a new coordinating board with more powers of coercion and with its jurisdiction extended to include the public junior colleges. This idea prevailed in 1965, despite the fact that many persons believed the same result might be better approached by enlarging the jurisdiction and expanding the powers of the 10-year-old Commission.

Late in 1964 Governor Connally's Committee on Education Beyond the High School released a handsomely printed and illustrated brochure of 64 pages, recommending the changes above suggested, and urging the establishment of a new Coordinating Board for Education Beyond the High School, which was in fact created. by the 1965 legislature and came to be styled the "Coordinating Board, Texas College and University System."

One of the financial features of the report, the projections of total biennial operating expenses for each of the three bienniums between 1963 and 1969, is now of especial interest because the projected sums can be compared with the sums actually appropriated for those fiscal periods.[9] The projected figures are slightly understated, because, unlike the "actual" figures, they exclude the Agricultural Experiment Stations and the Agricultural Extension Service. Also, while including the medical and paramedical schools, they exclude the teaching hospitals. Thus, they are somewhat further above the actual appropriations than the figures here literally indicate: For 1963-65, projected, $255 million (actual, $229 million); for 1965-67, projected, $420 million (actual, $330 million); and 1967-69, projected, $591 million (actual, $493½ million).

The point of the foregoing figures is that the Connally Committee, holding its predictions within a period of six years, succeeded in keeping them ahead of what the actual appropriations turned out to be, and hence need not suffer the humiliation that has beset many other makers of projections in other states who have very often undershot the mark so far as to appear almost ludicrous.

The statute of 1965, establishing the new Coordinating Board and defining its responsibilities, is probably the lengthiest and most detailed act of its kind in existence. The Board is composed of 18 members appointed by the governor with the advice and consent of the senate, representative of all areas of the state. No member shall be employed professionally for remuneration in the field of education during his term. Terms are for six years. The Board shall appoint a commissioner of higher education as its chief executive officer, and necessary staff employees.

It governs no institution or system—it is a coordinating agency; but its prescribed powers and duties are so numerous and explicit that it more than faintly resembles an administrative authority for the whole state-wide system as one institution. There seems to be no way of clarifying this generalization other than by quoting extensively from an already boiled-down digest of the statute.[10]

---

[9] *Education: Texas' Resource for Tomorrow.* Report of Governor's Committee on Education Beyond High School. Austin: Governor's Office, 1964. 54 pp.

[10] Robert L. Williams, *Legal Bases of Coordinating Boards of Higher Education in Thirty-Nine States.* Chicago: Council of State Governments, Midwestern Office, September, 1967.

First, some basic preliminary matters:

"The functions vested in the governing boards of institutions, not specifically delegated to the Board shall be performed by such governing boards. The coordinating function and other duties delegated to the Coordinating Board shall apply to all public institutions of higher education.

"The Board represents the highest authority in the state in matters of public higher education, and shall define junior and senior colleges, universities and university systems. Nothing, however, shall be construed to authorize the Board to establish or create any university system or to alter the present university system (existing) by virtue of the constitution of the state.

Among the duties of the Coordinating Board:

1. Classify, and prescribe the role and scope for each public institution.

2. Hear applications from the institutions for change in classification of role and scope.

3. Develop and publish criteria for determining the need for changing the classification, and the need for new institutions.

4. Review periodically all degree and certificate programs to assure that they meet the present and future needs of the state.

5. Order the initiation, consolidation, or elimination of degree or certificate programs. No new department, school, degree program, or certificate program shall be added except with specific prior approval of the Board.

6. Encourage and develop in cooperation with the State Board for Vocational Education new certificate programs, and recommend the elimination of certificate programs for which a need no longer exists.

7. Develop and promulgate a basic core of general academic courses for the junior colleges which shall be transferable among all public institutions in Texas which are members of recognized accrediting agencies.

8. Make continuing studies of the needs for research, extension, and public services, and designate the institutions to perform them, including limitation of credit programs to specific geographic areas.

9. Maintain an inventory of all research, extension, and public service activities by requiring yearly reports from each institution.

10. Develop and promote one or more degree or certificate programs to the highest attainable quality at each institution for which there is marked promise of excellence.

Each governing board shall submit to the Coordinating Board annually a comprehensive list—by department, division, and school— of all courses, course descriptions, prerequisites, etc., that will be required during the following academic year. The Board may order the deletion or consolidation of any such courses after giving due notice with reasons therefor, and after providing a hearing if one is requested by the governing board.

Elaborate detail regarding control of offerings and of the creation of new institutions:

"Any order of the Board affecting the classification, role and scope and program of any institution of higher education shall be entered only (1) after a written factual report and recommendations from the commissioner of higher education covering the matter has been received by the Board and distributed to the governing board and the administrative head of the affected institution, (2) after the question has been placed on the agenda for a regularly scheduled quarterly meeting, and (3) after the governing board of the affected institution has had an opportunity to be heard. Notice of the Board's action shall be given in writing to the governing board concerned not later than four months preceding the fall term in which the change is to take effect.

"No funds appropriated to any institution of higher education shall be expended for any program which has been disapproved by the Board, unless said program has been subsequently specifically approved by the legislature. No new department, school or degree or certificate program approved by the Board or its predecessor, the Texas Commission on Higher Education, shall be initiated by any institution until the Board shall make a written finding that it is adequately financed by legislative appropriation, by funds allocated by the Board, or by funds from other sources.

"Any proposed statute which would establish an additional institution of higher education, except a public junior college, shall be submitted, either prior to introduction or by the standing committee considering same, to the Board for its opinion as to the need of the state therefor, and the Board shall report its findings to the governor and the legislature, provided that a recommendation that an additional institution is needed shall require the favorable vote of at least two-thirds of the members of the Board. But a recommendation of the Board shall not be considered a condition to the introduction or passage of any proposed statute." (The legislature does not abdicate its lawmaking power!)

The statute plunges into another morass of administrative detail "to achieve excellence in the teaching of students." A saving grace is that the verb "order" does not appear in this segment, and the verbs "recommend," "encourage," and "explore" are the keys, leaving an implication that persuasive leadership is the touchstone, which is all to the good. But after all, the items are matters of administrative detail, and there is serious question as to whether a central state-wide governmental agency should concern itself with them:

1. Develop and recommend (a) minimum faculty compensation plans, basic increment programs and incentive salary increases; (b)

minimum standards for faculty appointment, advancement, promotion and retirement; and (c) general policies for faculty teaching loads, division of faculty time between teaching, research, administrative duties and special assignments; and faculty improvement programs, including a plan for sabbatical leaves, appropriate for the junior and senior colleges and universities, respectively.

2. Develop and recommend minimum standards for academic freedom, academic responsibility and tenure.

3. Pursue a goal of having all academic classes taught by persons with an earned master's degree or its equivalent.

4. Explore, promote and coordinate the use of educational television among institutions of higher education.

5. Conduct and encourage research into new methods, materials and techniques for improving the quality of instruction, and such other innovations as may offer promise for superior teaching or for meeting the need for new faculty members.

Embraced also is a detailed list of prescriptions "to assure the efficient use of construction funds and the orderly development of physical plants," here greatly condensed:

1. Determine formulas for space utilization.

2. Devise and promulgate methods to assure maximum daily and year-round use of educational and general buildings.

3. Consider plans for selective standards of admission.

4. Require, and assist in developing, long-range plans for campus development.

5. Endorse or delay until the next succeeding session of the legislature shall have opportunity to approve or disapprove, the proposed purchase of any real property by any state college or university.

The capacity for mischief inherent in number 5 is quite obvious. Not content with that, the statute goes on:

"(The Coordinating Board shall) approve or disapprove all new construction, and repair and rehabilitation of educational and general buildings and facilities financed from any source other than property tax receipts of the public junior colleges; provided, that the Board's consideration and determination shall be limited to the purpose for which such buildings shall be used, and their gross dimensions to assure conformity with approved space utilization standards and the institution's approved programs and role and scope."

These strictures, the statute recognizes, cannot apply to capital funds accruing to the older state universities by virtue of provisions in the state constitution; but they do apply to funds derived from fees and private gifts, and *ipso facto* they discourage private gifts for capital purposes. Obnoxious is the needless and humilating interference with the institutions' use of their own receipts from nontax sources.

On and on the statute goes into the processes of the current financing of institutional operations. The following is a much abbreviated version of its mandatory directives to the Coordinating Board:

1. Devise and periodically review formulas for use in making appropriation recommendations to the legislature; and require the institutions to use these formulas.

2. Recommend to the governor and the legislative budget board, supplementary appropriations to provide for increases in enrollment. (These may be made directly to the institutions, or to the Board, as the legislature may direct.)

3. Recommend to the governor and the legislative budget board, policies covering all agencies of higher education receiving state support concerning the fixing of tuition charges and student fees.

4. Distribute such funds as are appropriated to the Board for allocation for specified purposes. No allocation shall be made to any institution which has failed or refused to comply with any order of the Board.

5. Make continuing studies on its own initiative as well as upon the request of the governor or legislative budget board of the financial needs of public higher education, and all services and activities of the institutions, and issue such reports as may result from its studies.

The statute as a whole bears evidence of intent to invest the Coordinating Board with coercive administrative powers in many instances, so that if applied literally and unimaginatively, the authority of the institutional governing boards would be severely diminished, the autonomy of the institutions much impaired, and perhaps the morale of faculties and students permanently lowered, at great loss to the state. The words "order," "delay," "determine," "promulgate," "uniform," "require," and "formula," suggest a wooden administrative bureaucracy which could be a heavy incubus tending to suffocate initiative, originality and creativity among governing boards, presidents, faculties, and students.

In its permissive and stimulative aspects, the statute concerns itself too much in detail with notions widely popular in the early 'Sixties, some of which had already lost some of their glamor by 1969. This again illustrates the error of writing into the laws of the state in detail contemporary fads as long-range policies. Moreover, in the field of public higher education doubt must persist as to whether the improvement of institutional practices in personnel administration, business management, and the handling of curriculum and instruction at the different levels and of different types, which up to this point have developed locally with the stimulation of voluntary associations—national, regional, and state-wide—should now become a statutory function of the states.

It sounds good to direct an administrative bureaucracy to exercise leadership and initiative, to conduct and encourage research, and to provide a service of public information. It is another thing to get these admirable functions accomplished. How guarantee that the leadership will be wise and exercised with appropriate restraint, the initiatives unfailing and creative, the research not trivial or misdirected, and the public information candid and not designed mainly to promote the perpetuation of the agency from which it comes?

The answer is in the quality of the individuals who man the agency. May Texas always be fortunate in that respect! And may other states beware of freezing into their statutes lengthy prescriptions for the administration of state-wide higher education as a single institution. The Texas Coordinating Board, under the statute of 1965, has far too many atomized mandates to concern itself with matters of detailed institutional administration.

In December, 1968, the Coordinating Board recommended definite schedules for the early establishment of four new "Upper Division and Master's Level" senior colleges, to be located respectively at San Antonio, Midland-Odessa, Corpus Christi, and Dallas. Each of these institutions would have its own governing board. For Houston, a second campus and a third campus of the University of Houston were recommended. Total enrollments in all Texas higher education, recorded as 400,000 in 1969, were conservatively projected to 708,000 in 1980. The Board also issued in 1968 and early 1969 studies of medical education, dental education, and financial forecasts.[11]

---

[11]Among the reports: *Public Senior College Development in Texas to 1980.* (Policy paper 4), 1968. 24 pp.

A Proposal for the Development of Medical Education in Texas, 1969-1980. (Policy paper 5), 1968. 76 pp.

Dental Education in Texas. (Policy paper 6), 1968. 51 pp.

Financial Considerations for Planning for Higher Education in the Next Decade. (Policy paper 8), 1969. 21 pp.

Austin: Coordinating Board, Texas College and University System.

UTAH

The University of Deseret was chartered by the provisional government of the state of Deseret, and offered its first instruction in 1850. This was the institution that is now the University of Utah, operating under a new charter of 1892 which gave it its present name.

The Agricultural College of Utah (now Utah State University), the land-grant university, was chartered in 1888, opened for instruction in 1890, and conferred its first baccalaureate degree in 1894.

Within the present century some seven outlying state colleges, junior colleges, and technical colleges, of which the largest by a wide margin is Weber State College at Ogden, were established. All are small, and during the decade 1960-1969 they underwent frequent and somewhat bewildering changes of name, control, and two-year and four-year status. For example, Weber State was started as a state academy (secondary school) in 1899, gave its first college-level instruction in 1916, became a junior college in 1933, and a four-year college in 1963. Some recent changes in the names and governing bodies of the smaller institutions are observable in the Utah tabulation herein.

It may be surprising to many that in this sparsely-populated state of the mountain region, where private colleges are generally few and small, or wholly non-existent, in 1968-69 the largest institution of higher education in Utah was the private Brigham Young University at Provo. It is an institution of the Church of Jesus Christ of Latter-day Saints, founded in 1875 as an academy. Its first baccalaureate degree was conferred in 1893 and its present name adopted in 1903. Its enrollment of 32,893 students in 1968-69 was larger than those of the University of Utah (18,488) and Utah State University (9,265) combined.

Surveys of higher education in Utah were made in 1926 under the auspices of the United States Office of Education, and in 1939 by a team assigned by the American Council on Education. Both recommended a single state board of higher education, but both were happily ignored. In 1948 the Utah Legislative Council reported that it appeared that the legislature did not have the power to establish a single state board for the general control of higher education, because of language in the Constitution of 1894 and earlier Territorial statutes which created each of the two major institutions as independent corporations, guaranteed their locations, and perpetuated their "rights, immunities, franchises, and endowments" as existing in 1894.

For half a century, however, the two institutions had made the serious mistake of supinely submitting to infringements of their autonomy by various acts of the legislature and by rulings of several state administrative and fiscal agencies, until at length in 1956 the University of Utah instituted a suit for a declaratory judgment to define its status. Judge Martin M. Larson of the district court of Utah at Salt Lake City held that the University was a constitutional corporation free from control by the legislature, administrative bodies, commissions, agencies, and officers of the state.

On appeal to the supreme court of Utah, the judgment was reversed and remanded, in an opinion declaring that the Constitution did no more than fix the location of the University and the Agricultural College, and perpetuate their corporate existence and general purposes, none of which the legislature can change.[1] Justice Worthen wrote the prolix, repetitious, ill-organized opinion, in which not one of his four colleagues on the bench could concur unreservedly, though all agreed as to the result. Chief Justice McDonough and Justice Henriod concurred in the result without filing opinions, while Justice Crockett concurred specially in an addendum in which Justice Wade joined him.

The decision could have been exactly contrary if it had followed the historic Michigan, Minnesota, California, and Idaho cases which, from similar wording in the respective state constitutions, declared the state universities to be constitutionally independent. It was adversely criticized by scholars at the University of Michigan Law School, who intimated that the Utah court was provincial in its disregard of those precedents or its failure to comprehend their reasoning.[2] (See stories of Michigan, Minnesota, Idaho, and California, *supra* herein; also Arizona, Nevada, and Oklahoma.) A general rule of interpretation is that long-continued legislative or administrative practice contrary to a constitutional or statutory principle has no effect in a court test. This was directly and pointedly illustrated and applied by the Minnesota supreme court in a 1936 case, wherein it was held that the Regents of the University, having been for many decades appointed by the governor, must thereafter be chosen by the legislature, as stipulated in the Constitution.[3]

The Utah legislature of 1957 set up "a coordinating board of higher education" and provided for a survey of education beyond the high school to make a report and recommendations to the next regular

---

[1] *University of Utah* v. *Board of Examiners of State of Utah,* 4 Utah 2d 408, 295 P. 2d 348 (1956).

[2] See William P. Wooden's note in *Michigan Law Review,* Vol. 55, March, 1957, pp. 728-730.

[3] *State ex rel. Peterson* v. *Quinlivan,* (Minn.), 268 N.W. 858 (1936).

UTAH

Appropriations for Annual Operating Expenses of Higher Education in Utah, Alternate Fiscal Years, 1959-60 through 1969-70 (in thousands of dollars)

Institutions	Year 1959-60	Year 1961-62	Year 1963-64	Year 1965-66	Year 1967-68	Year 1969-70
U of Utah						
Medical School	6,267	6,308	7,396	9,488	13,208	15,211
Teaching Hosp		801	1,113	1,500	1,939	2,000
Rsch support[1]			500	750	312	250
Educ TV—KUED					680	1,000
Geol & Mineral Serv		158		182	201[2]	210
Ctr for Econ Devlpmt		25		67	100	100
Continuing education					80	180
Supplemental to U of U:						
Coal research				50		152
Patent develpmt proj				100		
Subtotal, U of Utah	6,267	7,294	9,009	12,062	16,521	18,293
Utah State U	4,102	3,701	4,251	5,230	6,211	7,585
Ag Exper Sta		692	829	905	1,017	1,050
Ag Exten Serv		509	605	665	715	800
Rsch support					230	250
Ecology Ctr					100	110
Water Rsch Lab				75	77	90
Educ TV—KUSU				27	31	50
Subtotal, Utah St U	4,102	7,294	5,685	6,903	8,337	10,115

State colleges:						
Weber St Coll	1,060	1,354	1,771	2,572	3,860	4,875
Coll of Southern U	437	510	657	888	1,227	1,491
Utah Tech Coll (Salt Lake)[3]		409	485	603	928	1,365
Utah Tech Coll (Provo)[3]		356	427	527	709	825
Dixie College	177	205	243	370	538	615
Snow College	237	277	317	398	502	672
Coll of Eastern Utah[4]	232	275	305	390	434	488
Subtotal, St Colls	2,143	3,383	4,206	5,750	8,200	10,331
Central agency						
Enrollmt adjusts						50
Acctg & computer serv						50
Police science						50
State-wide TV & components					228	100
Student loans				75	150	125
Comm on Interstate Coop				38	40	56
Coordinating Council				62	171	
Subtotal, Ctrl agcy						631
Total	12,514[5]	15,580	18,901[6]	24,891	33,695	40,000

[1]Includes $50,000 for coal research.
[2]Includes $65,000 for "county translator stations."
[3]Name changed from "Trade-Tech Inst."
[4]Name changed from "Carbon College" by 1965 legislature.
[5]Subsequent rectification has increased the total slightly.
[6]Additional sums aggregating $505,000, not included herein, were appropriated for the Geological Survey, the Water Board, and for educational broadcasting. These bring the biennial grand total to $38,307,300. This total is halved for entry in the 50-state summary table.

session. The two-year life of this board seems to have been entirely preoccupied with the survey; and the board was superseded in 1959 by the creation of a new Utah Coordinating Council of Higher Education— a research and advisory agency of the "soft approach" species—, as recommended by it.[4]

In one of its own reports of 1963, after it had had time to "shake down," this body said: "The Council conceives its role as advisory rather than administrative. Through its research and informational functions, it provides a unifying force in helping institutions analyze their common problems and work cooperatively toward resolving them." The Council consisted of six members appointed by the governor and senate for six-year terms, plus one representative of the State Board of Education and one representative of each of the institutional governing boards, the initial total membership being nine. The office of executive director was provided for, and a substantial and informative publication, the result of cooperative work on the part of many faculty members and administrators of the several institutions serving on technical and consulting committees, was produced in 1963.[5]

This Council, after a 10-year life of usefulness, was supplanted by an act of 1969 which also replaced all institutional governing boards (except the State Board of Education) with a 15-member State Board of Higher Education having all the powers of a governing board over all the institutions except the two technical schools. Nine members were appointed by the governor and Senate, three by the president of the Senate, and three by the speaker of the House of Representatives. Not more than eight may be of one political party.

This reversion to a scheme of completely consolidated and centralized governance took place under a conservative and business-oriented state administration, and was undoubtedly in part a result of the somewhat reactionary tendency, nation-wide and locally, of the state and national elections of 1968.

Governor Calvin L. Rampton, irked because he was not authorized to appoint all 15 members of the new Board of Higher Education, promptly challenged the constitutionality of that part of the act which empowered the president of the Senate and the speaker of the House to appoint three members each, on the far-fetched ground that this would be an intrusion by the legislative branch into the domain of the executive branch. He argued that since the Constitution provides that the governor shall appoint the members of the State Board of Education, it necessarily implies that he must appoint all members of

---

[4] *A Proposed Coordinating Council of Higher Education for Utah.* Salt Lake City: Coordinating Board of Higher Education, 1958. 64 pp.

[5] *Coordination of Utah Higher Education.* Salt Lake City: Utah Coordinating Council of Higher Education, 1963. 80 pp.

the Board of Higher Education. A state district court of Utah denied this contention in July 1969, pointing out that the legislature's power is residual, not delegated; that is, it has power to enact any measure not prohibited by the Constitution.

On the matter of the inclusion of members of the legislature as members of state-wide boards of higher education, compare the 1969 reconstitution of the state board of higher education in North Carolina, *supra*.

For years Utah has ranked near the top among all the states as to the percentage of its population of college age actually attending college. It also ranks high in investment of state tax funds per citizen in annual operating expenses of higher education ($32.75 in 1968, in eleventh place), and in the ratio of this sum to average total personal income (1.15¼ per cent in 1968, in fifth place). In rate of gain in appropriations for annual operating expenses of higher education over the nine years 1960-1969 it is relatively low (156½ per cent), but that is due in large part to the circumstance that its "effort" was high at the beginning of the period.

A legislative act of 1969 established a planning committee on higher education as an organ of the Legislative Council. The committee is composed of four members of the Senate and four members of the House of Representatives.

VERMONT

The ponderous statutory name of University of Vermont and State Agricultural College belongs to a corporation which joins the University of Vermont, chartered in 1791, and the Vermont Agricultural College, chartered in 1864. A legislative act of 1865 created the new corporation and transferred the property of both institutions to it, but did not terminate the existence of either of the prior corporations. On the contrary, it expressly continued the existence of both. Thus there are three legal entities, each capable of receiving and administering charitable trusts.

Bearing indicia of the union of the two institutions, the board of trustees of 21 members (in addition to the governor of the state and the president of the university *ex officio*) consists of one panel of nine who are "self-perpetuating" or coöptive for six-year terms (compare the boards of trustees of the universities of Alabama and Delaware), another panel of nine who are elected by the legislature (compare the Regents of the University of Minnesota), and a third panel of three appointed by the governor and senate. All have six-year terms.

There are three small state colleges having normal school antecedents at Castleton, Johnson, and Lyndon, and a state technical college at Randolph. Prior to 1961 the three first-named were governed by the State Board of Education, and the technical school had a separate board. The 1959 legislature set up an Advisory Council "to recommend a coordinated state program which will improve the services rendered by the educational institutions in meeting the teaching needs of the state." Reporting in 1961, this Council recommended that the three colleges (then teachers colleges) be removed from the jurisdiction of the State Board of Education and placed under a new separate board of trustees.[1] The 1961 legislature accordingly established the Vermont State Colleges Corporation and provided that not only the three teachers colleges, but also the technical college, be under the governance of its board of trustees.

This was in accord with a trend observable in several other states during the decade 1960-1970—relieving the State Board of Education of the governance of the state colleges. Here it occurred in one of the

---

[1] *Report of the Advisory Council on Procedures to Improve Teacher Education*. Montpelier: Governor's Office, 1961.

smallest state systems only a year after it had taken place in the largest, at the opposite side of the continent, when the California state colleges were similarly transferred by the Donahoe Act of 1960. It is apparently no longer credible that a lay State Board of Education can properly discharge its duties with respect to a state-wide system of elementary and secondary schools, and at the same time govern several institutions of higher education. Whether this latter function can be performed by a single board of trustees for several institutions is also questionable. It is probably better to do as Michigan did in the Constitution of 1963: give each of the institutions its own governing board when removing it from the jurisdiction of the State Board of Education. [2]

The board of trustees of the Vermont State Colleges Corporation has nine members appointed by the governor and senate for six-year terms, plus the governor and the Corporation's executive officer as nonvoting members. Notable is a lengthy section of the statute which exempts the Corporation from general statutes dealing with administrative departments of the state: classification of state personnel; the state employees' retirement system; the state teachers' retirement system; the pre-auditing of public disbursements; central purchasing of small orders; and the ministrations of the Board of State Buildings. The intent of the statute was obviously to give the Corporation a degree of fiscal independence in the exercise of its educational function.

The corporation's provost, in an article published in October, 1968, after explaining that the State Board of Education had been able to devote only very little time to the colleges, wrote: "Otherwise, they were governed by the state civil service. All purchases were made through the Purchasing Office, from chalk to coal. All out-of-state travel, including that of the basketball team, had to be approved by the governor. The professors were hired on the state merit system."[3] He added: "In 1962 the colleges were formally taken out from the Department of Education and placed under a new Board, with very broad powers, largely freed from state control." He meant only useless and self-defeating petty administrative and fiscal harassments fr. state administrative offices.

Vermont, with a population of 422,000 in mid-1968, had only three-fifths as many people as its geographic twin-sister, New Hampshire; but Vermont's annual appropriation for operating expenses of higher

---

[2] The change to separate institutional governing boards was also made in New Jersey (1967) and Alabama (1967). See also Virginia's creation of separate governing boards for three institutions in 1966.

[3] Robert S. Babcock, "The Creation of Three Swarthmores." *The American Oxonian* 55: 230-237 (October, 1968).

VERMONT

Appropriations for Annual Operating Expenses of Higher Education in Vermont, Alternate Fiscal Years, 1959-60 through 1969-70 (in thousands of dollars)

Institutions	Year 1959-60	Year 1961-62	Year 1963-64	Year 1965-66	Year 1967-68	Year 1969-70
U of Vermont and State Ag Coll		2,964	3,879	4,633	6,498	8,334
Educ'l TV					410	447
Subtotal, U of Vt		2,964	3,879	4,633	6,908	8,781
State colleges:						
Castleton		219[1]	355	1,492	800	918
Johnson		172[1]	228		550	762
Lyndon		140[1]	182		550	690
Vt Tech Coll (Randolph)		150	177		650	882
Unallocated			41			
Vt St Coll Bd					115	198
Subtotal, St Colls		681	983	1,492	2,665	3,450
Vt Stu Asstnce Corp Scholarships				215	576	1,135
New Eng HE Compact				15	90	90
					25	37
Private institutions:[2]						
Middlebury College		24	24			
Norwich University		90	100	40	40[3]	40
Total	3,331[4]	3,759	4,986	6,395	10,304	13,532

[1] Allocations to the three state teachers colleges are estimates, but substantially correct.

[2] Private colleges receiving state aid for operating expenses.

[3] Toward support of the Bureau of Industrial Research.

[4] This total is a state-wide appropriation.

education ($10,940,000), exceeded New Hampshire's $10,221,000. The figures would be almost exactly equal if the Vermont Technical College were removed from the picture, to balance the fact that New Hampshire does not report appropriations for technical schools as "higher education."

Vermont's state tax investment per citizen for annual operating expenses of higher education in 1968 was $25.92, ranking twenty-eighth; the ratio of this sum to total personal income was 0.86½ per cent, ranking twenty-fifth. Both rankings are near the national median. The corresponding figures for New Hampshire were $14.64 and 0.45 per cent, in both instances ranking forty-eighth among the states.

The difference could have been largely explained, no doubt, by the disparities in the tax systems of the two states. Specifically, Vermont's personal income tax was at the rate of 25 per cent of the federal income tax obligation. This made it simple to administer, economical to collect, automatically graduated, and an excellent producer of revenue. Vermont also had a corporate income tax at the rate of 5 per cent. Vermont's major missing link was a general sales tax, of which it had none, being one of only six small states without such a source of revenue. Effective June 1, 1969, the legislature enacted a 3 per cent general sales tax, increased the personal and corporate income taxes, and raised the rates of several selective sales taxes.

VIRGINIA

Public higher education in the Old Dominion has many distinctive features. The College of William and Mary at Williamsburg, dating from 1693, and now a state university, is one of the nine Colonial colleges which have survived and prospered to the present day. The University of Virginia at Charlottesville, established in 1819 at the urging of Thomas Jefferson, is not the oldest of state universities, but it marked the beginning of what were then new concepts of the potentialities of state institutions of higher education.

The Medical College of Virginia began as a department of the private Hampden-Sydney College in 1838, became a free-standing state institution in 1860, and in 1968 was merged with the Richmond Professional Institute to form Virginia Commonwealth University at Richmond. (The Richmond Professional Institute had begun in 1917 and become a branch of the College of William and Mary in 1925, but this connection was severed in 1962.)

Virginia Military Institute at Lexington was established in 1829. Virginia Polytechnic Institute at Blacksburg, the Morrill Act land-grant university, began in 1872. Radford College at Radford had normal school and teachers college antecedents (1910-1944), but became the Women's Division of Virginia Polytechnic Institute from 1944 to 1964, since when it has been a free-standing state college. Mary Washington College at Fredericksburg had similar origins (1908-1944), became the women's college of the University of Virginia in 1944, and continues in that affiliation. There are two other state colleges having the normal school-teachers college tradition, the oldest being Longwood College at Farmville (1884), having acquired its present name in 1949. The other is Madison College at Harrisonburg, founded in 1908 and given its present name in 1938. Both are largely populated by women students.

Virginia State College at Petersburg is an institution predominantly attended by Negroes. Founded in 1882, it granted its first baccalaureate degree in 1886 and acquired its present name in 1946. It maintains a large Division offering a variety of undergraduate courses in the city of Norfolk.

Old Dominion College at Norfolk, so named in 1962, was the former Norfolk Division of the College of William and Mary, begun in 1930 and severed from the parent institution in 1962.

From the foregoing brief but bewildering sketch of changes, it will be gathered that Virginia has some six principal state institutions of higher education, all at least three-quarters of a century old, and five of which are not located in or near large urban centers. Thus it is not surprising that the College of William and Mary planted and nurtured a branch in Richmond (1925) and a branch in Norfolk (1930) by way of "putting the college where the people are," and that Virginia State College placed a branch in Norfolk. The severance of William and Mary's urban branches brought about the inception of two important institutions of recent origin: Old Dominion College in Norfolk and Virginia Commonwealth University in the capital city of Richmond.

At least up to 1970 the College of William and Mary retained two outlying small two-year branches (in Newport News and Petersburg). The University of Virginia had as a branch George Mason College—a four-year institution at Fairfax in northern Virginia, accessible to the concentrated population in the Virginia suburbs of the city of Washington—and three other outlying small two-year branches.

Virginia Polytechnic Institute once had two-year branches at Clifton Forge, Danville, Roanoke, and Wytheville; but in 1966 and 1967 these were converted to "community colleges" which are in fact two-year state colleges under a State Board for Community Colleges. The Danville branch, combined with the Danville Technical Institute, became the Danville Community College, effective July 1, 1968. During the academic year 1968-69, the state had a total of 11 such community colleges operating. Two others, named vocational-technical schools, were also placed in that classification. The state-wide policy was to achieve eventually a state-wide network of two-year comprehensive community colleges, by "phasing in," where practicable, the university two-year branches and the vocational-technical schools, as well as by creating new two-year colleges.

In 1969 the number of state institutions offering programs of four years or more of study was 13. Three of these were branches of parent institutions. Each of the 10 "main-campus" or "one-campus" institutions has its own governing board. Virginia uses in all instances the archaic and somewhat inappropriate name of "Board of Visitors" for each of these boards. There is also a good deal of uniformity in the statutory provisions for their composition. They vary from 11 to 15 members appointed by the governor, usually for terms of four years, with the chief state school officer added as a member *ex officio*.

Into the foregoing picture in 1956 came the State Council of Higher Education for Virginia, created by a legislative act of that year. It is a "soft-approach" coordinating body, "to promote the development and operation of a sound, vigorous, progressive, and coordinated system of higher education in the State of Virginia."

The Council is composed of nine members appointed by the governor subject to confirmation by the general assembly for terms of four years, plus the superintendent of public instruction *ex officio*. No officer, employee, or member of the governing board of any institution of higher education, or of the State Board of Education, and no member of the general assembly or employee of the Commonwealth is eligible.

In general, the language of the statute is admirably urbane and considerate of the identity of each institution of higher education. It provides that the Council shall, insofar as practicable, operate in a manner tending to preserve the individuality, traditions, and sense of responsibility of the respective institutions. It expressly negates any authority of the Council over endowment funds now held or in the future received by any of the institutions.

The gist of the statute is perhaps best expressed in the provision that the Council shall study those questions requiring state-wide policies in higher education, and make recommendations with respect to such questions to the institutions of higher education, the governor, and to the general assembly. This is to be done only after seeking the views and advice of the governing boards and officers of each institution in arriving at the recommendations.

Regarding the addition or elimination of instructional programs, the Council has power, *with the approval of the governor in each instance*, to limit any institutions to such offerings as conform to the plans adopted by the Council, provided that any changes in the current general programs of the institutions shall not be made effective until sufficient time has been allowed to make the necessary adjustments in personnel and facilities. Actually the Council has been liberal in approving new programs, as needed and proposed.

As to the establishment of any additional branch or division, the institution is directed first to refer the matter to the Council for its information, consideration, and recommendation; and the crucial requirement is that the location and type of each such new branch or division *must be specifically approved by the general assembly*. (Compare with the North Carolina statute as amended in 1959, which withdrew certain powers from the State Board of Higher Education.)

As to the preparation of biennial budget askings for appropriations of state tax funds, the governing board of each institution transmits its operating and capital outlay budget requests to the Council at the same time it transmits them to the state budget office. The Council then studies them and after incorporating its own recommendations, forwards them collectively (and separately identified, both in their original form and with recommended changes, if any) to the state budget office as required by law. Nothing, however, says the statute, shall prevent any institution from appearing through its representatives, to present its case to the governor or his advisory committee on the budget, or the general assembly, or any committee thereof at any time.

In its early years the Council seems to have been a bit slow in developing its research and public information functions; and perhaps some of its emphasis was misplaced in more or less futile attempts to achieve instant uniformity among institutional practices in accounting and financial reporting, where no more than a fluid approximation of comparability is possible in a diverse system of higher education.

Since 1965 the Council has been prolific in producing informative statistical reports, factual summaries, and advisory statements, in varied series. Its *Biennial Report*[1] for 1960-62 predicted that total enrollments in Virginia's public institutions of higher education would jump from 26,378 in 1960 to 48,500 in 1970. In common with many other projections in scores of other states, this one had been shown by 1968 to have fallen far short of the mark. Opening fall enrollments for the academic year 1968-69 in the state's four-year public universities and colleges were reported as 52,757 *full-time* and 13,599 part-time, making a head-count total of 66,356. At the same time there were 12,674 *full-time* and 6,883 part-time in the state-controlled public two-year institutions. The total head-count for all public institutions was 85,913, of which 65,431 were full-time students.[2]

The biennial report, bearing date of November, 1961, recommended that local two-year community colleges be developed, in accord with Virginia custom, as branches under the wing of a major parent institution rather than as two-year colleges largely supported and controlled by the local taxing subdivisions; and this policy seems to have been followed until 1966, when it was abandoned by the enactment of the Community College Act of that year. This act was the result of a state-wide survey of higher education by a Higher Education Study Commission set up by the legislature of 1964.[3] This Commission employed the experienced and indefatigable John Dale Russell of Bloomington, Indiana, as its staff director, and a voluminous report in 12 mimeographed volumes was prepared by December, 1965. A central 206-page volume summarized the whole.[4]

First priority was given to the development of a state-wide system of two-year colleges.[5] Contrary to prior recommendations of the State

[1]*Biennial Report of the State Council of Higher Education*. Richmond: Governor's Office. Part I, September, 1961, 38 pp. Part II, November, 1961, 25 pp. (The projection of enrollments is at p. 9 of Part I; the recommendation of university branches, pp. 3-10 of Part II.)

[2]*Institutions of Higher Education in Virginia, 1968-69*. Richmond: Virginia State Council of Higher Education, 1968. An annual 4-page report of enrollments.

[3]Senate Joint Resolution No. 30, 1964 session of the General Assembly of Virginia.

[4]John Dale Russell, Staff Director, *Report of the Higher Education Study Commission*. Richmond: State Council of Higher Education, December, 1965. 206 pp. mimeo.

[5]*Ibid.*, Staff Report No. 4, by Aaron J. Brumbaugh, *The Two-Year College in Virginia*. 110 pp. mimeo.

VIRGINIA

Appropriations for Annual Operating Expenses of Higher Education in Virginia, Alternate Fiscal Years, 1959-60 through 1969-70 (in thousands of dollars)

Institutions	Year 1959-60	Year 1961-62	Year 1963-64	Year 1965-66	Year 1967-68	Year 1969-70
U of Virginia	4,322	5,118	5,735	6,427	9,764	13,956
Hosp Div			2,271	2,506	3,424	3,627
M Washington Coll	397	435	586	740	889	1,428
Sch of Genl Studies			400	455	670	819
George Mason Coll			129	143	464	1,045
Clinch Valley Coll			129	148	206	435
Eastern Shore Br					146	165
Patrick Henry Coll				48	109	110
Lynchburg Branch					71	
Scholarships			30			
Subtotal, U of Va	4,719	5,553	9,280	10,468	15,743	21,585
Va Polytech Inst	2,946	3,347	3,812	4,063	7,222	11,594
Ag Exper Sta[1]	1,449	1,719	2,071	2,139	2,440	4,855
Ag Exten Div	2,064	2,453	2,817	2,967	3,854	3,526
Research Div[1]						
Engr Exp Sta	57	70	72	98	267	138
Danville Br[2]			18	36	94	99
Regional Edn				82[3]	82	
Roanoke Tech I	7	31	49	72	115	
Clifton Forge Com Coll			20	29	108	
Radford College[4]	464	515	732	780	1,262	2,170
Wytheville Com Coll			30	35	83	650
Subtotal, VPI	6,987	8,135	9,621	10,301	15,527	23,032

Medical Coll of Va[5]	1,385		2,662	3,278	4,816	7,175
Hosp Div		2,036	3,597	3,953	5,627	6,242
Subtotal, M Coll of Va	1,385	2,036	6,259	7,231	10,444	13,417
Coll of Wm & Mary	1,203	1,498	1,819	2,214	3,631	5,617
Norfolk Div	523	634	974			
Petersburg Div		90	71	87	229	413
Chris Newport Coll		62	60	84	129	321
Richard Bland Coll				168	575	325
Va Asso Rsch Ctr[6]						
Subtotal, Coll of Wm & Mary	1,726	2,284	1,950	2,553	4,564	6,676
Va State College	1,920	2,206	2,155	2,216	2,999	3,544
Norfolk Div	561	719	902	1,171	2,027	2,860
Reg Edn & Schshps			267	273	262	80
Subtotal, Va St Coll	2,481	2,925	3,324	3,659	5,289	6,484
Old Dominion Coll	431	497	687	1,205	2,603	4,320
Richmond Prof Inst[5]	783	899	1,107	976	2,189	4,120
Va Military Inst	728	849	1,098	1,161	1,673	1,803
Madison College	630	724	814	860	1,696	2,559
Longwood College					1,266	1,780

(Continued)

VIRGINIA (Continued)

Institutions	Year 1959-60	Year 1961-62	Year 1963-64	Year 1965-66	Year 1967-68	Year 1969-70
State Board for						
Community Colls					7,323	1,728
Develop Insts						983
Existing						
Northern Va					1,220	4,374
Va Western						1,803
John Tyler						1,171
Thomas Nelson						1,058
Central Va						965
Blue Ridge						862
Southwest Va						609
D S Lancaster						475
Subtotal, St Bd for Com Colls					8,543	14,678
Governor's Office						
Impr faculty sals				1,000		3,000
Upgr coll libs						1,500
Plan st u (Richmond)						175
So Reg Edn Bd			33	33		33
Subtotal, Gov's off			33	1,033	7,323	4,708
St Council of H E						
Eminent scholars	80	51	61	95	156	255
Library coord				25		220
Undergrad schshps				50	125	125
Impr grad schshps					200	575
Grad schshps			250		500	
Matching, HE Acts					545	300
Instructional TV						300
						50
Subtotal, St C of H E	80	51	311	170	1,526	1,825

Tchr ed & schshps				2,947	2,478
Nursing schshps					45
Tchr in-serv trng					800
Law-enforce schshps					50
St Ed Asstnce Auth				183	196
Empl fringe benefits[7]				126	7,650
Other small approps					13
Total	19,943[8]	23,958[8]	35,458[8]	40,830	74,335	117,578

[1] The Agricultural Experiment Station and the Engineering Experiment Station at Virginia Polytechnic Institute were merged July 1, 1966, to form the Research Division.

[2] Effective July 1, 1968, the Danville Branch of Virginia Polytechnic Institute and the Danville Technical Institute combined to form Danville Community College.

[3] Includes forestry and scholarships.

[4] Formerly a branch of Virginia Polytechnic Institute. Became a free-standing college in 1964.

[5] Effective July 1, 1968, the Medical College of Virginia and the Richmond Professional Institute were combined to form Virginia Commonwealth University.

[6] Effective September 1, 1967, the Virginia Associated Research Center was placed under the administration of the College of William and Mary.

[7] The figures for "Empl fringe benefits" include employer costs of social security, retirement, and group life insurance. They are approximations, because exact calculations cannot be made until the end of the fiscal year.

[8] Subsequent inclusion of appropriations for the Hospital Division of the Medical College of Virginia, and other items, has increased these totals somewhat.

NOTE: Effective July 1, 1968, Frederick College, a private four-year college at Portsmouth, was donated to the state and became Frederick Community College. The donation included a cash gift of $1 million to operate the institution for the next two years.

Council of Higher Education, which had discouraged the founding of any additional four-year institutions, second priority was given to the development of a four-year state college or university in northern Virginia, in the populous Virginia suburbs of the national capital city. At the time, George Mason College, a two-year branch of the University of Virginia, was the only public facility in that area. A four-year state college was inevitable, and George Mason College almost immediately became that.

The strong emphasis on community two-year colleges led to the creation of a State Board for Community Colleges by the legislature of 1966. This Board was vested with broad powers over the establishment, location, financing, and operation of existing and future two-year colleges. The local governmental subdivisions were expected to supply the initiative in requesting the establishment of such a college, and to furnish land and utilities for the site. The state would finance all buildings and equipment, and pay all operating expenses except those derived from student fees, which were to be kept low. The State Board for Community Colleges would appoint a nine-member advisory board for each community college, but would itself actually be the power-clothed governing board for the whole system.[6] The Board consists of 15 members appointed by the governor for four-year terms. The Board and its director and staff are known as the Department of Community Colleges. Apparently not subordinate to the State Board of Education, but directed to be cooperative with state educational agencies, this setup is probably more nearly independent than any other junior college board in any state. It is nominally subject to the coordinative ministrations of the State Council of Higher Education.

At hand was an excellent basic document in the form of *Staff Study No. 1* of the Higher Education Study Commission, entitled *Prospective College-Age Population in Virginia, by Subregions, 1960-1985*.[7]

Turning now to the relations between higher educational institutions and state administrative and fiscal agencies in Virginia, observe that, as to academic personnel, "the central personnel agency (of the state) and the governor, following a review of institutional proposals, approve a general salary plan for each institution, and the institutions are free to establish individual salaries within that plan"; and "academic positions not in the budget require individual approval by the central personnel and budget agencies and such approval is usually granted."[8]

---

[6] *Policies, Procedures, and Regulations Governing the Establishment and Operation of the Program of Comprehensive Community Colleges in the Commonwealth of Virginia as Authorized by the 1966 General Assembly*. Richmond: State Board for Community Colleges, September 28, 1966. 12 pp.

[7] By Lorin A. Thompson of the University of Virginia. 25 pp. mimeo.

[8] These quotations, and those immediately following, are from *Higher Education and Financial Control by State Governments in Southern Association*

With regard to central state control of budgeted expenditures, we are told that "in Virginia, several of the larger schools have substantial sums which are managed totally outside the basic state budget system. These funds can be, and apparently are, used in such a manner that the basic control system is a neutral factor." This is a crucial, even if marginal, feature of the autonomy of a state university or college—control of the use of its income from non-state-tax sources, without interference from statehouse fiscal functionaries.

Again, "Virginia specifies in legislation the buildings which an institution may build," but "the legislature usually reflects priorities recommended by the institutions." Thus an insupportably detailed external control may generally be relatively harmless; but why maintain it?

Governor Albertis S. Harrison, Jr., expressed a noble sentiment in his inaugural address of 1962: "I would like to see a renaissance of education in Virginia, creating an atmosphere in which the minds of our people may grow in vision as the opportunities for the use of the mind can grow in scope." He set up a 15-member Commission to study the state's revenue system and to report by September 1, 1963. The Commission recommended no major changes, though it recognized the probable necessity of a general sales tax in the near future. The governor did not recommend a sales tax. No tax legislation of much consequence was passed by the 1964 legislature. The governor's recommendations for the support of higher education provided for only modest gains, for which the *Washington Post* smartly slapped him on the wrist: "The Governor of Virginia has chosen this moment to decelerate sharply the growth of his own state's system of higher education. Unfortunately higher education requires higher taxes, and the Governor cannot bring himself to recommend a sales tax."[9]

However, the governor set up another Commission to study the proper distribution of the proceeds of a sales tax, if and when enacted; and a 3 per cent sales tax was indeed enacted in 1966. The 1964 legislature accomplished one commendable task: it removed Longwood College, Madison College, and Virginia State College from the State Board of Education and gave each a separate governing board. It also created a separate governing board for Radford College, up to that time a branch campus for women of the Virginia Polytechnic Institute.

Within the period of three years between fiscal year 1965-66 and fiscal year 1968-69 Virginia's appropriations of state tax funds for annual operating expenses of higher education were nearly tripled ($41

States. Atlanta: Southern Association of Colleges and Schools, March, 1968. 20 pp. unpaginated.

[9]*Washington Post* editorial, January 15, 1964.

million to $107½ million); but in 1968 the average appropriation per citizen was only $24.37, ranking thirty-third among the 50 states. The ratio of this sum to average personal income in the state was 0.78 per cent, ranking thirty-first among the states.

The legislature of 1968 broke its long-standing custom of adhering to "pay-as-you-go" for capital outlays, and approved a proposal for a bond issue of $67,230,000 for higher education buildings; and the issue was approved by the electorate at the subsequent election.

WASHINGTON

Seattle and environs, metropolis of the Pacific Northwest, embraced a million and a quarter people in 1968. Of Washington's 3,276,000 population, nearly 70 per cent were classified as urban. Growth since 1960 was nearly 15 per cent, well above the national average of 11½ per cent.

The state has always been outstanding in support of public higher education. The University of Washington is, by many different criteria, among the top 12 state universities in the nation. Washington State University at Pullman, in the opposite southeastern region of the state, is respected among the land-grant universities. Three state colleges of the normal school-teachers college traditions are large and lively institutions of their type, known since 1961 as at least dual-purpose institutions for liberal arts and teacher education.

A fourth (new) state college, located at the capital city of Olympia, was authorized by the 1967 legislature, with an appropriation of $500,000 for planning and site selection. It is named Evergreen State College.

Washington was early in the establishment of local public junior colleges. By 1959 it had 10 of them, each based on a local public school district, and was planning two more. By 1967 it had 22. Around 1960 the state was paying approximately two-thirds of the operating costs of local public elementary and secondary school districts (the state's share being much above the national average); and a knowledgeable correspondent wrote that it was his estimate that the state was supplying approximately 80 per cent of the operating income of the junior colleges. This was perhaps prophetic of the change which occurred in 1967, when the legislature made provision for putting the junior colleges on a basis of full state support except for their income derived from low student fees.

The act of 1967 marked off 21 junior college districts, covering the entire area of the state. These are not taxing districts, but attendance and electoral districts, each to have its own board of trustees, but all to be within the purview of a new State Board for Community Colleges. The transition from partial local support and full local control by local school districts to the newly-defined status apparently involved a little time for adjustment of various details, but appears to have been accomplished without undue delay. Full state support and partial state control, with divorcement from local public school districts, is now the rule; but if some variations as to the details of control persist, these deviations may be educationally desirable.

The legislature of 1959 set up an Interim Committee composed of five members of each house, to study the organization, operation, and financing of education at all levels, and report prior to the 1961 session. An appropriation of $75,000 was made for the purpose. James F. Nickerson, dean of Montana State College at Bozeman, was employed as study director. The Committee created five citizens' subcommittees of about 15 members each, and assigned to each subcommittee a major facet of the study. Subcommittee No. 1 studied "Education Beyond the High School."

That part of the report contained 24 recommendations (some of them multiple). Two of these were notable because of their refreshing difference from what study committees in some other states were recommending at the time or had recently recommended. The Washington group advised: (1) "That the present state system for governing post-high-school educational agencies be continued, and that cooperative (voluntary) statewide coordination among such agencies should be continued and encouraged." (2) Expansions of scholarship opportunities should take place within the framework of such existing programs as the National Merit Scholarship Foundation; and a state-financed scholarship, loan, or gift fund is not the most desirable solution to the financial problem.

In short, the recommendation was against any statutory centralization of governance, and against any state scholarship or loan system. The latter, as in many states, was pleaded for by the private colleges, as an indirect way of channeling tax money into their coffers. The Subcommittee's recommendation to the private colleges was Spartan: They "should actively pursue their planned expansions in order that they may continue to bear their full share of the anticipated increase in enrollment." (Chimerical wish!) In general the private colleges have indeed grown, but their percentage of Washington's total college enrollments in 1959 (25 per cent) has declined steadily.

Also notable were the recommendations that the University of Washington should provide enlarged programs of undergraduate instruction in the evening; that the state should support such programs and not expect them to be self-supporting from student fees; and that all the state institutions should increasingly develop their summer sessions as regular full-fledged segments of their year-round programs, with additional state support.[1]

---

[1] Pages 15-34 in *Citizens' Committee Reports and Recommendations, Interim Study of Education in Washington*. Seattle: University of Washington, 1960. 113 pp.

The recommendations were also summarized in *Education in Washington*, a 13-page pamphlet from the same source.

In 1961 the Washington State Census Board issued a 20-page mimeographed document, *Enrollment Forecasts, State of Washington, 1961 to 1970.* It predicted that the University of Washington would grow from 18,143 students in 1960 to 30,000 in 1970, with the numbers of graduate students increasing more rapidly than the over-all enrollment figures. Total enrollments in the five major state institutions of higher education would go to 54,000 by 1970. As in the case of nearly all such projections, these were overfulfilled before 1970. The U.S. Office of Education reported in 1968 that fall enrollment in the University of Washington was 30,357. In Washington's five major state institutions it was 61,092. Increases in the two-year colleges were even more phenomenal.

Washington's principal source of revenue at the state level was the general sales tax. In 1959 the legislature raised the rate to 4 cents on the dollar from the former 3 – 1 / 3 cents, and also made small increases in the rates of business and occupation taxes and the levies on liquors, cigarettes, and other tobacco products. In that year there was a reported effort on foot to propose a constitutional amendment making state income taxes lawful. It seems that Washington, like Illinois and some other states, has a clause or clauses in the revenue article of the state constitution upon which conservative lawyers can base a "doubt" as to whether a state income tax is permissible without a constitutional amendment. In such a situation, the question of a state income tax sometimes remains on dead center for years or even decades, in a mood of negativism based on nothing more than speculations that the supreme court might declare an income tax act unconstitutional, or that the electorate might defeat a proposed constitutional amendment authorizing an income tax. At any rate, the absence of state income taxes, either personal or corporate, was a glaring defect in Washington's revenue system throughout the decade.

By 1968 the general sales tax rate had been raised to 4½ per cent. One other state (Maine) had the same rate. California, Kentucky, Mississippi, and Rhode Island had 5 per cent general sales taxes, and Pennsylvania's rate was 6 per cent.

At length the Washington legislature of 1969 enacted a flat-rate personal and corporation income tax at the rate of 3½ per cent, but subject to approval of the electorate at the popular election of 1970.

Despite the vacuum in the area of state income taxes, however, Washington's total of state and local tax collections per $1,000 of personal income was $112.12 for fiscal year 1966-67—somewhat above the national average. In 1968 Washington's state tax investment per citizen in the annual operating expenses of higher education was $42.76—highest among the 50 states except for Alaska's $42.80. The ratio of this sum to average personal income was 1.16 per cent—third highest in the nation, being exceeded only by Montana's 1.23 per cent and North Dakota's 1.21 per cent. These records put to shame

WASHINGTON

Appropriations for Annual Operating Expenses of Higher Education in Washington, Alternate Fiscal Years, 1959-60 through 1969-70 (in thousands of dollars)

Institutions	Year 1959-60	Year 1961-62	Year 1963-64	Year 1965-66	Year 1967-68	Year 1969-70
U of Washington (incl Med units)	22,719	27,954	31,754	42,923[1]	54,366	71,787
Environmental Rsch Lab			250	250[2]		
Infant autopsies (U Hosp)			10			
Subtotal, U of Wash	22,719	27,954	32,014	43,173	54,366	71,787
Washington St U (incl Ag Exp & Ag Exten)	13,386	15,966	18,577	22,071	27,796	35,288
Subtotal, Wash St U	13,386	15,966	18,577	22,071	27,796	35,288
State colleges:						
Western Washington State Coll	2,152	3,075	4,152	5,625	8,328	11,836
Central Washington State Coll	1,906	2,403	3,010	4,879	7,555	10,695
Eastern Washington State Coll	1,844	2,358	2,889	3,959	6,016	9,097
Evergreen State College[3]					250	1,271
Subtotal, St Colls	5,902	7,836	10,051	14,463	22,150	32,899
Community colleges	5,167	6,803	10,300	14,721	32,739	50,748[4]
Total	47,175	58,560	70,943	94,929	137,051	190,903

[1] Includes $85,594,690 from General Fund and $252,000 from Motor Vehicle Excise Fund (for biennium).

[2] Includes $250,000 from Accident Fund and $250,000 from Medical Aid Fund (for biennium).

[3] A fourth state college authorized by the 1967 legislature.

[4] The state-wide system of two-year local public colleges was removed from the control of the lower school system and is headed by a State Board for Community Colleges. The appropriation includes $300,000 (biennial figure) for expenses of the Board.

California's 0.83½ per cent, Illinois' 0.69 per cent, and Ohio's 0.48 per cent. Washington is a national leader in state support of higher education. This long-standing leadership can continue with appropriate improvement of the state's revenue system.

It can be said with complete confidence that no other state of comparable population has a system of education beyond the high school equal to that of the state of Washington in scope and excellence. The number, size, and eminence of Washington's universities, state colleges, and community colleges are unequaled in any state in similar circumstances. In fact, as recently as 1965 Washington's state system of public higher education was unquestionably superior in capacity and quality to that of New Jersey, a state with more than twice the population of Washington. There were several other states, smaller in population than New Jersey, but larger than Washington, whose statewide systems of public higher education could not equal that of Washington. Washington provides generous support and produces superior results.

Washington has always eschewed consolidation or other forms of overcentralization of the state-level structure for the governance of state universities and colleges. Each institution has its own governing board. Voluntary coordination—informal, nonstatutory and noncoercive—has prevailed. The mood was encapsulated in the famous aphorism attributed to the redoubtable President C. Clement French of the State University of Washington at Pullman, who, discussing the possible entanglement of the university in statehouse controls, either from state fiscal agencies or by consolidation of governing boards, was reported to have said, "You may gain another state department, but you will certainly lose a great university."

The legislature of 1969 set up a statutory central planning and research agency for higher education, named the Council on Higher Education. The Council is composed of 26 members. Nine "citizen members" appointed by the governor and confirmed by the Senate are the only voting members. There are 17 nonvoting members: two Representatives, two Senators, two members of the governor's staff; the presidents of each of the six public universities and colleges, two presidents of private colleges or universities, the executive director of the State Board for Community College Education, and one community college president appointed by the governor. The appropriation of $180,000 a year for the Council on Higher Education included $59,000 to be used for carrying on the functions of the Higher Educational Facilities Commission (preparing recommendations for federal grants and loans for building construction to private and public colleges and universities, and public junior colleges).

This latter, in loose language, is local administration of the Act of Congress known as the Higher Education Facilities Act of 1963 as subsequently amended, and affords one example of how unwitting federal pressures almost compel a state to set up one or more state-wide quasi-administrative agencies for higher education. In strict language, the state agency does not *administer* the Higher Educational Facilities Act, but only makes studies and recommendations and forwards them to Washington; but nothing can prevent interested citizens of the state from regarding it as an agency having a hand in the exercise of administrative authority. This abets an erroneous and unhealthy notion that state systems of higher education are and should be administered from the State Capitol.

So long as an agency such as the Washington Council on Higher Education abjures any mandatory powers and concerns itself with interinstitutional *liaison*, intercommunication, and cooperation in the public interest, and busies itself with pertinent research, recommendations, and the dissemination of public information about the role of higher education in the future of the state, it can fill a useful place. If it accumulates powers of coercion, it becomes a menace to optimum productivity in higher education.

The second section of the act creating the Council is a well-reasoned preamble: "The higher educational institutions, under the autonomous governance of their governing boards, and operating within guidelines set by statute for particular institutions, . . . have responded to the many kinds of educational needs of the people. . . . The state has been well served by the delegation to the institutions of a large measure of autonomy which has enabled them to cooperate in achieving educational and operating effectiveness. Opportunity for such institutional initiative and institutional voluntary cooperation should be preserved and encouraged to the largest possible extent. . . .

"To assure maximum effectiveness of the agency (the Council), its deliberations should be participated in by representatives of the governor, the legislature, and the institutions of higher education."[2]

---

[2]Chapter 277, *Laws of 1969, State of Washington*, First Extraordinary Session.

WEST VIRGINIA

How 55 mountain counties of the Old Dominion became the state of West Virginia in 1863 is a familiar story. Thus West Virginia is not a state of the Old South, nor is it of the North, for it is south of the Ohio River, and almost all of it is south of the symbolic Mason-Dixon Line. It is a border state.

In the geography of regional accrediting associations for educational institutions, West Virginia is the easternmost of 19 states covered by the North Central Association of Colleges and Secondary Schools, which run as far west and south as Arizona.

The governance of public higher education in West Virginia has a bumpy history. All the state institutions of higher education were placed under a State Board of Regents in 1909. This arrangement continued until 1919, when the Board of Regents was abolished and all the institutions were placed under the State Board of Education. Later West Virginia University alone was removed from the jurisdiction of the State Board of Education and given a separate Board of Governors.

Early in the century the fiscal functions of both the State Board of Education and the Board of Governors of West Virginia University were vested in the State Board of Control, a three-member salaried board of appointees of the governor and senate, set up to keep a tight fiscal rein on the state university and college governing boards, and to govern directly the eleemosynary, penal and correctional institutions supported by the state. This substantially reduced the powers of the governing boards of the institutions of higher education.

An act of 1935 removed the control of the Potomac State School at Keyser (a two-year college) from the State Board of Education and vested it in the Board of Governors, at the same time changing the name of the school to Potomac State School of West Virginia University.

The nine state colleges continued under the State Board of Education until 1969, when the legislature set up a new state-wide Board of Regents and transferred the state colleges to its jurisdiction, at the same time abolishing the Board of Governors and transferring West Virginia University to the same Board of Regents, thus achieving—superficially at least—the same degree of centralization that had existed from 1909 to 1927, half a century earlier.

The push for this kind of consolidated administration had been going on for several years, and several successive legislatures had defeated it. The general mood of reaction that permeated state and national elections in 1968 resulted in the change.

Effective July 1, 1969, the new Board of Regents, composed of nine members appointed by the governor with senate confirmation, plus the state superintendent of free schools, became the sole governing board of all public higher educational institutions. Each institution is permitted to have a small advisory board, wholly without powers of governance.[1] Somehow the overcentralized plan won over a much more appropriate scheme which would have retained the Board of Governors, given Marshall University a governing board of its own, and created a third board to govern the other state colleges, and placed a council of higher education at the apex of the state-wide system.[2]

As sometimes has happened in states whose people have a high level of understanding and appreciation of the service of public higher education to the future of the state, the 1969 legislature actually appropriated some $5 million more than the conservative incoming governor, Arch A. Moore, Jr., recommended for operating expenses of higher education for fiscal year 1969-70. This included raising the appropriations for scholarships and for the student loan fund from $25,000 each to $175,000 each, and adding $50,000 to continue the "awareness project" (previously financed by a federal grant), designed to emphasize to high school students the importance of attending college.[3]

Further evidence of West Virginia's relatively strong support of higher education appears in the fact that in 1968 the state ranked twenty-third as to the state tax investment per citizen in annual operating expenses of higher education ($26.93), and that the ratio of this sum to the average personal income in the state was 1.09½ per cent, ranking tenth among the 50 states. But despite this, the total of state and local tax collections per $1,000 of personal income in 1967 was

---

[1]The story is in *State Legislation Affecting Higher Education in the South*—Report Number One: West Virginia. Atlanta: Southern Regional Education Board, March 11, 1969. 5 pp. mimeo, under by-line of Don Marsh of the *Charleston Gazette.*

[2]This resembled the plan proposed by the West Virginia Committee on Higher Education authorized by joint resolutions of the House and Senate in 1965 and 1966, which issued a two-volume report in 1966: Volume I, *Summary of Major Conclusions and Recommendations*, 57 pp.; and Volume II, *Higher Education in West Virginia—A Self-Assessment.* 189 pp.

[3]This latter item calls to mind that an incorporated West Virginia Association of Colleges and Universities maintains a headquarters in Charleston and, among other publications, issues an informative brochure on *Attending a College or University in West Virginia* including data on each of the 21 private and public institutions, and information regarding scholarships and other student aids available.

only $102.11—more than 3 per cent below the national average. Support of higher education could hardly be said to be straining the economy, even if West Virginia had many of the ills of Appalachia: mountainous terrain, the near-collapse of the employment capability of the coal-mining industry on account of mechanization, and a slightly declining total population. West Virginia's people were reduced in numbers from 1,860,000 in 1960 to an estimated 1,805,000 as of July 1, 1968—a loss of 3 per cent.

Not only has the state been harassed for decades by recurring unanswered questions as to the appropriate state-level structure for public higher education. For a long period covering the 'Fifties the institutions were also repeatedly harried by an overaggressive and recalcitrant state auditor who again and again refused to issue warrants for various legitimate university and college expenses until ordered to do so by the state supreme court of appeals: medical expenses for a student injured in an athletic contest,[4] retirement benefits for superannuated professors,[5] institutional membership fees in the voluntary regional accrediting association,[6] sabbatical pay which was authorized by statute,[7] and institutional use of the expendable income of an endowment fund derived from a private gift, in the custody of the state treasury.[8]

The foregoing is only one example of many tales that have been told of ineptitude, maladroitness, and plain lack of integrity in West Virginia's state government and administration over the years. One syndicated columnist once acridly remarked that of all the 50 state governments, West Virginia's is the sorriest. That may be an exaggeration. Even if it may be pervasively permeated by partisan, personal, and pipsqueak politics, the spirit of humane progress is by no means smothered.

When Governor Hulett Smith addressed a joint session of the legislature January 12, 1967, he said: "To open new horizons of educational opportunity to all our young people, regardless of their economic station in life, I believe we must remove the burden of tuition and fees in the first two years of college training. I recommend that this program go into effect next fall for freshmen and sophomores who are qualified residents of this state enrolled in our colleges and universities."

---

[4]State ex rel. Board of Governors v. Sims, (W. Va.), 59 S.E. 2d 705 (1950).

[5]State ex rel. Board of Governors v. Sims, 136 W. Va. 789, 68 S.E. 2d 489 (1952).

[6]State ex rel. State Board of Education v. Sims, 140 W. Va. 64, 82 S.E. 2d 321 (1954).

[7]State ex rel. State Board of Education v. Sims, 139 W. Va. 802, 81 S.E. 2d 665 (1954).

[8]State ex rel. State Board of Education v. Sims, 143 W. Va. 269, 101 S.E. 2d 190 (1957).

WEST VIRGINIA

Appropriations for Annual Operating Expenses of Higher Education in West Virginia, Alternate Fiscal Years, 1959-60 through 1969-70 (in thousands of dollars)

Institutions	Year 1959-60	Year 1961-62	Year 1963-64	Year 1965-66	Year 1967-68	Year 1969-70
West Va U	7,109	9,888	11,363	14,167	19,691	23,464
Med Ctr[1]				4,000[1]	4,500[1]	5,000
Potomac St Coll	387	503	548	624	821	976
Kanawha Valley Grad Ctr					350	573
Parkersburg Branch					56	341
Subtotal, West Va U	7,496	10,391	11,911	18,791	25,418	30,354
Marshall U	2,095	2,601	2,967	3,791	6,067	7,506
Branch Colls					63	83
Subtotal, M U	2,095	2,601	2,967	3,791	6,130	7,589
West Va St Coll	1,081	1,324	1,466	1,768	2,570	3,068
Fairmont St Coll	694	872	1,030	1,257	2,282	2,938
West Liberty St Coll	492	658	828	1,239	2,130[2]	2,889
West Va Inst of Tech	656	855	975	1,250	2,120	2,728
Concord College	872	949	1,155	1,385	1,978	2,212
Glenville St Coll	468	614	690	832	1,324	1,680
Shepherd Coll	528	594	679	839	1,281	1,574
Bluefield St Coll	409	540	584	653	1,015	1,415
Total (gross)	14,791[3]	19,938[3]	22,286	31,805	46,248	57,005[4]

Less instit'l receipts at St Colls (est)[5]	-1,800	-2,000
Net Total	44,448	55,005

[1]The proceeds of a tax of 1¢ per bottle on soft drinks go to the Medical Center of West Virginia University, and need no current appropriation.

[2]This figure includes branch colleges.

[3]The figures for 1959 and 1961 totals above appear as somewhat larger in later revisions.

[4]Includes $558,000 for Board of Regents established in 1969.

[5]At all the institutions, "registration fees" and "tuition fees" are charged to students. At West Virginia University and Marshall University, all these fees are held in institutional funds and used only for capital outlays. At all the other state colleges, "registration fees" are treated in the same manner, but "tuition fees" are turned into the general fund of the state. It is necessary to subtract these fees in order to arrive at the net appropriation of state tax funds.

His recommendation was not implemented, partly because it seemed to be counter to the established practice of financing academic buildings by issuing institutional "revenue bonds" backed by contemplated collections of student fees. Such bonds, to be salable, have to bear a higher rate of interest than general obligation bonds of the state, or than bonds issued by a "State Building Authority" in states where such a public corporation has been created and authorized to borrow in its own name beyond the constitutional limitation of state indebtedness. In an effort to minimize this handicap, in 1956 the Board of Governors obtained a writ of mandamus directing the Secretary of State to affix his seal to each bond in an issue of $10 million of its "revenue bonds," though each bond recited on its face that it was not an obligation of the state within the meaning of any constitutional limitation of state borrowing. The presence of the seal could only give the bond some color of being backed by the power and prestige of the state. [9] At that time the statutes limited to 5 per cent the maximum rate of interest such bonds could be allowed to bear. In 1969, on account of stringency in the money market, the legislature removed that ceiling. All this works to the disadvantage of the students who pay fees which go into a fund to amortize the cost of buildings financed by bonds bearing increasingly high rates of interest. The ultimate answer may eventually be a refunding of such outstanding bonds by a new issue of state bonds or state building authority bonds.

West Virginia has long had a 3 per cent "consumers' general sales tax" and also a producers' "gross sales tax" which is said to justify in part the total absence of a severance tax on minerals and timber. In 1961 an individual income tax was enacted, simply requiring the taxpayer to pay the state an amount equal to 6 per cent of the amount he paid to the federal government as federal income tax. In 1962 the state supreme court of appeals sustained the constitutionality of this act. This type of state income tax act has merits, but in West Virginia by 1968 it had been superseded by a graduated state income tax at rates from 1.2 per cent to 5.5 per cent, rising in 24 steps on incomes of $2,000 to $400,000. In 1967 a corporation income tax at the rate of 6 per cent was enacted.

West Virginia's tax of 1 cent per bottle on soft drinks, with proceeds allocated to the Medical Center of West Virginia University, had been in operation a decade and a half by 1969, and was currently producing about $4½ million per year. Students of political science and public finance do not generally look with favor on "pre-allocated" or "earmarked" taxes, because in their view each successive legislature should have wide latitude in which to decide the distribution of the

---

[9] *State ex rel. Board of Governors* v. *O'Brien, Secretary of State*, 142 W. Va. 88, 94 S.E. 2d 446 (1956)

current financial resources. Nevertheless, this unusual state tax on sales of soft drinks has been apparently a relatively painless and satisfactory means of financing in large part both the construction and the operation of a great medical center.

WISCONSIN

The University of Wisconsin's old and often-repeated assertion that the state is its campus does not denote a condition unique to that institution or to that state. Nor does it convey a comprehensive impression of education beyond the high school in Wisconsin.

The University, dating from 1848, was later designated as the Morrill Act land-grant college of Wisconsin, and hence for more than a century has been both the principal state university and the land-grant university on one campus at Madison. This characteristic is paralleled in the history of the University of Minnesota; and in Illinois and Ohio the principal state university and the land-grant university are one and the same, though the history is different from that in either Wisconsin or Minnesota.

In the other three "Big Ten" states (Michigan, Indiana, and Iowa) the Morrill Act land-grant colleges have always been separate institutions located at a distance from the principal state university, and have themselves become cosmopolitan universities rivaling it in enrollments and financial support—all of which is commendable and wholly desirable as population grows and knowledge expands.

In 1950 the University of Wisconsin at Madison had nine "extension centers" (later to be known as University Centers), of which one was in downtown Milwaukee and the others in middle-sized cities distributed over the state. There were then nine state teachers colleges in the state, of which one was in Milwaukee. Also in Milwaukee was the largest of the locally-based vocational and adult schools, already having many students above the high school level and already offering a few courses of one and two years transferable for credit in the state university or other four-year institutions. Milwaukee also had Milwaukee-Downer College, a distinguished small private college for women; Marquette University, the well-known Jesuit institution; the Milwaukee School of Engineering; and a few other small denominational colleges.

None of the public institutions in Milwaukee had a large campus, and none had a campus where future large expansion would be feasible. Pressure for much larger and more varied facilities for public higher education in the region led the governor to commission a survey of higher education in the eight southeastern counties, of which Milwaukee was the urban focus. The author had a part in that work, under the chairmanship of Arthur J. Klein, who had recently retired as dean of the college of education at Ohio State University. For reasons already stated the survey team recommended that the existing institutions should continue with their current functions, with such expansions as practicable, and that a large new multipurpose state college, to have its own governing board, should be established on a large campus, of which there seemed to be several available choices obtainable in the near outskirts of the city.

This recommendation was not implemented. In 1956 the former Milwaukee State Teachers College in its 22-acre campus in the northern part of the city was linked with the downtown University of Wisconsin extension center to become the Milwaukee Campus of the University of Wisconsin, now styled the University of Wisconsin—Milwaukee. By 1968 this offshoot had nearly 17,000 students—over half as many as its parent at Madison—and was operating schools of applied science and engineering, business administration, education, fine arts, letters and science, library science, nursing, and social welfare, and offering doctoral programs in some departments. A school of architecture was added in 1969.

In 1964 the state acquired the 43-acre campus and plant of Milwaukee-Downer College, and added it to the adjoining campus of the former teachers college, thus giving the University of Wisconsin in Milwaukee some 65 acres in a desirable residential part of the city.

Nevertheless, by 1969 the continued expansion raised serious question as to whether the state would have to obtain another large campus in the outskirts of Milwaukee, as had been recommended nearly 20 years before. Certain it is that facilities for public higher education in the Milwaukee metropolitan region had been developed only on an increasingly inadequate scale until about 1960; and the great expansion since that time goes far to explain the gains in the state's investment in the annual operating expenses of higher education during the decade 1960-1970.

In the same period the two-year lower-division University Centers outstate grew in size and numbers, and two of them (at Green Bay and Kenosha) have been augmented by new two-year upper-division institutions to which they were attached.

By 1969 it appeared that former extension centers at Green Bay, Manitowoc, Menasha, and Marinette had become campuses of the degree-granting University of Wisconsin—Green Bay; two at Racine and Kenosha had become campuses of the degree-granting University of Wisconsin—Parkside; and there were seven two-year campuses of the University of Wisconsin—Madison, at Baraboo, Marshfield, Wausau, Janesville, Sheboygan, West Bend, and Waukesha, comprising the University Center System. The nine state colleges grew and were renamed Wisconsin State Universities. Three of them (at Oshkosh, Platteville, and Menomonie) each planted a small branch campus apart from its main campus.

Thus the picture of two large systems emerged: the University of Wisconsin System and the Wisconsin State University System, each governed by its own Board of Regents. A third system is that of the state-wide network of more than 60 Vocational, Technical, and Adult Schools, which had its beginnings as early as 1911. Each such school is based on its own local taxing district (separate and independent from the local districts for the regular public schools, but overlapping one or more of them). These districts have their own local governing boards. Recently these have been regrouped into 18 area districts. State supervision and the allocation of state and federal subsidies are vested in the State Board of Vocational Education—an agency of long standing and great importance in Wisconson, especially in view of the circumstance that the state has no other board of education at the state level—the state leadership and supervision of the regular elementary and secondary schools being wholly the responsibility of the state superintendent of public instruction and his staff constituting the department of public instruction.

The State Board of Vocational Education selects a director of vocational, technical, and adult education, who is thus in a position coordinate with that of the superintendent of public instruction. The importance of this structure for higher education derives from the fact that although the vocational and adult schools were originally on the high school level and were largely for pupils who preferred vocational training over academic education, and for "drop-outs" from the regular public high schools, they have long since become increasingly institutions whose students are in large part high school graduates. On account of the diversity and flexibility of many short-term programs, it is virtually impossible to say with precision exactly what proportion of their instruction is "beyond high school"; but a considerable part of it is of that nature, especially in the larger and better of these vocational, technical, and adult schools; and the whole system is properly regarded as in part an agency of education above high school, and increasingly so. The Milwaukee Vocational and Adult School (renamed Milwaukee Technical College) has long offered "college transfer sequences," accepted by the state university and other four-year colleges. Such programs are also available at the Madison Technical College, and have been authorized for the similar institution at Rhinelander.

A fourth system is much smaller. During most of the decade Wisconsin had some twenty-two "county teachers colleges" which were in fact only two-year normal schools, survivals of an earlier day. Most of them had fewer than 100 students, but had well-maintained plants on a Lilliputian scale. Once they had been essential facilities for the training of elementary school teachers in Wisconsin, at a time when the population was sparser and much more largely rural. For decades they were regarded as anachronistic, but efforts to abolish them did not succeed. For biennium 1967-69 appropriations aggregating $1,329,000 were made as state subsidies for them, and about that time they seem to have been renamed "county colleges." In 1968, 15 of these were in operation. The state's policy is to close them by 1971. There is a possibility that a few of them may continue and develop as the equivalent of community two-year colleges.

The foregoing is backdrop for the story of state-level structure. The legislature of 1955 set up the Coordinating Committee for Higher Education, at first composed of four members of the Board of Regents of the University of Wisconsin and the president of that board; four members of the Board of Regents of State Colleges and that board's president; four representatives of the general public appointed by the governor; and the State Superintendent of Public Instruction. Later the structure was modified to add four members of the State Board of Vocational and Adult Education, and two representatives of the county teachers colleges. Again in 1965 the composition was changed to give a majority of the seats to laymen appointed by the governor. The reconstituted body of 17 members consisted of 9 representatives of the general public appointed by the governor for overlapping terms of eight years; and a tenth, who must be a member of a county teachers college board, appointed by the governor on the recommendation of the Association of County Teachers College Boards. The representation of the "three big boards" was cut to two from each: its president and one other member, making six in all. The seventeenth member was the Superintendent of Public Instruction. The body was renamed the Wisconsin Coordinating Council for Higher Education.

This "laicizing" of the agency seems to have been forced by influential persons who were unappreciative of the good work done by the Committee and its joint staff over its first 10 years in developing *liaison*, research, and the dissemination of public information; impatient with persuasive and permissive methods; and unable to conceive of a state system of higher education as anything other than a monolith, ruled by an authoritarian bureaucracy. This concept will fail. To be sure, the central agency should not be made up entirely of professional people, or even of board members of the constituent institutions; but it is handicapped and half-blind without the presence of a heavy representation of institutional presidents and board members in all its deliberations, because these are the persons having intimate knowledge of what goes on in the state-wide system in its different parts.

Elsewhere the author has suggested that economy of time and money could be accomplished by having the "lay public" element of such a body composed of leading legislators from each House, members of an appropriate joint committee or joint subcommittee.[1]

---

[1] Pp. 186-187 and 210 in M. M. Chambers, *Higher Education: Who Pays? Who Gains?* Danville, Illinois: The Interstate Printers & Publishers, Inc., 1968. 302 pp.

WISCONSIN

Appropriations for Annual Operating Expenses of Higher Education in Wisconsin, Alternate Fiscal Years, 1959-60 through 1969-70 (in thousands of dollars)

Institutions	Year 1959-60	Year 1961-62	Year 1963-64	Year 1965-66	Year 1967-68	Year 1969-70
U of Wisconsin						
Madison campus		28,258	33,639	50,679	62,743	62,335
U hospitals		2,164[1]	3,261	4,362	4,407	3,779
Subtotal, U of Wis—Madison		30,422	36,900	55,041	67,150	66,114
Milwaukee campus					11,766	17,885
System of U Ctrs					3,922	4,417
Northeastern (Green Bay)					586	4,860
Southeastern (Parkside)					586	3,348
University-wide					897	4,159
Subtotal, U of Wis		10,473[2]		23,410[3]	84,907	100,785
State universities:						
Oshkosh			2,059		6,710	9,534
Fond du Lac					97	171
Whitewater			1,833		5,972	7,666
Eau Claire			1,667		5,031	7,141
Stevens Point			1,697		4,766	6,473
La Crosse			1,509		3,968	5,369
Platteville			1,558		3,783	4,703
Richland					323	453
Stout (Menomonie)			1,431		3,508	4,629
Barron (Rice Lake)					308	503
River Falls			1,310		3,278	3,781
Superior			1,192		2,755	3,696
Bd of Regents			334		939	1,375
Subtotal, St U's		10,473	14,590	23,410	41,438	55,927[4]

Board of Voc, Tech. & Adult Ed[5]

Coll level			9,550
Adult educ		550	
		4,778	
County colleges[6]		729	733
Total[7]	38,625	40,895	51,490	78,451	132,402	166,995

[1]This sum is only an estimate of the amount necessary to pay the state's share for the care of state patients. Actually the appropriation is for a "sum sufficient" which cannot be precisely predetermined in advance.

[2]A supplemental appropriation of $652,000 (for biennium) has been requested, because state college enrollments have substantially exceeded the estimates on which these appropriations were based.

[3]Allocations to the several institutions are at the discretion of the Board of Regents of State Colleges.

[4]Includes $171,000 for a new branch campus at Medford.

[5]Approximate allocations for beyond-high-school education in the Vocational and Adult Schools.

[6]The former county normal schools.

[7]State-wide totals for Wisconsin may be somewhat overstated because some work of less than post-high-school is carried on in some of the Wisconsin Vocational and Adult Schools.

This could sharply shorten the interminable seven-step gauntlet through which recommended improvements have to go in many populous states before reaching the legislature—a process involving much unnecessary and fruitless expenditure of time and effort in bureaucratic wrangling, and which, in many instances, simply "does not work" as intended.[2]

Wisconsin's central state administrative and fiscal offices and functionaries have long arms immersed in the affairs of public higher education. A State Building Commission tinkers constantly with construction priorities. The governor in 1960, apparently disenchanted with the Building Commission, was reported to have asked the State Commissioner of Administration for advice regarding state building policy for higher education. Came the reply that new building should be done at the state colleges and university extension centers, because the price of land and the cost of labor and materials was in general a little lower in the smaller towns than in Madison or Milwaukee. There was no prior consultation with educational administrators or board members, and apparently no attempt was made to assess accurately future educational needs. The idea did not dovetail at all well with careful plans already worked out by the Coordinating Committee for Higher Education and was abandoned; but the Commissioner of Administration, the Building Commission, and sometimes the governor himself, have continually been embroiled in this matter which is best understood by the governing boards and their Coordinating Committee.

The Coordinating Committee is almost always under heavy attack by power-hungry politicians, often through no fault of its own, other than its failure or refusal to operate all public higher education as a rigid hierarchy in accord with the dictates coming from sources in the financial and non-educational power structure. Such a mandate is impossible; and if it were possible, and were effected, the institutions would not be universities—they would become treadmills.

In April 1962, Governor Gaylord Nelson addressed a joint meeting of the Coordinating Committee, the University of Wisconsin Board of Regents, and the State Colleges Board of Regents, making 26 specific proposals, some of which were sound and others less than good. He already foresaw the need of another four-year state college in the southeastern region of the state. He recommended that the Vocational and Adult Schools be represented on the Coordinating Committee, which was later accomplished. He proposed that the University of Wisconsin place no limit on the enrollment of out-of-state graduate

---

[2]Representation of members of the legislature on the North Carolina Board of Higher Education, and on the Washington Council on Higher Education, was provided in statutes of 1969. (See *supra.*)

students. He urged an amendment to the state constitution (already rejected in the preceding two legislatures) to permit borrowing for capital construction on the general obligation of the state.

He advocated central processing of all applications for enrollment in the state institutions of higher education, adding that "this program is not intended in any way to restrict the student from applying for admission to the institution of his choice." Somehow, good though the governor's intentions undoubtedly were, that one smacked of an odious bureaucratic Big Brotherism, under which it could become possible for a student to be assigned to a college he never wished to attend, with disastrous effects upon his morale and the optimum fulfillment of his potentialities.

Illustrative of the rain of adverse criticism the Coordinating Committee has to endure was a plaintive and frustrated editorial in a Milwaukee metropolitan daily on the day before Christmas, 1966: "Where was the Committee when the State Building Commission hacked away at budget requests for starting new campuses in the Green Bay and Kenosha areas?" The same writer also noted that the Board of Regents of state colleges had "suddenly decided, unilaterally, that faculty salary requests should be revised"; and he asked, "Where was the Committee when the University of Wisconsin slipped to the governor a $216,000 request to start a new school of architecture at Milwaukee?" Instead of bewailing the first of these three items, the editorial writer should have advocated legislation to take the State Building Commission out of the business of higher education, as Governor Rockefeller had done in New York. Instead of lamenting the second and third occurrences, he should have celebrated them, for they were both obviously in the best interest of the state.

A refreshing feature of the scene in Wisconsin during the 'Sixties was the enunciation of adherence to the historic principle of low tuition fees or no tuition fees in public higher education. In March, 1961, the Board of Regents of the University of Wisconsin adopted a resolution: "Fees for students must not be expected to cover a greater percentage of the cost of education than they currently do. In fact, efforts should be made to return to the traditional concept of free public higher education, as the percentage of our young people attending college continues to increase, and as college-going becomes a part of the expected educational program for a majority of the state's youth."

In the same year the Coordinating Committee for Higher Education concurred: "The Coordinating Committee believes with conviction that the goal of the State of Wisconsin, concerning the impact of the payment of costs of higher education, should be to seek a return to the established principle of free public higher education, by gradually reducing the cost to the student until at some time in the future public higher education becomes available on a virtually free basis. The lowering of financial barriers to higher education certainly should enable our society more effectively to encourage the garnering and use of the full talents of its citizenry."[3]

Wisconsin has a good tradition of state tax support for public higher education. The state has both personal and corporation income taxes on graduated bases at comparatively productive rates. Late in 1961 a new 3 per cent sales tax on a long list of selected items was enacted. This measure was expected to produce $60 million of additional revenue annually. The same act increased the income tax rates and established a withholding system. On account of the withholding feature, taxpayers paying 1961 income taxes due by April 15, 1962, were allowed to deduct 65 per cent of the amount due for 1961. Thus the state got a "windfall" of 35 per cent of the 1961 amounts due, in addition to the regular collections for 1962.

In July, 1963, after a long deadlock involving a Democratic governor and a Republican-controlled legislature, new tax measures to produce $142 million per year of added revenue were enacted. The sales tax "package" of 1961 was extended to cover a great many more selected items and services, but excluding food, prescription drugs, and clothing; and there was a boost of 0.3 per cent in the state income tax rates. Wisconsin stands in the upper quarter of the 50 states with respect to total state and local tax payments per $1,000 of personal income, and with respect to state tax investment per citizen in annual operating expenses of higher education, and the ratio of that figure to average personal income. The situation is generally good, with some latitude for betterment; and the prospect is promising.

The 1969 legislature enacted tax measures estimated to produce $292 million over a 22-month period. The base of the sales tax was somewhat broadened and the rate raised to 4 per cent from the former 3 per cent. The rate of the cigarette tax was also stepped up, and a new real estate transfer tax enacted.

---

[3]A sketch of the scene in Wisconsin public higher education as of 1965 is available at pages 37-42 in M. M. Chambers, *Freedom and Repression in Higher Education*, 126 pp., now out of print, but accessible in many libraries.

WYOMING

"From the date of its establishment in 1886 to 1945, the University of Wyoming was the only institution in the state offering college-level instruction."[1] Under an act of 1945 authorizing public school districts to offer freshman and sophomore academic programs and terminal and adult education courses, three university centers and one junior college were established within four years. In the centers the University approved courses, maintained certain records, and jointly appointed faculty members. There was also close cooperation with the junior college.

An act of 1951 authorized the two-year institutions to become community colleges based on their own junior college districts and having their own local boards of trustees. This transformation took place (except for the original junior college which continued in its former status). Cooperation and service from the University continued. There was a Community College Commission composed mainly of representatives of the University and of each community-junior college.

The first appropriation of state tax funds as state aid for the operating expenses of community-junior colleges was made in 1957 in the sum of $80,000, to be distributed by the University. For the next biennium, the 1959 appropriation for this purpose was $400,000—$300,000 for the four existing colleges, and $100,000 for any additional ones that might be created during the biennium, all to be distributed on a formula basis by the Community College Commission. The biennial appropriations for state aid became successively $634,000 for 1961-63, $720,000 for 1963-65, $1,245,000 for 1965-67, and $2,216,000 for 1967-69.

In 1968-69 five local public community colleges were in operation, at Casper, Sheridan, Powell, Rock Springs, and Torrington. A two-year college at Riverton was listed as proprietary.[2]

---

[1]The quoted words, and the substance of the paragraphs of history which follow, are from George Duke Humphrey, "Evolution of Higher Education in Wyoming," in *Grapevine*, pp. 69-70 (October, 1959). Then president of the University of Wyoming, Humphrey is now president emeritus and head of the Division of American Studies at the University.

[2]*Education Directory, 1968-69, Part 3: Higher Education*. Washington: Office of Education, 1968. 459 pp. computer printout.

WYOMING

Appropriations for Annual Operating Expenses of Higher Education in Wyoming, Alternate Fiscal Years, 1959-60 through 1969-70 (in thousands of dollars)

Institutions	Year 1959-60	Year 1961-62	Year 1963-64	Year 1965-66	Year 1967-68	Year 1969-70
U of Wyoming						
Main operation	4,735	5,599	5,359	7,092	8,735	10,995
Ag Exten Serv			454	503	527	620
Retirement costs			498	502	665	1,193
Scholarships & loans			70	35	87	90
Subtotal, U of Wyo	4,735	5,599	6,347	8,150	10,015	12,898
State aid to Jr Colls	200	317	360	622	1,108	1,774
Total	4,935	5,916	6,707	8,772	11,123	14,672

Prior to the session of 1959 there was discussion of placing the community colleges under the governance of the board of trustees of the University of Wyoming in a centralized system; but no such act was passed. Thereafter the supervision and services which had been provided by the University to the community colleges were somewhat reduced, but full legal responsibility for the state accrediting of the colleges remained in the University. The University's policy was one of assisting and cooperating in the establishment of community colleges where practicable and desirable, and of providing some supervisory service during their infant years, but looking forward to their development as autonomous institutions capable of standing on their own feet.

The 1957 legislature requested its Legislative Interim Committee to make a study of higher education in Wyoming, but appropriated no funds for the purpose. The Interim Committee asked the University to assume leadership, and this was done, resulting in the assembling of a Steering Committee of 9 representatives of the University, an Advisory Committee of 25 prominent citizens, and 5 consultants from other states. An informative report was printed and circulated.[3]

It was explicit about the oncoming increases in enrollment and the capital needs and operating needs of the University and the community colleges. Apparently it had considerable favorable impact upon the legislature of 1959. That session increased the operating funds of the University for the next biennium to nearly $10 million, quintupled the formerly small state aid to the community colleges, and authorized the University to issue bonds up to $11,743,000 for capital outlays.

The program included acquisition of 135 acres of land adjoining the campus; construction of apartment units for 252 married students, a women's dormitory for 400, two 400-student men's dormitories with a dining hall, a building for the College of Commerce and Industry, a building for the College of Nursing and the student health service, and a warehouse-garage unit; remodeling of the former library building; and expansion of heating facilities and extension of the electric power system. All this seemed to place the University in an excellent position with respect to capital improvements to keep pace with increasing enrollments.

Between 1960 and 1968 Wyoming's total population seems to have declined from 330,000 to 315,000—a loss of 4½ per cent. Probably this explains in part why the gains in appropriations of state tax funds for operating expenses of higher education over the decade, while substantial, were not phenomenal in comparison with those of other

---

[3] *Higher Education in Wyoming.* Laramie, University of Wyoming, 1958. 45 pp. (A summary and digest of the study authorized by the legislature of 1957.)

states. The gain in Wyoming from fiscal year 1959-60 to fiscal year 1969-70 (10 years) was 197¼ per cent—just slightly less than a tripling. The weighted average rate of gain among all the states over the same period was more than a quadrupling.

This condition of a comparatively stationary population and a modest rate of gain in tax support of higher education is common to several of the northern mountain states—Idaho, Montana, and Utah. It is also common, in varying degrees, to the Great Plains states—the two Dakotas, Nebraska, Kansas, and Oklahoma.

In 1968, as to the state tax investment per citizen in the annual operating expenses of higher education, and as to the ratio of that amount to the average personal income in the state, Wyoming stood well up: $35.65 (fifth place) and 1.14 per cent (seventh place). The state had a 3 per cent general sales tax, but continued to be among the few having neither a personal nor corporation income tax. The 1969 legislature enacted a severance tax of 6¼ per cent on the value of minerals extracted.

APPENDICES

Appendix One

WHAT THE FIGURES ARE
INTENDED TO MEAN

The data are supplied by key persons in each state who report them to the small monthly mimeographed newsletter *Grapevine*. Their cooperation is indispensable. The ground rules used to achieve an approach to uniformity of reporting are enumerated in the following paragraphs. Diversities of practice among the fifty states make it impossible to eliminate all inconsistencies and accomplish absolute comparability among states and among institutions. We emphasize that comparisons are of limited usefulness, but have value if correctly interpreted.

(1) We *exclude* appropriations for capital outlay.

(Nevertheless, *Grapevine* appreciates informative statements and documentation regarding appropriations, bond issues, or other devices for providing capital funds. We can make occasional separate stories or exhibits of these, but never commingle or confuse them with appropriations for operating expenses.)

(2) We *exclude* any sums appropriated which clearly originated from sources other than state taxes, such as student fees or other institutional receipts. (Some states capture these non-tax funds for the state treasury, and appropriate them to the institutions as a part of the total appropriations for operating expenses; but many states do not. Hence, it is necessary to peel off the non-tax institutional receipts in order to report *Appropriations of State Tax Funds*.)

(3) We *include* any sums appropriated for the annual operating expenses of the institutions of higher education, even if appropriated to some other agency of the state for ultimate allocation and payment to the institutions. (Some states appropriate, either occasionally or habitually, sums for such items as faculty fringe benefits under conditions such that only the total made available at the time can be known, and the actual allocations to several institutions cannot be known until after the end of the fiscal period. *Grapevine* wants to report the total made available at the time of appropriation, and generally does not wait for subsequent institutional allocations unless they are obtainable without delay. *Grapevine*'s thrust is the prompt reporting of appropriations; not later reporting of actual expenditures.)

(4) We *include* any pre-allocated state taxes whose proceeds are dedicated to any institution of higher education, bypassing the process of periodic appropriation by the legislature. (For example, West Virginia has a tax of approximately one cent per bottle on the sale of soft drinks, currently producing about $4.5 million per year, which automatically goes to the West Virginia University Medical Center without legislative appropriation.)

(5) We would like to *include*, whenever practicable, *separate* appropriations for medical centers (including schools of medicine, dentistry, nursing, teaching hospitals, and other appropriate appurtenances of a medical education complex); *separate* appropriations for agricultural experiment stations and cooperative agricultural extension services; and *separate* ap-

propriations for branch institutions, regional campuses, and any other off-campus outposts of universities or land-grant institutions. We cannot request this except in instances where it is easily practicable and would not involve delay in reporting.

(6) We *include* sums derived from state tax funds and appropriated for *state* scholarships. This is regardless of whether such scholarships are tenable in public or private institutions, or tenable within or without the state.

(7) We *include* sums appropriated to *state-wide governing* or *coordinating* boards regardless of whether for the expenses of the board or for ultimate allocation to the institutions.

Appendix Two

THE TEN-YEAR FIFTY-STATE
SUMMARY TABLE

Appropriations of State Tax Funds for Operating
for Successive Fiscal Years from 1959-60 Through

States	Year 1959-60	Year 1960-61	Year 1961-62	Year 1962-63	Year 1963-64	Year 1964-65	Year 1965-66
(1)	(2)	(3)	(4)	(5)	(6)	(7)	(8)
Ala.	21,283	22,397	20,535	22,659	29,133	30,421	40,327
Alaska	2,111	2,323	3,023	3,301	4,817	5,300	6,108
Ariz.	14,042	16,218	18,305	21,007	25,683	29,742	35,459
Ark.	13,551	13,551	16,599	16,599	20,369	20,369	28,722
Cal.	188,604	221,592	247,172	277,708	301,304	351,982	413,103
Colo.	17,271	24,332	27,149	31,255	35,279	35,837	44,073
Conn.	12,273	13,080	14,855	15,948	18,585	19,706	31,060
Del.	3,731	3,734	4,368	5,094	5,831	6,889	7,390
Fla.	40,392	41,412	51,438	53,452	68,143	75,695	95,476
Ga.	24,058	26,605	29,046	32,162	35,270	41,770	50,859
Hawaii	4,958	5,825	7,254	8,515	10,867	12,580	17,006
Ida.	8,799	8,800	10,137	10,137	11,203	11,203	15,490
Ill.	90,289	90,290	116,293	116,293	148,170	148,170	204,403
Ind.	45,463	50,163	55,316	62,709	70,866	80,134	90,105
Iowa	34,630	34,861	39,682	39,705	48,275	48,328	61,284
Kas.	25,036	27,938	30,172	35,038	38,390	44,103	48,598
Ky.	14,954	19,672	24,491	29,573	32,164	42,782	49,507
La.	40,062	44,557	48,316	46,760	55,847	65,031	72,318
Me.	3,356	5,599	7,238	7,429	9,099	9,709	12,771
Md.	23,818	25,166	27,208	30,678	34,812	39,177	48,275
Mass.	12,167	13,361	15,281	16,503	19,874	28,415	32,022
Mich.	95,599	101,836	102,816	109,759	115,604	138,063	176,380
Minn.	36,173	38,920	43,908	45,117	49,710	55,059	65,211
Miss.	15,118	18,347	18,347	19,863	19,873	25,931	25,931
Mo.	24,744	25,641	29,251	33,603	44,526	46,847	62,168
Mont.	11,230	11,231	10,660	10,661	12,177	13,367	14,749
Nebr.	15,217	15,218	17,077	17,078	18,820	18,820	21,894
Nev.	3,682	4,107	4,863	5,325	6,042	6,518	7,114
N.H.	3,973	4,106	4,717	4,733	5,146	5,104	7,335
N.J.	21,982	24,457	28,421	34,179	40,020	45,816	50,826
N.M.	11,165	11,239	13,002	14,372	15,960	18,636	21,649
N.Y.	78,546	94,115	116,879	163,656	182,918	228,614	283,722
N.C.	28,419	30,574	36,087	36,815	46,768	51,431	76,323
N.D.	9,368	9,368	10,505	10,505	12,079	12,109	13,989
Ohio	43,331	45,326	52,014	55,620	60,670	67,670	85,045
Okla.	27,014	27,020	30,014	30,020	33,505	33,505	41,867
Ore.	28,719	28,719	34,796	34,263	39,923	39,998	49,252
Pa.	43,471	43,472	46,431	56,187	66,064	68,819	102,611
R.I.	4,477	5,271	5,826	7,697	7,963	10,283	12,868
S.C.	12,113	13,141	14,449	15,440	17,360	19,286	21,403

Expenses of Higher Education, in Thousands of Dollars,
1969-70, with Dollar Gains and Percentage Gains over Ten Years

Year 1966-67	Year 1967-68	Year 1968-69	Year 1969-70	1969-70 10-yr. Gain	%	States
(9)	(10)	(11)	(12)	(13)	(14)	(15)
54,782	58,192	58,462	72,518	51,235	240½	Ala.
7,314	8,619	10,400	11,876	9,765	462½	Alaska
40,492	46,281	55,121	65,611	51,569	367¼	Ariz.
28,722	38,985	44,547	47,630	34,079	251½	Ark.
489,102	534,075	637,788	749,162	560,558	297¼	Cal.
51,916	61,856	70,586	87,094	69,823	404¼	Colo.
34,897	53,655	61,513	80,270	67,997	554	Conn.
8,740	11,313	14,095	16,933	13,202	354	Del.
95,477	128,109	156,645	198,438	158,046	391¼	Fla.
59,193	87,369	112,524	124,207	100,149	416¼	Ga.
23,868	26,320	30,987	41,782	36,824	742½	Hawaii
15,490	20,101	20,601	29,862	21,063	239¼	Ida.
204,403	301,136	301,136	405,077	314,788	348½	Ill.
104,312	132,628	144,715	154,313	108,849	239½	Ind.
61,285	85,773	85,773	101,597	66,967	193½	Iowa
54,781	59,003	69,108	79,721	54,685	218½	Kas.
63,166	74,371	82,350	95,478	80,524	538½	Ky.
87,139	93,123	99,222	100,892	60,830	152	La.
13,457	18,167	17,873	25,984	22,628	674	Me.
61,567	67,700	79,742	92,132	68,314	287	Md.
43,940	57,667	69,097	85,278	73,111	601	Mass.
221,100	231,567	262,424	305,411	209,812	219½	Mich.
72,463	95,034	105,131	128,278	92,105	254¼	Minn.
36,720	36,720	47,804	47,804	32,686	216¼	Miss.
74,817	92,934	112,764	127,487	102,663	415	Mo.
16,784	21,375	24,418	26,715	15,485	138	Mont.
21,897	33,248	33,248	48,386	33,109	217½	Neb.
8,074	11,773	12,339	14,778	11,096	300	Nev.
7,185	9,201	10,221	10,685	6,713	169	N.H.
75,652	83,758	95,047	126,250	104,268	474¼	N.J.
26,088	28,954	31,262	36,126	24,961	223½	N.M.
353,793	431,212	482,986	625,341	546,795	696	N.Y.
81,194	106,550	114,709	175,931	147,512	519	N.C.
13,989	19,888	19,888	23,249	13,881	148	N.D.
93,269	150,527	174,136	239,891	196,560	453½	Ohio
41,867	46,858	52,858	59,552	32,508	120¼	Okla.
55,614	67,305	67,984	87,683	58,964	205¼	Ore.
137,509	179,212	264,693	250,000*	206,529	475	Pa.
15,387	18,401	21,545	28,935	24,458	546¼	R.I.
27,464	35,148	39,645	53,316	41,203	340¼	S.C.

(Continued)

States	Year 1959-60	Year 1960-61	Year 1961-62	Year 1962-63	Year 1963-64	Year 1964-65	Year 1965-66
(1)	(2)	(3)	(4)	(5)	(6)	(7)	(8)
S.D.	8,128	8,128	8,675	8,702	10,133	12,338	15,987
Tenn.	17,022	17,023	21,522	22,359	28,324	31,892	41,106
Texas	71,021	72,133	84,873	90,282	114,924	114,156	165,301
Utah	13,139	13,139	·15,580	15,580	19,154	19,154	24,891
Vt.	3,264	3,399	3,759	3,750	4,986	5,445	6,395
Va.	25,544	29,861	30,832	34,625	35,858	42,421	40,830
Wash.	46,909	47,441	58,733	58,387	69,913	71,973	94,979
W. Va.	16,919	16,919	23,518	20,743	21,875	23,761	32,294
Wis.	37,834	39,417	40,895	44,670	51,490	60,410	78,451
Wyo.	4,935	4,935	5,916	5,916	6,707	6,707	8,771
Totals	1,399,904	1,515,980	1,728,244	1,892,432	2,182,473	2,441,476	3,053,698
Weighted average percentage			-	-	-	-	-

Year 1966-67	Year 1967-68	Year 1968-69	Year 1969-70	1969-70 10-yr. Gain	%	States
(9)	(10)	(11)	(12)	(13)	(14)	(15)
14,251	16,992	17,152	18,227	10,099	124¼	S.D.
50,256	64,472	73,137	87,137	70,115	412	Tenn.
164,548	234,109	259,425	340,046	269,025	379	Texas
24,891	33,695	33,695	40,000	26,861	204½	Utah
6,998	10,304	10,940	13,532	10,268	314½	Vt.
64,134	74,335	107,524	117,578	91,614	358½	Va.
94,980	137,051	137,051	190,903	143,994	307	Wash.
32,294	44,448	49,033	55,005	38,086	225	W.Va.
95,160	131,505	155,957	165,851	128,017	338½	Wis.
8,773	11,123	11,123	14,672	9,737	197¼	Wyo.
3,541,194	4,422,142	5,050,424	6,124,624	4,724,120		
-	-	-	-	-	337½	

Appendix Three

AN ACT
TO PROVIDE FOR PUBLIC
HIGHER EDUCATION
IN A STATE

Preamble: Being cognizant that the extension, diffusion, and improvement of education beyond the high school among all the people of this State is essential to economic growth, industrial development, the public health and safety, the national security, and the elevation of the level of culture and well-being, the Legislature does hereby enact the provisions contained in this Act for the general support, organization and operation of public higher education in this State.

Definitions: "Higher education" includes all formal instruction beyond the level of graduation from an accredited high school.

"Institution of higher education" means any reputable institution offering programs of instruction or research, of any length, generally requiring a high-school diploma for admission, but not excluding vocational-technical schools not maintaining that requirement, but a majority of whose students are in fact high school graduates.[1]

"Community college" is an institution offering programs of instruction generally two years in length, and of the nature of (1) college-parallel courses, (2) terminal general education, (3) occupational or subprofessional and semi-professional training for work at what is defined as the technician level, and (4) educational and cultural activities for adults. The whole program is intended chiefly for persons residing within commuting-distance. A community college may include or be coordinate with a vocational-technical school in the same community. A community college may be supported in part and operated by a local taxing subdivision such as a city, county, public school district, or any duly organized combination of these, or by a public community college district[2] ;

---

[1]In Wisconsin there is a statewide system of Vocational and Adult Schools based on separate local taxing districts. Similar schools, often called Area Vocational-Technical Schools, exist in many other states. They are generally supervised by the Division of Vocational Education in the State Department of Public Instruction, which is a conduit for increasing federal subsidies to these types of schools. Often a majority of their students currently enrolled are high school graduates.

[2]Some 30 states have varying numbers of locally-based institutions of this type—notably California (which has about 80 of them), Texas, Florida, New York, Illinois, Michigan, and Mississippi.

or it may be a unit within any state institution of higher education such as a state university or state college, and in such event it may be on or adjacent to the same campus[3] or at a distance as a branch or regional campus.[4]

"State college" is a public institution owned by the State and supported in substantial part by appropriations of state tax funds, and offering programs leading to bachelors' and / or masters' degrees, usually requiring four, five, or more years for completion. A state college may include within its organization a community college and a vocational-technical school.

"State university" is a comprehensive, cosmopolitan institution, including a college of arts and sciences, a graduate school offering doctoral degrees in at least some departments of learning (except in the several instances where the institution is not yet manned and equipped to offer instruction at the doctoral level in any of its departments), and undergraduate and graduate professional schools, such as schools of education, schools of business, schools of technology or engineering, and often schools of law, schools of medicine and of related health professions, and others.

(In recognition of actual current usage, it must be noted state universities vary greatly as to size and comprehensiveness, and that in several of the larger and more populous states the state colleges have been given the name of "state university", while in a few of the least populous states the state university (which is in some instances the only state institution of higher education) has not yet developed any instruction leading to the doctoral degree, and may also lack some of the professional schools ordinarily found in a university. Thus there is some unavoidable ambiguity in defining "state university" and "state college", for sometimes a state college in a populous state may be larger and more comprehensive than a state university in a smaller state—[5] and some of these multi-purpose state colleges have been given the name of state university.[6]

Despite the proliferation of "state universities" in the larger states in recent years, there is generally no difficulty in identifying the *one principal state university* in each of the fifty states. In twenty states this is a "separated" state university (meaning that it does not include the Morrill Act land-grant institution of the state, which is located in a different part of the state, and usually does not have a school of law or a school of human medicine). In a few instances, nevertheless, the land-grant university in such a state is

---

[3]Many state universities and colleges offer one or more programs of a duration of only two years or less, on their home campuses.

[4]Wisconsin, Indiana, Kentucky, Ohio, and Pennsylvania are among the states having several two-year branches of the state universities. These are variously called "extension centers", "branch campuses", "regional campuses", and "community colleges". Nationwide, there are more than 150 two-year university branches of these types.

[5]Six of the older and larger of California's 19 state colleges currently receive annually appropriations of state tax funds for operating expenses of $21 million to $27 million.

[6]As in Wisconsin, Illinois, Indiana, Ohio, Kentucky, North Carolina, and Alabama.

larger and better-supported than the separated university—and here there may possibly be room for argument as to which is the "principal state university."

In thirty states the principal state university and the land-grant university are one and the same. Other state universities in the populous states can usually trace their origins to the normal school—teachers college—state college evolution. A state university may include a community college and /or a vocational-technical school, either on or adjacent to its main campus, or at a distance on branch or regional campuses.

NOTE: The foregoing definitions are limited to a minimum, in the interest of avoiding prolixity and maintaining flexibility. They do not include numerous special and unique types of institutions and programs, but sketch only the large outlines of a state system of higher education.

1. *Broad Policies.* It is hereby declared to be the public policy of the State that every child shall have accessible to him, without discrimination as to sex, race, religion, national origin, social status or economic underprivilege, opportunity to receive formal education to the highest level he is capable and desirous of obtaining with benefit to himself and to the State and nation.

It is hereby declared to be the public policy of this State that at least two years of further education, aimed primarily at intellectual growth, shall be made available tuition-free to all high school graduates.[7]

It is hereby declared to be the public policy of this State that a return to the historic principle of free public higher education is to be accomplished by gradually reducing the cost to the student until public higher education becomes available on a free basis to all qualified persons.[8]

The financial support of public institutions of higher education is primarily an obligation and responsibility of the State itself; and although substantial supplementary support may be received from private donors, the federal government, and local taxing subdivisions of the State, it is the policy of the Legislature that, in its consideration of revenue laws and other fiscal measures, including its acts appropriating state tax funds for the support of the several functions of State government, provision for adequate and satisfactory support of higher education shall have first priority, in keeping with its recognition as a paramount and uniquely important activity of the State, somewhat apart from and comparable with all other functions of government as a whole.[9]

It is hereby declared to be the public policy of this State that its public institutions of higher education shall operate in each instance to the greatest practicable extent under the leadership of their own presidents and consonant

---

[7]This is practically the exact wording of the noteworthy recommendation of the Educational Policies Commission, published in January 1964.

[8]This policy has recently been declared both by the Regents of the University of Wisconsin and the Wisconsin Coordinating Committee for Higher Education. California public junior colleges are tuition-free. In the City University of New York City, no tuition fees are charged to regular full-time undergraduate students, and the tradition is strongly defended against pressure from Albany.

[9]The California Constitution, Article XIII, Section 15, declares: "Out of the revenues from state taxes for which provision is made in this article, together with all other state revenues, there shall first be set apart the moneys to be applied by the state to support of the public school system and the State University."

with an ongoing consensus among their own faculties and students as academic communities, under the general governance of their own lay governing boards in accord with the provisions of Sections 2 and 3 of this Act; and that their internal academic and fiscal affairs shall be entirely free from interference from central administrative and fiscal officers of this State, in accord with the provisions of Sections 4 and 5 of this Act. The purpose of this policy is to create an environment in which public higher educational institutions can be operated with high morale and rising quality of accomplishment, and with the highest possible return from the investment of the taxpayer's dollar;—with, in short, "the efficiency of freedom."[10]

2. *The Basic Unit is the Autonomous Institution of Higher Education.* Each public institution of higher education (excepting only such institutions as are for the time being in the status of branches or regional campuses of some other major institution of higher education, and subject to administrative control by it) shall be a *public corporation,*[11] having its own corporate identity distinct from that of the State or of any other corporation, public or private; and shall be governed by a board of citizens elected or appointed as may be provided by law, which board may be styled "Board of Trustees", "Board of Regents" or by any other name deemed suitable; and said corporate board (known generically as the governing board of the corporation) shall have no other public responsibilities or authority other than the governance of the one institution of higher education under its jurisdiction.[12]

Eight hundred years of history have demonstrated that a university or college is essentially and inherently an autonomous academic community, if it is to approach successful performance of the functions for which it exists. Three centuries of history in the United States have indicated that a governing board devoted to one institution will generally succeed in maintaining empathy with and understanding of the aims of the constituency of that institution and of its students, faculty, and administration; that the board will exercise a wise restraint in abstaining from interference in administrative details and in fostering the governance of the academic community by an ongoing consensus, which is in turn indispensable to the high morale upon which the highest quality of instruction and research unavoidably depends.

3. *The Powers and Duties of the Institutional Governing Board.* The institutional governing board shall hold all property of the institution in trust for the State, which is the real owner. In the case of property received as gifts in trust from private donors, the institutional governing board shall, as agent of the State, serve as trustee for the execution of the terms of the trust instrument and for the lawful operation of the trust.[13] The institutional governing board

---

[10]This phrase was used as the title of the landmark report of the Committee on Government and Higher Education, headed by Milton Eisenhower. The trenchant 44-page pamphlet was published in 1959 by the Johns Hopkins Press in Baltimore, and had wide influence.

[11]Occasionally state universities have sought to deny their corporate entity when this facilitates their escape from liability under the cloak of sovereign immunity. The advantages are far outweighed by the opposite practice of consistently maintaining and asserting their corporate status and identity under all circumstances.

[12]"Each institution should have its own governing board, with the maximum of autonomy that can be provided to it . . . Only as the board has authority to act can there develop the community of consensus which for higher education is an essential of governance." These are the words of Thad L. Hungate, at page 226 in *Management in Higher Education.* New York: Teachers College, Columbia University, Bureau of Publications, 1964. 348 pp.

[13]The West Virginia Court of Appeals recently corrected an incipient breach of trust when the state auditor asserted his right to divert a legacy in trust to

shall have power to purchase, sell, lease, rent, and otherwise manage and dispose of all manner of property, real and personal, for the educational purposes of the institution, including power to invest and re-invest permanent funds to produce income for those purposes.

The institutional governing board shall have authority to enter into contracts and-or receive grants from the Federal Government, without the intervention of any officer or agency of this State.

The institutional governing board shall have power to appoint and fix the duration of employment and salaries and other compensation of a president, other administrative officers, and members of the faculties of the institution; and to establish rules governing the employment and compensation of all other employees of the institution. All appointments other than that of the president shall be made only upon the recommendation of the president.

The institutional governing board shall establish general rules governing the appointment, pay, promotion, tenure, leaves of absence, suspension and dismissal, retirement, and other conditions of employment for the president, administrative officers, and members of the faculties of the institution, such rules not to be in conflict with any law of this State;—but it is expressly provided hereby that nothing in the statutes of this State shall be construed to prevent or disable the institutional governing board from employing selected members of the faculties of the institution under "indeterminate contract" or "permanent tenure" in accord with such rules as the board may have formulated and adopted for that purpose, after the manner of leading institutions of higher education in the United States; and any part of the statutes of this State which may have been judicially construed as proscribing the said type of employment, or which purports to make it unlawful or legally impossible or unenforceable, is hereby repealed and declared to be null and of no effect.14

It is hereby declared that no part of the Civil Service or State Personnel statutes of this State is applicable to any employee of any state institution of higher education in this State; but that the employment and conditions of employment of any and all such persons shall be governed by rules adopted by the institutional governing board in accord with the usages, customs, best practices, and advancing needs of leading universities and colleges in the United States. The purpose of this provision is hereby declared to be to prevent waste of time and public money caused by efforts to apply inappropriate personnel regulations in the management of a university or college, and to facilitate and encourage economical and efficient practices in the personnel management of such an institution by vesting in the institutional governing board sole and exclusive authority to adopt appropriate personnel rules at its own discretion.15

Bluefield College (a state institution) to the general common school fund of the state. *State ex rel. West Virginia State Board of Education* v. *Sims*, 143 W.Va. 269, 102 S.E. 2d 190 (1957).

14 The purpose of this proviso is to remove doubt as to the authority of a state university or college governing board to establish tenure regulations and confer indeterminate tenure upon selected professors; such authority having recently been denied in certain state supreme court decisions such as *Posin* v. *State Board of Higher Education*, (N. D.), 86 N.W. 2d 31 (1957), and *Worzella* v. *Board of Regents of Education*, 77 S.D. 447, 93 N.W. 2d 411 (1958). See "Academic Freedom, Tenure, and the Law," by Clark Byse, in *Harvard Law Review* 73: 304-322 (December 1959).

15 A classic judicial decision on this point is *Hernandez* v. *Frohmiller*, 68 Ariz. 242, 204 Pac. 2d 854 (1949), in which Article 11, Section 2 of the Arizona Constitution was construed as giving the Board of Regents exclusive power to

The institutional governing board shall have and exercise all the powers customarily appertaining to universities and colleges from time immemorial, save and except such as may be prohibited by this Act or by other laws of this State not hereby repealed. These powers include, but are not limited to, the enactment of rules for the admission, classification, suspension and dismissal, and graduation of students; the conferring of degrees, including earned and honorary degrees, upon the recommendation of the faculty; and the adoption and amendment and publication of rules governing student affairs, faculty affairs, the non-academic staff, and the affairs of the board itself in the conduct of its own business.

In accord with time-tested practice, the board shall have plenary legal authority in the governance of the institution and all its affairs; but shall exercise a wise restraint in abstaining from direct action in the normal management of the institution, and shall be expected ordinarily to receive and approve, after deliberation, proposals originating with the president after his consultation with the faculties, or originating with the faculties and submitted to the board through the president and with his approval; and it is normally anticipated that the board will delegate all executive authority to the president of the institution, who will in turn delegate much of it to deans, department heads, and other administrators; and it is normally to be anticipated that the board will delegate, subject only to its own power of approval, the great bulk of the large amount of quasi-legislative work required in the operation of the institution to the organized faculties and to appropriate faculty committees.

It shall also be lawful and permissible for the board to delegate, with the approval and upon the recommendation of the president and faculties, appropriate spheres of its quasi-legislative and quasi-judicial authority to institutional councils or courts composed wholly of students, or composed of any combination of students, faculty members, and administrative officers.[16]

Within the traditional framework of institutional governance, it shall be a paramount duty of the board to foster and promote an ongoing consensus among students, faculty members, parents, alumni, taxpayers, public officers, and all affected citizens regarding the plans and progress of the institution, to the end that there shall be a continuing esprit-de-corps and a rising morale among all classes of persons concerned, springing from a well-founded belief that the institution is in the main wisely and democratically governed in the public interest of the State as a whole.

In view of the increasing necessity of prolonged and detailed negotiations between representatives of the board and representatives of the faculties and of the student body regarding numerous matters of mutual and legitimate concern, such that neither board members nor the president of the institution can devote the amount of time required for this work, it shall be lawful for the board to appoint, upon the recommendation of the president of the institution, one or more vice-presidents or assistants to the president who shall be able to spend full time as representatives of the board and of the president in conducting

---

appoint and supervise all employees of the state university; and a statute of 1948 purporting to place the non-academic employees of the university under the jurisdiction of the state civil service system was declared unconstitutional and void.

[16]This would remove uncertainty as to the lawfulness of delegating quasi-judicial powers in disciplinary cases which may involve heavy penalties against offending students, to an adjudicatory body composed wholly or partly of students. Apparently the only state supreme court decision on the point is *In re Carter*, 262 N. C. 360, 137 S.E. 2d 150 (1964), which holds that such delegation is lawful.

negotiations with duly elected representatives of legitimate organizations of faculty members or of students, for the purpose of illuminating matters of dispute regarding affairs of mutual interest to the board and the faculties, or the board and the students.

"Negotiation" does not mean "capitulation", and it is hereby understood and declared that when a governing board agrees to negotiate with organized teachers or students, and provides machinery for negotiation, it does not thereby surrender any of its plenary legal prerogatives, and that its powers as defined herein continue unimpaired. The purpose of the machinery of negotiation is merely to facilitate the transmission of information and opinion between the board and the personnel of the institution, to the end that many matters at first thought to be in dispute may be amicably illuminated and agreed upon with mutual satisfaction and with benefit to the institution and to all concerned if adequate time and effort can be devoted to their presentation and appraisal.[17]

4. *Statewide Liaison in Public Higher Education.* It is hereby recognized and declared that in the statewide academic community, consisting of the student bodies, faculties, and governing boards of several institutions, there is no necessity and no place for that precise coordination of effort which may be required in a large industrial organization or in a military force. The goal of higher education is realized in the minds and actions of individual students, as inspired by scholars and as influenced by the academic environment. The actual advances made by students are as individuals, inspired by interest, initiative, inventiveness and voluntary consensus rather than by authoritative command from a pyramidal hierarchy. Scholarly professors, deans and presidents have generally a somewhat different mode of operation from that of the "man in the grey flannel suit", or that of the officer in the armed forces. Their work requires a different mode.[18]

An institution of higher education can not function well as merely one of several "branch offices" of a vast and highly-centralized "system", receiving daily directives on teletype, and shaping its operations entirely on the dictates of a distant central headquarters.[19] The essential spirit of the thing is wholly different from that concept. It is of course desirable, however, that there be ways and means of facilitating the liaison and cooperative activities that already go on everywhere among public institutions in any single state, as well as regionally and nationwide. The public institutions of higher education in any state compose a statewide "system"; and the concept is in the public interest if it is free of notions of mandatory control of the institutions by one or several central administrative agencies at the state capital. Instead, the appropriate

---

[17] The idea of formal channels of "professional negotiation" between the board and its teaching and research employees has made great strides in large city public school systems, and offers a promise of allaying some of the traditional lack of communication between the board and the faculty under the conventional practice of channeling all communications through the president. New machinery is necessary, especially in large institutions.

[18] John D. Millett has written: "I believe ideas drawn from business and public administration have only a very limited applicability to colleges and universities," in *The Academic Community: An Essay on Organization.* New York: McGraw-Hill Book Co. 1962. 265 pp.

[19] Homer D. Babbidge has remarked that a thoughtless and naive push toward increased centralization of state systems of higher education could reduce the state institutions to such a status that the state university would have "no more distinctive institutional character than the local post-office."

"system" for statewide public higher education is an elastic and flexible federation of the institutions, in which the utmost care is taken to continue unimpaired the autonomy of the institutional governing boards, while providing a small central agency charged only with the duty of collecting statistics and information, making annual statewide surveys of higher educational needs and accomplishments, and providing advisory reports for the governing boards, the legislature, the governor, and the public, including "long-range" studies in which the needs and developments of as much as a decade or two ahead may be projected, for the information of the public and the legislature.[20]

A State Council on Public Higher Education is hereby established for this State, to be composed of the presidents of each of the four-year state universities and colleges; the chief academic officer or dean of the faculties of each such institution; the chief business officer or financial vice president; and one member of the governing board of each such institution; plus four additional members of the governing board of the principal state university, plus two additional members of any state university or college having a head-count of 15,000 students or more; plus one representative of each ten two-year public colleges in the state (or fractional part of ten); plus one representative of the state or area vocational-technical schools in the state.[21]

The Council shall elect its Chairman and other appropriate officers annually in January, and shall meet at least twelve times a year in monthly sessions, and otherwise at the call of the Chairman. It shall adopt rules for its own procedure, and shall appoint and fix the salaries of an executive secretary and other staff members upon the recommendation of the executive secretary and as deemed necessary by the Council, and as financed by the Legislature, or by the participating institutions of higher education, or from philanthropic sources, or any combination of these sources.

It is hereby stipulated that neither the Council in its collegial capacity, nor any of its officers or members, nor any of its professional or clerical staff members, shall ever exercise any executive, administrative, or other mandatory or directive authority over any institution of higher education in this State, or any officer, faculty member, other employee, or student therein or thereof.

The executive secretary and such other professional staff members as may be appointed shall be selected primarily on the basis of their experience, education, and ability to study and report upon state systems of public higher education and to act as advisory consultants to the Council.

The Council shall have power to request, but not to require, such reports at such intervals as are deemed desirable for the conduct of its research, advisory, and informational functions, from each state institution of higher education, public two-year college, and area vocational school in this State. It shall invite the voluntary cooperation of each of these institutions in the conduct of all its work. It shall invite them to submit as early as possible copies of their

---

[20] This terminology is preferred over the inappropriate and distasteful phrase "master plan" currently in use in California and New York.

[21] In the present preliminary draft, these provisions for the composition of the Council are admittedly inadequately developed. A perfected draft capable of adaptation to states of widely varying population and numbers of institutions would probably have to provide two or more optional plans for the composition of the Council, with the recommended choice depending chiefly upon the number of institutions in the particular state. In any event, the theory of constituting the Council as chiefly an agency of lateral liaison among autonomous institutions, rather than a hierarchical administrative agency and source of mandatory orders, would be unchanged.

annual operating budgets and of their capital outlay budgets and projections, and as a result of its inspection, study, and conference on these budgets, may make recommendations regarding the general level of support of the institutions to the governing boards, the Legislature, the Governor, and the public.

The Council shall have as its principal and continuing duty the making of studies and recommendations and the dissemination of information regarding ways and means of implementing the five "Broad Policies" as declared in Section 1 of this Act.

5. *Institutions of Higher Education in Relation to Political, Administrative, and Fiscal Officers of the State Government.*[22] It is the policy of this State that partisan or personal political considerations shall be excluded as completely as possible from the governance of the state institutions of higher education. To that end the terms of office of members of the respective institutional governing boards shall normally be of not less than eight years' duration, and shall be overlapping in such manner that a sudden influx of new members sufficiently numerous to constitute a majority shall be an improbable occurrence. The purpose of this provision is to minimize the possibility of any board's falling under the domination of any Governor or other powerful politician, or of bending too easily in response to passing political fads.

It is the policy of this State that the institutional governing boards shall have an optimum degree of autonomy and independence in the governance of the administrative and fiscal affairs of their respective institutions, to the end that their faculties and administrative officers shall not be subjected to unnecessary and self-defeating controls from multiple administrative and fiscal offices at the state capital, entailing delays and annoyances deleterious to the morale of the institutions and hence destructive of the quality of their performance.

Consonant with that policy, it is hereby mandated that relations between the institutions of higher education and the central administrative and fiscal agencies of the State government shall be as stipulated in the remainder of this Section; and all statutes or parts of statutes, or administrative regulations hitherto promulgated and now in effect to the contrary are hereby repealed and rendered null, void, and of no effect.

(1) No institution shall be required to deposit in the state treasury, or in any other state depository, any of its funds derived from any source or sources whatsoever other than legislative appropriations of state tax funds; and no such funds derived from any sources other than state tax funds shall ever be required to be appropriated by the State Legislature before being lawfully expended by the institution.[23]

---

[22] The whole of Section 5 is a comprehensive "declaration of fiscal and administrative independence" designed to provide for the correction of the many disadvantages of over-centralization in the governance of state systems of higher education which has been imposed during several decades of *"administrative reform" without recognition and largely in disregard of the essential character and unique functions of public institutions of higher education; but which has become discredited in recent years by administrative theorists even for business and governmental bureaucracies.*

[23] A considerable number of states, especially in New England and the Northeast, adhere to the primitive practice of requiring all institutional receipts from student fees and other non-tax sources to be transmitted to the state treasury immediately upon receipt, and held there unavailable for institutional expenditure until appropriated by the legislature. In some instances

(2) Each institutional governing board shall appoint its own treasurer and prescribe his duties and his required surety; and shall never be required to accept the state treasurer or any other state officer as its treasurer *ex officio*; and the institutional treasurer shall have custody, subject to the regulations of the institutional governing board, of all funds of the institution from whatever source derived, including those derived from legislative appropriations of state tax funds from and after the point at which they are allotted and paid to the institution.

(3) Each institutional governing board shall have power to employ attorneys to represent it in litigation and to perform other necessary legal services in the operation of the institution, either as full-time salaried staff members or on a retainer basis or otherwise; and shall never be required to depend upon the services of the attorney general or his staff for such services, though each board shall have the privilege of requesting and using the services of the attorney general when deemed advantageous to the public interest.

(4) Each institution shall prepare its annual or biennial budget in complete detail for its own internal use; but no state budget director, comptroller, or finance officer, by whatever title designated, shall require the budgeted requests for appropriations of state tax funds to be presented in minute detail as "line item" budgets, or require such budgeted requests to be in a form identical with those of other state agencies and departments; and it is hereby declared to be the custom and tradition of this State that successive legislatures appropriate state tax funds for operating expenses of institutions of higher education generally in lump sums to each institution, and not in the form of minutely detailed "line item" appropriation acts.[24]

(5) Each institutional governing board shall have power to appoint and establish personnel practices for all employees of the institution of all grades from that of president downward through the lowest ranks, subject to the law of contracts applicable to such employments, and subject to such valid ordinances as may be enacted by the board touching the tenure of specified classes of employees; and no such board shall ever be required to submit to regulations adopted by any Civil Service Commission, State Personnel Board, or any other central state personnel authority, by whatever name styled.

(6) Each institutional governing board shall have power to purchase every sort of materials and supplies deemed necessary in the operation of the institution, either directly from vendors or, when deemed desirable, through the agency of such cooperating national or regional associations of educational buyers as may be selected by it; and shall never be required to purchase any article or commodity through the agency of a State Purchasing Officer except when it adjudges this procedure advantageous to the public interest and requests the services of such central purchasing agency.

---

they are held in a special fund, but in others commingled in the state general fund. In 1965 the legislature of Ohio enacted a statute providing that all receipts from student fees shall remain in possession of the institution to which they are paid, and be available for expenditure by its governing board without the intervention of the legislature.

24 A wise and eloquent statement against unnecessary minute itemization of university appropriation acts is in the opinion of Justice House for the unanimous Illinois Supreme Court in *Turkovich* v. *Board of Trustees of University of Illinois*, 11 Ill. 2d 460, 43 N.E. 2d 229 (1957), in which he said: "The General Assembly cannot be expected to allocate funds to each of the myriad activities of the University and thereby practically substitute itself for the Board of Trustees in the management thereof."

(7) Each institutional governing board shall have power to authorize such printing, publishing, and distribution of publications as it deems in the public interest, by the institution in its governance; and shall never be required to let printing or publishing contracts through the agency of a State Printer; and no State Printer or State Editor or other similar functionary shall ever exercise any authority in determining what any institution of higher education shall print or publish or disseminate.[25]

(8) Each institutional governing board shall have power to issue "revenue bonds" payable solely out of the income of the buildings which the proceeds are intended to finance, or out of the revenues of other similarly financed facilities at the institution so financed in the past or which may be so financed in the future. The said "revenue bonds" shall not in any sense or in any contingency ever constitute a debt of this State. The power to issue such bonds shall be at the sole discretion of each institutional governing board, and shall never be conditioned upon the consent or approval of the Legislature or of any state administrative or fiscal officer or agency.

(9) Each institutional governing board shall have power at its own sole discretion to let contracts for the construction of necessary buildings and appurtenances, for academic and instructional purposes as well as for the purpose of providing for students and / or faculties necessary living quarters, dining facilities, and any and all the related and other services suitable for maintaining and improving the health, safety, and convenience of its campus and environs as a dwelling place, and conducing toward the improvement of the quality of living among all members of its academic community.

(10) The architectural planning of new buildings and or of remodeling projects, the preparation of specifications and blueprints therefor, and the inspection and supervision of construction, and the acceptance of completed structures on behalf of the governing board as agent and trustee for the State, shall be within the sole discretion of the institutional governing board, acting upon the recommendations of the president of the institution; and these several functions shall be accomplished by qualified employees appointed by the governing board upon the president's recommendation. No state building commission, state department of public works, state architect, or other similar state agency or functionary, shall have any part in these functions, save and except as such agency or functionary may be invited by the governing board to advise it regarding the best current practices conducing toward improved protection of the health, safety, and convenience of the occupants of and visitors in any type of university or college building or related facility. The purpose of this subsection is to expedite the completion of building projects and to avoid or minimize the added costs and delays that have occurred on a great scale as the result of having the several complex and time-consuming services performed twice—once necessarily by university or college officers and employees, and again by state officers or employees; and to maintain the reasonable degree of autonomy in the governance of its institution which properly belongs to the institutional governing board and which is important to the morale of the academic community.[26]

---

[25]If this subsection were couched in more positive terms, it would expressly authorize the institution to own and operate printing presses, binderies, and any and all appurtenances of a publishing house, which in fact many state universities do; but this authority may readily be implied in the statements of the plenary powers of the institutional governing board contained in Section 3, *supra*.

[26]In New York State's complex and interlocking bureaucracy, the lapse of time between the financing of a building and its readiness for students recently

(11) In the disbursement of its funds from whatever source derived, for the purpose of discharging its financial obligations lawfully incurred, each institutional governing board shall, upon the recommendation of the president of the institution, employ qualified disbursing officers, accountants, auditors, or comptrollers who shall be under the direction and supervision of a chief business officer or vice president for finance and business affairs, who shall be appointed by the board upon the recommendation of the president, and who shall be under the direction and supervision of the president. The organization of the institutional office for business and financial affairs shall be as directed by the president and approved by the governing board. All writing of checks and drafts in payment of lawful financial obligations of the institution shall be accomplished in that office, and such pre-auditing as the practice of the best institutions of higher education and such as the rules of the institutional governing board may require shall be performed by appropriate officers or employees in that office. In no event and under no circumstances shall a lawful expenditure duly authorized by the institutional office of business and financial affairs be required to await pre-auditing or other prior approval from any state office or officer external to the institution.

The general policy shall be to approve expenditures requested by the president, deans, or department heads upon evidence that such requests are approved by appropriate academic officers at or above the levels of deans or directors of colleges, schools, divisions, or independent departments of instruction and research; that the expenditure is lawful; that funds are or will be available for the purpose; and that the request is not unreasonably beyond the limits of the current budget allotments to the unit involved. The purpose of this subsection is to prevent unnecessary and wasteful delays that inevitably occur when institutional expenditures are required by law to be approved in advance by pre-auditors or comptrollers in a distant central fiscal agency of the state.[27]

(12) Promptly after the termination of each fiscal year the financial affairs of each institution shall be post-audited by a qualified agency external to the institution, for the purpose of affording evidence that all expenditures and other fiscal functions of the institution were made with accuracy and in conformity with law, or of identifying any deviations from these standards which may have occurred; and of affording advice to the institution regarding any suggested improvements in its fiscal procedures. To obtain this indispensable annual post-audit, the institutional governing board may at its own discretion request the service from the state auditor or other appropriate state fiscal officer or agency; or it may on its own initiative employ for the purpose the temporary services of a qualified and disinterested private accounting firm known to be reputable and to have special competency in auditing the fiscal operations of institutions of higher education.[28] The report of the annual post-audit shall be

---

stretched out to as much as six years in some instances. In 1963 Governor Nelson A. Rockefeller cut through the red tape by an executive order which removed the Department of Public Works from the program of construction of the State University of New York, and appointed General Traub as special expediter of the program. Substantial reduction in the loss of time has subsequently occurred.

[27] There is a practically insurmountable temptation on the part of state auditors to go beyond the limits of their statutory authority (to check on the lawfulness of the expenditure and the availability of funds) and assume to pass on the wisdom and expediency of the expenditure. Numerous decisions of many state supreme courts have repeatedly rebuked state auditors for this practice, especially in West Virginia and Arizona.

[28] The annual post-audit of the University of Michigan, one of the nation's greatest state universities, is made by private accounting firms.

published and copies kept available for inspection by the public. Typically it should constitute a part of the published Annual Financial Report of each institution.

(13) Each institutional governing board shall have sole discretion as to the investment and re-investment of all trust funds and other funds in its custody. For this purpose it may employ a full-time investment officer who shall be a member of the staff of the institutional business office, or it may retain the services of a qualified trust company or trust department of a reputable bank, or obtain the necessary continuing consultative management of its investment function from other reputable sources or from a combination of sources. Normally the treasurer of the institutional governing board will be also the chief business officer or vice president for financial affairs of the institution.

(14) It is hereby declared to be the policy of the Legislature not to attach conditional clauses to institutional appropriation acts, in order to subvert the authority of the institutional governing boards and usurp their functions, in derogation of the declared public policy of this State that the institutions of higher education shall be autonomous in their academic and fiscal affairs.[29]

(15) Once a legislative appropriation of state tax funds has been duly made by the Legislature and the Governor, either for annual operating expenses or for capital outlays by any institution of higher education, under no circumstances shall any executive, administrative, or fiscal officer or agency of this State, or any interim legislative committee, or any combination of such individuals, bodies, or agencies, have authority to reduce the full amount appropriated or to withhold, temporarily or permanently, any part or fraction of any periodic allotment of such amount to the institution to which it has been appropriated; and any statute or statutes of this State now in force, purporting to contravene this provision for any reason or in any manner whatsoever, is hereby expressly repealed and declared null and void.[30]

The purpose of this subsection is to prevent the waste of money and talent which is made inevitable by the existence of statutes which, though innocently intended to prevent any possible deficit at the end of any fiscal period, actually severely impair the possibility of efficient planning by institutional governing boards and presidents by maintaining a continual uncertainty regarding the exact amount of funds that will become available for any specified fiscal period. It is the policy of this State that the losses of efficiency thus incurred are the cause of much greater damage to the public interest than is the possibility that a temporary decline in state revenue receipts below the estimates on which the budget was based may cause small temporary dollar deficits to be incurred in order to execute fully and efficiently planned operations which have been budgeted by an institutional governing board and president in justified anticipation of good faith on the part of the state's chief legislative and executive officers in making a definite appropriation for a specified fiscal period.

(16) The institutional governing board shall have sole authority, within the limits of the funds allotted for travel of state university or state college em-

---

[29] In a few states "conditional appropriations" and "riders on appropriation acts" are limited or prohibited by the state constitutions or by the rules of both houses of the legislatures.

[30] Many states have such statutes, enacted in deference to "the fetish of the balanced budget" and designed to prevent absolutely the occurrence of any operating deficit, however small, at the end of any fiscal period. The theory is that any deficit is the one supreme unpardonable sin. The inefficiency and waste caused by the uncertainties thus introduced into institutional planning of operations is seemingly entirely overlooked.

ployees, to establish policies regarding such travel in the interests of the institution, and shall authorize the president of the institution to approve or disapprove all individual requests for payment of the expenses of such travel, in accord with the policies relative thereto established by the board. The decisions of the president in all such cases shall be final.[31]

6. *Repealer.* All acts and parts of acts which conflict with any provisions of this Act are hereby expressly repealed to the extent that they so conflict. Rights acquired prior to the effective date of this act by university and college officers and employees under Civil Service or Retirement System statutes of the State shall be protected, and the State shall take care to discharge its lawful obligations under such statutes.

-----

[31]Some states retain the incredible requirement that some or all individual travel requests must be approved by the Governor. In most instances this type of statute is probably a vestigial hangover from the Great Depression years.

Representative Guy A. Kistler of Pennsylvania said in his address to the Pennsylvania House September 1, 1965: "Today the travel of employees, both in-state and out-of-state, is vitally important to the administration of any institution of higher education. College presidents must authorize attendance at professional meetings for administrators and college teachers. This applies at state colleges as well as at other state institutions of higher education, and it applies to out-of-state travel the same as in-state travel. The fact that all out-of-state travel must be approved by the Governor's Office delays the administration of out-of-state travel and subjects professional decisions of state college presidents to review and approval. The state college presidents should have the authority to administer all travel of employees whether it be to professional meetings, or for the recruiting of professional personnel, or the general administration of the institution."

INDEX

INDEX